The Holy Book of Destiny

The Holy Book of God's Eternal Universal Religion
The Holy Adhyatma-Yoga-Dharma of
Maitreya The Friend of All Souls

Published by Kaivalya International Sanctuary
by Permission of His Holiness
Maitreya Adhyatma Bhagavan Sri Babajhan Al-Kahlil The Friend

Kaivalya International

P.O. Box 4002
Redondo Beach, Ca. 90277-1734

Telephone USA (310) 540-6044

www.maitreyathefriend.com

First Edition © Copyright 59 A.F. (2011)
Second Edition © Copyright 62 A.F. (2014)
Maitreya Adhyatma Bhagavan Sri Babajhan Al-Kahlil The Friend
All Rights Reserved

Regarding the Continuous and Immediate Nature of God's Revelations and Awakening Within Man

"And I will ask of my Father, and He will give you another Comforter, to be with you forever. Even the Spirit of Truth, whom the world cannot receive, because it has not seen Him and does not know Him; but you know Him because he abides with you and is in you."

St. John XIV, Verse 16 and 17

"And Moses said unto Spirit 'Behold, when I go to the children of Israel and say to them, The Spirit of your fathers has sent me unto you; and they shall say unto me, What is His Name? What shall I say unto them?' And Spirit said unto Moses, 'I AM THAT I AM!'".

Exodus II, Verse 13 and 14

"Whenever there is a decay of True Religion and a rise of ignorance, then I embody myself in this world, O Wise One. For the protection of The Right and The Good, for the destruction of Darkness and Ignorance, and for the renewal of True Religion I am born age after age. He who knows my Divine birth and action in their True Light, is not born again when he dies, but enters into Perfect Union with Me."

The Bhagavad Gita
Chapter IV, Verses 7, 8 and 9

"And Ananda, holding back his tears, said to The Buddha: 'Who will teach us when you are gone?' And the Blessed One answered: 'I am not the first Buddha who has come upon the earth, nor shall I be the last. In the right time, another Buddha will arise in the world, a Holy One, a Supremely Enlightened One, endowed with wisdom in conduct, auspicious, knowing The Truth, an incomparable leader of men, a master of Spirit and mortals. He will reveal to you these Eternal Truths. He will preach his Dharma, Glorious in its Origin, Glorious in the Middle, and Glorious in its end, in the Spirit as well as the letter. He will proclaim a life of Dharma, wholly Perfect and Pure, even as I now proclaim'. Ananda said: 'How shall we know Him?' And The Buddha said: 'He will be known as Maitreya, which means, The Friend.'"

The Mahaparinirvana Sutra
Chapter V, Verses 1 - 14

Rise and Rise Again

*"O' Maitreyian,
go out into this world
bold and unafraid.
Initiate all willing Souls
in my Name and in The Name
of The One Universal God
who has sent me unto you;
and bring forth The Age
of Universal God's Pure Divine Truth
for the Salvation and Liberation
of all suffering Souls.
And when the bigots
cast stones against you,
take every stone they cast,
and use them
to build My Church
in this world.
And when they seek
to oppress you
and destroy you;
rise and rise again
and again
like The Phoenix
from the ashes;
until the lambs
have become lions
and the rule of Darkness
is no more."*

~ Maitreya The Friend of All Souls ~

Foreword

The Living Book of Destiny

As the instructions given to a child
must change as the child grows;
As the orders of a General
must change as the battle goes;
As the steersman at the helm
must turn the wheel
to keep the ship on course
accordingly as the current flows;
Even so do God and The Friend
change this Holy Book of Destiny
as God's Religion grows.
As the Sun and the Moon
remain not in one place,
but move through The Heavens
according to God's Universal Command;
As the light that The Sun pours down upon the Earth
is new at each moment
where ere we stand;
As the circumstances and situations of Man
are not fixed, but are ever-changing
due to the Gift which God has given unto
every Soul of Will that is Free;

Even so, do I reveal God's Eternal Universal Religion
of Holy Adhyatma-Yoga-Dharma
unto you according to the needs
of a suffering Humanity.
As the day and the night do not contradict one another;
As the Earth and the Sky do not negate one another;
As the Sun and Moon are not enemies,
but Sister and Brother;
As all apparent opposites of this, God's Infinite Creation
compliment one another and find perfect harmony and unity
in Him, and no other;
Not one thing do I give unto you
that, in Truth contradicts another,
for all of these are joined in perfect harmony
in God, and no other;
Whosoever sees contradiction in any of these things,
sees only the appearances of the contradictions
deep within his own heart hide.
But he who is wise and will follow the threads
of apparent contradiction to their Source
will come to know their harmony and unity
for truly are these joined in The One God
who is all around, yet dwells inside.

Maitreya Adhyatma Bhagavan Sri Babajhan Al-Kahlil The Friend
14 Honor 45 A.F.
Kaivalya

A Work Unfinished

God's Divine Work is fully complete in itself at each moment; yet it is ever unfinished. This World, being God's Divine Work, is fully complete in itself at each moment; yet it is ever unfinished, unto the End. Man, being God's Divine Work, each man and woman is fully complete at each moment; yet is ever unfinished unto the end.

This Holy Book of Destiny, being God's Divine Work, is fully complete in itself at each moment; yet it shall remain unfinished until I have left this world and dwell in the Spiritual Realm and within The Secret Inner Sanctuary of each Soul's Heart.

Though The One Universal God is the Source of all Art, only the artist who paints a picture may rightfully change his art or tell its true meaning. Though The One Universal God is the Source of all Poetry, only the poet who writes the poem can rightfully change his verse or tell its true meaning. Though The One Universal God is The Source of my Religion, only I may rightfully interpret this Holy Book of Destiny or change it in any way.

Let, therefore, those who would take up God's Eternal Universal Religion and follow me Home to Self-Realization and Liberation within this life; and Perfect Final Union with The One Universal God, I AM THAT I AM, at this life's end; not attempt to interpret what is written herein or change it. Instead, let each who would follow me and fulfill God's Supreme Promise of Universal Salvation and Liberation accept, Preserve, Practice and Propagate what I give and strive to understand it exactly as it is.

Paratpara Ji Kijai!

All Glory to God The Beloved!

Maitreya The Friend of all Souls left this world on July 29, 60 A.F. (2012).
He now dwells in the Spiritual Realm and within
The Secret Inner Sanctuary of each Soul's Heart.

The Mission

Divine Critical Mass

And The One Universal God Said To Maitreya The Friend of all Souls:

{G} "I say unto you that when your Maitreyians have given My Supreme Promise to the Souls of this world such that the Sun never sets upon the Maitreyians and there are enough of The Faithful who have received your Holy Initiation and who give heed to the letter of your teachings and instructions and examples in their lives and are following you Home to Perfect Final Union with Me in True Faith and Devotion in Spirit, they will form a Divine Critical Mass; and in that moment, I will spread My Supreme Promise and Gift of Perfect Final Union with That I AM THAT I AM, to all Souls. And no Soul shall be left behind.

{G} "And in that Day, all Souls shall come straightaway into Knowledge of Perfect Final Union with Me at the end of their lives. And Hell shall be emptied. For the wretched Souls who suffer therein shall be redeemed and made Holy and I shall take them into Perfect Final Union with Me and the gates of Hell shall be closed forever. And the Heaven world itself shall become empty of Souls. For in that day, I shall take every last Soul into Perfect Final Union with That I AM THAT I AM, as countless drops of water are taken into The Sea. This is The Great Dispensation that your sacrifices and Vow have won for all Souls.

{G} "Make this the highest Goal and Purpose of all that you do and all that is done by your Faithful Maitreyians who are, truly your Soldiers of The Light and My own and it shall come to pass."

All Glory To God The Beloved!
Victory To The One Universal God and The Friend!

The Soldiers of The Light

Our Purpose and Mission

We are Soldiers of The Light. Our one Purpose and Mission in this world is to defeat The Force of Darkness with the Sharp Sword of Universal God's Pure Divine Truth; end The Age of Ignorance, Darkness, Chaos, Confusion, Delusion, Illusion and Destruction; restore God's Eternal Universal Religion to all the peoples of the Earth; and bring The Age of Universal God's Pure Divine Truth into fullness and Reality for the continued survival of Humanity and the Salvation and Liberation of all Souls for all time; that all Souls may attain Perfect Final Union with God at the end of this life and be set free, forever.

Soldier of The Light Pledge

"I am a Soldier of The Clear Light of Universal God's Pure Divine Truth. The Friend's Religion is my Religion.

"My Holy Mission is: to defeat The Force of Darkness with the Sharp Sword of Universal God's Pure Divine Truth; end The Age of Ignorance, Darkness, Chaos, Confusion, Delusion, Illusion and Destruction; restore God's Eternal Universal Religion to all willing peoples of the Earth; and bring The Age of Universal God's Pure Divine Truth into fullness and Reality for the continued survival of Humanity and the Salvation and Liberation of all Souls for all time; that all Souls may attain Perfect Final Union with God at the end of this life and be set free, forever.

"I will fulfill my Holy Mission and this Sacred Pledge by my own Free Willed discipline, determination and obedience to God and God's Eternal Universal Religion, helped and guided by The Divine Guidance and Grace of The One Universal God and The Friend and by right use of the Divine Gifts The Friend has won for me and His Faithful by His two Supreme Self-Sacrifices of giving up Perfect Final Union with The One God for the sake of all Souls and His Vow of Compassion.

"I profess that God's Eternal Universal Religion is the Religion He has given unto all Souls through His Awakened and Ordained One, The Friend and no other. God's Eternal Universal Religion is the Absolute standard by which I live my whole life and judge all things.

"I surrender totally to The One Universal God. I submit totally to God's Infinite Divine Will as God reveals His Will to me, directly and personally within The Secret Inner Sanctuary of my Heart and through His Awakened and Ordained One, Maitreya Adhyatma Bhagavan Sri Babajhan Al-Kahlil The Friend. I accept, love and revere all of God's Prophets, Saints, Buddhas, Saviors and Avataras alike, without being bound to accept what has been said or written about them. No man or woman is my enemy. The Force of Darkness alone is my enemy. The Sharp Sword of Universal God's Pure Divine Truth is my weapon. I will destroy The Force of Darkness with The Sharp Sword of Universal God's Pure Divine Truth wherever I find it.

"I commit myself totally to seeking, finding and living The Highest Truth, The Whole Truth and Nothing but The Truth, for better or worse.

"I pledge myself and commit my life: to liberate all willing Souls from The Force of Darkness and restore them to The Clear Light of Universal God's Pure Divine Truth - starting with myself, by changing and being changed by The One Universal God and The Friend; to extending God's Eternal Universal Religion to all willing Souls through The Friend's Holy Initiation; and to doing everything I can possibly do to help create an ever-growing Community of The Friend's Enlightened Faithful Believers throughout the world.

"I will refrain from doing anything that would harm God's Eternal Universal Religion, the Holy Community, the progress of The Friend's Holy Mission or The Friend Himself. I will go about this world alone and in concert with others of The Friend's Faithful, doing all things that fulfill my Holy Initiation and move me closer to full Salvation and Liberation; and doing all that I can do in every possible way and at all times taking every good action that I can take to help The Friend accomplish The Holy Mission for which The One Universal God has Awakened within Him and Ordained Him - and me through Him.

"I will not use force, threat, coercion, intimidation, bribery, violence or deception to bring any Soul to Universal God and The Friend or God's Eternal Universal Religion. I will not fear aggression or give in to it. I will advance our Holy Cause ever forward to Victory by using all of my thoughts, words, deeds, resources and my very life itself in every possible way to create Belief, Faith and Confidence in Universal God and The Friend, in God's Eternal Universal Religion and in The Age of Universal God's Pure Divine Truth - in the Hearts and Minds of all people.

"In all things I will do all that I can, the best I can. With the help and Grace of The One Universal God and The Friend, I will make myself into the highest possible example of God's Eternal Universal Religion and a living Lamp shining The Clear Light of Universal God's Pure Divine Truth out into this world for the Salvation and Liberation of all Souls. I will give no quarter. I will never give up."

All Glory To God The Beloved!

Victory To The One Universal God and The Friend

Book One

God's New Covenant

Won for The Salvation and Liberation of All Souls

by Maitreya Adhyatma Bhagavan Sri Babajhan Al-Kahlil The Friend

On The Twelfth Day of March Nineteen Hundred & Seventy Seven

Chapter One
The Friend's Declaration

The First Declaration of

Maitreya Adhyatma Bhagavan Sri Babajhan
Al-Kahlil The Friend
Bringer of the Age of Universal God's Pure Divine Truth

By The Will and Grace of The One Universal God:

Rejoice, for The One Universal God has Awakened within me for the Salvation and Liberation of all Souls!

2. The Breath of God, The Eternal has come upon me, burning away illusion and confusion and washing me clean of the Darkness and Ignorance which had clouded my Spiritual Sight.

3. It is Clear! Of this there is no doubt! The One Universal God, That I AM THAT I AM, The Eternal One, is The Source, Substance and Self of all Creation and The One True Self of all Souls. He has Awakened within me and anointed me and Ordained and Commissioned me to carry The New Covenant of His Promise of Perfect Final Union for all Souls and His Pure Divine Truth of the Oneness between Man and God unto all Souls.

4. Let your eyes see and your ears hear and let God dispel all of your doubts. For The Gift I bring unto you from The One God, The Beloved, is Eternal Truth, New Hope, Renewed Faith, Infinite Joy, Everlasting Life and True Salvation and Liberation for all Souls. The Gift I bring is a New Covenant and God's Divine Promise of Perfect Final Union with Him for all who will receive my Holy Initiation and follow Him through me, to the end of this life.

5. The One Universal God has Revealed unto me this day my Oneness and Identity with That I AM THAT I AM which He is, Absolute, One without a Second. And He has sent me forth unto you to bear witness that:

6. God Alone is Real! This whole Universe and all that is within it is God's Dream and Image, Created by That Absolute One within His Own Being out of His Own Being. Soul and Spirit are One and Identical with God and no other.

7. Between man and God, there are no separations. Nothing is there that stands between man and God, The Beloved, but man's own sleep of belief and ignorance.

8. For, The Truth that has been shown unto me is Clear. Beyond the illusions of this world, you are each One and Identical with God. That I AM THAT I AM is The One True Self within all selves; One, Whole and Complete.

9. As God Is, so you are; though you know it not! As God is Good, you are Good; as God is Great, you are Great; as God is Love, you are Love; as God is Wisdom, you too are Wisdom; as God is Beauty; you are Beauty; as God is Eternal, you are Eternal; as God is Infinite, you are Infinite; as God is Immortal, you too are Immortal; as God is all of This, yet beyond all of This, you too are all of This, yet beyond all of This! The True Self of each of you is Pure Divine Spirit which is One and Identical with God and no other.

10. And, as when two pictures are identical to a third they are also identical to one another; you are each One with each other, though you know it not. And in your unknowing you do all manner of cruel and evil things unto one another.

11. He alone knows God who knows Him as his own True Self and knows Him within even the least of his Brothers and Sisters.

12. No greater Worship is there than a man shall know God in all and Love God within them even as he Loves God within himself and make sacrifices of his own good and life for the sake of his Brothers and Sisters.

13. For, whatever you do unto one another, you do unto God and unto your own True Self, That I AM THAT I AM, which you are.

14. You have two selves. A Greater Divine Self which is One and Identical with God and a small false self that separates you, with a wall of ignorance, from knowledge of your Greater Divine Self.

15. It is your identification with your false self that separates you from God who is your One True Self. Verily, it is this confusion that binds you to the eternal Wheel of Birth, Suffering, Sorrow, Sickness, Fear, Pain, Old Age, Death and Rebirth.

16. Untangle your Greater Infinite God-Self from your small false self. For, all this to which you cling shall surely perish, as The Real Alone endures.

17. Cast off your attachment to this world of temporary and passing illusion and things. Come with me Home to God! What else is there in this world for you to do that is Truly Worth doing?

18. Take up your Divine Self and come with me to God, your One True Self. For in Realizing your Oneness and Identity with God, all else shall be added unto you and you shall dwell in Perfect Final Union with God, Forever.

19. Fear not! For The One Universal God, That I AM THAT I AM has Awakened within me and sent me unto you, as Maitreya Adhyatma Bhagavan Sri Babajhan Al-Kahlil The Friend, the Awakened One, Bringer of Oneness with God, The Friend of all Souls. Not to destroy any of Universal God's Prophets, Saints, Buddhas, Saviors or Avataras, but to affirm them and fulfill God's Truth on Earth.

20. I have not come to answer earthly desires or understanding, or to mystify men's minds with Miracles. Neither have I come to answer the tests and challenges of men. I have come to give unto each The Water of Life and The Fire of That I AM THAT I AM, that alone satisfies the burning thirst for Knowledge of Oneness and Identity with God, The Beloved - The All Father - The One True Self of every Self!

21. For your earthly desires, I give you a smile and a flower. For your burning thirst, I give you The Water of Life Eternal. To lead you out of the Darkness, I give you the Divine Fire and Light of God's own Divine Spirit! To defeat The Force of Darkness and bring forth The Age of God's Pure Divine Truth for the Salvation and Liberation of all Souls and win the continued survival of Humanity, I give you The Sharp Sword of Universal God's Pure Divine Truth and make you Maitreyians and Soldiers of The Light.

22. Not of my earthly self, but of God, The All Father, I am sent unto you, a Living Bell tolling to Awaken all Souls to their own True Nature and Being, and set each upon The Way Home to God.

23. Because you Quest, I give you a smile and a flower.

24. Because you thirst for God, I give you The Water of Life.

25. Because your Heart Sleeps and your Spiritual Sight is shrouded in The Darkness of Ignorance and Belief, I give you The Divine Fire of God's own Divine Universal Spirit.

26. Because The Force of Darkness assails you, I give you The Sharp Sword of God's Pure Divine Truth with which to cut away the fetters of Darkness.

27. I am sent unto you of The One God - I AM THAT I AM - as a Bell, tolling to Awaken you, as a Living Fountain to quench your burning thirst and a Lamp to Light your Way Home to Him.

28. Hear me and Awaken! Drink deeply of That I AM THAT I AM, and you shall never Thirst again! Turn within; Follow The Light of this Lamp; and you shall know Perfect Final Union with That I AM THAT I AM; and be set Free forever!

29. The Road is steep and The Way is narrow. But fear not, for with each step, the effort of your climbing will strengthen you for the next. And, hidden within the pain of climbing, awaits the Infinite Bliss and Joy of your Awakening!

30. For The Way, narrow and straight though it is, leads all who dare to travel upon it, beyond pain, darkness, sorrow, suffering, death and rebirth; and onward to Awakening, Salvation, Liberation, Eternity, and Home, to Perfect Final Union with God - That Beloved Universal, That I AM THAT I AM, which you are!

31. The Goal of your Journey is that you will Know, of your own Direct Experience, that you are One with The One God That Is All, yet beyond All!

32. To this end have I been Reborn of God. To this end has He bid me call Him Paratpara - God who is within, yet beyond all. To this end has Paratpara,

The One Universal God of Countless Names and Forms, Who Is Beyond All Names and Forms Awakened me from the Sleep of Ignorance and Illusion and wiped The Darkness from my Spiritual eyes. To this end I have answered the Call of Calls; To this end I have come among you as Maitreya Adhyatma Bhagavan Sri Babajhan Al-Kahlil The Friend, The God-Awakened Bringer of Oneness with God - The Friend of All Beings - a Ray of God's own Divine Light, sent out from That I AM THAT I AM to Light The Way Home to Him with The Light of His Pure Divine Truth;

33. To this end, and no other, has He sent me to you that you might know, without doubt or reservation, that God dwells not in faraway places, but within the Hearts of all Beings.

34. Go! Each of you, and do likewise! For you are each One with The One God and a Friend; though you know it not! Go Forth into this world and give God's Promise to all Souls and get all Souls Home to God.

35. Fear not that you are unworthy or too weak. For, whatever has been done by The Prophets, Saints, Buddhas, Saviors and Avataras is open unto you. And Greater things than these shall you do! For the Unfoldment of God's Love is never ending and moves ever onward! And whatsoever anyone has done can, with the help and Grace of God, be done by you!

36. Worship not that which you see of me; worship not that which you hear of me; worship not that which you feel of me and which you call Maitreya Adhyatma Bhagavan Sri Babajhan Al-Kahlil The Friend. For, far beyond that which you see of me; far beyond that which you hear of me; far beyond that which you feel of me; am I and The Gift that I bring unto you from God! Of myself, I Am Nothing. With God, All Things are Possible.

37. No name or Form is there that can contain That I AM THAT I AM - All in One, and One in All. And to Worship only the apparent is to admire only the hands of The Eternal Sculptor who is the Source of All.

38. Of what use, Beloved Soul, are the hands without the body? Of what use is the body without a mind to form and guide it? Of what use is a mind without a heart to join it to The Source of All that Is? And, of what use is even a heart, if it knows not The Presence of The One God within it?

39. I do not come to be Worshipped, but as fingers pointing the Way Home to The One God, I AM THAT I AM! Not that you might admire the fingers; but that you might have Perfect Final Union with That I AM THAT I AM who has Awakened within me and sent me unto you!

40. And I say unto you, worship not The Prophets, Saints, Buddhas, Saviors and Avataras of yesterday, in name or form of wood, earth, metal or words in books as apart from God. For he who Worships Name and Form alone without True Knowledge of God, is an Idolater.

41. Neither shall you deny or degrade any one of God's Beloved Prophets, Saints, Buddhas, Saviors and Avataras. Instead, let your Worship be a Celebration, and a seeking after your own direct experience of The One God, Who is All in All.

42. The Divine Spirit of God is beyond, yet within every single thing

of this Earth. That I AM THAT I AM is the one Source, Substance and Self of all Creation, all Existence and all Being. Therefore, worship That I AM THAT I AM within every Brother or Sister Maitreyian, stranger, friend, foe and flower in your field as Worthy of your Worship. But do not worship the apparent alone. For, it is through worship of the apparent without The Spirit that man falls under the spell of The Force of Darkness and is led into The Great Sleep of Illusion, suffering, sorrow, death and rebirth.

43. A race of idolaters have the vain and pious religionists made of you! They frighten you with fear of God to cause you to Worship Name and Form and Doctrine and Dogma, and demand your belief in the emptiness of their words under the most terrible penalties. But in Truth, they are powerless.

44. I say unto you that The One God which you seek is That I AM THAT I AM - The One Universal God of Countless Names and Forms Who Is Beyond All Names and Forms. All this that Is, Is within The One God and The One God within it but not limited to it. The Creator Uncreated, The Unmanifest source of all manifestations is He. First Cause without a prior. The Namers of names and The Former of forms, is He.

45. Let it be, Beloved Brothers and Sisters of The Water of Life, that your Worship shall be in seeking to Realize The One God, who is The One True Self within every self, within The Experience of all Experience.

46. Do this, and I promise you, even as the gentle rain washes the greatest of mountains into the Sea, Perfect Final Union with The One God, That I AM THAT I AM, shall be yours!

47. I Proclaim and Bear True Witness unto The Truth of The New Covenant of The One God as it has been Revealed unto me, that:

48. There is One Universal God: Manifest and Unmanifest; Personal and Impersonal; Immanent and Transcendent. There is no other. Universal God alone is Real. As all in a dream is of the dreamer; as a drop of water taken from the Sea is Sea; all that is, is Universal God. There is nothing but Universal God everywhere. All Soul is Pure Divine Universal Spirit which is One and Identical with Universal God and no other. I am Universal God's Awakened One, Bringer of The Holy Satya Yuga, whom Universal God has Ordained to end the Age of Spiritual Ignorance and bring forth The Age of Divine Pure Truth on earth. Out of My Universal Love and Compassion, I sacrificed Perfect Final Union with Universal God for the sake of all Souls for all time. In reward for my Supreme Sacrifice, Universal God has Promised that all who receive the Enlightenment of my Holy Initiation and follow me to the end of their lives, shall attain Self-Realization and receive the Supreme Gift of Perfect Final Union with Him that I sacrificed for their sake.

49. There is no I but God! All that Is, I Am! All that Is, You Are! You and I are not we, but One! For, That I AM THAT I AM, is The Beginning, The Middle, and The End of All that Is.

50. As a potter, knowing the essence of clay, knows all things made of clay; as the Goldsmith, knowing the essence of gold, knows all things made of gold; even so shall he who Awakens

to Universal God's Pure Divine Truth know All Truth!

51. Arise! Awaken! Thy Dawn has come! The Day is at hand! Unto he who knows The One Universal God as his True Self is given Life Eternal! Fire cannot burn him; sword pierce him; nor cold freeze him! Free from the illusions of your false self, knowing that you are not this, or this, or this, or this; but One with That I AM THAT I AM, you shall endure forever. For always have I been; and always will you be; One with Paratpara, The One Universal God of Countless Names and Forms Who Is Beyond All Names and Forms, That I AM THAT I AM - All in All!

52. Seek, therefore, to know your own True Self. For in that knowing, you shall Know The One God - All in All. And you shall Know, without doubt or reservation that you are not this body or this mind or this personality - but That One Universal God, who is your True Source, Substance and Self - and no other!

53. And no longer shall the Sun be your Light by Day; nor the Moon your Light by Night. For The One God, The Beloved, shall have become an Eternal Light shining out from you unto all the Earth! Your Sun shall never set, nor your Moon wane. For The Light of The Eternal is yours and your days of sorrow are at an end.

54. In His Eternal Love He has always Loved you. In His Infinite Being He has always held you. Come with me to God and take your place among The Twice Born of Eternity! This time you shall be truly made One with God - a Pure One, Reborn in God!

55. There is no I but God! There is no you but God! I am with you always.

56. Awaken! All you who sleep the sleep of The Living Dead. And come with me Home to God!

57. This is The Water of Life: God Alone is Real! This whole Universe and all that is within it is God's Dream and Image, Created by That Absolute One within His Own Being, out of His Own Being! And, Soul and Spirit are One and Identical with God and no other!

58. Whoever shares The Water of Life, shares Maitreya Adhyatma Bhagavan Sri Babajhan Al-Kahlil The Friend and that I AM THAT I AM! Whoever shares The Divine Fire of The Spirit, shares Maitreya Adhyatma Bhagavan Sri Babajhan Al-Kahlil The Friend and That I AM THAT I AM. This do often for the Salvation and Liberation of all Souls.

59. You and I are One within The One that is All in All. Whenever one of you appears to be separated from the rest, know that this is but an illusion cast by The Force of Darkness that hides your True Self from you. For, outside the sleeping minds of The Living Dead, there are no separations within God's Infinite and Eternal Being and we are forever One in Him.

60. This is The Holy Water of Life! May You Never Thirst for The Holy Water of Life!

61. This is the Testimony of Maitreya Adhyatma Bhagavan Sri Babajhan Al-Kahlil The Friend of all Souls. The God Awakened One - Bringer of Oneness with The One God.

Om So'ham Tat Tvam Asi!
Om! I Am That - Thou Art That!

Jai Bhagavan Ji!
Victory To God The Beloved!
That Beloved Universal
I Am That I Am
Which You Are!

**Here Ends The Chapter Entitled
The Friend's Declaration**

Chapter Two
The Friend's Profession

The Second Declaration of

Maitreya Adhyatma Bhagavan Sri Babajhan
Al-Kahlil The Friend
Bringer of the Age of Universal God's Pure Divine Truth

By The Will and Grace of The One Universal God:

The Spirit of The One Universal God, The Eternal, I AM THAT I AM, The One True Self of every self, has Awakened within me and Consecrated and Commissioned me to carry His New Covenant unto all Souls; to awaken their Sleeping Spirits; to reveal The Way of Salvation and Liberation; restore sight to their Spiritual eyes and hearing to their Spiritual Ears; to Free each Soul from Darkness and false self; and to Proclaim and bear True Witness that the time to overthrow The Force of Darkness and bring forth The Age of Universal God's Pure Divine Truth on earth for the Salvation and Liberation of all Souls, is Now!

2. This is the Promise I bring unto you from The One Universal God: Whoever receives the True Enlightenment of The Friend's Holy Initiation; and follows Him to the end of this life; shall Attain Self-Realization and receive the Supreme Gift of Salvation and Liberation which He Sacrificed for the sake of all Souls.

3. The expression of Universal God in Activity is That One Immortal Universal Spirit, that animates and gives life to all Beings. This Universal Spirit is inseparable from Universal God, The Eternal Principle, who is One In All and All In One! I AM THAT I AM! You Are That!

4. You have two selves. A smaller self made of Spiritual Darkness which you mistakenly call I; and a Divine Self which is That I AM THAT I AM, which you Know not. You Are That!

5. Accept the Divine Light of this Supreme Truth that I bring unto you from The One God. Light it up within your heart of hearts and it will dispel the Darkness that enslaves.

6. Unburden your self of your false self! Take up your True Divine Self; which is The One True Self of God; and come Home with me to God!

7. The One Universal Spirit is Universal God-Unmanifest, I AM THAT I AM, the One Source, Substance and Self of all Creation

who is beyond all names and forms and manifestations.

8. All things are Manifest by That I AM THAT I AM; not one thing exists without It. It is The Life and The Light of all That Is.

9. Having received my Holy Initiation and followed me to the end of this life according to God's Promise, that Soul attains Perfect Final Union and becomes One with That Absolute One without a Second who is beyond the beyond. By this, a Soul awakens and realizes Its True Self as Pure Divine Spirit that is One with That I AM THAT I AM and no other.

10. Although this God-Self is aglow within the unawakened, they know it not. That True Self, when Realized by the mortal man, Liberates The Spirit from its prison of flesh - forever.

11. The True Self of Universal God is The One Source, Substance and Self of every Soul. Though they know not the reason why, it is through that God-Self alone that each Soul grows from the darkness of separation from God into The Clear Light of Oneness with That I AM THAT I AM.

12. Though The True Source and Self of each Soul is That I AM THAT I AM, the uninitiated fail to Realize it. And failing to realize it, they cling to their false self like a drowning man clinging to a bag of gold.

13. But, unto those who receive my Holy Initiation and follow me to the end of this life, God has given The Power to Be Reborn as The Children of God; those who Know that they are more than body and mind and personality born of carnal desire; those who know that they are Soul, which is Pure Divine Spirit, which is One and Identical with The One Universal God, I AM THAT I AM, and no other.

14. Truly, at the end of this life, these Souls enter straight away into Perfect Final Union with That I AM THAT I AM and are born into suffering and death no more.

15. God is hard for the earthbound to reach. Because of this, are Souls bound to the eternal Wheel of Suffering and know Birth, Suffering, Sorrow, Fear, Pain, Sickness, Old Age, Death and Rebirth; again and again.

16. Due to the influence of The Force of Darkness, the earthbound cannot grasp The One God. But, as two pictures that are each identical to a third picture are also identical with one another, whosoever Realizes Oneness with One in whom God has taken into Perfect Final Union with Himself also attains Oneness with God.

17. The One God, I AM THAT I AM, is merciful and compassionate. He does not abandon Souls. When mankind has lost the light of Universal God's Pure Divine Truth and the Force of Darkness rules the earth, That I AM THAT I AM awakens within an ordinary mortal man for the renewal of the Age of His Pure Divine Truth and the Salvation and Liberation of all Souls from the Wheel of Suffering, Sorrow and Death.

18. This which I have spoken has come to pass in me in this day.

19. Because of this, whosoever Realizes Oneness with me knows Oneness with The One Universal God Who Is Beyond All Names and Forms,

That I AM THAT I AM - Who has Awakened within me and sent me here to give all Souls His Supreme Promise and get all Souls Home to Him.

20. Awaken and dispel the illusion of separation from God. None is there which is separate from That I AM THAT I AM.

21. God, alone, is Real. In Truth, you are not a body or a mind or a bundle of experiences or memories. In Truth, you are Soul which is Pure Divine Universal Spirit that is One and Identical with The One Universal God, The One True Self of every self, and no other!

22. No one can become One with God - ever, for, you are each, already One with The One God and no other. So have you always been. All other impressions are illusions woven of ignorance and darkness. As you always have been, so shall you always Be.

23. Fire cannot burn you, sword cannot pierce you, knives cannot cut you. Nothing is there that can harm that True Self which is That I AM THAT I AM and no other.

24. The appearance of separation from God is but an illusion born of Spiritual ignorance and wrong belief. Truly, it is this illusion that blinds the unawakened to Knowledge of Universal God's Pure Divine Truth and keeps all suffering Souls enslaved to this world.

25. Receive God's Gift of My Holy Initiation. Follow me to the end of this life according to God's Supreme Promise. Strive to Awaken and Realize that you are One with That I AM THAT I AM who is The True Self of every self. What else is there to be done that is truly worth doing?

26. For as long as men have walked the earth, Souls have struggled, endured austerities and sacrificed their lives in their quest to Realize God. Of the millions who seek, only one-thousand find The Way Home. Of the thousand who find The Way Home, only one-hundred travel far upon it. Of the one-hundred who travel upon it, only one attains The Goal.

27. In this Age, out of His infinite Mercy, Paratpara, That I AM THAT I AM, has awakened within me and taken me into Perfect Final Union with Him twice. Twice have I sacrificed my own Perfect Final Union with Him and returned to this world, that all Souls may find their Way Home and have Perfect Final Union with Him before me.

28. For, I have vowed that I will never again take my own Perfect Final Union with God until I have seen all Souls safely Home into Perfect Final Union with Him before me.

29. As a result, That I AM THAT I AM has promised that whosoever will receive my Holy Initiation and follow me to the end of this life, will attain that Perfect Final Union with Him that I sacrificed for the sake of all Souls. This is The New Covenant of The One Universal God, I AM THAT I AM.

30. The key is turned. The lock is loosed. The Gate is opened. Now every Soul who will receive my Holy Initiation and follow me to the end of this life may enter into Perfect Final Union with God at the end of this life.

31. How shall a Soul who receives my Holy Initiation follow me Home to God? No one can say fully, for all Souls have their own burdens to bear and their works to complete in his life. But I tell you, there are five things that each who would follow me and win Perfect Final Union with God must do.

32. He must Strive within this life with all of his heart to Realize his Oneness with That I AM THAT I AM, while still living in the body;

33. He must fight and defeat The Force of Darkness wherever he finds it and do his best to advance our Holy Mission to victory in this world;

34. He must strive to live by The Two Rules:

35. The First Rule is this: Love The One Universal God with all of your heart, all of your mind and all of your Spirit; Love yourself and one another even as you love God; Accept, love and revere all of God's Prophets, Saints, Buddhas, Saviors and Avataras alike, without being bound to accept what has been said or written about them.

36. The Second Rule is this: Seek, find and live by The Inner Divine Inspiration, Insight, Guidance and Revelation of The One Universal God and The Friend, and the counsel of your own True and Essential Conscience within The Secret Inner Sanctuary of your Heart, according to my Instructions, in all things, great and small.

37. He must take regular fellowship and Sanctuary with other Maitreyians and contribute of his time, energy, knowledge, wealth, Spirit and talent to support and further God's Eternal Universal Religion and our Holy Mission toward victory;

38. And, he must take Inner Divine Communion with God twice every day in the morning and in the evening according to my Instruction, which is:

39. With your Heart and Mind firmly set on Seeking The Highest Truth; Call Upon Me to become active in Spirit within The Secret Inner Sanctuary of your Heart by holding My Presence within your mind and calling out within your Heart "Bhagavan Ji! Bhagavan Ji! Bhagavan Ji!" Ask for and open yourself to The Inner Divine Inspiration, Insight, Guidance and Revelation of Paratpara, The One Universal God of Countless Names and Forms and The Friend and your own True and Essential Conscience. Take Refuge in The Four Pillars of Bhagavan, Dharma, Sangha and Satya Yuga and enter into The Secret Inner Sanctuary of your Heart through the repetition of My Holy Dharma Mantra "Jai Bhagavan Ji!" (Jay Bhag-wan Gee). Immerse yourself in The Divine Ocean of Paratpara's Supreme Truth and Being therein, like a drop of water in The Sea and dwell steadily therein, like a candle flame in a still place, INJIA (Instantaneously Non-Judgmentally Insightfully Aware) and accepting of whatever comes, while it is coming, whatever lingers, while it is lingering and whatever goes, while it is going; Speaking that which is right to be Spoken when it is right to Speak it; Doing that which is right to be Done when it is right to Do it. Offer each part and the whole of these to Paratpara in the Sacrificial Fire within The Secret Inner Sanctuary of your Heart at each instant and receive whatever returns to you as Divine Gifts, given unto you by

Paratpara and The Friend for your own Self-Realization and Liberation and the Perfection of The Holy Satya Yuga in this world for The Self-Realization and Liberation of all Souls everywhere for all time. This do, in a spirit of harm to none and benefit to all. And you shall Know The Truth and The Truth shall set you Free.

40. God has made me the captain of the ship of His Eternal Universal Religion in this world. The captain of a ship must guide her to her destination according to the weather and condition. No captain can therefore say, 'I will always go North or I will always go South.'

41. Still, there are five things that I will not ask of a Soul who follows me.

42. I will not ask him to harm himself or another. Neither will I ask him to refrain from acting in his own defense, the defense of his family and friends, or in defense of the innocent and his country;

43. I will not ask him to violate his own conscience, his morals, or his ethics;

44. I will not ask him to abandon his family or his duties to his family unless these duties require him to serve the Force of Darkness;

45. I will not ask him to abandon his duties to his nation unless these duties require him to serve The Force of Darkness.

46. And, I will not ask him to do anything that would require him to violate his Sacred Vows of God's Eternal Universal Religion.

47. When a Soul knows in his heart of hearts the true Self that he is, is One with That I AM THAT I AM and no other, that is Self-Realization.

48. Self-Realization is rebirth in The Spirit that reveals to every Soul his eternal Oneness with The One God. It liberates each Soul from Darkness and bondage to this life of illusion through Realization of Oneness with Paratpara - The One Universal God, The One In All - The All In One. You are That, though you know it not.

49. What can keep you blind to this Truth, but The Force of Darkness that clouds your Spiritual Sight and covers you with ignorance and wrong belief? And what is the Purpose of living, if not to throw off the chains of Darkness and Awaken to God's Pure Divine Truth and be Free?

50. As a man awakening from a bad dream becomes happy upon realizing that his dream was not real; even so does every Soul rejoice upon Realizing his Oneness with God and knowing that God Alone is Real and that this whole World is but God's dream!

51. In that moment, the ignorance and false self by which the Force of Darkness imprisons the Divine Spirit as Soul is shattered and it is absorbed in the Divine Ocean of God's Infinite Divine Being, like a drop of water in the sea. Then, the Truth that you are Pure Divine Spirit which is One and Identical with God and no other is Realized, and that Soul is set free - forever.

52. I am sent unto you of That I AM THAT I AM as a bell tolling to awaken you to The Divine Presence of That I AM THAT I AM within you and as a ship to carry you to the far shore of Perfect Final Union with

Him. Awaken to the Truth! Then you shall behold God's Radiance shining forth from All who have become Reborn into Oneness with Universal God, That I AM THAT I AM, and are consumed with the Reality of Universal God's Pure Divine Ever-Presence and Truth.

53. Because God is everywhere Present and all Knowing; all Souls may come to Eternal Truth and attain True Salvation and Liberation through my Holy Initiation and God's Divine Grace earned through my two Self-Sacrifices and Vow.

54. Men may hoard earthly things and keep them from others. But no one can hoard God's Pure Divine Truth or God's Supreme Promise and still have Perfect Final Union with God for himself at the end of this life.

55. Those who seek to hoard God's Supreme Promise for themselves alone bring woe upon them of their own wrong doing. Truly, they deprive themselves of Perfect Final Union with God at the end of this life.

56. They also bring woe upon themselves who deny The One God or any of His Prophets, Saints, Buddhas, Saviors or Avataras, or His Awakened One or cause the people to fall into wrong belief.

57. And greater woe do those bring upon themselves who turn one Soul away from That I AM THAT I AM or The Supreme Gift of Perfect Final Union with Him, which He has sent me forth to give unto all Souls. Such as these shall answer to God for the full burden of each who is turned away from That I AM THAT I AM.

58. Divine Law is taught by every God-Freed One, but Self-Realization and Perfect Final Union with That I AM THAT I AM are attained only through the Divine Grace of God's Supreme Promise, given unto all Souls by The New Covenant The One Universal God has made with all Souls through me in this day.

59. No earthbound one can know Universal God Unmanifest, That I AM THAT I AM - ever! Only those whom God sends forth, The First Emanation of The One Universal God, is Revealed to the earthbound! That I Am.

60. Though taken up into Perfect Union with Universal God, I have sacrificed Perfect Final Union with God twice and returned into this world of suffering, sorrow, death and rebirth yet another time to give Universal God's Promise and Divine Grace unto all People; to set all Souls Free from Darkness, Ignorance, Illusion and free all Souls from Birth, Suffering, Sorrow, Pain and Death.

61. The Gift that God has sent me to give unto all Souls, is The Gift of Eternal Life in Perfect Final Union with That I AM THAT I AM, and no other. Through my Holy Initiation and God's Supreme Promise, Realization of Perfect Oneness with Universal God, That Absolute Universal I AM THAT I AM, The One True Self without a Second, is now opened to all Souls everywhere for all time.

62. This, is my Profession: Universal God Alone is Real! This Universe, and all that is within it, is Universal God's Divine Dream and Image; created by God out of His Own Being! You are Soul which is Pure Divine Universal Spirit that is One and Identical with

Universal God and no other! I AM THAT I AM. Thou Art That.

63. Each Soul lives only to fulfill God's Universal Design. Nothing is there, other than Darkness, ignorance and wrong belief, to keep you apart from That I AM THAT I AM, your True Divine Self.

64. This is The Truth! Know The Truth! And The Truth Shall Set You Free.

**Om So'ham Tat Tvam Asi!
I Am That - Thou Art That!
Jai Bhagavan Ji!**

**Here Ends The Chapter Entitled
The Friend's Profession**

Chapter Three
Universal God's Divine Design of Creation

By The Will and Grace of The One Universal God:

Before The Beginning, there was neither Being nor Not Being. Neither Space, nor Time, nor Energy, nor Matter existed, nor did they not exist.

2. Before The Beginning, there was Only The One Universal God Unmanifest. Total, Silent, and Absolute within Its Self, One without a Second. Neither Infinity nor Eternity was there; neither Existence nor Non-existence; for these, too, are born of Creation and Space and Time. Universal God, That I AM THAT I AM, wanted to Know, and Creation was born.

3. Within the nameless and formlessness of The One Universal God Unmanifest there arose the question "Who Am I?" And, being One Alone, without a Second, there was no answer to this question.

4. For a hundred thousand Eternities, That Absolute One without a Second brooded upon how It could come to Know Its Self, and answer this question "Who Am I?"

5. And it came to pass, that The One Universal God Unmanifest thought, in formless thoughts, "I shall come to Know The One by Manifesting My Own Self and Being within This Self and out of This Self which I Am. This I will Be and yet, beyond this which I Create, I shall neither Be nor Not Be, for That is This My Nature.

6. "And within this Creation will be all possible possibilities to be fulfilled. And That which I shall Manifest, shall fulfill this Creation by doing all of the possible doings within it. By this means, I shall come to Know this Self by what it has done and I shall Know Who I Am by This, My Creation."

7. Universal God, Absolute and One without a Second conceived within Its Self, "This which I will make manifest shall be Created out of the very essence of That Which I Am, It shall be This One, and This One shall be It. Of this, there is no doubt. And I shall Be within each and every least and greatest part of this Creation and shall Be It and yet beyond It at one and the same time."

8. By this Self-Sacrifice, Universal God Unmanifest, who is beyond All-Knowing, All-Wisdom, and All Creation and Being, set forth a portion of His own Self as God Manifest - The Creator, The Preserver, and The Destroyer of all Creation; all in One and One in all. From Universal God made manifest, came forth all Matter,

all Souls and all Life. From Being and Life, came forth Mind. From Mind, the Truths. From the Truths, the Worlds. From this, all actions and their results. So it is that all within Creation is Created, Preserved, and Destroyed by The One Universal God Manifest alone.

9. "And," that Absolute I AM THAT I AM, One without a Second thought, "while within This Creation, This One must come to forget that It is The Creator and Know this Creation as if it were Real and Independent and Complete within itself. For, if this Second continues to Know that we are One, This One shall continue viewing it from this all encompassing and All-Knowing Oneness that I Am, and nothing shall come of it."

10. And, it came to pass that The One Universal God Unmanifest designed this whole Creation and each part of it to fulfill this Quest that It might know the answer to the Question "Who Am I?" And, That Absolute One imaged Universes and Worlds without number. And all of the forces and Natures of each world and the means of their existences were included in this Divine Design.

11. There being nothing but God, The Creator brought forth this whole Creation and all within it out of That One's Own Substance and Being. Because of this, this whole Creation is the very Substance and Being of God made manifest in the countless myriads of names and forms.

12. There being no Spirit and no Soul but God, The Creator brought forth The One Universal Spirit and the infinite numbers of Souls, out of That One's limitless Spirit. Because of this, The True Essence of every Soul is Pure Divine Spirit which is One and Identical with The One Universal God and no other; and The Supreme Spirit of God is, verily, The One True Soul of every Being.

13. There being no Self but God, The Creator brought forth The True Self of every Being out of That One's Own Self, and instilled it within every Being. Because of this, The One True Self of every Being is The Self of The One Universal God and no other.

14. There being nothing but Paratpara, The One Universal God of Countless Names and Forms Who Is Beyond All Names and Forms, before Creation, verily, The One Universal God is The One Substance, Spirit, Soul and Self of all Creation, all Existence and all Being. Of this there is no doubt.

15. When this Imaging was through, The One Universal God Unmanifest considered Its Creation and saw that all was ordered by Nature and System and that it was Good.

16. And That Absolute One moved upon Its Creation and saw that there were none who could fulfill Its Quest, for all was fixed and in its place, from the Universes, to the very Creatures themselves.

17. That Absolute One considered Its Creatures and, choosing the most likely of them, Created Man in Its own Image to be the greatest of all Creatures.

18. And That One set all this Creation into motion and decreed that each smallest part of The Second should work its way from the least of Its Creation unto the Greatest. And this smallest part was called Soul. And It Decreed that the Greatest and Final

Doing that each Soul should do within this Creation, shall be to Realize that it is One and Identical with That Absolute One and return unto It through this Realization, knowing, I AM THAT I AM.

19. To insure the independent Nature and faultless continuation of Its Creation, That Absolute One made each part of Its Design Interdependent, one upon another. And each action to give rise to a reaction, which would become, in turn, the creator of still another action and reaction, in an endless chain of Cause and Effect, Action and Reaction, Infinite and Eternal; and this came to be called Karma.

20. When The One Universal God Unmanifest had finished Its Design of Creation, That Absolute One, Father of all the Universes, issued forth, within Its own Self, The Image, Total, Infinite, Eternal, and complete unto itself. And, like unto Its Divine Design, That One made this whole Existence to be filled with all possible Dualities of Light and Dark, Up and Down, Inner and Outer.

21. And when it was finished, That Absolute One withdrew Its Knowingness from Its Creation, giving unto it and all within it, its independent existence.

22. And there was one alone among the Creatures of Its Creation from which That One did not withdraw Its Knowingness, but unto whom It gave the Highest Gift of Total Knowledge of Its Oneness and Identity with That One. And this Creature was called Man.

23. In The Beginning, There was The Image. And The Image was God and God was The Image, for The One Universal God Unmanifest had made Its Self Manifest. Thus came into Being all of the Universes and Worlds, and all within them.

24. And, within The Image there were Manifested all of the Universes, and all of The Dualities of Existence and Non-Existence, all of The Worlds and the Creatures and Qualities thereof.

25. And there came forth The Heaven and The Earth; The Light and The Darkness; The Solids, Liquids, and the Gasses; and all of Space, Time, Energy, and Matter and their opposites; and all other Manifestations of this Infinite and Eternal Existence were Manifest.

26. And That Absolute One without a Second entered into Its Own Creation and filled it in Perfect Innocence and found it was Perfect within itself.

27. And The One Universal God Unmanifest filled the many Universes of Its Creation with all manner of Beings from the least knowing to the most; and set into motion, the progression of Souls through them, that Its Design might become fulfilled.

28. And Spirit meshed, blended and merged into matter to become life. And Spirit wanted to know light, so the eye came into being. Spirit wanted to know sound, so the organ of hearing was brought forth. Spirit wanted know flavor, so the organ of taste came into being. Spirit wanted to continue what God had begun, and the organs of reproduction came into being. All things that Spirit desired, that, The One Universal God brought forth into being.

29. And That Absolute One Created, in Its Own Image, the Being called Man and gave unto Him the Power and Ability to Exist within Its Creation while Knowing that He is One and Identical with That One Unmanifest.

30. So it was, that in The Beginning all Men lived within The Perfect Paradise of Total Knowledge of Oneness and Identity as The One Universal God Unmanifest and were untouched by The Illusion of Duality.

31. And it was Universal God's Command that Soul should not taste of The Fruits of Action born of The Tree of Duality and Illusion, but that all Soul should Fulfill Universal God's Design of Creation. And, The One Universal God Ordained that Man should have two selves, a Greater Self, which is Soul, which is Pure Divine Universal Spirit that is One and Identical with God and no other which exists beyond all Creation - forever; and a smaller self, which is made out of God's own Creation alone and exists only within it. And God called Man's Greater Self Adhyatma and his smaller self, Adama. And God ordained that Man should be like unto the Great Tree of Duality and Illusion and that his two selves should be like two birds that live, verily, in that same tree. And God commanded that Adama, the bird of Man's smaller self, should act and eat of the fruit of the Tree of Duality and Illusion but never leave it; and, that Adhyatma, the bird of Man's Greater Self should neither act nor eat of the fruit of the Tree, but should be ever an unattached eternal Witness to all of Creation, untouched by actions and their results, and ever free to come and go by Its Will according to God's Divine Design.

32. And Adhyatma was above and beyond suffering, sorrow, pain, death and birth again, for, in His Perfect Paradise of Total Knowledge all Souls were One in their Oneness with The One Universal God Unmanifest. For this was Universal God's Design of Creation.

33. And with His Perfect Paradise, The One Universal God gave unto Adhyatma the gift of Freedom having five aspects which are: Free Will, Free-Choice, Self-Determination, Individual Freedom and absolute, inescapable Personal Responsibility. And these were all born of God's own Perfect Free-Will. For this was, truly, God's very own Nature itself. And, without this Freedom, all possible possibilities could not be fulfilled.

34. And all Men lived in the perfect freedom and independent Unity of Adhyatma and, all Men were Adhyatma and only later became Adama after The Fall from Perfect Paradise. For Adhyatma is, Truly, The Divine Self and Adama the animal self and creature. And The Divine Self dwells within The Creature and is ever One and Identical with The One Universal God, That Absolute One without a Second, within whom this whole of Existence has its Name and Form and Being. And they were, Adhyatma and Adama, as God had intended as two Birds in one tree.

35. But Adhyatma became fascinated with The World of Duality and Illusion and, partaking of the Free Choice given unto Him by The One Universal God, forsook Universal God's Design for Him. And, merging with Adama, partook of The Fruits of Action, born of The Tree of Duality and Illusion and fell from The Perfect Paradise of Total Knowledge of Its Oneness

and Identity with The One Universal God Unmanifest. And The Force of Darkness was born.

36. All Souls and all Men, Being One with one another in Spirit, straight away, entered into the Illusion. In that moment, Adhyatma forgot Its Oneness with The One God and became confused and identified Itself with the false self and He came to believe upon the Idea that Duality created. And Adhyatma became caught up in the web of Illusion and was differentiated into Man and Woman; and into many Men and Women, each separate and isolated from the other. And through each man and each woman came to know Birth and Death and Birth again and again; and the suffering, sorrow, and pain that lies between these. And struggle and strife were born among and between all men and between all women, everywhere.

37. Having forsaken The Perfect Paradise of Knowledge of their Oneness with The One Universal God by their Free-Choice, all men and all women fell under the Spell of This World of Duality and Illusion to endure The Ordeal of Birth, Suffering, Sorrow, Pain, and Death over and over again; until each should, as with all other Beings of Universal God's Creation, struggle up the Ladder of Spiritual Knowledge and, once again, attain Realization of their own Oneness and Identity with The One Universal God Unmanifest, That Absolute One without a Second and in His Attainment regain The Perfect Paradise and know Salvation and Liberation from Birth, Suffering, Sorrow, Pain, and Death. And, The Divine Adhyatman was called among Men, The Unspeakable and was known by the Mark +.

38. Slow, difficult and unbearably painful was the progress of men and women toward return to The Perfect Paradise. Due to Adhyatma's Great Sleep of Ignorance, Man fell further and further away from His True Divine Nature and Identity. Thinking The One Universal God, His Own True Self, to be other than That, He came to believe in a Fierce and Jealous and Vengeful God that was far removed from Him. And He made Idols of wood and metal and, believing these objects to be His God, He fell upon His face and Worshiped and Sacrificed others of God's Beings unto them. Knowing not that He worshiped and Sacrificed unto His own Sleep and Ignorance, and no other.

39. And those who had eyes with which to see, were blinded; and those who had ears with which to hear, were deafened. Fearing that which could go beyond their blindness and deafness, they fell upon those who had begun to Awaken from The Sleep of Ignorance set upon them by their confusion with The World of Duality and Illusion, and cursed them; and killed them without mercy.

40. The One Universal God Unmanifest, knowing this Abomination which had arisen within Its Design of Creation; it came to pass that That Absolute One's Mercy, Love, and Compassion that surpasses all Understanding, moved Its Grace within Its Creation and gave unto all Men this Gift: That in each age, when men and women of the nations have fallen into darkness and Ignorance rules the land; one shall be Awakened within their midst who shall Light up The Clear Light of Universal God's Truth within their Hearts and Minds. He shall be their Savior and Liberator from their Sleep and Ignorance.

41. And whosoever among them shall Love this Awakened One and, taking True Faith in Him shall become as One with Him shall also Awaken and Attain Salvation and Liberation from Birth, Suffering, Sorrow, Pain, and Death and shall re-enter The Perfect Paradise of Total Oneness and Identity with The One Universal God and no other; within this life or at its end.

42. So it is, that in each age, when men and women of all Nations have fallen into the deepest depths of Duality and Illusion and sleep the Sleep of Ignorance; The One Universal God, That Absolute One without a Second, moves upon the face of Its Creation and Awakens One who has come The Way farthest toward The Goal of Self-Realization.

43. It is The One Universal God's Eternal Promise that all men may Attain Salvation and Liberation and Regain The Perfect Paradise of their own Free Choice and Doing, even as they have lost it.

44. But slow and steep and narrow as the edge of a razor is The Path Home and few are they who travel upon it that attain The Goal. And often is it that this World falls from the Truth to enter the realm of Darkness, failing to know The Clear Light of The One Universal God's Truth, though It shines within and all around them.

45. For this reason, and in this age, The One Universal God's Infinite and Eternal Mercy, Love, Compassion, and Grace has brought forth The Awakened One, The Friend, that all Beings might Know the Truth of their Oneness and Identity with The One Universal God and no other, and be set Free from Ignorance, Birth, Suffering, Sorrow, Pain, and Death, Forever; and regain The Perfect Paradise within this Life and Perfect Final Union with The One Universal God, That I AM THAT I AM, at the end of this life. To the end that The Force of Darkness shall be banished and The Age of Universal God's Pure Divine Truth shall become manifest for the Salvation and Liberation of all Souls and the continued Survival of humanity.

46. For this reason and in this age, I sacrificed Perfect Final Union with The One Universal God twice and vowed that, never again will I enter therein, until I have seen all Souls safely Home into Perfect Final Union with That I AM THAT I AM before me.

47. Because of this, The One Universal God, I AM THAT I AM, has made a New Covenant with all Souls through me and Promised that:

48. {G} "Whosoever, having received The Friend's Holy Initiation shall follow Him to the end of this life, shall have the Supreme Gift of Perfect Final Union with That I AM THAT I AM which The Friend of all Souls sacrificed for My sake and the sake of all Souls everywhere for all time."

49. Whosoever shall do these that are Commanded by That Absolute One through The Awakened One, shall drink the Water of Life and be Free.

50. This is The One Universal God's Divine Truth as It has come upon me and become One with me, making me One with It.

51. I did not ask that it should be so, neither may I turn away from my God's Command. Though this very Heaven and Earth should pass away,

and these mortal bones be ground to dust, nothing could change my task, for this is The One Universal God's Appointment, made Manifest for the Salvation and Liberation of all Beings, given for the sake of The World that all Beings might Awaken from The Sleep of Ignorance and take up their Divine Nature and follow me Home to Paradise.

52. I AM THAT I AM! Whosoever becomes One with Me attains Salvation and Liberation from Ignorance, Birth, Suffering, Sorrow, Pain, and Death; and regains The Perfect Paradise of Total Oneness and Identity with The One Universal God, That Absolute One without a Second, and no other; either within this Life or at its end.

53. This is my Testimony of The One Universal God's Mercy, Love, Compassion, and Grace; This is my Testimony of The One Universal God's Pure Truth as it has come to pass in me in this day.

Paratpara Kijai!
All Victory and Glory
To God The Beloved!

Jai Bhagavan Ji!
Victory To That Beloved
Universal I AM THAT I AM
Which You Are!

Here Ends The Chapter Entitled
Universal God's Divine
Design of Creation

Chapter Four
The Mission and the Million

By The Will and Grace of The One Universal God:

Before Creating the Universes, Paratpara, The One Universal God, Created His Eternal Universal Religion and His Holy Adhyatma-Yoga-Dharma, The Way by which all Souls could Realize their Eternal Oneness with Him; to insure that all Souls would have an Eternal Way to Realize The Truth, be set free and return Home into Perfect Final Union with Him.

2. Universal God's Divine Pure Truth is Eternal, Unchanging, and Immutable. Nothing can change it. Nothing can destroy it. Though the affairs of men and civilizations rise and fall as with the tides, Universal God's Divine Pure Truth remains ever One, ever Pure, ever Unchanging amidst this ever-changing world of Illusion.

3. As a mirror left in a field slowly becomes clouded with the dust of this world until no image can be seen within it; even so do the Souls slowly lose the Knowledge of Universal God's Pure Divine Truth to the dust of Ignorance that they allow to settle upon its mirror face.

4. Out of His Infinite Love and Compassion, Paratpara, The One Universal God of Countless Names and Forms Who Is Beyond All Names and Forms has given unto men and nations Four Ages of Truth.

5. In the first Age of Divine Pure Truth, all people Live God's Pure Divine Truth, Know The Truth fully exactly as it is, and follow His Holy Adhyatma-Yoga-Dharma, The Way to Perfect Final Union with Him.

6. In the second Age of Truth, the dust of Ignorance covers one-quarter of The Full Holy Adhyatma-Yoga-Dharma. This, truly, is called The Age of Three-Quarter Truth.

7. In the Third Age of Truth, the dust of Ignorance obscures another quarter of The Holy Adhyatma-Yoga-Dharma from the hearts and minds of the people. This, Truly, is called The Age of One-Half Truth.

8. In the Fourth Age of Truth, the dust of Ignorance hides yet another quarter of The Holy Adhyatma-Yoga-Dharma from the hearts and minds of the people. This, Truly, is called The Age of Ignorance, Darkness, Chaos and Destruction.

9. Countless thousands of years ago, when darkness had covered the earth and the people had begun to turn their hearts and minds away from Universal God's Divine Pure Truth of Holy Adhyatma-Yoga-Dharma; Universal

God sent forth His Divine Call unto all Souls to come to Him of their own Free Will. Of the infinite numbers of Souls, only one million answered Universal God's Divine Call.

10. And Paratpara, The One Universal God of Countless Names and Forms Who Is Beyond All Names and Forms, gathered the million Souls together within the Highest Heaven World of Holy Adhyatma and bid them to take part in His Divine Design, whereby all Souls might be saved from the horrible ravages and fiery destruction which The Force of Darkness and its minions of Chaos and Destruction would surely bring upon the earth thousands of years in the future in The Age of Ignorance, Darkness, and Chaos if they were not stopped.

11. And The One Universal God offered every Soul gathered therein who would choose it of pure Free Will, a place within His Divine Design. And He called each Soul one-by-one to step over the invisible line that divided those who accepted from those who refused. And all of the million Souls accepted Universal God's Divine Offer of their own Free Will, and stepped over the line. And not one Soul refused.

12. And when they had all accepted His Divine Offer and stepped over the line, Universal God Revealed unto them His Divine Design for the Creation and The Holy Sanctuary of His Eternal Religion and The Great Wheel of Holy Adhyatma-Yoga-Dharma. And Universal God told them that, in the appointed time, He would Awaken within one Soul among them who would be an ordinary man or woman who would become The Friend of all Souls. And The Friend of all Souls would, twice, attain Perfect Final Union with God; the first time by God's Grace alone and the second time by His own works. And The Friend of all Souls would, twice, make the Supreme Self-Sacrifice of giving up Perfect Final Union with God and returning to this World for the sake of all Souls. And, that it would be this Supreme Compassion and Self-Sacrifice of an ordinary man or woman, which would set The Wheel of Holy Adhyatma-Yoga-Dharma into motion in the appointed day and restore The True Salvation, and Liberation of Universal God's Pure Divine Truth and The Way Home into Perfect Final Union with Him, to all suffering Souls.

13. And Paratpara, The One Universal God of Countless Names and Forms Who Is Beyond All Names and Forms brought The Million Souls together in Divine Organization such that they, and all Souls who would heed The Call in that day, would come together in groups of Three; and the groups of Three in groups of Twelve; and the groups of Twelve in groups of Forty-eight and so on; such that these very Souls should form the rim, the spokes, and the Hub of The Great Wheel.

14. And Universal God showed unto them how The Great Wheel of Divine Truth would be set into motion and The Age of Ignorance, Darkness, Chaos and Destruction brought to an end and His Eternal Divine Pure Truth of Holy Adhyatma-Yoga-Dharma restored on earth for The Salvation and Liberation of all Souls and not one least Soul would be lost.

15. And The Million returned into the World of Creation and drew around them the Cloak of Spiritual Sleep, Ignorance and Illusion, to walk their individual paths toward

Enlightenment and Self-Realization and await The Awakening of The Friend of All Souls and His Call To Awaken and carry out Universal God's Divine Design for The Salvation and Liberation of the world.

**All Victory and Glory To
God The Beloved!**

**Victory To That Beloved
Universal I AM THAT I AM
Which You Are!**

**Here Ends The Chapter Entitled
The Mission and the Million**

Chapter Five

The New Covenant Revealed

*The First Testament of
Universal God's Revelation of His New Covenant
As Given By God to All Souls
Through His Awakened One
Maitreya Adhyatma Bhagavan Sri Babajhan
Al-Kahlil The Friend*

*On The Seventh Day of August
Nineteen Hundred & Fifty-One*

By The Will and Grace of The One Universal God:

While wandering aimlessly in the wilderness of life, I heard The Call of God that surpasses all calls.

2. Crying out, I threw the Gate of my heart open wide in search of The One God in All.

3. And, from the very wilderness itself, the voice of God arose, saying:

4. {G} "In this wilderness you have been called John of Douglas, but from beyond this one called John of Douglas this cry has come!

5. {G} "Fear no more my Beloved One. Your cry is heard. Your Faith has made you Whole. Your Quest has been answered!

6. {G} "Quest no more. For in your seeking after Me, your Lord, your God, you have found The Answer to all quests!

7. {G} "From this day forth, you shall be known unto men of all Nations as The God-Realized One, Teacher of Oneness, The Friend - Bhagavan Sri Babajhan Al-Kahlil The Friend!

8. {G} "And you shall be the Living Testament and Seal upon a New Covenant, I shall make between Man and God through you. And your number shall be called Seven Hundred Seventy and Seven; and you shall be called Blessed among men, for you shall unite all of My people upon The Pure Way, that leads to Oneness with Me!"

9. Within that single moment, all of the Veils of Darkness and Ignorance that had blinded my Spiritual Sight were torn away; and out of The Eternal

abode of The One God came forth a Clear Light such as would light up the Sun.

10. And the Breath of The One God came upon me, searing my flesh from my bones, winnowing The Real from the unreal and scattering my false self to the far corners of Eternity!

11. Within that Eternal moment, Light and Darkness met in Divine Battle that shook the very Foundations of Existence. And, when the Battle was ended, Light came forth in Victorious Glory; and Darkness was conquered, Forever.

12. And the One that I Am became harkened to The One God that is All In All. And I answered The One in Formless Thoughts through Silent Words, saying "Yes! Verily! Thou Art The One God my Lord! Truly Thou Art All In All! There is no other!"

13. And the soundless Voice of my Lord came again unto me saying:

14. {G} "You are My Beloved who has found The Truth and The Truth has set you Free. As I Am, so Thou Art! There is no I in you but That I AM THAT I AM. Through you, I shall make a New Covenant with all Souls and give My Promise unto all Souls. A New Covenant and Promise that will resurrect their Spirits and bring them into Perfect Final Union with Me, I AM THAT I AM!

15. {G} "And my New Covenant and My Promise shall be this: that all who Believe in Me and in You and receive your Holy Initiation and follow you Home to Me to the end of their lives; I shall give unto them Freedom from the suffering and sorrow of this World, Freedom from the endless rounds of birth and death, Supreme Happiness, and Eternal Life in Perfect Final Union with Me. As a drop of water returning into the sea becomes The Sea, so shall they be One with Me!

16. {G} "Unto those who know Me in thee, My Beloved, and have Faith in you and this, My New Covenant and Promise made through Thee, I shall give The Gift of Perfect Final Union with Me. And they shall no more be born or die but shall abide in Eternal Oneness with Me.

17. {G} "I Am The Alpha and the Omega, The Goal and The Purpose of all Existence, all Creation and all Being. You, are The Gate and The Way that leads all Souls Home to Perfect Final Union with Me - I AM THAT I AM. You are My Light made manifest in this world. Whosoever comes through you abides in Me, forever. So Be It!"

18. In that single moment, the True I that is One with God, The Lord of all Creation, was Awakened from the Sleep of The Living Dead and I was reborn, Bhagavan Sri Babajhan The Friend, The God-Realized One, Teacher of Oneness, The Friend! Of this there is no doubt!

19. And I cried out to The Beloved once again, saying:

20. "My Lord, my God, my own True Self. Haunted am I with doubts of my worthiness. Ignorant and impure am I, living among the ignorant and impure! How can it be that I shall be the One You have Chosen, when I am so unworthy of this Great Work?

21. "How shall I be the Living Testament and Seal upon Thy New Covenant and Promise? How shall I be

Thy Perfect Instrument? When Jesus of Nazareth, Thy Beloved Messenger before me, was Perfect from the moment of his Birth?"

22. Out of The Clear Light, Eternal beyond the first day of Creation, came the Breath of my Lord, my God. And His Breath drove straight to the Center of my Being, making me One with It.

23. And I heard with the ears that know no sound:

24. {G} "Thy Life is Touched! Thy Heart is cleansed! Thy Ignorance and impurity is dispelled.

25. {G} "Even as the darkness of the night flees at the coming of The Light of The Dawn, so have I purified you in The Sacred Fire of My Presence!

26. {G} "The division within you that kept you from True Knowledge that I Am your True Self, is healed. You are made Whole! Awaken, Bhagavan Babajhan The Friend! Arise and shine forth My Light into The Darkness of this World!

27. {G} "Thy Light is come. My Glow-ray is alight within you! It shall be seen within you by all who have eyes and will see!

28. {G} "My people are sleeping in ignorance of Me and darkness surrounds them. But I have Awakened within you and made you My Radiance in this, My Creation!

29. {G} "Go forth into this Age of Darkness for Me as Bhagavan Babajhan The Friend. Proclaim and Bear True Witness to this New Covenant and Promise I have given unto all Souls through you this Day.

Give this, My New Covenant and Promise to all Souls and bring them Home to Perfect Final Union with Me. I AM THAT I AM.

30. {G} "Good people of all Nations shall be drawn to Thy Light. Rulers and Great Ones shall take Joy in Thy Awakening and shall open their hearts unto Me and all people.

31. {G} "Lift up your eyes, My Beloved. See the multitudes gathering to come unto Thee! From beyond Eternity thy Source has come unto Thee! I AM THAT I AM. My Presence can be seen upon Thee. I have made you one with Me. There is no longer any I in Thee but Me. I am your one True Self and your Heart!"

32. Again, the essence of The Word without sound issued forth from The Clear Light of God saying:

33. {G} "Go forth Bhagavan Babajhan The Friend, My Beloved! Let The Truth of My Covenant be Revealed unto all men. Carry My Word into this sleeping world. For you are My Truth, My Light, and My Way. You are My Gift of Salvation and Liberation I give unto all people!"

34. Then, once again, I heard my Lord, my God calling The Call of Calls saying:

35. {G} "Who will make the greatest sacrifice and go forward for Me?"

36. And I said unto My Lord, That Beloved I AM THAT I AM, "Here I am. I will go forth for you!"

37. Suddenly a Great Light was struck in me and the soundless Voice of The One Universal God said unto me:

38. {G} "You are My Beloved! In you I am pleased!

39. {G} "Go forth for Me! Tell the sleeping ones that they see and hear, but fail to understand. Tell them that they must close their eyes and close their ears to this world and open wide the Gate of their hearts unto That I AM THAT I AM.

40. {G} "Tell them that they must See, but not with their eyes; and Hear, but not with their ears. Tell them that they must see with Divine Sight that needs no light; and hear with Divine Hearing that needs no sound.

41. {G} "Then, they will come Home to Me through you and My New Covenant and Supreme Promise given unto them this day through you.

42. {G} "Tell them that through you I have also given them The Supreme Way to Realize their Oneness with Me while living in this life. Tell them that this Way is My Eternal Universal Religion which I embody in you.

43. {G} "Whosoever receives your Holy Initiation and follows you faithfully shall have Direct Experience of his Oneness with Me. And I will Awaken him from the sleep of spiritual ignorance. And he shall be Born Anew even while living in this world.

44. {G} "Tell them that My New Covenant and Knowledge of Oneness with That I AM THAT I AM, are the keys that unlock the prison cell of suffering, sorrow, death and rebirth and set all Souls free.

45. {G} "Following you to the end of this life and keeping Worship, Prayer and Spiritual Practice in Faith, according to your Teachings and instructions and examples; these are The Way that fulfills My Promise.

46. {G} "I will Awaken all Faithful Maitreyians who heed these words, to The Supreme Truth that they are One with Me their Lord, their God, their One True Self; All In All!

47. {G} "This is The Way. There is no other way by which a Soul may certainly come Home to Me.

48. {G} "Truly, My Beloved, The Path before you is filled with treachery and danger for you and those Faithful Maitreyians who take up their Divine Nature and follow you. Even as it has been for all Mercies I have sent unto them before you.

49. {G} "In those Days which are yet to come, The Sleeping, who are The Living Dead, will call you and those who follow you and teach this, My Word; blasphemer, heretic and all manner of evil names. And the Spiritually blind will despise you and spit upon you, out of their own ignorance of Me, their Lord, their God. For I am The One Universal God. The One Source, Substance and Self of all Creation, all Existence and all Being. I AM THAT I AM. There is no other. But in their Spiritual blindness and ignorance, they do not know Me.

50. {G} "I am The God of Abraham and all of The Prophets and Mercies that I have sent unto Man in all times and places.

51. {G} "Though the Spiritually ignorant and the bigots will curse and defile you as they have cursed and defiled all of My Mercies, My Faithful have no fear. Nor shall any Maitreyian who follows you faithfully

Home to Me with all his mind and all his heart have need to fear.

52. {G} "Whosoever will hear My Word; and enter My Gate through your Holy Initiation; and heed your teachings and instructions; and, making Me his Purpose and his Goal, will follow you who are My Way and My Light; is My Own. And at the end of his life, I will take him Home into Perfect Final Union Me.

53. {G} "No Fire can burn him. No spear can pierce him. No water can drown him. Nothing is there that can touch the Maitreyian who knows that he is not a body, but Pure Divine Spirit that is One and Identical with That I AM THAT I AM.

54. {G} "Whoever will go forth into The Darkness for Me, Proclaiming and Bearing True Witness to you and My New Covenant; I will hold fast in My Heart.

55. {G} "Even as I held Abraham, Moses, Buddha, Jesus, Rama, Krishna and my Prophet Mohammed fast in My Heart; so will I protect and guide you and all who accept My Truth and take up their Divine Natures and follow you Home to Me.

56. {G} "Let all men know that in each age, when My people have fallen into ignorance and darkness, I Awaken within an ordinary man and send him forth into this sleeping world as My Representative, who brings My Divine Light unto Man in such manner as fulfills the needs of that Day.

57. {G} "Some I have Commissioned to bring Man the Iron Fist of The Law. Others I have sent forth to soften The Law with Mercy and Compassion and redeem Man from its sting.

58. {G} "Woe be unto those foolish ones who accept only one of My Mercies to Man. Greater woe unto those who deny or denounce any of My Mercies.

59. {G} "As a man does unto the least of men, so does he do unto all men and unto That I AM THAT I AM The Lord thy God. Such as these may be forgiven.

60. {G} "But whosoever shall deny and denounce even one of My Mercies, setting man against man and Nation against Nation in My Name, is guilty of the most grievous sin. He shall suffer without measure.

61. {G} "For, as you deny and denounce a single one of My Mercies to Man, even so do you deny and denounce The Lord Thy God. And My Face shall be turned away from you and you shall live out your days in Darkness.

62. {G} "Unto those who challenge you, saying that theirs is the only True Way and their Messenger the only True Messenger, make this Truth Known:

63. {G} "Brahma I revealed unto Man that he might know the Essence of Creation.

64. {G} "Vishnu I revealed unto Man that he might know Endurance and Preservation.

65. {G} "Shiva I revealed unto Man that he might know that Death and Destruction are no more than the compassionate plowman readying the earth for new Seed.

66. {G} "Rama I did send unto Man that he might know the True meaning of Righteousness.

67. {G} "Krishna I did send unto Man that he might know Order and Right Conduct.

68. {G} "Abraham I did send unto Man that he might know the Necessity of ceaselessly seeking after Me.

69. {G} "Moses I did send unto Man that he might know the Iron Hand of The Law.

70. {G} "Zoroaster I did send unto Man that he might know the essence of Duality.

71. {G} "Lao-Tsu I did send unto Man that he might know the One Unity within All Duality.

72. {G} "Confucius I did send unto Man that he might know the Right Conduct of Affairs.

73. {G} "Sakyamuni Buddha I did send unto Man that he might know the Cause of Suffering and a Way to its end.

74. {G} "Bodhidharma I did send unto Man that he might learn the lesson of giving My Light to all Nations Equally.

75. {G} "Jesus of Nazareth I did send unto Man that he might know My Love made Perfect within him.

76. {G} "Muhammad of Mecca I did send unto Man that he might know that I Am The One God who speaks through all of The Prophets.

77. {G} "Baha'u'llah I did send unto Man that he might know the value of Perseverance in the face of all Adversity.

78. {G} "Gandhi I did send unto Man that he might know the value of unswerving Truthfulness and Non Violence.

79. {G} "Ramakrishna I did send unto Man that he might know the Way of Bliss as a direct road Home to Me.

80. {G} "These and all other of My Messengers and Prophets I did send unto Man that the steps of men should be turned ever more steadily toward Me.

81. {G} "Now Bhagavan Sri Babajhan The Friend, My Own Divine Radiance, I send you forth as I sent those who came before you.

82. {G} "Go forth for Me. Unite all people into a new people through this Covenant I make with all Souls through you This Day!"

83. {G} "Go forth for Me, not as one who is Perfect by Earthly measure as judged by those who are yet earthbound, but as One made Perfect in Oneness with Me through the Knowledge that You and I are not we but One.

84. {G} "Listen not to those who pridefully proclaim against you. For the character of each man's Faith is a matter that is between that Soul and Me. And no man hath the wisdom to judge such things; but That I AM THAT I AM, who is within yet beyond all, and knows every man's heart.

85. {G} "And when Men would revile you and do harm unto you and those who are My Faithful through you, say unto them for Me these words:

86. {G} "'What business have you with me? If I offend The One God who has sent me unto you, He will punish me directly without need of your sword. Have you so little Faith that you must make your understanding into Reality by force, thus interfering with God's Great Plan for all Men? Did not the blind of your Prophet's time seek to do unto Him even as you now seek to do unto God's Compassionate One sent again to you?'

87. {G} "Think not if you choose for Me, your road will be easy, or your burden lighter than that of any other man. Nothing shall I do for you that would not be done for any other of My People. And I shall cast a net of forgetfulness over you and none of what you know of Me now shall remain, save the smallest thread and shadow to guide you back Home to Me.

88. {G} "But, when you attain The Goal, in that day, all that has been taken will be restored, and more. For, to fulfill The Covenant for which I have Awakened within you, that I shall make with all Souls, you must lose all Knowledge of your Oneness with Me and regain it by your own works.

89. {G} "Go, therefore, and make ready this Heart and Mind and Body as fitting vessels for My Spirit that My Radiance may shine forth unto all Men as a Lamp uncovered and set upon a high place!

90. {G} "And, how could this be otherwise? Unless you do these things of your own actions and efforts, the Sleeping and The Living Dead will only excuse their sleep and ignorance by saying of you as they have of all those I have sent 'He is blessed and far beyond our ability to do like Him, so let us return to the stillness of our Illusions, Sleep and Ignorance.' For, it is just this that they have done with all others of those I have sent unto them!

91. {G} "You, My Beloved Bhagavan Babajhan The Friend, have seen The Light. You have known The Truth. You have traveled The Way and come Home to Me! We Are One. No longer is there any other I in you but Me.

92. {G} "Go now and do that for which you were made upon this Earth. Go among My People, Proclaiming and bearing True Witness to This, The New Covenant of The One God, and tell them for Me:

93. {G} "There is but One God. There is no other! As all in a dream is of The Dreamer; as a drop of water taken from the Sea, though it be taken to the Stars, Is Sea; All that Is and all that is not, Is This I; for there is no I but God! And, everything Is! There is no one thing that Is and another that is not. There is no one thing that is True and another that is not True. All Is. And it is All True. True and not True are illusion born only of the sleeping minds of the Living Dead who dwell in darkness and Ignorance. There is no I but God! All that Is, Is of God! All that Is, I Am. All that Is, Thou Art. You and I are not we, but One. And I Am The Lord Thy God. The Beginning, The Middle, and The End of All that Is! As a Potter, by knowing the Nature of clay, knows the Nature of all things made of clay, even so will he who Awakens to My Truth know All-Truth!

94. {G} "Arise! Awaken you who sleep the sleep of the Living Dead. Thy Lord has come! The Day awaited is at hand! He who knows That I AM

THAT I AM within himself is Great among Men. But he who knows That I AM THAT I AM, truly, as his own True Self is given Eternal Life and Freedom from Suffering and Sorrow in this Life.

95. {G} "Whosoever shall take Me as his True Self shall find everlasting Peace. Fire cannot burn This Self; sword cannot pierce It; nor cold freeze It. Freed from the illusion of the false self, knowing that you are not only this, or this, or this, but One with Me, Thy Lord Thy God, you shall endure Forever. For always have I been and always will I Be and Thou Art, in Truth, One with Me, The Lord Thy God-All In All! Though you have always been One with Me, you know It not! Seek you first to know your True Self. For in this knowing, you shall come to know Me. And, knowing Me, you shall come to know I Am All In All. And you shall know, without doubt or reservation that you and I are not we, but One!

96. {G} "Do then, this which I give unto you and no longer shall the Sun be thy Light by day; nor the Moon thy Light by night. For The Lord Thy God, Thy Beloved, shall have become an Eternal Light shining out from Thee unto all the Earth! Thy Sun shall never set and Thy Moon shall never wane. The Light of The One God is Thine and Thy day of suffering and sorrow are at an end.

97. {G} "In My Eternal Love, I have always Loved Thee. In My never ending Being I have always held Thee though you have known it not. Once more I have remade Thee. This time you are Truly Made One With Me. A Pure One Reborn in Me!

98. {G} "There is no you but I, The Lord Thy God who is with you all ways. Of this there is no doubt!

99. {G} "The journey is long and the mountain steep. But each step that you take for Me shall not break you down, but shall make you stronger for the next. And a New Covenant between That I AM THAT I AM and Man shall come to pass in you!

100. {G} "In that day, all who hear thy Word and follow thy Teaching and walk upon The Way are thy Brothers and Sisters and The Brothers and Sisters of That I AM THAT I AM, The One Universal God.

101. {G} "In fulfilling The New Covenant that I shall make with all souls through you and doing Its Work with Faith and unbounded Devotion, all error and illusion and sleep shall be wiped from their eyes and they shall know The Truth and I shall make them Free!

102. {G} "Whosoever shall believe, within his Heart and Mind, in you and this New Covenant I make through you; and shall take up his Divine Nature and follow you Home to Me, shall enter into Perfect Union with you and through you, into Perfect Union with Thy Lord, I AM THAT I AM, The One God, All In All.

103. {G} "Do this that I ask of thee and you shall render unto all Mankind a service so wondrous that the Doctrines of the learned Philosophers and the Intellectuals shall be cast aside, and the interpretations of the conveniently wise shall pass away.

104. {G} "For in that Day, The Wisdom that surpasses all understanding shall be knowable to all Souls. And those

who were Spiritually Deaf shall Hear and the Eyes of the Spiritually Blind will be opened. And they shall pierce the Veil of Ignorance, Sleep, and Illusion. In that day, all who shall accept My Word and accept you within their Hearts and Minds will rise up out of darkness and ignorance into the Clear Light and attain Oneness with The Lord, The One God, All In All.

105. {G} "For it shall come to pass that in that Day, My People will return to True Worship and Knowledge of Me. For, there is no I but God.

106. {G} "And, knowing True Worship and Practice of My Presence, each of My Faithful will stand, uncovered and unashamed, before Me and before all men, saying without doubt or reservation:

107. {G} "There is One God. There is no other! As all in a dream is of The Dreamer; as a drop of water taken from the Sea, though it be taken to the Stars, Is Sea; as a wave rises from the Sea, lingers but for a time and returns into the Sea which is its very self; all that Is and all that is not, Is this I; for there is no I but God! And, everything Is! There is no one thing that Is and another that is not. There is no one thing that is True and another that is not True. All Is. And it is All True. True and not True are illusion born only of the sleeping minds of the Living Dead who dwell in darkness and ignorance. There is no I but God! All that Is, Is of God. All that Is, I Am. All That Is, Thou Art. You and I are not we, but One. The Lord Thy God is The Beginning, The Middle, and The End of All that Is! As a Potter, by knowing the Nature of clay, knows the Nature of all things made of clay, even so will he who Awakens to God's Truth know All-Truth.

108. {G} "Arise my Beloved! Awaken all who sleep the sleep of the Living Dead. Tell them The Lord I AM THAT I AM has sent you unto them. The Day Awaited is at hand! He who knows That I AM THAT I AM within himself is Great Among Men. But he who knows That I AM THAT I AM, as his own True Self is given Eternal Life and freedom from suffering and sorrow in this life.

109. {G} "Whosoever shall realize That I AM THAT I AM as his True Self shall find everlasting Peace! Fire cannot burn this Self; Sword cannot pierce It; nor cold freeze It! Freed from the illusion of the false self, knowing that you are not only this, or this, or this, but One with thy Lord thy God, you shall endure Forever! For always have I been and always will I Be and thou art, in Truth, One with Me, The Lord thy God-All In All!

110. {G} "Though you are One with God, you know it not! Seek you first to know your True Self. For in This knowing, you shall come to know That I AM THAT I AM, All in All. And you shall know, without doubt or reservation, that you and I are not we, but One!

111. {G} "Do this which is given unto you, my Beloved One. Go forth into the darkness of this world for Me as The One Who Is Sent and no longer shall the Sun be thy Light by day; nor the Moon thy Light by night. For The Lord thy God, thy Beloved, shall have become an Eternal Light shining out from thee unto all the Earth! Thy Sun shall never set and thy Moon shall never wane. The Light of The One God is thine and thy days of suffering and sorrow shall be at an end.

112. {G} "In My Eternal Love, I have always Loved thee. In My never ending Being I have always held thee though you have known it not. Once more I have remade thee. This time you are Truly Made One with Me. A Pure One, Reborn in The Lord thy God!

113. {G} "There is no I within you but That I AM THAT I AM! The Lord thy God is with you all ways. Of this there is no doubt! So It Is!

114. {G} "Your journey shall be long and treacherous and many times you shall fall. Care not for the falling, for all men fall. Care only for how many times you rise and continue on. For each time you shall rise, I, The Lord thy God, shall rise with you and always shall I be with you.

115. {G} "And when you have attained the Goal, you shall say unto them 'I bring you The New Covenant of the One God, for it has come to pass in me, Bhagavan Sri Babajhan The Friend, The God-Realized One, Teacher of Oneness, The Friend. And so shall it be!'

116. {G} "Go forth now, Beloved Bhagavan Sri Babajhan Al-Kahlil The Friend, seeker of Oneness with God, and do that for which you are reborn!

117. {G} "Go out into the desert of this World sharing This, The Water of Life, with each who thirsts for It. That he who has eyes may See; and he who has ears may Hear; and they shall know within their hearts The Truth of This Truth. For whosoever shares The Water of Life shares Bhagavan Sri Babajhan The Friend. Of This there is no doubt!

118. {G} "Gather together The Faithful of all Nations into a Holy Community so that My Word shall cover the Earth from Sun to Sun.

119. {G} "Gather together My People. For, wherever two or more who shall have thy Holy Initiation are gathered together in quest of Oneness with The Lord thy God, in your Name and the Name of That I AM THAT I AM, who has sent you, there I Am and there is My Church and therein dwells The Lord thy God.

120. {G} "It is My Promise unto all Mankind through you, that whosoever will declare himself unto you and, Sharing The Water of Life, shall receive your Holy Initiation of The Water of Life and the Fire of My Divine Spirit and shall call himself yours and your Religion as his own; and will go forth Proclaiming and Bearing True Witness of the New Covenant and Promise I shall embody in thee, shall Know Me as his One True Self within this life and at the end of his life, I will take him into Perfect Final Union with Me. And, as a drop of water falling into the Sea becomes The Sea, he shall become That I AM THAT I AM and he shall thirst no more!

121. {G} "Go forth now, you, who have Awakened The Dawn, Proclaiming and bearing True Witness to This Covenant.

122. {G} "Dispel the sleep of ignorance of those who would know Me. Lead them to know Me as their One True Self. For it is not within Temples made by the hands of men that they shall find That I AM THAT I AM, The Lord thy God, but within The Secret Inner Sanctuary of each of their

Hearts; even as I Am within the Wind and the Flowers of your fields.

123. {G} "Many will there be in that day who would act as givers of The Truth, but who are as a hollow drum within, who prattle on without knowledge of Me. Know that such as these are but like unto strangers in a strange land who, for the sake of studying their charts and maps have missed the Truth that is before them.

124. {G} "Truly, My Beloved, shall such as these seek to enslave the heart and mind of one who has set his foot upon Thy Way Home to Me, and turn them away from Me saying 'God is this and not that' and laying down all manner of many laws and regulations that all might see them and marvel at their knowledge of such things.

125. {G} "Be not as these, you who Love Me. Neither give your heart or your mind into the keeping of such as these. For, though a man have all the knowledge of this Earth and its heavens and know Me not, he is lost and shall not attain Perfect Final Union with Me, but shall wander in the wilderness of this world life after life without end!

126. {G} "Do not argue and debate with the sleeping, who have endless ideas and opinions; for opinions are as many as there are men to have them and their opinions do not change or define Me any more than opinions about the sun change or define the sun.

127. {G} "Instead, speak this, My Truth with certainty from Heart to Heart and Mind to Mind and Spirit to Spirit. For, though the sleeping have hearts and minds, they have confused them, putting their hearts where their minds should be and their minds in the Place of The Heart!

128. {G} "You, who know Me and Love Me and would come unto Me, exchange them! And you shall find The Way Home to Me that all Souls can travel!

129. {G} "Seek to Know Me as your One True Self, within the Heart of your Heart and the Mind of your Mind and you shall Truly find Me therein, All In All and you shall Know The Truth and The Truth will set you free. This is The Work. There is no other!

130. {G} "And when you have found Me and Know The Truth, do not hoard it for yourself, but go out and give it to all people and all nations and Initiate all Souls and bring them Home to Perfect Final Union with Me, I AM THAT I AM, One in All and All in One.

131. {G} "When you do My Work, seek not after earthly rewards that wind and rain and sun may destroy and robber and thief may steal. But give your Heart and your Mind unto Me without doubt or reservation; and surrender all your actions and their fruits unto Me and follow My Divine Guidance that you will not stumble and fall into darkness and death. For it is only through Devotion, Surrender, and Selfless Service to Me, that The Way to Salvation and Realization are found and won.

132. {G} "Bear not False Witness of this New Covenant. Neither compel another to bear False Witness of My Truth. For, only when you have Known Me directly, once again, within My Kingdom; and the Heart of your Heart and the Mind of your Mind has drunk of The Water of Life;

and your Spirit has become God-intoxicated with its direct experience of Oneness with Me, shall The Truth of this New Covenant become a Living Reality for all Souls and you shall set them free and they, too shall become Reborn in Me.

133. {G} "Beware! My Beloved. For all men take great delight in pretending to speak for Me, saying 'This is God's Word' and 'This is God's Will'. Such as these seek dominion and mastery over their Brothers and Sisters in My Name, saying 'You shall do this' and 'You shall not do that.'

134. {G} "But I say unto you that you shall not use The Name of The Lord who is your God vainly to satisfy your earthly wants and desires. Neither shall you condemn others or confuse their Hearts and Minds with vain mouthings of this and that Requirement and this and that Prohibition.

135. {G} "Let man's laws be man's laws and God's Laws be God's Laws. For all of My Beings, large and small, follow My Design of Creation and return Home to Me according to the results of their Actions and their True Knowing of their Oneness with Me.

136. {G} "And when the vain and ignorant who sleep the sleep of Duality and Illusion, lay their many Prohibitions before you in My Name, Know that there are none other than these that are given unto you of The Lord thy God:

137. {G} "You shall not hold anything higher or more dear than attainment of direct experience of your Oneness and Identity with Me.

138. {G} "You shall not bear False Witness of this Covenant, nor shall you compel another to bear False Witness of it.

139. {G} "You shall not use My Name vainly to satisfy earthly wants and desires, or to gain dominion or mastery over your Brothers or Sisters.

140. {G} "You shall not deny Me in any of My Creation from the greatest even unto the very least.

141. {G} "You shall not spread or encourage Ignorance, Illusion, or allow of any man or woman to alter or pervert these My Words and Teachings; Nor shall you allow those who follow you Home to Me to interpret them to another.

142. {G} "You shall not yield unto temptation and be turned away from The Way Home to Realization of Oneness and Identity with Me; Neither shall you allow any man or woman to distract or divert you from The Way or bar your Way Home to Me; Neither shall you allow any man or woman to discourage you from your Quest of Oneness with Me.

143. {G} "You shall not deceive, harm, or degrade another man or woman in so far as you can do so without giving up your very life.

144. {G} "You shall not believe, nor shall you set forth the belief that The One God is limited to any time, place, or object. For, though I Am In All and All Is In Me, no one is there that can limit Me; and, to do so is to fall under the spell of Idolatry and Ignorance; for I Am All-Present equally save that, wherever two or more are gathered together in My Name there shall My Presence be made Known.

145. {G} "And, when the Vain and Ignorant shall seek to place the yoke and burden of man-made Requirements upon you, saying that they are Mine; Know, without doubt or reservation, that My Requirements are these:

146. {G} "You shall Love and Cherish The Lord, Thy God, That One Universal I AM THAT I AM without Second, with all your Heart and all your Mind and all your Spirit.

147. {G} "You shall make The Goal and Purpose of your life and actions to regain direct experience of Oneness and Identity with Me, That Beloved Universal I AM THAT I AM, which you are.

148. {G} "You shall make your whole Life a Worship and a Meditation by surrendering all and each of your actions and their fruits unto Me without doubt or reservation.

149. {G} "You shall have Love and Compassion for All Beings as I have boundless Love and Compassion for you.

150. {G} "You shall seek to bring forth this New Covenant and bring All Beings to Realization and Knowledge of their Oneness and Identity with Me and That, Which I Am.

151. {G} "You shall be The Way Home to Me. And you shall be The Guardian of The Way Home to Me, preserving and protecting The Way, My Eternal Universal Religion, keeping It Pure and True in word and in meaning. You shall command each Brother and Sister within the Community of My Faithful to do likewise.

152. {G} "This, which I have spoken unto you this day, is The Work and The Way. There is no other!

153. {G} "When you do it, be quick! When you do it, be strong! When you do it be Truthful! When you do it, cast aside all doubt and reservation and be filled with Faith and Confidence and Certainty! When you do it, be Bold and Courageous without vain pride or arrogance.

154. {G} "You, My Beloved, are The Gift of The One God-Unmanifest, That Absolute One without a Second, given unto all Souls for The Salvation and Liberation of All Beings.

155. {G} "Covet not The Gift. Cast it not before those who would deny and degrade it; neither shall you hide it away from those who thirst after Knowledge and Realization of Me. For no man lights up a Lamp only to have it hidden away. And, whosoever shall be ashamed of you or My Eternal Universal Religion or your Teachings or My Community while within this World shall find no Home with Me beyond it; but shall return to it time after time to endure its Birth, Suffering, Sorrow, Pain, and Death over and over until he shall know the error of his ways and repent.

156. {G} "Go! Attain The Goal. Then, go out among those who sleep The Sleep of The Living Dead and Awaken them, proclaiming The One God who is All In All, and bearing True Witness to The New Covenant I shall have made with all Souls in you; Initiate them and Consecrate them in thy Name and I shall receive them, for I Am The One God who has Commissioned you. And whosoever believes in you, shall live in Me.

157. {G} "And when you Proclaim; and when you bear True Witness; speak not with words alone. For words alone are but empty vessels that are easily misunderstood and twisted astray by The Sleeping.

158. {G} "When you Proclaim; and when you bear True Witness, call upon Me! And I will be there, in the still small places within your words; and I will guide them to the mark "+"; and they shall have The Power to lift the Veil of Darkness from the Spiritual Eyes and Awaken men's Souls.

159. {G} "When you Proclaim; and when you Bear True Witness; Speak not to the ear of the hearer alone. For I Am within each Being, and only The I that is, within each one, can hear The Message of The I That Is All In One and One In All.

160. {G} "Let, then, The Heart of your Heart and The Mind of your Mind reach out and speak unto the Heart and Mind of the hearer.

161. {G} "Let, also, the I within, that is One with Me; speak unto The I within the hearer that I Am also. For, in Truth, you are not two, but One in The One God who is One In All and All In One.

162. {G} "Be you, then, not as two divided; for that, Truly, is the way of The Living Dead; but as One speaking unto your own Self; for there are no divisions between you but the ignorance and illusions which are born of the darkness of those who sleep The Sleep of The Living Dead.

163. {G} "Ask not for special favors or miracles, my Beloved. For the ways of this dream world are sufficient unto it. Guide your Heart and your Mind and your Spirit, instead, constantly toward direct experience and Realization of Oneness and Identity with That One That I Am. If you were to gain the whole universe and fail to Realize Me, you would have gained nothing. Ask not, then, for the ways of this world to be taken away for your sake; for nothing is there that I shall do for you that is not done for any other.

164. {G} "The Prophets, Seers, and Messiahs of all ages have pointed The Way Home, but few are they who take up The Way. You shall show many The Way; you have opened up The Gate, for you are The Gate and The Way and The Light upon The Way. But, before The Clear Bright Light will shine forth from you, you must put your own house in order. For, even though this Light is aglow within you now, you Know it not. You are like unto a Lamp whose glass has not yet been polished clean; and because of the dirt thereupon, your Light cannot be seen.

165. {G} "Make your House ready for The Liberation of your Spirit. Wipe clean The Glass of your Life that The Clear Bright Light of The Lord thy God may shine forth into this World.

166. {G} "A deep sleep has settled upon the People making them deaf and blind to Me and The Truth.

167. {G} "Each man's vision has lost the meaning of My Scripture and the very Life of his Life wanders aimlessly in the wilderness of this World.

168. {G} "Greater in numbers grow those who know of words and symbols. But few are they who will read The Book of Life I have written

within their Hearts and understand The Truth therein.

169. {G} "Even the so-called Religious Ones, the Teachers, Prophets, Preachers and Seers have become confused. Moved only by fear of man-made demons and devils and false fear of Me resulting from false doctrine and false belief, they create and spread man-made beliefs, calling them My Doctrine and My Truth, and encourage other Sleeping Ones to vain attempts at Spiritual Progress by raising their voices in empty mouthing of words to no avail; for their understanding of True Religion and Worship is far removed and amiss from the True Meaning.

170. {G} "Beware, you who would find Salvation and Liberation, for The Way is long and narrow and few are there who walk alone to its end.

171. {G} "Be awake always, lest you too shall become lulled into the drowsy state and fall into the ways of the Ignorant and sleeping who sleep The Sleep of The Living Dead; and do all that they do for the awe, admiration and approval of their neighbors.

172. {G} "Truly, I say unto you, that they shall realize their fondest desires in this World and shall return into it time after time for the sake of their desires and attachments. But, no rest or peace shall they find. For this whole world is temporary and passing. All things which are put together, must come apart; and within this world, everything changes; nothing remains the same; and each pleasure brings with it, its opposite of pain, sorrow, and suffering even as life in the flesh brings death.

173. {G} "Seek not after the things of this world that are passing and as hard to hold onto as vapor; but seek, instead, to attain direct experience of That I AM THAT I AM, your own True Self, and all else shall be added unto you.

174. {G} "Nothing is there that endures save that One Spirit which I Am, which you call Soul; for this is One and Identical with Me and no other. This, is the Eternal Treasure I send you forth to restore unto all Beings; whosoever seeks it through you shall find it and shall Know The Truth and The Truth shall set him Free, Forever.

175. {G} "Seek Me, then, within The Heart of your Heart and The Mind of your Mind that you might Know Realization and attain The Goal.

176. {G} "And when you seek within, do not do so publicly out of desire for approval and admiration of others. Neither hide yourself away out of shame or fear of hate or rejection.

177. {G} "Be, instead, as one balanced upon the fine edge of a razor; falling neither one way or the other; and let your doing be such a part of you that the one on the left will not know what is happening on his right!

178. {G} "Prayer, Meditation, Devotion, Surrender of all Actions and their Fruits, and Direct Knowledge of Me; These are the Paths Home to Oneness with Me.

179. {G} "Some are there who will abuse and misuse you and My Way to selfish and evil ends. But, I say unto you that the Road is not at fault that the robber does his evil acts upon it. And the Road shall be held blameless

and suffers not. But the robber shall not be held blameless; and shall suffer the results of his own actions again and again until he sees the error of his ways and repents and turns his face unto Me.

180. {G} "Even so, you and The Way shall be not blamed for any man's abuse of these. But each who misuses you or My Eternal Universal Religion or your Teachings or Instructions shall be held guilty and shall suffer the fruits of his actions again and again until he sees the error and repents and comes Home to Knowledge of his Oneness and Identity with Me through you.

181. {G} "Beware of prayer, my Beloved. No Road is so fraught with the hidden dangers of selfishness, desire, greed and arrogance and vain pride as is Prayer.

182. {G} "As Selfless Action seeks Me through Compassion and the surrender of all actions and their fruits; As Meditation seeks Me through watching, listening, and waiting; Even so does Prayer seek after Knowledge of Me through desiring and asking. Truly, such is their vain pride that they deceive themselves that they must tell Me what they believe I do not know. And, it is desire that fans the fires of the False Self and makes strong the chains that bind each Being to this World and the Birth, Suffering, Sorrow, Pain, and Death herein. And few are they who do not abuse and misuse this Road Home.

183. {G} "I say unto you that all these Roads, Truly, lead Home to Me. And the Highest of them is Direct Experience and Knowledge of Oneness with Me. Blessed are they who walk The Highest Way.

184. {G} "If you must follow the Way of Prayer, know that it is a tempting and cautious path to tread. When you Pray, let not your Prayer become the mouthing of empty words for the sake of fulfilling your earthbound desires and cravings, as do The Living Dead who, knowing Me not, imagine that they must be heard by one who hears only words. Believing Prayer to be but the speaking of words, such as these are as one speaking unto himself in the empty forests of Duality, Darkness, and Ignorance.

185. {G} "Imitate them not! For not one True Thought is thought, but that it is I who think it. Not one Right Feeling is felt, but that I feel it! Not one Right Action is done, nor its Fruit Surrendered, but that it is done and surrendered by Me. For I Am The One who is The True Self within every self's self; there is no other!

186. {G} "When you Pray, turn inward to The Secret Place Within; and closing your Heart and Mind to all else, seek Therein your own Divine Self, The One God, That I AM THAT I AM, All In All, who dwells within The Secret Inner Sanctuary of your Heart!

187. {G} "And when you Pray, seek not after the things of this World of Illusion that fire can burn and thief can steal and which pass away like vapors in the air. For nothing is there of this Dream World that remains the same from moment to moment. And the companion of all worldly pleasure is the pain of its passing and the sorrow of its loss. Of desire and attachment to this World and the things herein is all Birth, Suffering, Sorrow, Pain, and Death born. But, instead, Free your Self! Throwing off Desire, Greed, Attachment, and Selfishness; and

casting off your small false self, let your Prayer be of this essence:

188. {G} "Oh my God, My Beloved, My own True Self, I surrender completely unto Thee! Restore Thy Authority! Manifest Thy Presence within this little self until it has become One with Thee, shining forth with Thy Own Clear Light!

189. {G} "Let me know, this moment, my Oneness with Thee; The one thing I lack; through which all else is made Perfect.

190. {G} "Heal the division in me; that I may Know Thy Oneness in all this that is!

191. {G} "Consume this little self in the Sacred Fire of Thy Presence; That I may find my way through The Ordeal and be Liberated from it; Realizing my Oneness with Thee.

192. {G} "From darkness, lead me to The Light; From the unreal, lead me to The Real; From the temporary, lead me to The Eternal; From death, lead me to Immortality; From division, lead me to Wholeness!

193. {G} "O Beloved One! I would be One with Thee fully this moment! Make my Doing One with my Speech! Make my Speech One with my Mind! Make my Mind One with my Heart! Make my Heart One with my Will! And my Will One with Thy Will!

194. {G} "Shatter this prison of false self; and absorb me, in the Ocean of your Infinite Being, as a drop of water in The Sea!

195. {G} "That I shall Know without doubt or reservation that You and I are not we, but One.

196. {G} "For Thou Art my Only True Self; Majestic, Splendorous, Immortal!

197. {G} "There is no I but Thee!

198. {G} "So Be It With Me!

199. {G} "This is The Work and The Way! That you shall each, of your own direct experience, Know that you are One and Identical with Me and That Absolute One without a Second with whom I Am One. There is no other Work. There is no other Way that brings Peace born of Certainty and Knowing and through which each may attain Salvation and Liberation without doubt or reservation. For, within all belief there lingers the darkness of doubt and reservation; only in True Knowing does the Clear Bright Light fully illuminate The Way Home!

200. {G} "Unto you, who Know That I Am within The Heart of your Heart and The Mind of your Mind and The Self of your self; and have True Knowledge of The Truth of this New Covenant that I bring for the Salvation of all Beings; The Journey is Certain! The Goal is Won! Within this Life or at its end, you shall enter into The Perfect Paradise of Union with The One God who is One In All and All In One; and shall be born into The Grand Illusion no more!

201. {G} "Go forth! My Beloved in whom I have Awakened and whom I have Anointed and sent forth. Raise up among you a New Race of God-Men who shall multiply themselves and cover the Earth and Awaken all Souls to their Oneness and Identity with That I AM THAT I AM, and no other.

202. {G} "Truly I say unto you that if you choose to do My Will, you shall lose all memory of these things that you have Known this day. And you shall wander in the wilderness of this world and grope through the Spiritual Darkness and find your Way back into Perfect Union with Me as would any other man.

203. {G} "But through your journey back Home to Me, I Am with you and will Guide you if you will hear Me and heed My Divine Guidance. But if you will hear Me not, it shall not be because I am not Guiding you, but because you are deaf to Me.

204. {G} "And, when you have Freed your Self, turn not your back upon those who suffer birth after birth in Darkness and Ignorance and Illusion; and Know not who they Really Are!

205. {G} "But have Compassion for every very least of these Beings until all shall have awakened down to the very stones themselves! No greater Love is there than a Being shall sacrifice Final Union and take up yet another Life for the sake of all Beings. For this is the greatest sacrifice of all!

206. {G} "This is The One Work. This is The One Way. This is The New Covenant of The One God as it has been Revealed unto This One. This is The Testimony of Bhagavan Sri Babajhan The Friend, The Awakened One - Bringer of Oneness with God - The Friend of All Beings.

207. {G} "Know The Truth and be Free!"

Paratpara Ji Kijai!
All Glory to God The Beloved!

Jai Bhagavan Ji!
Victory To That Beloved
Universal I AM THAT I AM
Which You Are!

Here Ends The Chapter Entitled
The New Covenant Revealed

Chapter Six
First Light

Universal God's First Awakening within John Douglas and His Ordination as Bhagavan Sri Babajhan The Friend On The Seventh Day of August Nineteen Hundred & Fifty-One

By The Will and Grace of The One Universal God:

The house in which I lived when I was a child had a large basement where my brother and I used to play. My father had a workshop in the basement, just below the stairs. I would often sit or stand at the top of the stairs watching my father work in his shop. One day, while standing at the top of the stairway watching my father, my younger brother crept up behind me and grabbed me around the waist as a joke. But there was no rail on the side of the stairs and we both fell over the side and down onto the hard pavement of the basement floor below.

2. From the time I was born into this world, I had always had a natural tendency to sacrifice myself for the sake of others, though I did not know the reason why. When I felt myself and my brother falling off of the stairs, I naturally grabbed him and held him to my chest so that he would land on top of me to protect him being hurt.

3. As Divine Destiny would Will, my younger brother landed on top of me unhurt, and I was knocked "unconscious" and badly injured and for a moment I died to this world.

4. Then, a wonderful thing happened. As my mortal body and mind lost consciousness, I myself Awakened to a whole new world within! When I realized that I was fully conscious without my body, I became frightened. I tried to call out to my parents, but I could not. The pain was terrible. I felt as if my whole body were going to explode with pain.

5. Just as I was certain that I could not stand any more pain, the pain began to fade away like smoke in the wind. Blessed relief came upon me. But my relief from pain was quickly shattered by my growing awareness that I was drifting away from my broken body.

6. Now, ice cold fear replaced pain. I feared that I was dying and, indeed I was. I held onto my physical body with all my might. But it was to no avail. I continued to drift farther and farther away from my body in spite of my efforts and pleadings. Suddenly, there was a silent snap as my connection with my body finally broke apart. Panic and white-hot fear shot through my Being for an eternal instant, and then was gone.

7. And I heard a soundless Divine Voice calling out, in a language I had never heard:

Satyam nasti paro Dharmaha!
Satyam lokasya dipaha!
Sruyatam!
Drishyatam!
Kriyatam!
Uchyatam!

Paratpara Sharanam agachati!
Bhagavan Sharanam agachati!
Dharmam Sharanam agachati!
Sangham Sharanam agachati!
Satya Yugam Sharanam agachati!

Om! Jai Paratpara Ji!
Om! Jai Bhagavan Ji!

8. And, as if in answer to my lack, that same voice called again, saying:

Truth is The Highest Religion!
Truth is The Light of The World!
Let it be heard!
Let it be seen!
Let it be done!
Let it be told!

Come take Refuge in Paratpara,
The One Universal God of
Countless Names and Forms
who Is beyond
all Names and Forms!
Come take Refuge in
God's Awakened One, The Friend!
Come take Refuge in
His Eternal Universal Religion!
Come take Refuge in
The Holy Community
of His Enlightened Faithful
Believers!
Come take Refuge in
His Holy Cause of Universal God's
Pure Divine Truth!

Om! Victory to Universal God,
The Beloved!

Om! Victory to God's Awakened One, The Friend!

9. Far off in the distance, I thought I faintly heard my mother's fearful voice calling my name. I wished I could comfort her, but my body seemed thousands of miles away now. I feared that I was dead.

10. But I didn't die. My fear gave way to child-like fascination as I realized that my body still surrounded me. But now, instead of being bruised and broken, my body was perfect and strong and radiant. My new body was not made of flesh and blood and bone. My new body was made of the very substance of mind.

11. This mental body lingered for quite some time. Then, just when I had taken solace in my new mental body, it began to slowly fade away. Again, fear and panic overcame me. I tried everything I could, but nothing I could do could stop my new mental body from fading steadily away. Suddenly, there was another silent snap, like the one I had felt when my connection with my physical body was broken. Then, my mental body was gone.

12. Again, I became aware that a new, still finer and subtler body, finer than the finest gauze, now surrounded me. Then, I realized what was happening. I realized that these various bodies, each one finer and more subtler than the one before it, were not coming to me anew. But that they had always been there, one and continuous with one another. A moment of fascination vanished as the full realization that my new and more subtle mental body was fading away even faster than the one before it. The full reality that the fading away of each of my subtler bodies brought the moment of my own

fading away closer and closer, came crashing in upon my consciousness. I was filled with a strange mixture of pure fear and pure excitement, amazement and anticipation.

13. Suddenly there appeared before me a long road that led up a hill to a Sanctuary that I could not see clearly. And along both sides of the road stood many different people. Some of them I recognized. Some of them I did not believe I had ever seen. Somehow, I knew that I was commanded to take "The Long Walk" along this road toward the Sanctuary on the hill. And as I walked, I was made to face each person standing along the road. And those who were on the left were those I had wronged in some way. And those along its right side were those I had blessed in some way. And I was made to stand before each of them and answer their charges for me and against me. When I had faced the anger and hostility of one who stood on the left side of the road and spoke against me - and when I had faced each who thanked me for some kindness and spoke for me - that one would step back and vanish. Those I could not or would not face, but passed by, would remain standing - waiting. So, on and on it went for such a very long and painful time. Some of them were those I knew in this life. Many were they who were from some former time I did not know. When I was finished, I was still a long way from the Sanctuary high on the hill which I could see only vaguely. Then, it was over and another body began fading away.

14. Body after body, each one finer and more subtle than the one before it, continued to fade away into eternity, until six bodies had vanished. I was certain that I was about to cease to exist all together, but I didn't. Just as I was bracing for my last covering to fade away, the fading stopped and I was left with the finest and subtlest of coverings. This was no longer a body with form, but an indescribable and unimaginably fine and subtle covering.

15. Here, was ego, identity, personality. Here was the storehouse of all of my experiences, all of my good deeds and all of my bad deeds. Not one instant of my life was missing. Every heartbeat, every eye-blink, every thought, every anger, every joy, was therein, recorded faithfully in complete and absolute detail. I recognized my life fully, every bump, every fall, every tenderness, every pleasure and every pain. But, there was more, far more. There, in that finest of coverings, so fine that the finest particle of matter was made gross by comparison, was History. History of lives lived, deeds done, and deaths died. Thousands of them. Only much later would I know that this subtle covering, that would stay with me until the moment of my full Liberation, was The Soul-Covering: The final Veil that separates Spirit from True Knowledge of its Perfect Oneness and Identity with The One Universal God, The Supreme Truth that sets all Souls Free, forever. Here too was the Storehouse of Karmas. The Storehouse of all my good and evil thoughts, feelings and deeds, and the penance that I would have to endure to balance my sins and karmas before I could be Liberated and return into Perfect Final Union with God. For, no Soul can enter into Perfect Final Union with God while laden with sins or Karmas. While sins can be forgiven by God's Mercy, and are, there is no escape from God's Infinite Universal Justice of Karma and Karmas must be burned up in The Divine Fire.

16. Then, I had to choose. Would I avoid experiencing the fruits of my evil deeds and go on to enjoy the fruits of my good deeds and be reborn in the flesh again? Or, would I insist on Perfect Final Union with God and endure the pain of experiencing the results of my bad deeds as required to attain Perfect Final Union? I chose True Knowledge of my Oneness with God.

17. Suddenly, I was in Hell. I suffered the results that my every bad thought, my every bad feeling, my every bad deed had caused. Torment was everywhere. Pain was unending and merciless. I endured unimaginable eternal pain and agony as The Divine Fire of God's Presence burned away my wrong and evil thoughts, feelings and deeds. There was no end and there was no escape. This was Eternal Hell. The Divine Fire of God's Pure Truth and Being was everywhere, eternal and unrelenting. I cried out in unbelievable agony as The Divine Fire of God's immediate Presence burned all wrongness and evil from me. As the goldsmith sears the raw ore in the white-hot fire of his furnace to burn away the dross from the gold, God was searing me in The Divine Fire of His Truth and Being to burn away the dross of my wrong doing and evil deeds from me. It went on and on, eternally. Then, as suddenly as it had begun, it was done.

18. I had passed through The Wall of Fire into The Paradise that is beyond it. The Peace that surpasses all understanding came upon me like a wave and I was taken up into the Paradise of Heaven. Where there had been pain, there was Pure Joy and Bliss. Where there had been agony and loathing, there was Peace and Happiness Eternal. The Divine Fire of God's Ever-Presence was here too. But here, That Divine Fire rained down upon me and rose up in Blissful Waves as The Supreme Water of Life. And I was amazed, for The Fire was in The Water and The Fire was the very Water of Life. Here, too, The Divine Fire of God's Presence and Truth was at work, burning away even the smallest traces of good thoughts, feelings and deeds and their results. For even good deeds and their results are too gross to be taken through The Eye of The Needle and into Perfect Final Union with God.

19. Now, another time for choosing came upon me. Would I choose The Path of The Sun, by which all Souls return into Perfect Final Union with God? Or, would I choose The Path of The Moon and return to the world from which I had come and gather up yet another body for yet another life? I chose The Path of The Sun. As soon as I had made my choice, a great sea-horn was blown the likes of which I had never heard. And the sound of that ancient sea-horn seemed to echo throughout all Creation. Then, suddenly, out of nowhere, there appeared before me a Divine Being dressed in clothing of Radiant Clear White Light. The Radiant One reached out his hand and touched me on the forehead and said "Be at Peace, there are no accidents, you have been long awaited and the time is at hand!" The Radiant Divine Being vanished as suddenly as he had appeared and a deep sense of profound Peace and Understanding came upon me, and for the moment, I forgot all about my accident and my plight.

20. Soon, other Divine Shining Ones came to me. They gathered around this bodiless Soul who I still thought of as "John" and seemed to be studying

me very carefully. From time to time the Radiant Ones would withdraw a short distance as if discussing me like I had seen my parents do with my teachers at school. Soon, one of the Radiant Beings who was larger than the rest approached me and tested me for my "Readiness," whatever that was. No words were exchanged, but the Radiant One seemed to be very satisfied and returned to the others. After a short while, all The Shining Ones vanished as suddenly as they had come. I was all alone once again.

21. Then, from within and all around me I heard countless Heavenly Beings chanting with one Divine Voice:

Om Paratpara!
Tat savitur varenyam
Bhargo devasya dhimahi
dhiyoyonah prachodayat

22. Seven times The Divine Voice repeated these Holy words. Then, chanted:

Om
Asato ma
sad gamaya!
Tamaso ma
jyotir gamaya!
Mrityor ma amritam gamaya!
Om Shanti, Shanti, Shantihi
Om Jai Bhagavan Ji!

23. Then, as if to, once again, answer my wondering mind, that all encompassing Voice chanted:

Om Universal God!
All Radiant Universal Light!
As we turn our minds to you
fill our hearts and minds and lives
with Your Clear Light

Om!
From the unreal,
lead us to The Real!
From darkness,
lead us to The Light!
From death, to Immortality!

Om!
Peace! Peace! Peace!
Om!
Victory to Universal God
and The Friend!

24. After a pause, the Divine Voice chanted:

Bhagavan sharanam gachaami!
Dharmam sharanam gachaami!
Samgham sharanam gachaami!
Satyayugam sharanam gachaami!

I take Refuge in
The One Universal God
and His Awakened One,
The Friend!
I take Refuge in
His Eternal Universal Religion!
I take Refuge in
The Holy Community of His
Enlightened Faithful Believers!
I take Refuge in
The Age of His Pure Divine Truth!

25. One time was this sounded within and all around me, but this time, I heard it in the Sanskrit and in the unspoken Universal Language that all Souls understand.

26. Suddenly, my whole being was fixed upon an Angel who was coming toward me, so Divine, so Radiant, and so Beautiful that I could think of nothing else. Unlike the others, this Radiant One had no definite form. Instead, within this brilliant Clear Light I sensed the Totality of all Humanity, all Life and all Existence, though there was no definite sense of a single man or a specific existence! It was as though all Humanity, all Life

and all Existence of all time stood only a breath away from this center which I still called, "I."

27. After what seemed like an eternity, this All-Encompassing Presence began to expand. It grew and expanded until it was everywhere, yet no one place alone, all at the same time. It was within me and yet I was also within it. Divine Bliss arose within me in great waves until I knew I was as old as Creation itself.

28. Then, The Shining Ones returned. But now, instead of a few, there was a great multitude of them. They each approached me, one by one, and Initiated me and Baptized me and taught me their Wisdom and their Ways in turn. Unlike the Great Presence which had come to me a little while before, these Shining Ones appeared to me as men and women of definite form.

29. First one, then another Radiant Being would approach me and bow deeply, shining with such brilliance that I thought I would surely be blinded by their Clear Light. But the Radiant Angel came forward and put my fears to rest, saying, "Fear not, for you see with the sight that is beyond eyes and you hear with a hearing that is beyond ears. You are The Awaited One who will be The Friend of all Beings who shall Awaken them to the Clear Light of God's Truth in this age. You are The Maitreya, The Kalki, The Mahavatara, The Satguru, The Universal World Teacher. You are The One Awaited by all Beings, whose Holy Number is 777."

30. "These Radiant Divine Beings are all of God's Prophets, Saints, Buddhas, Saviors and Avataras. These are now your Teachers whom The One Universal God, I AM THAT I AM, has sent forth to guide you. But, when this Work is finished, we shall all be your friends and Brothers and Sisters who will shelter you and walk beside you and help you to bring about the Age of God's Pure Truth on Earth!" All these things were given unto me without words, in a way that no words can explain.

31. And I said unto The Angel, "Oh my Lord, why am I called 777?" And the Divine One said unto me, "I am not your Lord, Blessed One, but His servant and messenger whom He has sent forth unto thee." And he showed unto me Three Realms, Seven Worlds within Seven Worlds within Seven Worlds. Each world leading to the World above and beyond it; such that each Realm was like unto a great ladder of Seven Steps leading to that which was above it. And the lowest World in each Realm was ignorance and materialism and Spiritual Blindness compared to that which was above. And this World was called Shin. And the highest World of each Realm was The Unspeakable. And each of these highest Worlds led, straightaway to the lowest World in the Realm above it. And the first Realm was called Material and the second Realm was called Mind and the third Realm was called, truly, Spirit. And I said unto the Angel of God, "What is this that you have shown unto me?" And the Angel of God said unto me, "This, verily, is the Ladder of Yakov that leads all who climb it to The Supreme Unspeakable and onward into Perfect Final Union with The One Universal God, I AM THAT I AM. It is this ladder that you shall climb. Jai Bhagavan Ji!"

32. There were many Shining Ones. I did not recognize most of them. But one of the Shining Ones was familiar

to me, for He had come to me in a dream when I was hardly one year old. This one I knew as Jesus Christ, but did not look like the pictures in the church had shown Him. He corrected the pronunciation of His name, saying, "The worldly, yes even those who believe they follow me, call me Jesus The Christ, but you, Beloved Brother, should call me Yohoshuay." Only many years later would I discover that I had been in the presence of all of the Great Masters, Prophets, Saints, Buddhas, Saviors, Messiahs, Avataras and Mahavataras of all times, for I did not recognize their names, though they told them to me.

33. Each Divine Being approached me in turn, Initiated me with both Water and Fire, and taught me their Wisdom and their Ways of Worship, Prayer, and Meditation one after another. One of them, who was a tall dark and regal warrior said unto me, "Be careful in the small things, Beloved of God, for even the smallest fault can defeat a great warrior." Another said unto me, "Tell them that they must not make camels out of rope. Tell them to use my words only as a mirror to look in their own hearts for the Truth."

34. Yet another said unto me, "The people hear, but they do not understand. Tell them for me that The Law of The Spirit is Supreme." Still another said unto me, "Let my people know that I saw the Angel in every direction because He was in my heart and mind and eye, not upon the mountains. Tell them that each man and woman must know the meaning of my words for themselves alone and be a light unto themselves."

35. And, yet another said, "Tell them that I mean only what I say. Tell them that I came, not to make them fishers of men, but to make them Fish-Men, God-freed Souls who live equally, on the land of this world and in the Holy Ocean of The Spirit of God, That Beloved I AM THAT I AM." And yet another said, "Tell them to be like the birds in the air. No bird can soar into the sky while tied to the ground. Tell them that they must give up all attachment to this world and all within it before they will know The Truth and be set Free."

36. These and many more things did they each say unto me. In this way, I learned all of the highest and most ancient and righteous methods of Prayer and Worship and Repetition of the Names and Holy Words of Universal God from all of the Prophets, Saints, Buddhas, Saviors, Avataras and Mahavataras of all times. As each Divine Being completed his Initiation, Baptism, Instruction and Counsel, that One would come to me and reach out and embrace me and we would Mesh, Blend and Merge into One!

37. After many had come and Initiated and Baptized and Instructed and embraced me, I discovered that I could no longer think of myself as "John", for I was becoming One with all who had joined with me. Soon the very idea of "John" and "I" became only vague labels that I used to refer to this ever growing and expanding Beingness I was rapidly becoming.

38. Among the Shining Ones who came and Initiated and Baptized me and became One with me were Rama, Krishna, Abraham, Moses, Shankara, Buddha, Yohoshuay, The Prophet Mohammed, Vasishtha, The Angel Gabriel; and many other Saints, Masters, Prophets, Messiahs, Avatars,

and Mahavataras from all of the ages and Religions man has ever known!

39. And each Divine Being who Initiated and taught me agreed and vowed that the divisions between the Religions of man were not of God, but of the People's own ignorance and desire and attachment and identification with the things of the False Self within them. And they all taught me the same Wisdom: that Universal God's Manifest Saviors have never been opposed to one another, but have always been One with one another and, that I was chosen by Paratpara, The One Universal God, to restore the Ancient Universal Truth of God's Eternal Universal Religion to all Souls, to renew and unite all of God's Religions with The One True Religion of Eternal Divine Truth, to Awaken all Beings to The Eternal Divine Truth of their Oneness and Identity with Paratpara, The One Universal God and with one another through their Oneness with The One Universal God and, to end the Kali Yuga, The Age of ignorance, darkness, chaos and destruction and bring forth The Holy Satya Yuga, The New Age of Universal God's Pure Divine Truth upon Earth!

40. My Divine Initiation and Training continued for what seemed like centuries. Still, the Initiating, Baptizing, Teaching, Counseling, Meshing, Blending and Merging into Oneness of one after another went on and on. I did not feel like I was getting any smarter, but I had no trouble keeping up with the steadily increasing difficulty of the Wisdom I was being given.

41. Then, suddenly, I began to doubt myself and the experiences I was having. I began to question my own worthiness and even doubted that these Shining Divine Beings were real. Sensing my distraction, Yohoshuay approached me and explained that the Knowledge which I was being given had nothing to do with worldly knowledge such as I had learned in school, but that this Knowledge was Divine Knowledge which was above and beyond worldly knowledge.

42. The Buddha too, approached me and explained that worldly knowledge was artificially put together and would eventually come apart, but that the Eternal Knowledge which was being given to me was never put together, for it existed before time itself was created, and would never come apart.

43. Other Divine Beings came and gave me their Wisdom. They all agreed and taught me that The Adhyatma-Yoga-Dharma is The Way by which all Souls can Know their Oneness with The One God and that God's Eternal Universal Religion is The Sanatana Dharma, The Supreme Eternal Knowledge and Truth that is beyond all earthly and relative thought and understanding. And they told me that if I accepted what was to come, I would still have to learn the ideas and ways of the world as would any other boy of my physical age.

44. I agreed that it would be so with me. And thus, I became The Maitreya Kalki Mahavatara, The Divine Sanctuary and Vehicle of Universal God's Ancient and Eternal Universal Religion, Bringer of The Age of His Pure Divine Truth and Supreme Adhyatma-Yoga-Dharma.

45. When the very last of these ascended Prophets, Saints, Buddhas,

Saviors, Avataras and Mahavataras had given me his or her Initiation, Baptism and Teaching and had meshed and blended and merged into Oneness with me, all was Perfectly Still, Peaceful and very dark. And this One I had become, who had been just a young boy playing in an Iowa basement a few moments before, knew that "I" no longer existed as a young boy but that I was growing and expanding just as I had witnessed The Universal All-Encompassing Presence do, what now seemed like many thousands of years ago.

46. First, I became One and Identical with all of the Prophets, Saints, Buddhas, Saviors, Avataras and Mahavataras of all time. Then, I became One with all Beings upon the earth. Then with all Life. I became One with the very earth itself and went on expanding to become One with all Souls and Beings throughout Creation. I continued to expand for many Eternities, out-reaching even the most distant corners of time and space, transcending the many universes until, finally, I had become One with all Creation all at once!

47. Suddenly, all became One and I entered the Supreme Divine Stillness. I had transcended even time and space and gone beyond motion itself. I began to consider "Am I dead?", but I stopped before I could begin, because there was no longer any "I" to do the considering! So I waited silently while suns and galaxies were born and died away into ashes. I had gone beyond time and space and for me all things were here and now. I waited in silent Divine Knowledge that my waiting would eventually fulfill its Purpose.

48. Then, came The Presence. It went Beyond even The All-Encompassing.

Here was Paratpara, The Infinite beyond Infinity, The Eternal beyond Eternity. I had outreached the entire Realm of Creation and encompassed it within my Being. I had become One and Identical with I AM THAT I AM as God Manifest. I had become One with The Holy Spirit, with The Son, with Brahma, Vishnu and with Shiva. Yet, so All-Pervasive and Comprehensive was The Presence of Paratpara that I felt small and insignificant by comparison. The Formless Universal I AM THAT I AM surrounded me and stretched out into all directions far beyond the entire Realm of God Manifest and all Creation. This alone, was The One Universal Source, Cause, Substance, and Self of All; here was Paratpara, The One Universal God who is both Manifest and Unmanifest and yet neither, God beyond God, The Father of The Father, Omnipresent, Omnipotent, Omniscient beyond all Existence and Manifestation!

49. {G} "Hear me My Beloved! For, I AM THAT I AM! In this wilderness you have been called John of Douglas, but from beyond this one called John of Douglas this cry has Come! Fear no more My Beloved. Your cry is heard. Your Faith has made you Whole. Your Quest has been answered!

50. {G} "Quest no more. In your seeking after Me, The Lord, your God, you have found The Answer to all quests! For I Am The One God whom men call Brahman, Allah, Jehovah, and countless other names. But you may call me Paratpara, for I Am The One Universal God of Countless Names and Forms who is beyond all Names and Forms. I AM THAT I AM! I Am The One Universal God whom all Souls worship, though they know it not.

51. {G} "I Am God beyond God. I Am The One Universal Spirit. I Am The Father of The Father, The Mother of The Mother, The Creator of The Creator. I Am The One Source, Substance and Self of all Creation, all Existence and all Beings. I AM THAT I AM.

52. {G} "In this that I shall ask of you in this day, I shall not command thee, for you must choose, you may in no way avoid choosing. If you choose for Me, you shall be My Chosen One. And from this day forth, you shall be known as Bhagavan Sri Babajhan Al-Kahlil The Friend. For you shall have become The God-Realized One, Bringer of Oneness with God, The Friend of all Souls and your number shall be Seven hundred Seventy and Seven!

53. {G} "And you shall be called The Blessed One. For I shall have Blessed you in this day and invested in you My Power to Bless all Souls. Whosoever you shall Bless and in whatsoever manner you shall Bless any man, woman or child, that one shall I Bless in kind.

54. {G} "And you shall be called Maitreya. For you shall have become The Awaited One. And you shall be called Kalki. For you shall be The One within whom I Am Awakened to end The Age of Spiritual Ignorance, Darkness and Chaos.

55. {G} "And you shall be called Mahavatara. For you shall be The One within whom I Am Awakened to bring forth The Age of My Pure Divine Truth on Earth for The Self-Realization, Salvation and Liberation of all Souls.

56. {G} "And you shall be called Satguru. For I shall make you The True Teacher who shall Awaken all My People from the living death of Spiritual Ignorance and Darkness.

57. {G} "And you shall be called The Friend of all Souls. For through you I shall make a New Covenant unto all Souls. And you shall unite all My People and send them forth upon The Pure Way and lead them Home to realization of their Oneness with Me!

58. {G} "All of these shall you be, for I shall have Awakened within you and remade you, My own Self and Radiance made manifest in this world. I shall Embody My Pure Divine Truth and Eternal Religion within you. And you shall call The Way Home to Me, My Holy Adhyatma-Yoga-Dharma. All who receive your Holy Initiation and follow you and profess this, My Eternal Religion, and follow this, My Holy Adhyatma-Yoga-Dharma, as I give it unto them through you, shall be My Chosen. And they shall be Blessed among men and women of all Nations.

59. {G} "And you shall go about this world as an ordinary man struggling with all things with which ordinary men must struggle. And yet, within this ordinary man you shall be, verily, all of these things I have spoken unto you. And those who have eyes that cannot see beyond this ordinary shell and ears that cannot truly hear beyond this ordinary voice, will deny you and revile you. And this shall you endure for My sake. But those who have eyes that truly see, they shall see thee within an ordinary man and, verily, Me within thee. And those who have ears that truly hear, they shall hear The Truth even in thy most

ordinary and mundane utterances and shall Know That I Am within you and your words.

60. {G} "Truly, wherever a Soul, a People or a Nation shall receive you, that Soul, that People and that Nation shall be My own. Truly, they shall be Supremely Blessed. For, whosoever shall receive you and follow you, shall receive Me and follow Me. I say unto you, that Soul who discerns The Truth of this, which I have spoken unto you and will take up his Divine Nature and follow you shall be My own. But whosoever shall reject you, shall reject Me. And, whosoever shall deny you, shall deny Me. And Whosoever shall revile you, degrade you or persecute you or your Faithful, who are My Faithful, that Soul shall have reviled, degraded or persecuted Me.

61. {G} "And, whosoever shall revile or deny this, My Divine Revelation or this My Holy Covenant or The Supreme Pure Divine Truth of My Eternal Universal Religion or My Holy Adhyatma-Yoga-Dharma, shall also revile or deny Me. As swine trampling upon precious jewels shall they be.

62. {G} "Woe unto that man or Nation who shall revile you, deny you, degrade or persecute you or your Faithful. For you shall be My Living Testament and My Seal upon a New Covenant, I make, between That I AM THAT I AM and Man through you this Day and your number shall be Seven Hundred Seventy and Seven."

63. And out of The Clear Light, Eternal beyond the first day of Creation, came the Breath of Paratpara, my Lord, my God. And His Breath drove straight to the center of my Being, winnowing the chaff from the wheat, burning away the dross from my Soul, making me One with Him. And I heard with the ears that know no sound:

64. {G} "Arise My Beloved! Thy Life is Touched! Thy Heart is cleansed! Thy Ignorance and impurity are dispelled. Even as darkness flees at the coming of The Light, so are you Purified in The Sacred Fire of My Presence! Thy division is mended and you are made Whole!

65. {G} "Awaken, Bhagavan Sri Babajhan Al-Kahlil The Friend! Arise and shine forth into The Darkness of this World! Thy Light is come. I Am Awakened within you! Although My people are sleeping in ignorance of Me and darkness surrounds them, I have Awakened within you and My Glow-ray can be seen upon Thee!

66. {G} "People of all Nations shall be drawn to Thy Light. Rulers and Great Ones shall find Joy in the brilliance of Thy Awakening and shall open their hearts unto Me and all people. Lift up your eyes, My Beloved, and see the multitudes gathering to come unto Thee! From beyond Eternity thy Source has come. From this moment, you and I are not we, but One. From this moment, you shall be One with Me beyond Eternity. You have attained The Supreme. My glow-ray can be seen upon Thee! For That I AM THAT I AM, The Lord, Thy God, lives within The Secret Inner Sanctuary of your Heart!"

67. Then, I was taken up into Perfect Union with Paratpara, The Lord, My God. And I became That I AM THAT I AM. No other was there, anywhere. And in that Blessed moment, I saw all of the countless Souls, they that had lived, they that were living and those who were yet to live. And they

were wrapped in cloaks of ignorance that hid The Truth of their Oneness with The One God from them. And they wandered endlessly in the Wilderness of darkness and illusion. And they were beset with endless birth, suffering, sorrow and death. For they were drowning in the Ocean of Ignorance, Illusion and Delusion. In that moment, my fear was swept away and I was overcome with compassion.

68. For many Eternities, I, who had Realized my True Nature as One and Identical with God Manifest, contemplated this Mighty Revealed Truth. Then, in one final mighty leap of expansion I stepped over The Threshold, I crossed over The Line and became One and Identical with Paratpara and I Awoke! And in the instant of my Awakening, I gave forth the Cry of Victory "Jai Bhagavan Ji!" And my Cry went out through all Creation and all The Seven and Nine Worlds of Existence and became The Supreme Holy Dharma Mantra that can lead all Souls Home to Paratpara and me and True Liberation. And in that moment, I Knew that it was I who had been Dreaming all of these Spiritual Realms and Universes, and Galaxies, the Seven Worlds, the Prophets, Saints, Buddhas, Saviors, Avataras and Mahavataras, the Earth, its cities, John and my mother, father, brother and sister. I Realized That I AM THAT I AM and no other, as the Uncaused Cause of all Existence, The Unknown Knower of all Knowledge, The One without a prior or a second. I Realized and became That I AM THAT I AM, the Totality of All beyond All.

69. And in that instant, I looked inward upon The Creation of This Image, This Dream, and I saw that it was Good and Beautiful and Perfect; this Dream that I am within, and which was always within That I AM THAT I AM, for I had Created it out of none other than That I AM THAT I AM and there was none other than That I AM THAT I AM in all! Nothing was there in all Existence which That I AM THAT I AM is not and which is not in Me. But even in my Perfect Rapture, I was also aware of each and every one of the Beings of this Dream from the greatest to the smallest. For all Beings are that Universal I AM THAT I AM, and I Am them. But they did not know that they were I and I Am Their True Self. They did not know that they are That I AM THAT I AM within which this whole Creation exists as a dream exists in a man. And, because they do not Know this Truth of their Nature, they fight one another, suffer and believe themselves to die and they are reborn again and again. Because of their Ignorance and Illusion they suffer endlessly, never knowing that there is neither birth nor death for The Dreamer which They Are, and that this suffering and hell exist only for those caught within the appearance of The Dream!

70. And my heart went out to all unawakened People and Beings of my Dream who were still caught up within the Dream. My heart went out to all Souls who, covered as they are by the veils of forgetfulness, ignorance, Desire, Attachment and Identification, did not know the Perfection and Beauty of This Dream, but only its hardship, pain, suffering and death. And I knew that, to these still suffering Souls, Peace, Happiness and Joy meant little more than those very short intervals between one pain, struggle or suffering and another when the agony became a little less than usual.

71. Truly, I thought, if there really were any place in creation that deserved to be called "Hell" this state of forgetfulness, ignorance, suffering and endless dying and rebirth would be it. And I Knew that there was no such place as Hell, other than within ignorance and delusion. For, That I AM THAT I AM had Created it all and That I AM THAT I AM had not Created any such thing as "Evil" or "Hell." But the myriad of unawakened Souls, who are really That I AM THAT I AM, had forgotten me out of their Desire and had fallen into Ignorance, Suffering, Death and Rebirth again and again. These Souls had entered into that state of Being which is completely cut off from That I AM THAT I AM Which They Are, which I had now realized. The unawakened had come to believe that they are, now and forever, different and isolated from That I AM THAT I AM. And in place of The Truth, they created for themselves a false god who was outside of them and was jealous and vengeful and cruel. A false god, who was full of anger and fury and fire and brimstone and would torture them mercilessly for the least transgression of the most petty rule. So forgetful and asleep were they, that they created for themselves, good and bad and a heaven and a hell and even their god in their own image. Because of this, the unawakened Souls live out their lives, time after time, in fear and loathing of their own creation of ignorance, never truly Knowing That I AM THAT I AM which they are!

72. And, their religions taught separateness and their Priests killed those who Awakened enough to Realize their Oneness with That I AM THAT I AM; leaving only the Spiritually Dead to populate the Churches and fill the streets of the cities! On and on they went, driving themselves deeper and deeper into the Illusion they had created. Generation after generation they became more and more cruel, heartless and destructive, just like the false god they had created in their own image, until they were ready and able to destroy themselves and all other creatures in that part of this Beautiful Dream with their self-made "Hell" and "Evil"!

73. From beyond eternity, I knew, "This must not go on!" Yet, That I AM THAT I AM had given this whole Dream the Gift of the same free-choice that I possessed, each according to its nature. I would not violate that condition of this Divine Dream, as that was one of its aspects that gave it its Beauty and Perfection.

74. From my Consciousness as The Dreamer, I could experience this whole Dream at once, for I had Awakened and Realized Oneness and Identity with That One Universal I AM THAT I AM, The One Universal Source of all Being and Existence and was everywhere at once, and yet, beyond it all! In this All-Knowing I knew, too, that a tiny sparrow had fallen and that the small Dream-body that I once lived within was being carefully carried up the stairs of an old house in Iowa and being placed upon a bed. I knew, also, the concern and agony of those who cared for this body I had once called "I". Infinite Compassion poured forth within my Being for all who were still trapped by their own forgetfulness and ignorance within The Dream.

75. Then, Paratpara, The Presence that I had become, gave forth the choice to remain in Perfect Final Union, or to return to the small body I had been, to endure forgetfulness of all but a

fine thread of my Self-Realization and to struggle through the Dream until I should regain what I had lost of my own doing and find The Way back Home to Oneness that all Souls could travel.

76. In less than an instant, I had decided: That I who had become I AM THAT I AM, Dreamer of the entire Dream of Existence, would make the Greatest of all possible Sacrifices for the sake of all Still Suffering Souls. I would give up the Infinite and Eternal Bliss and Joy of Awakening and Realization of my Nature as One with Paratpara, Universal God Manifest and Unmanifest and return to the limp and unconscious Dream-body that was being laid upon its bed in this small Iowa house. I would, once again, willingly and consciously descend back into the Hell of this forgetfulness, ignorance, suffering, misery and death to find a way by which all Beings could awaken from their sleep of Ignorance and rise again from the Living Dead. I would imprison myself within the small Dream-body from which I had escaped and discover The Way to Awaken myself again for the sake of all Souls. A Way which all Beings might then use to Awaken to their Oneness and Identity with Paratpara, The One Universal God of Countless Names and Forms, That Universal I AM THAT I AM and be Free. I would discover The Way back Home and then, I would go out into The Dream, among the Sleeping and the Living Dead and teach them how to Awaken. That each Soul might attain the Salvation and Liberation of Self-Realization and know their True Self as The Dreamer of this whole Dream of Existence and know the Infinite and Eternal Consciousness, Reality and Bliss of their True Nature and Identity, which is One and Identical with Paratpara, God Manifest and Unmanifest, That One Beloved Universal I AM THAT I AM and no other!

77. I chose to return to this world knowing that I would return and forget all but a faint trace, a thin thread, of what had happened. But I knew that I had to do this. Because this first Self-Realization was by Universal God's Infinite Divine Grace alone. And I knew that I would have to forget this Self-Realization, this transcendence of all Creation and the step that I took across The Threshold into Perfect Final Union with Universal God. And I agreed to return to this world to pursue yet a second Self-Realization with my own intelligence and my own mind and my own heart and my own will in this world until I had regained it by Works.

78. So, I made The Supreme Self-Sacrifice. I gave up my Realization of my True Self as The Infinite and Eternal Dreamer of the Dream, for the sake of all suffering Beings. I gave up Perfect Final Union with Paratpara, The One Universal God and returned to the world of the Sleeping and the Living Dead. And, as the veils of forgetfulness were drawn over me I looked up and said: "My head hurts real bad." And no one, not even I could say exactly what made it so, but I was very different from that day on.

Om So'ham Tat Tvam Asi!
I Am That - Thou Art That
Jai Bhagavan Ji!
Victory To That Beloved
Universal I AM THAT I AM
Which You Are!

Here Ends The Chapter Entitled
First Light

Chapter Seven

Pilgrimage

Maitreya The Friend's Journey Home

By The Will and Grace of The One Universal God:

My life went on. I grew and gained knowledge and experience. I was always seeking - something. I didn't know what I was seeking. All I knew was that I had an important and urgent mission to accomplish. Important and urgent to myself and the whole world. I knew that the answer was always right there, just out of reach, but no matter how hard I tried, I couldn't remember what it was. Still, there was always this urge, this nagging, hazy sense of some plan, some Purpose, and some Destiny that was set into motion long ago and far away that I had to fulfill!

2. From time to time, a small crack would form in the armor of my self-chosen forgetfulness that God had wrapped around me. Then, some of the things I had experienced and learned during the Rapture of my first Perfect Final Union with God many years before, would suddenly flash through my mind like sheet lightening on a hot summer's night in Des Moines, Iowa. At these times, I would have sudden flashes of clear awareness that I was faced with fulfilling some unspeakable Destiny with each step that I took. At other times, I felt totally alone and lost. Sometimes, upon visiting some place I had never been before or upon meeting someone I had never met, I would have an unmistakable flash of having been there or known them once before. But the details were always hidden away behind these veils of my forgetfulness.

3. During my first Perfect Final Union with The One Universal God, God revealed to me some of the events I would go through in this mortal life and how they would unfold. God had shown me that my Grandmother would soon give up her body and that my Aunt, her sister, would soon follow her. I was also shown that my family would move to Los Angeles, California soon after these events; and that I would find my Spiritual Guardian and Friend in that place! I did not know my Guardian's name, but God had shown me his face and more important, God had let me experience my Guardian's Spirit during the Rapture.

4. I knew that these things would happen and that I would recognize my Guardian when I saw him. Though I could not recall my Perfect Final Union with God, God let me recall these things and they came to pass just as I had seen them.

5. As God had shown me, we moved to Los Angeles. I started school. I was timid by nature and in a strange city in the fifth grade. I didn't know

anyone. I was easily intimidated. My mother gave me money for lunch, but the bigger boys would come and take it away from me. I didn't eat lunch for almost six months. I was very discouraged. But God never deserted me and always gave me what I needed most, though not always what I wanted most.

6. My first teacher in Los Angeles was my fifth grade teacher. He was a good Soul. His name was Robert Content but, we always called him "Mister" Content. He had been an officer in the Air Force and carried himself with an air of proud Dignity. Still, while stern, he was open and free and kind of wild, while being gentle and caring in a way I had never known.

7. Mister Content did things that I never expected a teacher to do. If you were talking in class, he could throw a dusty blackboard eraser and hit you every time faster than you could duck. He once chased my friend Ron Carr; a particularly unruly boy, out of school and all the way home to his house, three blocks away, and then into his own house and pulled him out from under his bed where he was hiding, while Ron's parents stood by wide-eyed and amazed. They thanked Mister Content afterwards.

8. Though he never spoke to me about it, he seemed to sense that I was going through something very difficult. It was not so much what he said to me, although his words were always good and wise. It was more the way he treated me and his living example of his love of Freedom, his courage to do what was Right in spite of suffering penalties. His steady Wisdom, caring and compassion and the way he treated everyone, stranger and friend alike, as a member of his own family, really moved me. It took me six months to absorb what he had to teach me through his own life. Then, one day I finally understood.

9. That day, after morning class, the bully kid who always took away my lunch money, came up to me with two of his friends. He told me to hand over my lunch money, as he always did. But this time I did not hand over my lunch money. Instead, as if Mr. Content were standing inside of me, I looked right into the eyes of all three of them and, simply walked away and went and bought my lunch. Neither the bully kid or his two friends ever said one word to me. And, they never asked me for my lunch money again.

10. I knew I had received God's Gift of Love of Freedom, Courage and Human Dignity through my teacher, Mr. Robert Content. My life would never be the same again.

11. For a time, I went on through life, as any other boy. But I didn't have the interests of any other boy. While other boys played baseball, during the summer, I became interested in hypnosis. I was a natural and rapidly became so good at it that I was paid as a hypnotherapist before I was fifteen years of age. My first subject was my best friend Ron Shepherd. Ron was an excellent subject and could achieve a very deep state of hypnosis easily and quickly.

12. One of my first and most important experiments was to find out how much the mind could affect the human body. I hypnotized Ron and told him that I would touch his wrist with a red hot piece of metal, but that he would feel no pain. Having told him this, I touched the inside of his left wrist with an ordinary yellow pencil that had

been laying close at hand. As I had instructed him, he felt no pain.

13. I awakened Ron and we talked at some length about the experience. Just before Ron left, I noticed him rubbing his left wrist where I had touched him with the pencil. I asked him if anything was wrong. He said his wrist itched and thought he might have been bitten by something. He said good-bye and went home.

14. Twenty minutes later, Ron called me and said, "I want you to see something." We met a few minutes later and he showed me a blister that had raised in the shape of a rod the size of a pencil on the inside of his left wrist.

15. This experiment taught me the power of the mind to create conditions within the human body. I again hypnotized Ron and tried to make the blister go away. Still, no matter what I did, the blister took nearly a week to heal. This taught me that what is done to the body by the mind, must often be undone by the body through its own healing methods. This was a mystery that caused me great concern for some time.

16. As a result of this experiment, I decided that hypnosis, while useful for many worldly reasons, was not the answer to my Destiny, though I still didn't know what that Destiny was.

17. So, I turned to the ancient eastern art and science of Yoga. There I learned that Yoga came from the root word "yuj" which meant "Union," but in its broader meaning meant "Union with God." I studied but quickly went beyond Physical (Hatha) Yoga. I turned my attention and practice to the more esoteric and Spiritual forms of Yoga such as The Way of Love of God and Devotion to God, called Bhakti Yoga; The Way of Surrendering all Actions and their results to God, called Karma Yoga; and The Way of Direct Knowledge of God, which is called Jnana Yoga.

18. It was summer and I had time to study and practice. During that summer I began and completed a fourteen day fast taking only water. During that time I often meditated as much as eight or ten hours a day. With such intensity, self-discipline and desperation, I advanced steadily and rapidly in these Spiritual Disciplines and soon acquired some of their worldly powers called "Siddhis."

19. Amazing things began to happen. One day, as I sat absorbed in Inner Divine Communion with God, I became annoyed that that my brother had left the bedroom door open. I wanted it shut, but did not want to disturb my meditation to get up and close it. I quickly flashed my intention toward the door and a second later it slammed shut with a loud bang. There was no wind. No one was there.

20. A week or so after that, on another occasion, as I sat in Inner Divine Communion, deeply absorbed in God Consciousness, my mind touched upon a coke bottle that had been left on top of my dresser. In a flash, I heard a loud thud. Opening my eyes, I found the coke bottle stuck neck first into the bedroom wall. There was no one else in or near my room. I called my brother in to see what had happened, but he only said I must have put it there.

21. Then, something happened that put an end to my quest for these worldly powers. A few months after summer had ended, as I was sitting in a class

in English, I had one final experience with the worldly power, or Siddhi, of moving objects. My mind was far away from English grammar and absorbed in thinking about God. As the teacher talked on and on, I began to absentmindedly roll a pencil up and down the slanted desk top with one finger. First giving it a little push so that it rolled up the slanted desk top and equally absentmindedly watching it roll back down of its own weight.

22. Then a strange thing happened. As the pencil was rolling back down the desk for the tenth time, I thought into the pencil, not at the pencil but into the pencil, "Stop!" Suddenly the pencil froze in place half-way down the desk top even though my hands were nowhere near it. Then, I thought into it, "Move up the desk!" The pencil obediently rolled back up to the top of the desk while I kept my hands away from it. Then, without surprise or excitement, I thought into the pencil, "Roll down the desk!" The pencil obediently rolled back down to the bottom of the desk and stopped. I should have been excited or shocked or, something. But I was completely detached from the whole affair and only mildly interested in it or concerned by it.

23. I continued rolling the pencil up and down the desk in this same way three or four times. The thoughts that I placed into the pencil were not in words and my mind was completely unattached to them. Instead, my mind was firmly fixed on God. In reality, I did not care at all whether the pencil moved or not. At that moment, I cared only for The One Universal God. I had discovered the Spiritual Principle of detachment and surrender to God, without even knowing it.

24. The boy who was seated next to me suddenly gasped and then shouted "Look! The pencil! It..." My attention snapped back to the classroom to find the whole class staring at me and at him. With my communion with God broken, the pencil rolled off the right side of the desk and clattered to the ground.

25. Silence was all around. All eyes were upon me. I picked up the pencil and calmly said to the boy who had yelled, "What is the matter?" The boy sputtered and started to explain to the class what he had seen, but stopped. I guess he knew that no one would believe him, and broke down and cried.

26. I had no intention of hurting anyone. But, my worldly powers had already hurt another in this way. From this experience, I realized that worldly powers are only the gross outer manifestations of Spiritual Practice. I also understood the ancient admonition to avoid the Siddhis as temptations that can become a distraction and stop Spiritual progress.

27. I decided not to exercise any of the powers that came to me in any way that could hurt others. The last thing I ever wanted to do was to bring more grief and suffering to any living Being. The Siddhis themselves would no longer have a place of importance in my life.

28. I tried to make friends with the boy who had seen me moving the pencil, but the boy's parents were fundamentalist Christians and believed that all such things were "evil." They would not let the boy associate with me even though he

wanted to be friends. I contemplated this event for a very long time.

29. How, I wondered, could just moving a pencil by God's Divine Power be "evil"? Was not my entire mind and heart in inner communion with God at that moment? I certainly knew there could be no "evil" in communing with God. Had not Yohoshuay, the God-freed One, who people call Jesus healed the sick and raised the dead Himself? Why were so many of those who called themselves Christians always seeing "evil" and living in darkness and fear when The Clear Light of God was all around them?

30. I also wondered how those who claimed Yohoshuay for their Savior and Teacher could preach separation between the individual Soul and God, when Yohoshuay Himself had told me personally that His life had been sacrificed to awaken all people to the Oneness of every man's Soul with God?

31. Most of all, I wondered how I could know these things that I should not be able to know. How could I know that Jesus' true name was Yohoshuay? I didn't know where or when Jesus himself had told me these things, but I knew that He had done so.

32. Though I didn't know it, the answer to these and many other perplexing questions lay hidden behind the veils of forgetfulness that God had wrapped around me when I sacrificed Perfect Final Union with Him and returned to this world of suffering to do His Will.

33. Such questions haunted me day and night. I knew that I had been told and shown these things, and I knew that it was truly Jesus The Christ who had given me many of these Truths! Further, I knew that those of all ages and times who had Realized their Oneness and Identity with God, including Yohoshuay, called those religions that teach the separation of man's Soul from God "The Church of the Living Dead." And, I loved others without wanting to, even those who hated me.

34. To gather greater insight into these questions, I set aside my practice of The Way of Union with God (Yoga) and became part of a new Lutheran Church which was being built a block away from my parent's home. I put my back, my hands and heart to work helping the Minister, a wonderful young Pastor named Monroe Husfeld, build the church during the day. At night my friends Ron Shepherd and Mike Crossley and I guarded it from vandals.

35. I put my energy, my heart and my very Spirit into every stone and board I touched. In the moments when we stopped working, I asked Pastor Husfeld many questions that had been weighing heavy upon my mind. His answers were always very kind and wise in God's Ways.

36. I loved Pastor Husfeld, but was saddened, because I sensed he knew more answers than the Doctrine of his Church would allow him to give to my many questions. The only answer his Doctrine would allow him to give to my questions that went directly to the heart of things, was all too often: "Son, you cannot understand these things; no man can understand these things; we are Souls that are separate from God. We are like pots and God is the Potter. He makes us, but we can only be close to Him, we cannot be

Him! You cannot know these things. Just believe, and when you die you will go to Heaven and be close to God forever!"

37. I never told him, but it was not enough for me to just be "close" to God. My love and longing and desperation for God was too great to be satisfied with even the smallest separation from God. For me, nothing less than everything would do. Besides, I knew, deep in my heart, that what this Minister had said was far from the Truth and was the Doctrine of the Living Dead! I didn't know how I knew. I knew that all Souls were One with God with greater certainty than I knew that I existed. I also knew that I had to find The Way by which to experience and realize this Divine Truth.

38. One day something happened that filled in a small piece of the puzzle. When we were moving out to California from Iowa, we stopped in Yuma, Arizona for gas. Next to the gas station, there was a souvenir stand run by an old Indian. There were many things to buy, but I took my allowance and bought a small piece of wood laminated with a picture of Jesus guiding a young sailor at the wheel of a ship on an angry and stormy sea. I would not know it until years later, but the picture was a famous Christian Classic titled 'Christ Our Pilot.'

39. It was just a cheap trinket that tourist places sell to tourists, but I treasured that little picture. When I was fourteen, I hung it in a special place in the hallway of my parents home, just inside the front door, so I would be sure to see it every time I went out and came in.

40. When I came home from Junior High School one day, I was shocked to see that someone had cut out a small picture of my face and pasted it over Jesus' face in that picture. I was shocked, hurt and angry. I blamed my brother, who had a habit of doing things like that to upset me. But, my mother stepped in and said that she had pasted my face on that picture. I was heartbroken. I demanded that she tell me why. All she would say is, it was the right thing to do.

41. In a burst of anguish, I told her, "I am not Jesus and you shouldn't have put me in Jesus' place. I am who I am and have a different Mission than Jesus." As these words left my lips, I heard them as if someone else were saying them. Suddenly, another awareness of a greater Truth arose in me. It was vague and undefined but very powerful and pointed me in a new direction and changed me at my core. No, I wasn't Jesus. But somehow, I knew that I knew Jesus and many others of God's Mercies to Man in ways that I didn't even know myself.

42. I wiped as much as I could of the picture of my face off of Jesus' picture. But no matter how hard I tried a tiny bit of glue remained that would not come off without ruining the picture. It stayed on that picture, as if to remind

me of something important I had to do. I lost track of the picture many years later but the awareness never faded.

43. I kept on going to The Lutheran Church, partly to please my parents and friends, but mostly in the hope that I might yet discover a kernel of God's Reality and Truth there. But, in my private moments, my heart and attention always returned to The Way of Union with God. Even this was not satisfying my purpose. I had studied and practiced all of the many kinds of Yoga. I had studied the Bible, the Koran, the Bhagavad Gita, the Vedas, and the Upanishads. I had studied the Talmud and the Torah. I had looked into Spiritualism and Psychicism. Though all of them held some kernel of God's Truth deep within them, none of them held the complete answer. The road I was following seemed bleak and hopeless.

44. My Faith was unraveling. I had to know if God was real or, if it was all just a figment of my imagination. So, I set out to perform a series of "experiments" to find out whether or not my natural Faith was justified or not.

45. I gathered together my good friends John and Ron Shepherd and several other interested brother and sister seekers. I told everyone that the purpose of our meetings would be to study unusual phenomena, such as mental healing, moving physical objects with our minds and the like. That was true. However, my greater purpose was to find out whether so-called "miracles" were evidence of God, or only tricks of mental physics. I covered my real purpose so that the results of our efforts would not be biased by the members' beliefs about God.

46. Our first experiment was centered in telekinesis, moving physical objects with the mind alone. We gathered together every Wednesday night from eight o'clock until ten o'clock. Our laboratory was John and Ron's parent's living room. Our experimental equipment consisted of a huge two hundred pound coffee table and a glass of tap water. The goal of our first experiment was to move the glass enough to make the water splash out of it, using only our minds.

47. We were as devoted and determined as any scientists had ever been. We sat without moving, our eyes glassy, staring at that glass of water for two solid hours every Wednesday evening for two months. Nothing happened. When I was completely satisfied that our own efforts could not move the glass, I embarked on the second part of my experiment.

48. One Wednesday evening, about two-thirds of the way through our session, when all of our minds were exhausted from concentrating and our eyes red and tired from staring, I said, "You know, the Bible and other Holy Books say that when people have complete Faith in Him, God does what they cannot do by themselves. Maybe we should try that."

49. Then, I suggested that we all turn within and call upon God, according to our own conceptions of God, with the single-minded intention of having the glass BE moved. To demonstrate our Faith, I conducted everyone out into the kitchen, out of sight of the table and glass. There I asked everyone to "wait in Faith" knowing without a doubt that, "it will be done."

50. Perhaps because everyone was so tired and frustrated, everyone

quickly agreed to this plan. Each of us communed with God, according to our own conceptions of God, for ten minutes. Then, we all waited in Faith for God to do as we had asked.

51. After about fifteen minutes, John Shepherd and I both felt a strong urging to go into the living room. At first I thought this might just be our lack of Faith rising up, so I hesitated for another few minutes. Finally, the urging spread to the others and became so powerful we could not resist. When we walked into the living room, we were astonished to see the glass of water intensely vibrating on the coffee table and water splashing out of it. After we walked in the vibrating decreased and the glass just sat there and sort of shivered, throwing tiny droplets out onto the massive table.

52. Being self-avowed "scientists" and die-hard skeptics, we immediately phoned Griffith Observatory and asked if there had been an earthquake or any tremors of significant size to cause what we had seen. The answer was, positively, "no." Thus the first of my "experiments" ended with my conviction of the reality of God much increased.

53. Our meetings continued. We went back to the old method for a comparison and to see if we could make it work. We kept on staring at the unmoving glass week after week for another month. As before, despite our best and most intense efforts and stares, nothing happened.

54. Finally, I decided to embark on the next phase of my experiment. I had seen that God, or at least complete Faith in God could move a physical object. But what about moving the hearts and minds of people? Was that just something that happened in books or, was that Blessing available to us, here and now?

55. We began again. During one session, when everyone was again tired and frustrated, I said, "I have an idea, suppose we just completely surrender to God and God's Will and see what happens?" A couple of people began to object to bringing "God" into things and I was afraid they would see through my rather thinly disguised intention. But, after some intense discussion, they agreed to try it.

56. I suggested that we should sit for thirty minutes and put forth the greatest effort of mind and Spirit that we each could manage into reaching for God. Then, instead of asking God to move glasses or do anything in particular, that we should simply completely immerse ourselves in God, surrender totally to God and let "God's Will Be Done." All agreed and we began. We were still hoping for the darned glass to jump up in the air, but managed to put this desire out of mind.

57. After thirty minutes, something happened. It grew slowly within us. It was as if we were all joined together in a way that went far beyond our bodies or our minds. It was as if we shared a common consciousness that was much more and far greater than any one of our own.

58. Suddenly, we each knew, together, beyond all doubt, that we had a choice: we could either see our efforts fulfilled and God would raise the glass straight up into the air; or, we could have God and God's Divine Presence within our hearts. There was no question or hesitation. We all chose God and

God's Presence within and the glass was completely forgotten.

59. Then, a most miraculous thing came upon us. We were filled with God's Divine Spirit to overflowing. Tears came to our eyes and the inner book of each of our lives was opened to us. Our "sins" and karmas were shown to us and, as we repented of each of these they were wiped clean. Following this, we were each given the answers to the main questions that were burning the brightest within each of our hearts and minds.

60. We were amazed by this Divine Blessing which we had neither called for nor anticipated. We sat in stunned, tearful and blissful silence for many minutes and then took to hugging one another and rejoicing.

61. Independent testimonies, given after The Blessing, proved that we all felt and knew that this was happening with one another, at the same time; even though none of us knew what God had revealed to the others. We all agreed that we now knew what the Disciples of Jesus and Buddha and all of The Prophets, Saints, Buddhas, Saviors and Avataras themselves must have felt. We all knew that we would never be the same again. There were no further arguments against God.

62. These experiments had given me abundant Faith that God is God and that God is immediate and available to every person at all times. Still, the feats of strength and courage that I had read about in nearly every Holy Book haunted me. Were they real? Did they really happen? Could they actually happen today, or are they only relics of long ago and far away? I determined to conduct yet another simple experiment to settle my mind.

63. My good friend Ron Shepherd was an amazingly strong man, even at sixteen. His body was like a powerful spring. He was fully three or four times stronger than I. We had arm wrestled many times. I was no match for him. He would take me down and pin my arm to the table or floor in two or three seconds no matter how desperately I tried to resist. Because of this, I planned my experiment around our tremendous difference in strength.

64. One evening, while we were sitting around in Ron's living room talking, I purposely started a roughhouse play with Ron, as teenage boys often do. With this as a rationale, I challenged Ron to arm wrestle, with the person who won two-out-of-three, being the winner of the match.

65. I weighed more than Ron. So, to eliminate my having any weight advantage, I insisted that we should wrestle lying belly down on the floor.

66. Our first round went just as usual. In less than three seconds Ron's massive spring-like strength had slammed my right arm to the floor and I was completely helpless to move it. I asked for a few minutes to "rest up" before the second round. During this time, I prayed and called upon God to be my self and my strength and then, surrendered myself completely to God and God's Divine Will. I should mention that I had no least "faith" or "belief" that this would result in anything at all.

67. We faced off and joined hands and the second round began. I felt

not one bit stronger. I accepted in an instant that my experiment had already failed. I did not notice that my arm was moving toward the floor much more slowly than usual. I only became aware of what was happening when I heard Ron grunt loudly. Then, I was astounded to find that he had pushed my right arm to within two or three inches of the floor, but was completely unable to move it any further!

68. My body felt like it belonged to someone else and I was nothing but an impartial Witness to what was happening. Or, more precisely, what was not happening! Beads of sweat appeared on Ron's forehead and his face became so red I began to fear for his health. Suddenly, I thought, "Let's get on with it." Ron and I both stared in utter amazement as my right arm pushed his right arm up and up and over and pinned it to the floor on the other side! Ron was completely helpless to raise his arm or even get up so long as that amazing Divine Power and Grace flowed through me into him. Finally, I said silently within myself, "Release him." At that very instant, The Power stopped flowing and Ron pushed his arm up with no trouble at all.

69. He asked me and then begged me to tell him what was going on. He said that he had never felt anything like that in his life. I told him it was part of an experiment I was doing and that I had one more phase to complete before I could talk about it. Then, without willing it, I heard myself, "Of myself I am nothing; with God all things are possible." Ron looked shocked, but said no more about it.

70. We quickly started the third and final round. Without God, Ron had once again pinned my now aching right arm to the floor within two seconds. This pleased him greatly and the first phase of my experiment with God's Personal Power came to an end.

71. The second phase of my experiment in the bodily manifestation of God's Personal Power came the following Wednesday evening at the Westchester Y.M.C.A. Each Wednesday evening, Ron and I studied Judo and Jujitsu under the expert guidance of Joe Penwell. Joe was a veteran Marine and tough as nails. Unfortunately, I was about as tough as warm butter and miserably slow at mastering these arts. Ron, on the other hand, was like a steel spring and fast as lightning and mastered everything Joe taught well and quickly. I spent the days following each class, nursing multiple bruises and mat burns resulting from being thrown about by Joe and Ron. Here, was more fertile ground for finding out if calling upon God and surrendering to God's Will and Divine Power could make a martial artist out of a lump of butter.

72. We went through the class as always, with Master Penwell and my "friend" Ron bouncing me off of the walls of the gym; and I, being the world's first human volley ball. When the teaching and practice portion of the class was over, I told Master Penwell and Ron that I wanted to do an experiment in Meditation and Concentration, and asked Master Penwell if I could Meditate for a few minutes before Ron and I sparred. Having received Joe's permission, I sat in the middle of the mat and, once again, called upon The One Universal God to fill me and be my self, my courage, my strength and my skill. After five minutes of prayer and meditation, I heard myself softly say,

"Of myself I am nothing - with You Father all things are possible. Make me an instrument of your Divine Grace." Stunned, I announced that I was ready to begin.

73. When I stood up this time, I was a different person. My stiffness had turned into a strangely relaxed and loose but powerful energy. My bent over, fearful posture had become easily and naturally straight, as if my whole body were suspended from a wire tied to the crown of my head and held by someone far beyond that gym. I felt as though I were a cat and my movements reflected my feelings. Instead of being made into fists, my hands were open and relaxed while at the same time being like steel traps. I moved about with a grace of a ballet dancer.

74. Each time I would turn my awareness in a certain direction, it felt like God's limitless Divine Power from beyond me was flowing into the very center of my being and out through my body, my legs or my arms and into infinity beyond. "Is this path circular and does this Power that now flows through me return to its Source only to flow through me again?" I wondered casually as Ron and I circled each other.

75. Suddenly, Ron grabbed my left arm. Normally, I would have tensed and been quickly thrown across the room. This time, my left arm swung in a graceful arc and it was Ron who went flying across the mat. Next, Ron tried a leg sweep. A move that always caught me off guard and put me flat on my back. This time, however, my leg cooperated with his so fully that I did a beautiful pivot and he went up in the air and landed flat on his back.

76. This last move made Ron very angry. He jumped up and came roaring after me. I should have been scared. Normally, I would have been scared, and with good reason. But I wasn't scared. It was as if time had suddenly slowed down. I saw Ron attacking me from every possible angle, as if I were watching a movie in slow-motion. By the time he made his move, I had already met it and countered it and executed my own move and he was down again.

77. After fifteen or twenty minutes, Ron finally called for the sparring to stop. He had not captured me or thrown me once and I had captured or thrown him an amazing number of times, without effort and with perfect detachment. If Master Penwell was impressed, he did not show it. He merely mentioned that he had seen such things when he was in some of the Asian countries and understood what I was doing.

78. I wanted to make sure that my performance was really the result of calling upon and surrendering to God and had not come about because I had suddenly understood Judo. So, I did my sparring the following week without calling upon God. Needless to say, Ron got more than even and I spent the whole next week nursing my many bruises and mat burns.

79. After this experiment, my Faith increased one hundred-fold. I gave up Judo and returned to my Spiritual Practice with a desperation and determination I had never before known or felt.

80. Then, one day after completing my prayers and while sitting deep in communion with God, a Holy Book was opened within my heart and mind

and a new Way was opened unto my Spirit. This Way had no name that I had ever heard of. This Book had no title I had ever seen. This Supreme Holy Book was called "The Sanatana Dharma, God's Eternal Universal Religion;" and, this Supreme Way was called, simply "The Holy Adhyatma-Yoga-Dharma."

81. A still small voice within me said, "This is the Highest and most Ancient Religion and Way to God. Before The Beginning, It was. After The End It shall be! This is your Religion and your Way! Follow The Way to The Goal for the Salvation and Liberation of all Souls! For thousands and thousands of years The Way has been lost due to man's ignorance, desire, attachment and identification with this world of illusion. The sleeping and the Living Dead have suppressed it in all ages. Revive It! Follow It! Practice It! Preach It to all beings, for this is the Great Answer you have asked after and it is given!"

82. Thinking back on the ideas of evil I had heard about from my friends who claimed to be followers of the Christ this voice worried me. I thought, "From whom does this Answer come? From God, or from another?" And the answer came, "From That I AM THAT I AM. I Am The One True Universal Living God, Father of all Creation, Thy Own True Self and the True Self of all Beings Forever! I Am The Father of The Father! I Am The One Without a second! I AM THAT I AM! You may call me Paratpara for I am The One Universal God of Countless Names and Forms Who Is Beyond All Names and Forms!"

83. My heart leapt for joy! Bliss flowed within and all around me. I had found The Way at last and could begin the long journey Home and fulfill The Universal Purpose! I had been given The Book of Life and shown The Sanatana Dharma, The Eternal Truth and Way of God's Eternal Universal Religion: The Friend's Way of Self-Realization, The Way of Union with The Highest Self, which is none other than The One True Universal Living God! I began reading The Holy Book of Life within my own heart and practiced The Way without doubt or reservation. But in idle moments I often wondered why it was called "The Friend's" Way of Self-Realization and who this "Friend" might be.

84. Still, my worldly life continued to unfold. I met a wonderful girl named Patty Stein, who captured my heart. I could put aside all other desires with ease, but my young love for this beautiful girl haunted me day and night. I would awake in the middle of the night calling her name. She became an obsession with me and I could not bear to be parted from her for even a short time. She too, was devoted to me, a fact which made my heart tremendously happy, but which made it all the harder to cut the strings of desire and attachment that bound me to her.

85. My Spiritual Practice fell apart. Soon, she and she alone became my object of worship! I dreamed of nothing but carrying her off and marrying her and raising a family together in peace and harmony.

86. But there was not always peace and harmony between us. Instead, jealousy and fear and conflict were often woven into the fiber of our love. I suffered in sorrow, fear and misery. Some days I could do nothing by my own will. I began to have severe

migraine headaches and suffered greatly under this overwhelming love and attachment, which was all my own doing.

87. One day while I was visiting a friend in Playa Del Rey, a nearby city, I happened to mention something about my practice of yoga. The mention of yoga instantly caught the attention and interest of my friend's mother who had been involved in eastern philosophy and Spiritual study for many years. Her name was Virginia Sietz. My newfound soul-friend and I spent many hours involved in intense discussion in the weeks that followed.

88. Finally, my incessant questions exhausted her knowledge. One day she said "The questions you are asking are beyond ability to teach you. I don't know where you have been or what you have done, but I, with all of my many years of experience, I can't keep up with your thirst for insight. I want you to go and see a man who has deeper and greater knowledge in these matters than I, who can take you the next step of The Way." She gave me the name of an electronics engineer by the name of Hank Frazier. She said, "He is a brilliant man, but he rambles a lot."

89. I was very disappointed. He was not even from India and had a most common name. But, I promised to contact this engineer and go to see him. As I was leaving her house, this wise woman looked deeply into my eyes and said "Who are you and what have you brought to us?" All that I could say was "I wish I knew. I really wish I knew. That is what I am trying to find out."

90. That same evening, I phoned the mysterious engineer who my friend said could take me the next step of the way to my Destiny. He said that Virginia had called him and I made arrangements to have a meeting with him. Two days later, I was standing on the doorstep of a common looking house in an ordinary middle class neighborhood.

91. When the door opened, my heart leapt for joy! Here was the very man I had known would become my Spiritual Guardian and friend. In that moment, a small crack opened in the wall of forgetfulness that God had wrapped around me when I sacrificed Perfect Final Union with Him. A flash of future-sight showed me a long association and the eventual loss of my Spiritual Guardian and friend, whom I had only just found. I stood there, speechless. "Howdy. Come on in," my new found Guardian said in a deep resonant cowboy-like voice, that reminded me of John Wayne.

92. It was 6 p.m. when I and my good friends, Ron Shepherd and Mike Crossley arrived at my new Spiritual Guardian's house. Mike had to leave early. Ron and I stayed. It was 6 a.m. the following morning when I finally left. We had talked the whole night through.

93. None of us had slept. None of us noticed the lack of sleep. I had forgotten all about time and the fact that I had promised my parents that I would be home before midnight. But this night was too precious to waste thinking about possible punishments. I had found a huge piece of the puzzle and was not going to let it go. Here was a true Master who understood life and the world and The Spirit in the same way that I, myself, understood

these things. But Hank had gone much further! Disciple and Spiritual Guardian said good-bye and vowed to meet again the following week.

94. Strangely, when I arrived home at seven in the morning, my mother and father did not scold me or even ask where I had been or what I had been doing. I had never thought of them as particularly Spiritual people, but my father was a Thirty-Second Degree Mason and seemed to have a deep insight into what I had been doing. Still, not a word was spoken about my long absence.

95. Many meetings followed this first one. These meetings often lasted into the early hours of the morning. I noticed some annoyance on the part of Hank's wife, Barbara, over our long late night conferences and wondered why he would upset their relationship for my sake. After all, I had only met him; why would he have such a deep concern for me?

96. Patty was also becoming upset at all of these meetings; and I sensed deeply that the forces of attachment to this world, which I would later realize as The Force of Darkness; and the forces of The Way Home to God, which I would know as The Force of Light; were lining up on either side of me. I was frightened.

97. During these early meetings, I learned and absorbed Hank's own Spirit with a thirst that could not be quenched. For every question my Guardian would answer, I would raise three more. Then, one evening, in pure surprise, I heard my own mouth speak out "Someday, I will bring Salvation and Liberation to all Souls with The Clear Light of God's Truth, Awaken them from this Illusion, and Restore to them the Knowledge of their True Nature as One and Identical with God and no other!"

98. I tried to stop myself from speaking these words, but I could not! It was as a Divine Force, infinitely greater than I, was speaking through my mouth. This Divine Force would have its say in spite of my feeble attempt to stop it.

99. My Guardian sat back in his chair and gazed intently, with furrowed brow, as was his manner. He looked like an old wise Scotsman. He said nothing, he only looked. I waved my arms helplessly in the air and tried to make myself deny what I had said. No denial came. No matter how hard I tried I could not make my own mouth say "I didn't mean it," For, deep down inside, despite fear and embarrassment, I knew that I did mean it! Hank continued to gaze intently for some time and then said only, "It's been a long night. I'll see you next week."

100. Our meetings went on week after week. Many subjects were discussed. We investigated many different ideas from Astronomy to Zen Buddhism. My Guardian, who was also becoming my most trusted friend, showed me the most brilliant means of delving into the heart of a subject, discriminating the Real from the unreal, and capturing the Essence of it.

101. During the months that followed nearly all aspects of life and living became objects of our discussion, investigation and understanding. I awaited the moment at which my Guardian would respond to my mysterious outburst. That moment never came. Finally, out of desperation, I asked him to comment

upon this strange occurrence. Was it "psychic?" Was it a disembodied Spirit speaking through me? I had read about such things happening to people and wondered if this was what happened to me.

102. My Guardian was surprisingly firm and urgent about it. "Absolutely not!" he said, softening a little, "It was no such thing. Stay away from such things with regard to yourself. Study them, learn about them, understand them if you must, but do not get lost by applying them to yourself! You are very special in this world. Someday you will understand, but I will not be here when you do!" He would say no more about it.

103. A short time later, Hank moved to a city further away. Because I could not yet drive, our meetings became fewer and farther between. Soon, my attention was being drawn more and more to Patty, whom I had neglected since meeting my Guardian and Friend. Our love and attachment to one another grew quickly once I was out of my Guardian's immediate influence. Soon, I nearly gave up seeing my Guardian at all.

104. I was growing up and it was not long before I had a license to drive and a small car to enable me to get around. Once again, I began making regular journeys to my Guardian's house, which was twenty miles away.

105. Occasionally, I would take Patty and we would meet all manner of wonderful men and women who were following different Spiritual Paths who were drawn to my Guardian's house. There were psychologists from all over the country. One was a researcher with J.B. Rhine, the famous parapsychological investigator at Duke University. There were physicists, doctors, and experts of all kinds. There was even a wonderful man named Fred Kimball, who claimed that he could actually see the auras around people, look into their lives and histories, and "read the minds of animals."

106. Hank introduced me to Mr. Kimball and told him that I needed to talk to him. At my first meeting with Mr. Kimball, I was amazed to find that this wonderful man could tell all about my life. The moment I shook his hand, Mr. Kimball said "You fell out of an apple tree when you were eight years old and hurt your back right here," he said, pointing to the place. He was right about the fall and the place my back was hurt. Then he said "Oh, yes. You had another fall when you were eight years old, but it is strangely sealed with a seal that I can't break. I can't see into it." Mr. Kimball looked very puzzled by this. He told me that I had a very difficult time ahead because of a strong ability to deal with the world that would pull me toward worldly things and a special Spiritual Nature that would constantly try to draw me away from the world.

107. Mr. Kimball rightly said that my father occasionally drank more than he should and that I would be in danger of becoming an alcoholic within the next ten years because of the conflict between this great Spiritual Destiny and my longing to be part of the world!

108. Mr. Kimball also shook hands with Patty and told her that she would be taking a far different path and that she could not follow me where I had to go! But, that we might be reunited

in a far different way many years later in our lives.

109. I was shocked and hurt. Fear arose in my heart over the possible loss of my beloved. I left Hank's house that day vowing never to return. I even thought there was a conspiracy to separate us and that this conspiracy was the work of my Guardian and Mr. Kimball. Little did I know that these wise men were but reporting the plan that I, myself, had set as my Destiny, so many years ago, while immersed in Total God-Realization and Perfect Final Union with God.

110. A year passed. As Mr. Kimball had predicted, Patty and I began to grow apart. Panic stricken over what I knew must eventually happen, I began clinging ever tighter to her. But my clinging soon stopped being an embrace and became a strangle hold on her life. I was the agent of my own undoing. The tighter I held on, the more she, naturally, wanted to run away. Sooner than I had expected, it was over between us. Alone and desperate, I, once again, turned to my Spiritual Guardian and Friend for help.

111. One evening as we sat talking about the things of the Spirit, my Guardian mentioned a cactus that American Indians had used for thousands of years to unlock Spiritual secrets and grow closer with God, The Great Spirit. My mind leapt to life. "How can I have this experience?" I urgently asked. My Guardian explained that the cactus was called "Peyote."

112. Hank said that one had to know exactly where and how to find it in the desert and when to take it from the ground with Religious ceremonies. He went on to explain that, even though the Indians had used it for many hundreds of years, little was known about it and that it could be very dangerous and maybe even deadly unless I was properly prepared for it.

113. The thought of danger or death didn't sway me. I was aflame with the possibility of discovering another piece of the answer to the riddle of my life. I vowed that I would do anything to make myself ready for this experience and, I did.

114. For more than six months I prepared and prepared. Once every two weeks, I would meet with my Spiritual Guardian and report my progress. Hank would always ask the same question: "Why do you want to have this experience?" I would answer and he would furrow his brow and shake his head, saying "No! Go and work on it some more."

115. Then one day after six months of preparation, I gave up. I met with Hank as usual. He asked his question as usual. Only this time, I answered, "I have absolutely no reason." Hanks eyes lit up. He leaned forward and said, "You are ready."

116. Finally, after six long months, I was "ready." I took the weekend off from my job at a service station and slowly drove the twenty miles to my Guardian's house. Five times I nearly turned back. I firmly believed that there was a fifty-fifty chance that I would never come out of this experience alive. Still, the risk was worth it if I could only find the answer to my quest.

117. Taking the cactus was a trial of the Spirit in itself. It was horribly bitter.

All the while I was suffering through the sour and foul taste, my Guardian was right by my side giving final words of instruction and preparation. It was late when we began and, after choking the Peyote down with a whole quart of milk to prevent my throwing up, I and my Guardian sat facing one another, talking softly.

118. "The Peyote" he explained "is but a key that opens the lock upon your mind and Spirit. Where you go and what you experience once the lock is opened, depends completely upon the state and condition of your own heart. If you are filled with sins and Karmas you will have to experience them and conquer them. But, if your heart is pure you will go directly to The True Spiritual Realm and see the world anew from there. Never allow yourself to be attached to the Peyote or any other earthly substance for they can only give you a look through the window of the world at The Reality beyond. But, once you have seen The Reality from the window, you must stand up Spiritually, find the door, and pass through it into that One Reality without any support or aid at all!"

119. I did not die. I did not suffer past sins and Karmas. Instead, I stepped lightly through the "eye of the needle" and inside the Gates of Heaven. For three full days and nights I explored the Realm of Spiritual Reality from within, that was beyond! No least corner was left unexplored, no stone was left un-turned. I broke through the veils of darkness and ignorance and grasped The Truth with both hands of my Spirit.

120. For seventy-two hours I was Pure Consciousness, True Reality, and Boundless Bliss! I turned my attention to the World of Illusion and mastered its principles. I found, perfected, and mastered Soul Travel until I could be many and all places and realms at one and the same time. I mastered Perfect Harmony with the world of Illusion.

121. On the second day of my Peyote journey, I came upon a bush that was filled with honeybees. After communing with them in Spirit for some time, I meshed and blended and merged with them. Then, I gently slid my hand into the midst of the bush and brought it out covered with bees. I communed with them on my hand and arm for some time, then I placed my hand back into the bush and bid them to leave me and return to their work. The bees cooperated with my wishes fully; not one of them had stung me.

122. I also discovered and mastered harmony with my body and its relationship with its world. Around mid-morning, my Guardian's daughter and another friend took me for a walk. While beginning to walk up a steep hill, I suddenly saw my situation through Awakened eyes, and decided that it would be much easier if my body would keep going the same direction but walk downhill. Suddenly, though I had not changed direction, I was walking quickly and easily downhill while still walking up it! When I reached the top of the hill, it changed back to its normal state. I looked back down at the others, who were only beginning to struggle up the long hill. I was not even out of breath!

123. The area in which we were walking was having trouble with small packs of stray dogs killing pets and biting people. As we were returning to my Guardian's house we were attacked by two snarling dogs.

124. Earlier in the day, I had discovered that I could "see" in all directions at once. I could not explain it, but it was as though my vision covered all of the space around me on all sides and above and below, in a complete sphere.

125. Suddenly, out of one side of my greatly expanded vision, I saw two dogs stalking us from behind a garage. I saw the dogs break into a run straight toward the backs of those who had come with me on this walk, one of whom was my Guardian's daughter!

126. I Spiritually meshed and blended and merged with the two dogs in perfect Unity and Affinity. Then, waiting until the last moment, I swung around, put my right arm straight out with my palm facing the closest dog's nose; and thought straight into them, Soul-to-Soul, "I love you beyond measure for I am one with you! But if you come any closer, I will destroy you! Stop! Go back where you came from!" Both dogs stopped dead in their tracks. The hair upon their backs stood straight up. The closest and bigger dog yelped, put his tail between his legs and ran back down the lane as fast as he could. The smaller dog was close behind the larger dog, running as fast as he could. The weekend was over. I had seen and experienced much. The experiences I had contained many amazing, wondrous and beautiful things I would never mention to any living person. Still, even this experience had not revealed to me the Answer to the riddle of my life. But, it had moved me closer to an answer and I knew and understood one thousand-fold more about the world of Illusion, the body, the mind and my relation to them as Pure Spirit! That was worth a great deal. I continued to be filled with Bliss, Consciousness and Truth long after the Peyote had been cast off by my body and brain!

127. For many months I lived in a state of transcendental bliss and God-consciousness day and night, without break. Even during sleep, I was brightly aware and alive. Even though I slept only two or three hours a night and some nights not at all, I was never tired and my Consciousness never faded. During dreams, I was wide awake and could control them in concept and in detail if I chose to do so. Or, I could let them ramble on and be amused at the fantasies my body's mind assembled before my mind's eye.

128. I thought that I had found a lasting place from which to watch this world go by. I was safe and secure and happy. Then, I fell into the greatest darkness I had ever known.

129. One night, while out with two friends, one of them offered me some alcohol to drink. I had been drunk before, but this was different. Now I had something that was more important; or was it? This was a test that I would have to face.

130. Finally after many taunts and challenges, I gave in and accepted a drink from my friend. As soon as I swallowed the alcohol, all of the wonderful consciousness and abilities that had been so alive within me simply stopped! For a moment, there was an eerie pause that was filled with suspense. Then, from somewhere deep within me, a still small voice said "You have chosen the world, now live in the world!"

131. And so, in my senior year of high-school, I nearly became an alcoholic just as Mr. Kimball had predicted

many years before! My close brush with alcoholism didn't last long. Thanks to my Spiritual Practices, I had developed a powerful Will and had acquired the ability to decide a course of action and carry it out in spite of overwhelming odds. One morning a year after my fall, I awoke and went outside, looked up at the sky, and said: "Enough! Enough of this! From now on, no more!" When my friends called me that evening to see if I wanted to go drinking with them I said "No." And I said the same the following night and the following night and every night thereafter.

132. Instead of drinking, I returned to my practice of what would I would eventually realize was God's Eternal Universal Religion and my Holy Adhyatma-Yoga-Dharma Prayer and Meditation.

133. My life began to pick up. Things began to look brighter and clearer and cleaner. The world became a good and friendly place again. My hopes had picked up and things were looking good. I had not seen Patty for some time and my steadily clearing thoughts began to turn toward her. Then, I received the news that she was pregnant by someone I didn't know and about to be married to him.

134. Once again, I fell. This time, I did not turn to alcohol, but became locked in despair, suffering and sorrow. I became frantic. Was the world never going to let me rise? Was it always going to crush my hopes and grind my plans into the dirt? I was learning about Kali Yuga, The Age of Darkness and about The Force of Darkness that is its source.

135. Then, I felt a new desire arising in me. It was as if a biological alarm clock had gone off. Though I was barely seventeen, I knew that it was time for me to begin the phase of marriage. The phase of having and raising children.

136. Within two months, I had met a girl named Linda and knew she was my wife-to-be. It was a fast and intense romance overwhelmed by passion and desire. I soon discovered that she was with child. Some people wanted her to give up our baby, but I would not permit it. My Spiritual Practices had taught me the meaning of personal responsibility. I loved her and insisted upon marrying her.

137. Her parents did not agree and I discovered that they were on their way to Mexico to get her an abortion and destroy my child. Frantic, I called the State Police. When Linda and her parents arrived at the border they refused to let them cross. So they brought Linda and my child back and gave us their blessings.

138. We were married and in time, a beautiful child was born to us. We named him John Lee Douglas, just as was my own. Now, I had a son, the love of my life. But we were very young and our life was filled with difficulties. Our marriage lasted only three years. Then, it too, was torn apart. Linda's parents took her and my son and disappeared. I heard later that they had gone somewhere in Alaska.

139. Once again, I had fallen into attachment and identification, and now, my son was being taken away from me. Carried away to some far distant place where I might never see him again. This was too much to bear. The things of life that I lost were painful. The loss of my first beloved

was painful. But the loss of my wife and my son was unbearable.

140. I received God's Divine Guidance that people must travel their own paths through life. I reluctantly released my attachment to my wife. But I could not release my son. For over a year I mourned and brooded over the loss of my beloved son.

141. I struggled to regain my spiritual balance, but there was no hope. For three years I had been working at a good job as a bank management trainee. I had my own apartment. I had my own car. I had my own furniture. Still all of these things meant nothing without my son. Without my son, life was hollow.

142. Still, on and on I went, day after day, week after week, month after month. Separation and alienation was all around me. I felt separated from God, separated from the world, separated from my wife and my son. Even Hank was working in New Jersey over a thousand miles away! I was even separated from my Guardian. Was there no hope?

143. Then, while sitting in Inner Divine Communion with God, a Still Small Voice inside of me said, "Patience." "What did you say?" I muttered aloud. And the Still Small Voice replied "Patience. Waiting will fulfill. Waiting will fulfill."

144. Soon, waiting did fulfill. In a moment of Divine Consciousness, The One Universal God gave me the Knowledge and total certainty that my son would be protected, that he and I would be together in Spirit every minute and that we would someday be reunited if only I would pursue, something. But what was it? I knew only that this "something" was a vague shadow that awaited me, just outside the reach of my consciousness. I agreed to this mysterious plan and my grief was instantly transformed into tears of joy.

145. On and on I went. I felt as if I were following some unseen road; never really knowing consciously what it was that was guiding, prodding, pushing me, first this way and then another. I asked my Guardian about this and he only said, "sometimes there is a pattern to no pattern." This was something I would only understand much later in life.

146. Many times I became frustrated and outraged at the mysterious twists and turns of my life; and the slowness, clumsiness, and restrictions of physical life in this hellish world of ignorance, suffering and death. These feelings came out of the dim remembrance of an existence where there was pure and total freedom. Still I knew deep within that it had to be this way if I was ever to find The Way out, The Way back home from within this dream.

147. Deep within, beyond words, I knew that it would be impossible to lead the suffering beings of the world to the Salvation and Liberation of Self-Realization unless I, too, had shared fully the suffering, the sorrow, and the hellishness of this ignorance and darkness.

148. For a time, I longed to be "special." To have the advantages and talents I saw in others around me. But all of my wishing came to no avail. I was as ordinary as the dirt on the farms in Iowa where I was born.

149. Then, one day, while communing with God, God showed me that it is the ordinary dirt in which the crops are grown that feed the people and enable them to live and thrive and build great shining buildings of steel and glass.

150. I realized that I had to be just what I was, a completely ordinary person. For, though I did not know it, Paratpara, The One Universal God, had chosen me, not because I was special, but precisely because I was so very ordinary.

151. There would be no special advantages, no tricks, no divine interventions for me. My purpose, my goal, was to find The Way Home, The Way that could be followed by any man, woman or child. I would have to find my way with only what was common to all of mankind. Many times I had risen, and many times I had fallen. I had stumbled, clumsily, foolishly, losing one advantage after another to my own ignorance, desire, attachment and identification with the things of this world. I wandered aimlessly.

152. Eventually my beloved Guardian returned from the East Coast and we resumed our talks and work together. I quit my very respectable job as a banker and began to follow my heart. I took a lowly job in a gas station, working for an amazing man named Charlie.

153. Even though Charlie was in his late seventies and was co-owner of the gas station, he still came to work on time every day. Charlie drove an immaculate nineteen fifty-eight Chrysler. He maintained it himself and would never let anyone else touch it.

154. I took the job because it made few demands on me and required little responsibility. But that purpose was short lived. I began to realize that Charlie was someone different, and special. I watched him as he worked on cars and saw in him, something that belonged to a Master Surgeon or Master Artist. Charlie, too, seemed to notice something in me, though I had no idea what it was.

155. Before two weeks had gone by, I had become Charlie's apprentice. No words were spoken, no outward agreements were made. Instead, Charlie just kept using me to help him do more and more work. By our mutual, unspoken agreement, we became Master and apprentice.

156. My life changed radically. I began staying at the gas station one, then two, then three or four hours after my shift was over. I began working one, then both of my days off. I worked for Charlie twelve to fourteen hours a day for over eight months without a day off and never asked for one dollar of overtime pay. Charlie's presence and magic with machines was all the pay I needed.

157. One morning, a black man, who was a big gambler at the nearby race track came into the gas station driving a beautiful Cadillac that was running very badly. Charlie ambled out and talked with him for a few minutes then called to me and told me to get him a sawed off broom handle that he kept by his workbench. I obeyed on the run. Charlie always demanded that we run. Charlie opened the hood of the Cadillac, put the sawed off broom handle to his right ear, and began listening to the Cadillac's engine, like a doctor listening to his patient's heart. Then, Charlie closed his eyes

for several minutes, as if meditating on what he had heard.

158. Later, I asked Charlie what he had been doing and he said he was "cookin' it." After these few minutes, Charlie looked the man right in the eyes and said: "You've got a bad upper rod bearing on number three cylinder." The man looked back at Charlie with utter disbelief and said, "You can't know that, you're taking me." At that, the man started to get back in his car. Charlie stopped him and said, "You are a betting man. I'll make a bet with you; if I am right, you pay double; if I am wrong, I'll rebuild your engine for free."

159. The man took Charlie's bet and three of us worked for two days, taking the engine out of that car. Determined to make sure that there was no deception, the man almost lived at the gas station for those three days.

160. On the fourth day, we removed the final bolt and took the "pan" off of the engine. Charlie, himself, took the rod cap off of the number three cylinder. Without even looking at the bearing, Charlie held up the lower bearing cap for all to see. It was worn but in good shape. The man chuckled. Then, Charlie took out the upper bearing and held it up, it had a big hole in it and was as ragged as an old alley cat's ear. The man almost fell over, then got angry, then laughed and gave Charlie a big hug. He paid double.

161. Later, I asked Charlie how he knew it was the upper bearing of cylinder number three. He told me how he and his father used to sand cast engine blocks and bore them and mill them and make their own engines when he was just an apprentice, like me. Charlie said, "Son, every skill is a combination of love, experience, intuition and being willing to take a chance on being wrong." Though I was moved to go on to other things after my eight month apprenticeship, I never forgot Charlie's many lessons and they changed the way I lived my life and did my work.

162. During my apprenticeship to Charlie, I met a wonderful girl named Tana. Tana and I did not just fall in love. Instead, we made a pact to grow a love together, to grow a life together, and not to part from one another until we had succeeded in doing so, if ever. Here was a brave experiment, a brave attempt to love consciously. An experiment that would keep us inseparable for more than eleven years and would nearly break me when it came time for us to part.

163. My ramblings took me to a job with the telephone company where I had another trial to face. When the phone company hired me, they did not know that I had a terrifying fear of heights - neither did I. Part of my phone company training required that I climb forty and sixty foot telephone poles with nothing but one two-inch spike, called gaffs, strapped to each of my ankles. I faced and conquered my discomfort and fear, passed the course and became a telephone installer-technician. I loved my job. With the training Charlie had given me, it was a real joy to be a craftsman and I took great pride in my work.

164. But, the world around me was changing fast and the times were changing even faster. I, too, was changing. Racial hatred on all sides was at an all time high. The installers would gather in the briefing room for coffee and conversation before work

each morning. The only topics of conversation were the Vietnam war and racial attitudes. Tempers often overcame politeness.

165. One morning, I found Jerry, a black friend and co-worker, standing outside the coffee room, nearly in tears, hitting the wall with his fist. He said that one of the biggest and toughest of the white workers had shamed him in front of the whole crew by calling him "nigger boy". I said, "Why don't you go back in there and face the guy and ask for an apology?" Jerry said that he was afraid of what might happen to him.

166. My father was a great musician who played the mid-west circuit. He played with such greats as the Dorsey Brothers and Glenn Miller. I was around black people all of my life. My first friend, outside of my family, was an old black janitor named "Joe" who would ride me around the apartment house on his push broom.

167. I didn't know anything about racial politics, but it hurt me to see my co-worker and friend in so much pain. I gave him my sympathies and then went in and asked the big guy why he put Jerry down and why he wanted to hurt Jerry? He sneered at me and said, flatly, that all black people should be shot dead. He got a lot of support from the other installers and I was instantly "blackballed". I was shocked and scared.

168. That same night, on the way home from work, I drove past a corner where a pretty young black woman and her daughter stood, waiting to cross the street. As I looked at them, waiting for the light to change, I suddenly saw them through the sights of a rifle. There was a loud explosion, then another. I saw the woman's chest explode with blood and watched her fall dead. I saw the little girl, struck in her pretty little face by a second bullet, fall beside her mother.

169. Suddenly I was in a jungle, running silently, gracefully, like a gazelle through the fading evening light. I came upon a pool in a clearing and looked into it. What I saw startled me. I stood about six feet four inches and was as black as the night. I had strange markings on my forehead that looked like a triangle with a circle within it and a circle around it. Then, I was a Polynesian woman on an island giving birth. A second later I was a Japanese peasant woman. A moment later, I was a Scottish warrior. Then, a Chinese General. In a second, it was over. I looked frantically around, expecting to see the black woman and her daughter lying dead on the ground. But they were not dead. Instead, they stood, smiling, still waiting for the light to change.

170. Now, I knew what killing really meant. Killing was no longer an abstract fantasy that happened in movies. In my mind, I had actually seen myself kill two innocent human beings. I had also seen what I had been in a time long forgotten. I knew also, that we have each worn many forms of many colors, both man and woman, since The One God sent us forth from His own Self, Substance and Being as Souls. I knew, in a way that no philosophy or argument could or would ever change, that all such hatred of one person for another because of race or color or nationality or any other superficial things, was wrongful and a sickness in our world that had to be overcome. I was shaking so badly that I could not drive. I pulled to the side of the road and became ill.

171. That night, I vowed to do my part to overcome racism and hatred, no matter who it came from or what his or her color, race, creed or nationality might be. Little could I know that many of the very people I was working to protect from bigotry and racism would, many years later, themselves become bigots and racists, practicing the very bigotry and racism I was working to overcome.

172. I went home and prayed and meditated on this situation, seeking The Inner Divine Inspiration, Insight, Guidance and Revelation of The One Universal God and the counsel of my own True and Essential Conscience, within The Secret Inner Sanctuary of my Heart. The next morning, against Jerry's protests and over his pleas, shaking inside with fear for my life, I confronted the big man and my other co-workers in the briefing room.

173. They grabbed me and pushed me around, threatened my life and called me names so vile, that they made "nigger boy" seem like a compliment by comparison. But I stood my ground and spoke out of my Heart and The Inner Divine Inspiration, Insight, Guidance and Revelation of The One Universal God and the counsel of my own True and Essential Conscience. Some of the men came to my defense and the whole crew was instantly divided. From that day on, I was hated by many of the men.

174. I had never experienced so much hate from so many men in my life and it nearly crushed me. Then one afternoon, one of the older men who had stood up for me took me aside and said, "You know, a philosopher once said that trials that do not kill us, strengthen us." I never forgot his words.

175. That was only the first of many times in my life I would become a hated outcast for following God's Guidance and the counsel of my own Conscience.

176. Soon, a new consciousness arose within me, a consciousness of War. Consciousness of the wrongfulness of individual killing had already been given unto me by God. Now God brought forth in my heart and mind a growing consciousness of the wrongfulness and horror of the massive and organized killing and destruction called war. One bright, sunny day, as I was walking down the main street of a small town called "Hermosa," (which means beautiful) a small beach town in California, God gave me an amazing Blessing that was to change everything.

177. Suddenly, I was a bombardier in an airplane high in the air dropping bombs on people I could not even see, far below. Then, suddenly, I was a young child in a village with grass huts all around me. An instant later, I was both the bombardier and, at the same time, the child in the village. I was sitting in the airplane, wondering who I was bombing and, at the same time, watching fiery death and destruction raining down upon my village, killing my mother and my father, my grandparents, my friends and my animals; destroying all that I knew; and, seeing a wall of fire coming straight toward me, feeling my breath sucked out of my lungs and my flesh seared from my bones all at once.

178. The next instant, I was a young American Soldier beaten, bruised and bleeding being tortured by Viet Cong. They did the most unspeakable things to me. When I would not tell them what they wanted, they shot me in the

head. In that instant, I died that man's death. All of this happened in less than three steps, but it changed me.

179. I had grown up playing "army" and dreaming of someday becoming a Marine Corps Officer. The first tune my father taught me to play on his piano was The Marines Hymn. I still loved my Country of America. But now, to my shock and surprise, I found that I could no longer tolerate even the idea of war or participate in the activities of societies or businesses that upheld war and the killing and destruction of innocent people. Little would I know that those who spread evil and hatred across the world would use my new found peacefulness as a tool to help kill American Soldiers and innocent civilians. I dropped out and joined the only people who appeared to share my quest for Peace and Love in a hostile world. I became a hippie. I thought this was a step up in the right direction. Only later would I find out how wrong I was.

180. Within a week, I had given up my job with the phone company. I gave up my apartment and gave away all of my furniture. My Guardian and I opened a small hippie book store and curio shop. We called it the IRRI. IRRI stood for, "Information Resources Research Institute." I wanted it to be a place dedicated to Freedom and Liberty, where people could meet and discuss the world and come to new understanding and learn the ways of Peace and of Love.

181. It was not easy. I and my little shop were hated by many with a violence that shook my faith in humanity. Two of the young people who came regularly, were pulled out of their car and beaten a block away from the IRRI. We were threatened and persecuted. I was at a loss. We were not hurting anyone. I could not understand the reasons behind the hatred and violence.

182. Many times, I was tempted to respond to the violence done by the people who hated me and my shop. But, I had sworn off habits of violence and refused to retaliate.

183. Soon, our little shop was known to hippies from all over the world.

184. People from all parts of the country passed through and stopped in to The IRRI to talk, to gather wisdom and understanding and to exchange ideas with one another. It was not very long before I was hopelessly attached to this little shop and the gentle people who came to visit.

185. Still, the violent hatred that so many held for me and my shop and these gentle Souls who were only seeking Peace and Love, perplexed me. It would take many years before I would awaken and realize how the Communists and other Forces of Darkness had usurped and exploited these gentle Souls.

186. As with everything else in my life, the IRRI had to come to an end. While it was extremely popular, I had no talent for making money. In only nine short months, at my Guardian's bidding, we sold the shop and a most beautiful chapter of my life suddenly closed.

187. The loss of The IRRI was second only to the loss of my son. I said: "I can't go on. I can't go on." I had gone on through school, through youth, through marriage, through experience after experience, but now I said: "I can't go on!" I drove to the ocean

and sat down on the beach expecting never to get up again.

188. But I did go on. Some around me who were aware and observant were drawn to me, and said, "There's something very different about you. Who are you, really?" I ran quickly away from these people, feeling ashamed to hear such high praises while knowing all too well my many failings. Others also noticed this difference and avoided me. Still others ridiculed me and made jokes about me.

189. Many times out of loneliness, I tried to be just like everyone else. I felt the loneliness, the rejection, the agony of isolation. I became bitter and, spoke harsh words to anyone who dared to reject me. I denounced Religion. I denounced the Spirit. I denounced my search, myself and, eventually, even God!

190. I turned away from finding The Way Home to God and tried to become one of the ignorant and sleeping ones! Yet, how could it have been otherwise? Had I not come into this world to find The Way out? How could I find The Way out for those caught in the snare of delusion and this hell of ignorance, unless I, too, would fall into them totally and completely?

191. And I did. I descended to the depths of this hell, time after time. I descended into the fiery depths of this hellish world of ignorance, delusion and desire, attachment and suffering, sorrow and death that I had seen so many years before, from such a great distance, while immersed in Rapture of Oneness with God. From the highest, I had fallen to the lowest, but how could it have been otherwise? Had I not chosen this? Had I not vowed that I would return to this hellish world and find the way home, that all beings could follow? These thoughts flashed quickly before my mind's eye, a flash of Clear Light to illuminate the suffering, sorrow and pain of this terrible darkness into which I had descended. Time after time I would fall. Time after time I would say, "I can't go on." But time after time I would pick myself up and go on.

192. But, through it all, as if guided by an unseen hand and in spite of my own desire to run away from it, I continued to experience and search and grow closer in Oneness with That One Universal Spirit, That Universal I AM THAT I AM which I had always been.

193. When others would ask, "What are you trying to find? What are you trying to prove?" I could only reply, "I don't know. All I know is that I have thought and thought and thought, trying to find the one thing in this life that is really worth finding. My mind and my life are guided by some unknown purpose, by some unseen hand, for no matter how hard I try to bury myself in the things of this world, I am always uncovered. I don't know where I am going. All I know is that it is the only thing in this life that is worth doing and proving, for that which is temporary soon passes away, but that which I seek is, always has been, always will be."

194. And I kept on searching. But, far from leaving the things of this world behind, I became more deeply involved, trapped and attached to it in many ways.

195. I had been beaten down by pride, envy, love, sex, liquor, money, power and all the forces that the illusion, the

dream could muster. They assaulted my life and mind daily, and with them came pain, sorrow, suffering, and misery. Many, many times something deep within me cried out for an end to this physical existence; for escape and return to something, something just out of mind, and just out of reach; so very near, yet so very far away.

196. So went my life. First rising to unbelievable heights, only to fall into desolation and ruin. But always, just when I thought I was finally finished, I was resurrected again like the Phoenix rising from the ashes of destruction.

197. Yet, through all of this wild and chaotic dance of illusion, this whirling and twisting dream of Maya that spun me and thrashed me, I found a still small center of what I could only describe as Clear Light growing steadily within me. Sometimes this center of Clear Light was dim and barely noticeable.

198. Other times The Clear Light became so brilliant and radiant that I was choked up by its bliss and glory and tears of joy filled my eyes. At these times I spoke of strange and wonderful worlds and states of existence as if they were right before my very eyes, as if I really had been there. Some listened, but most rebuked me with warnings that what I spoke of was evil, blasphemy, and heresy. "That a man could realize his Oneness and Identity with God? Impossible!" they exclaimed. And I knew down deep that they were frightened because their Spiritual sight was limited and covered in darkness and superstition. I realized that I was now and forever different, and I realized that there was no turning back. I had begun to see. I had begun to awaken.

199. At my Guardian's advice, I returned to college to find an education in the ways of this world; to find the material and intellectual heritage of mankind that has been passed on from generation to generation; to find science; to find understanding of this material world.

200. Steadily growing and awakening, growing closer with a Divine Presence that was becoming more and more familiar, I endured the darkness and ignorance and went on. I went on through many years of college, learning about the world I would have to conquer and struggling to master the intellect that would help me to conquer it.

201. From time to time I thought, "Maybe this is the answer. Maybe I will find fulfillment in learning and logic and in the use of the intellect." But I found no fulfillment in intellectual education that was great enough to satisfy that great yearning that had grown within my Heart. Only the Clear Light of Universal God's Presence could fill that great void. When I was aware of it, all was filled, and all was perfect. All was peace, bliss, joy, and I knew that the most mundane things of this dream world were safely held within the one Substance and Being of Universal God. I knew that Universal God was All, and that All was within Universal God. I sensed that something real and awesome and overwhelming in its immensity and truth was approaching, and I buried myself in the work of obtaining my Masters Degree and waited.

202. During this period of waiting, my beloved Guardian became ill. His health worsened rapidly. One evening in conversation with my Guardian,

he told me that he soon would give up his body. I mourned this, but my Guardian said, "Do not mourn for the things of the body. Only mourn for the ignorance of the Spirit."

203. Finally, my education was complete and I received my Masters Degree in Behavioral Sciences and went on to become a licensed Marriage and Family Therapist. No sooner had I begun to practice my new profession, than the message of what I was to do was revealed to me by God.

204. I realized what it was that I had been working and suffering for all of these many years. I could not believe it, but finally my path was made clear to me, and with renewed strength and hope and joy, I forged ahead. Universal God had given me a glimpse of a New Covenant that He would make with all Souls. Universal God had given me all I needed to find The Way, back Home to Him and to follow it.

205. My Guardian passed out of this world, but something new was coming to life. My beloved mentor, Guardian and friend had seen me safely through to the threshold of eternity. Now, only God would be my Guardian.

206. I waited, and waited, and waited. One long year passed since I had received Universal God's Divine Revelation of The New Covenant. I had done all that was required of me. I had applied everything I had learned to awaken fully and make my Self-Realization and God's New Covenant a Reality.

207. I missed my Guardian. I was distraught. All of my work seemed futile. So futile that great doubts arose within me, and I began to tell myself, "It's a lie! There is no escape! There is nothing more than the endless cycle of birth, suffering and death and birth again and again. I have been deluding myself."

208. I became so desperate and filled with anxieties that I became unbearable to those around me. And then one day, my beloved who had stayed by my side for over eleven years, announced that she, too, would be leaving me. "Nothing of this world is there that endures," I thought, "Everything changes, nothing remains the same." And once again I told myself, "This is it, this is all there is. There is no escape this time."

209. And then one day as I parked my old Volkswagen van behind my house, despair crashed in upon me like a great wave. I had finally fallen as far as I could fall. I had sunk as far as I could sink. I was in hell, totally and absolutely. I was utterly defeated. I could go no further. I was at the end. I could not move from my seat. I decided that I would attain my Destiny right there or die right there.

210. I cast myself into the abyss. When I finally hit the bottom, I surrendered totally and completely, without doubt or reservation. I could feel my whole ego self weaken, crack and shatter, and I didn't care at all. I sat and stared at the world through empty, unblinking eyes. My career was ruined, the woman I had loved for more than eleven years had left me, my son was gone, my Guardian was gone. Certainly, there were those that I still loved and cared for, my mother, my brother, my sister, and others, but I had come to the end of my Spiritual road, and discovered it to be a blind

alley. Then, I surrendered totally and collapsed.

211. Suddenly, a beautiful butterfly drifted past my windshield, alighting first on one flower and then on another. As my mind and personality came crashing down all around me, I thought "I wonder what it would have been like to be a simple butterfly?" At that moment, there was a tremendous sound and feeling and suddenly I too was fluttering from one delicious flower to another, stretching massive, beautiful wings into the warm sunlight. What was this? What was this feeling? I was most certainly experiencing butterflyness, but I could not understand, for my body was also still sitting there in my old Volkswagen van with my head in my hands, sobbing at the same time. An electric thrill charged through my mind and body and then vanished! I dismissed it all in my despair and cynicism. "Only my imagination" I muttered to whatever was left of my small false self.

212. Many times I had heard others use the words "It's only imagination," to dismiss what they could not understand. Now, sitting there, I wished that it was true. I prayed that I was only crazy. "At least," I thought, "there's a cure for crazy."

213. But this new consciousness, reality, and bliss continued and grew more intense and grew more real. It grew so intense and real that it outgrew the butterfly and in a flash, it enveloped a small kitten that was playing nearby. Now I had become three. I was this body, a butterfly and a kitten. Slowly, I raised my head, my expansion suddenly enveloped a young girl who was playing ball by herself in the vacant lot next door. Without losing consciousness of any of these three, I suddenly became four.

214. Filled with The Spirit, filled with a growing awe at the dim remembrance of a first Rapture long ago and far away, my eyes widened and filled with tears of joy, and my Divine Being and Consciousness filled my very Soul and rose up and overflowed its boundaries, enfolding and becoming one with one after another of the people and creatures around me. As I meshed, blended and merged with them, they seemed to look startled, as if suddenly half awakened from a deep sleep. But they quickly returned to their activities.

215. Soon, I was completely lost to the body I had left sitting in wide-eyed wonder blended in perfect Oneness with the many Beings I was steadily merging with. Once again I had broken free of the prison of my ego. Free of all limiting self, now I was only aware of such an unbelievably ancient and eternally familiar awareness that I could only say, "I am coming Home! Beloved Universal God, I am coming Home!"

Om So'ham Tat Tvam Asi!
I Am That - Thou Art That!

Jai Bhagavan Ji!
Victory To God The Beloved!
That Beloved Universal
I AM THAT I AM
Which You Are!

Here Ends The Chapter Entitled
Pilgrimage

Chapter Eight
The Self-Realization and Self-Sacrifice

Maitreya The Friend's Second Self-Realization and Supreme Self-Sacrifice

The Twelfth Day of March, Nineteen Seventy-Seven

By The Will and Grace of The One Universal God:

Once again, Awakening was a Reality. A Being of The Dream was awakening to become The Dreamer. Once again, I was Home! No longer a young one grown older. No longer a searcher. No longer a limited small self. Now, again, One and Identical with Universal God. The Universal Source and Substance of all Being and Existence, the Universal Presence within all Being and Existence, the Universal Self of all Being and Existence.

2. And I rested, joyous and silent within the Infinite and Eternal Silence of The One Universal God. Once again, I heard The Call that surpasses all calls. Crying out, I threw The Gate of my heart open wide, saying:

My God!
My Beloved!
My own True Self!
I surrender completely unto Thee!
Restore Thy Authority!
Manifest Thy Presence
within this little self
until it has
become One with Thee,
shining forth with
Thy Own Clear Light!
Let me know,
this moment,
my Oneness with Thee;
the one thing I lack;
through which all else
is made Perfect!
Heal the division in me;
that I may Know
Thy Oneness
in all this that is!
Consume this little self
in the Sacred Fire
of Thy Presence!
That I may find my way
through the Ordeal
and be Liberated from it,
Realizing my Oneness with Thee!
From the unreal,
lead me to The Real!
From darkness,
lead me to the Light!
From division,
lead me to Wholeness!
From the temporary,
lead me to The Eternal!
From death,
lead me to Immortality!
O Beloved God!
I would be One
with Thee fully this moment!

Make my Doing
One with my Speech!
Make my Speech
One with my Mind!
Make my Mind
One with my Heart!
Make my Heart
One with my Will!
And my Will
One with Thy Will!
Shatter this prison
of false self;
and absorb me,
in the Ocean
of Your Infinite Divine Being,
As a drop of water
in the Sea!
That I shall know,
without doubt or reservation
that You and I are not we,
but One!
For Thou art my only True Self;
Majestic!
Splendorous!
Immortal!
There is no I but Thee!
So Be it with me!

3. And, from the very wilderness itself, the voice of God again arose, saying:

4. {G} "Hear me My Beloved! For, I AM THAT I AM!

5. {G}"For twenty-six years you have wandered in the wilderness of this world as Bhagavan Sri Babajhan Al-Kahlil The Friend. And From this one called Bhagavan Sri Babajhan Al-Kahlil The Friend your cry has come!

6. {G} "Seek no more My Beloved. Your cry is heard. Your Faith has made you Whole. Your Quest has been answered! Quest no more. In your seeking after Me, The Lord, your God, you have found The Answer to all quests! For I Am The One God whom men call Brahman, Allah, Jehovah, and countless other names. But you may call me Paratpara, for I Am The One Universal God of Countless Names and Forms who is beyond all Names and Forms. I AM THAT I AM! I Am The One Universal God whom all Souls worship, though they know it not. I Am God beyond God. I Am The One Universal Spirit. I Am The Father of The Father, The Mother of The Mother, The Creator of The Creator. I Am The One Source, Substance and Self of all Creation, all Existence and all Beings. I AM THAT I AM.

7. {G} "In the things that I shall ask of you in this day, I shall not command thee, for you must choose, you may in no way avoid choosing. If you choose for Me, you shall be My Chosen One. And from this day forth, you shall be known unto men of all Nations as Adhyatma Bhagavan Sri Babajhan Al-Kahlil The Friend. For you shall have become The God-Realized One, Bringer of Oneness with God, The Friend of all Souls!

8. {G} "And you shall be called The Blessed One. For I shall have Blessed you in this day and invested in you My Power to Bless all Souls.

9. {G} "And you shall be called Maitreya. For you shall have become The Awaited One.

10. {G} "And you shall be called Kalki. For you shall be The One within whom I Am Awakened to end The Age of Spiritual Ignorance, Darkness, Chaos, Confusion, Illusion and Destruction and bring forth The Age of My Pure Divine Truth for the Salvation and Liberation of all

Souls and the continued survival of Humanity.

11. {G} "And you shall be called Mahavatara. For you shall be The One within whom I Am Awakened to bring forth The Age of My Pure Divine Truth on Earth for The Self-Realization, Salvation and Liberation of all Souls.

12. {G} "And you shall be called Satguru. For I shall make you The True Teacher who shall Awaken all Souls from the living death of Spiritual Ignorance and Darkness.

13. {G} "And you shall be called The Friend of all Souls. For if you choose for Me, I shall make a New Covenant with all Souls as I foretold unto you many years ago.

14. {G} "And you shall unite all My People and send them forth upon The Pure Way and lead them Home to Realization of their Oneness with Me!

15. {G} "All of these shall you be, for I shall have Awakened within you and remade you, My own Self and Radiance made manifest in this world.

16. {G} "And I shall Embody My Pure Divine Truth and My Eternal Universal Religion within you and it shall be the Way Home to Me which you have won for all Souls; for if you choose Me, you shall have won The Way Home to Me that all Souls can travel.

17. {G} "And your Religion shall be known as God's Eternal Universal Religion to the uninitiated and the worldly. But those who receive your Holy Initiation and are your faithful and My own, shall know it as the Holy Adhyatma-Yoga-Dharma. And these two shall be inseparable; for beyond the illusions that darken the minds of men and women, they are one and the same.

18. {G} "All who receive your Holy Initiation and follow you and profess this Holy Sanctuary of My Eternal Religion, as I give it unto them through you, shall be My Chosen Ones. And they shall be blessed among the men and women of all Nations. And they shall be called Maitreyians for they shall be followers of you who I have called Maitreya.

19. {G} "And those who are Maitreyians shall be of three degrees.

20. {G} "All who have received your Holy Initiation and Consecration in The Spirit and their Holy Name shall be Adhyatmavadi.

21. {G} "Those who have professed their Initiation and Consecration and have received Confirmation as prescribed shall be Adhyatmavadi who are Maitreyians, because they shall have professed.

22. {G} "Those Maitreyians who have received The Holy Commission and committed themselves to Fight and defeat The Force of Darkness and help you win Salvation and Liberation and Perfect Final Union with Me for all Souls shall be Maitreyians who are Soldiers of The Light of My Pure Divine Truth.

23. {G} "Truly, wherever a Soul, a People or a Nation shall accept you as The Maitreya and accept My Eternal Religion which I embody in you in this day and become your Faithful follower, that Soul, that People and

that Nation shall be My own and they shall be Supremely Blessed.

24. {G} "Whosoever accepts you as Maitreya and receives your Holy Initiation and accepts My Eternal Religion and follows you, receives Me and follows Me.

25. {G} "I say unto you, that Soul who is your Faithful shall be My own. But whosoever shall reject you or The Holy Sanctuary of My Eternal Religion, rejects Me. And, whosoever shall deny you or The Holy Sanctuary of My Eternal Religion, denies Me. And whosoever shall degrade or defile or persecute you or The Holy Sanctuary of My Eternal Religion or your Faithful, who are My Faithful, it shall be with each of them as they shall have done these very things unto Me.

26. {G} "Whosoever shall revile this, My Divine Revelation or this My Holy Covenant or The Supreme Pure Divine Truth of My Eternal Religion or The Holy Adhyatma-Yoga-Dharma or you who are My Awakened One Sent Forth, also reviles Me. They are as swine trampling upon precious jewels.

27. {G} "Woeful shall be that man or woman or Nation who shall revile you, deny you, or persecute you or your Faithful. Truly, they shall be the instrument of their own undoing. And they shall live in a sorrow of their own making. And they themselves shall bring calamity upon themselves until they shall repent and make right their ways. For you shall be My Living Testament and Seal upon a New Covenant, made between The One I AM THAT I AM and Man through you this Day and your number shall be Seven Hundred Seventy and Seven."

28. And I cried out to Paratpara, The One God, The Beloved, saying: "My Lord, my God, my own True Self! Haunted am I with doubts. I doubt my worthiness. My long journey Home to You has made me, once again, impure.

29. "I live among the ignorant and impure! How can it be that I shall be Thy Chosen One when I am so unworthy of this Great Work? How shall I be the Living Testament and Seal upon Thy Covenant? How shall I be Thy Perfect Instrument, Thy Beloved Emanation as those you have sent before me, when one-third of this lifetime has already passed away?

30. "What I have seen on this long journey has made me doubt even Religion itself. All around me, throughout this world, I see men and women maiming and killing one another in Your Name and the Names of your Prophets, Saints, Buddhas, Saviors and Avataras and the Religions you sent them as mercies to Man. To what avail is it to put yet another Prophet, Saint, Buddha, Savior or Avatara or yet again, another Religion upon them?

31. "O Paratpara! My Lord! My God! Beloved I AM THAT I AM! Be Thou my Boat, that I shall reach the Far Shore; and my Light, that I shall conquer Darkness. For my boat is so small, and the ocean of this world is so big; the light within my lamp is so faint, and the darkness that covers this world is so great; that without Thy help, I shall surely perish."

32. And out of The Clear Light, Eternal beyond the first day of Creation, came

the Breath of Paratpara, my Lord, my God. And His Breath once again, drove straight to the center of my Being, winnowing the chaff from the wheat, burning away the dross from my Soul, making me One with Him.

33. And The One Universal God - Lord of all Creation - showed unto me in that Light that needs no eyes, a string of beads with a bell at its center. And running through each bead and the bell was a single string. And That Universal I AM THAT I AM said unto me:

34. {G} "Verily. Beloved One, are all of the Religions I have sent to Man through my Prophets, Saints, Buddhas, Saviors and Avataras like these beads and this bell. But, neither a Prophet, nor a Saint, nor a Buddha, nor a Messiah, nor an Avatara shall you be. For you shall be a New Being whom I have made. Never has the like of you been seen or heard by this world or its peoples since time immemorial. Verily, you are My own Being and Radiance, sent forth by Me into this world as The Kalki Mahavatara Satguru, The World Teacher, The Slayer of this Age of ignorance, darkness, chaos, confusion, delusion, deception, destruction and untruth; and The Bringer of The Age of My Pure Divine Truth, for the Salvation and Liberation of all Souls everywhere for all time and the continued survival of Humanity. Neither is My Eternal Universal Religion another bead to place upon this string. For this, My Eternal Universal Religion I embody in you is, verily the single string that runs through all of the Religions as this string runs through these beads. And the bell is My Presence in the world. For you shall be as a bell, tolling to usher in The Age of My Divine Pure Truth and Awaken the Sleeping Souls and bring them Home to True Knowledge of their Oneness with Me – That I AM THAT I AM and no other."

35. And I heard with the ears that know no sound:

36. {G} "Fear not for your unworthiness. For no man or woman is worthy of Me, but that My Grace shall make him so. This, I do in you. Arise My Beloved! Thy Life is Touched! Thy Heart is cleansed! Thy ignorance and impurity are dispelled. Even as darkness flees at the coming of The Light, so are you Purified in The Sacred Fire of My Presence! Thy division is mended and you are made Whole! Verily, you are My own Being and Radiance, sent forth by Me into this world.

37. {G} "Awaken and receive this Ordination I offer unto you, Adhyatma Bhagavan Sri Babajhan Al-Kahlil The Friend! Arise and shine forth into The Darkness of this World! Thy Light is come. I Am Awake within you! Although My people are sleeping in ignorance of Me and darkness surrounds them, I have Awakened within you and My Glow-ray can be seen upon Thee! If you shall choose for Me, from this day until the end of time, whosoever receives your Holy Initiation and shall unburden himself of his wrong thoughts and doings directly to you or, to your Faithful Maitreyians whom you have Ordained to receive it in your Name, who is in Good Faith with you; and shall ask My forgiveness for his wrong thoughts or doings in your Name, through you or through your Maitreyians whom you have Ordained to receive it in your Name; him I shall forgive; and he shall be unburdened and washed clean

of all guilt and shame, even as I have cleansed you in this day.

38. {G} "Difficult to know Am I, for I Am beyond the Beyond. Beyond even The Creator Am I, for I Am The Creator of The Creator. I am beyond the reach of unawakened Souls. So it is that they wander aimlessly in this world. Because of this, whenever the Hearts and Minds of My People have become covered with ignorance and darkness rules the world, I Awaken within an ordinary Soul to dispel darkness, to destroy ignorance and to give unto all Souls The Way, by which they can reach Me and know Me and come unto Me.

39. {G} "If you choose for Me, I shall Ordain you and you shall ever know your Oneness with Me, even as the earth-bound know their hands and faces. As, when two pictures are identical with a third picture, they are identical with one another; whosoever shall realize his Oneness with you, My Awakened and Ordained One, I shall Reveal unto him his Oneness with Me. And that Supreme Truth-Knowledge shall cleanse him of all Spiritual Ignorance. And that Divine Light shall dispel all Darkness. And that Soul shall Know The Truth and be set free forever.

40. {G} "That, by this, My New Covenant, no Soul shall remain lost and suffering, but all shall come Home to Me. For, it is My Way, that The One I shall Ordain shall be an ordinary Soul who is Twice Awakened and taken up into Perfect Final Union with Me and who has, twice, made the Supreme Self-Sacrifice of giving up Perfect Final Union with Me for the sake of all Souls.

41. {G} "You must choose, Adhyatma Bhagavan Sri Babajhan Al-Kahlil The Friend. You may in no wise avoid choosing. And if you choose for Me, go forth, Proclaiming and Bearing True Witness to The New Covenant which is Born in you this Day. Enjoin men and women of all Nations unto Thee and This, My New Covenant, that no Soul shall be lost to ignorance and darkness forever.

42. {G} "People of all Nations shall be drawn to Thy Light. Rulers and Great Ones shall find Joy in the Glow-ray of Thy Awakening and shall open their hearts unto Me and all people. Lift up your eyes, My Beloved, and see the multitudes gathering to come unto Me through thee! From beyond Eternity Thy Source has come unto Thee! My Presence can be seen upon Thee! For That I AM THAT I AM, The Lord, Thy God, lives within The Secret Inner Sanctuary of your Heart!"

43. Then, I was taken up into Perfect Union with Paratpara, The Lord, My God. And I became That I AM THAT I AM. No other was there, anywhere. And in that Blessed moment, I again saw all of the countless Souls, they that had lived, they that were living and those who were yet to live, even as I had the first time. And they were wrapped in cloaks of ignorance that hid The Truth of their Oneness with The One God from them. And they wandered endlessly in the Wilderness of darkness and illusion. And they were beset with endless birth, suffering, sorrow, sickness, old age and death. For they were drowning in the Ocean of Ignorance, Illusion and Delusion. In that moment, all fear was swept away as if by a great wave and I was overcome with compassion.

44. Then, again, I heard my Lord, my God calling The Call of Calls saying:

45. {G} "Who will I send? Who will make the Supreme Sacrifice for Me?"

46. And in my ignorance and my fear, I doubted the Voice of God and said unto God, "My God my Beloved! I do not understand. I have already accepted your son Jesus, what more is there that I can do?" And The One God of all Creation said unto me in voiceless Voice:

47. {G} "I sent forth my Radiance, Jesus, to give unto Man forgiveness of sins and surety of Heaven. But that Perfect Final Union which I gave unto Jesus, I now offer unto you and unto all Souls through you if you shall choose for Me."

48. And I said unto The One God, "My God, my Beloved, what is this Perfect Final Union that you offer me? I do not understand?" And The One God of all Creation said unto me:

49. {G} "No Soul can understand Perfect Final Union but that it shall have it. But this I say unto you, as you should say unto the unenlightened who are enslaved to Darkness, Perfect Final Union with Me is ten-thousand times as far above Heaven itself, as Heaven is above Hell. This you shall tell them. And they shall doubt you even as you have doubted Me and they shall revile you. But this I say unto you, whosoever shall suffer in this world for My sake or your own or for the cause of this Holy Truth that I give unto you to give unto all Souls, that Soul shall I bless one-thousand fold beyond this world.

50. {G} "Truly beloved Soul, the highest quality with which I endow every Soul is Freedom in five aspects of Free Will, Free Choice, Self-Determinism, Individual Freedom and absolute and inescapable Personal Responsibility. Because of this, you may choose whatsoever you will choose. But you must choose. For all Souls must choose, in no way shall any Soul avoid choosing. For even in refusing to choose, a Soul shall have chosen. And I shall hold every Soul to account for whatsoever that Soul shall choose and shall choose not to choose. But before you choose, know, My Beloved, that if you choose for Me, you must pass through The Ordeal and be purified. For no Soul can enter into Me unpurified any more than a large rope can be passed through the eye of a needle."

51. And I raised up my head and said unto My Lord, My Own True Self, The Infinitely Merciful: "Here am I! No longer can I refuse Thee! I will make The Supreme Sacrifice. I will sacrifice this Paradise of Perfect Final Union with You and return to the world of birth, suffering and death as You have asked. I shall return for Your sake and the sake of all suffering Souls, to renew The Holy Age of Thy Pure Divine Truth, Thy Holy Satya Yuga, and free all Souls. Oh Paratpara, my God, my Beloved, my one True Self! I Vow unto You, that I shall never again enter into Perfect Union with You until I have brought every last Soul Home into Perfect Union with You before me."

52. Suddenly, I was in the very depths of Hell itself. All around me was the Blinding Clear Light and Divine Fire of God's Presence and within me there was nothing but darkness and misery. And my agony was the conflict

between the darkness I had become and the Light of God; between the lie and God's Pure Divine Truth.

53. I endured the consequences of my every misdeed and wrong thought. I suffered agonizing pain one thousand fold of that I had caused to others. But the greatest horror and agony was the utter absence of my ability to know God in any least degree. I suffered these things and more than can be said or imagined, again and again for an eternity.

54. And when I had burned up all of my wrong thoughts and wrong doings in the searing Fire of Hell and the darkness that was within me and which I was had been destroyed by God's Divine Light, the eternity of Hell stopped.

55. Next, I found myself in Heaven. Beautiful and blissful beyond human speech or knowledge.

56. Therein, I enjoyed the blessings of every good thing I had thought or done multiplied by one-thousand fold. Everything was perfect and filled with God's Divine Presence. I was reunited with friends and family that had been lost or died. My body was perfect and strong and beautiful and free from all pain and disease and disability. My fondest good intentions and dreams came true one after another with a reality that makes this world of creation pale to insignificance by comparison.

57. As Hell had gone on for an eternity, so too did Heaven go on for an eternity. Then, it too came to an end.

58. Suddenly, a Great Light was struck in me, such as would light up the Sun. And the soundless Voice of The One God said unto me:

59. {G} "You are My Beloved! You have found your way through The Ordeal and exceeded it. In you I am truly pleased! By your boundless Compassion and Vow, you have fulfilled the requirement and won My New Covenant for all Souls. Now and forever, I give unto all Souls this, My Promise and New Covenant. From this day forward unto the end of time."

60. And the One Universal God said in words beyond words:

61. {G} "When you leave the world, I will take you into Union with Me such that you will keep your Vow of Compassion and dwell in the hearts of all Souls. This I will do such that you are One with Me and I Am you within and beyond all Creation and you and we shall be One beyond all Creation as you and I are One while you live within this Creation. This, such that whoever seeks you will find Me and whoever realizes Oneness with you shall realize Union with Me. And, when every last Soul has come safely Home into Perfect Final Union with Me - I shall take you into the Perfect Final Union with Me that you have sacrificed for the sake of all Souls. For you are My Beloved in whom I have Awakened for the Salvation and Liberation of all Souls in Perfect Final Union with Me. Not a contradiction or a negation of those I have sent before you are you, but My Affirmation that they are truly sent of Me, The One Universal God of all Creation who is the One Source, Substance and Self of all Creation who is beyond all Creation.

62. {G} "Whoever receives your Holy Initiation; and follows you to

the end of this life; shall Attain Self-Realization within this life and know his Oneness with Me while yet living. And, whosoever has received your Holy Initiation and follows you to the end of his life, that Soul I will bless with the Supreme Gift of Perfect Final Union with Me, which you Sacrificed for the sake of all Souls this day.

63. {G} "Whosoever shall receive The Gift of your Holy Initiation, I shall place within The Secret Inner Sanctuary of his Heart the Four Treasures of, this My Promise; True Enlightenment; The Power For Good That Can Do No Wrong; and your Holy Ordination which will Purify and Sanctify that Soul and give unto him thy Power and Authority and My Own to give The Gift of your Holy Initiation unto all Souls. And he shall have become like unto a Living Temple within which thy Presence and Mine Own and My Eternal Universal Religion shall Dwell as the Indwelling Spirit.

64. {G} "Go forth! Beloved Adhyatma Bhagavan Sri Babajhan Al-Kahlil The Friend! Reveal My Supreme Truth and this, My New Covenant unto all men. Carry this, My Pure Divine Truth, into this sleeping world. For Thou Art My Truth, My Light, and My Way. Thou Art My Gift of Salvation unto all Souls!"

65. And out of The Eternal abode of The One Universal God came forth another Clear Light such as would light up the Sun, and in that Eternal moment, Light and Darkness met in Divine Battle that shook the very Foundations of Creation. And, when the Battle was ended, Light came forth in Victorious Glory; and Darkness was conquered, Forever. And the Veils of Darkness and Ignorance that had blinded my Spiritual Sight were torn away; and the Breath of The One God came upon me, searing my flesh from my bones, winnowing The Real from the unreal and scattering my false self to the far corners of Eternity!

66. And I cried out within the far reaches of eternity: "Om! Jai Bhagavan Ji! Victory to That Beloved Universal I AM THAT I AM Which You Are!" And my Victorious cry went out through all time and Creation and became, verily, the Supreme Mantra inscribed within the Hearts of every Soul, from the Beginning. And The Age of Universal God's Pure Divine Truth, was set into motion within all Souls.

67. And The God-Awakened within me, hearkened unto The One Universal God that is All In All. And I answered The One Universal God in Formless Thoughts through Silent Words, saying: "Yes! Verily! Thou Art The One God! My Lord! My One True Self! Truly Thou Art All In All! There is no other! Jai Bhagavan Ji! Victory To That Beloved Universal I AM THAT I AM, Which You Are!" And I prayed:

Paratpara!
Beloved Universal
I AM THAT I AM!
My God!
My Beloved!
My One True Self!
Through Thy Holy Initiation
Thou hast revealed
my Oneness with Thee!
I surrender completely unto Thee!
Thy Authority is restored!
Thy Presence has become
manifest within this little self!

I shine forth
by Thy Divine Clear Light!
The division in me is Healed!
I know my Oneness with Thee!
I know Thy Oneness
 in all this that is!
All is made Perfect!
I lack for nothing!
Thou hast consumed my Ignorance
in The Sacred Fire of Thy Presence.
Thou hast led me through the
Ordeal!
Through Thy Holy Initiation,
Thou hast revealed
my Oneness with Thee;
and liberated me
from the endless rounds
of birth and death!
From the unreal,
Thou hast led me to The Real!
From darkness,
Thou hast led me to The Light!
From division,
Thou hast led me to Wholeness!
From the temporary,
Thou hast led me to The Eternal!
From death,
Thou hast led me to Immortality!
O Beloved God!
I am One with Thee this moment!
My Doing is One with my Speech!
My Speech is One with my Mind!
My Mind is One with my Heart!
My Heart is One with my Will!
And my Will is One with Thy Will!
Thou hast shattered my prison
of ignorance and false self;
and absorbed me,
in The Ocean of
Thy Infinite Divine Being;
like a drop of water in The Sea!

I know, without doubt or reservation
that Thee and I are not we, but One!
That which Thou Art, I Am!
Thou art my Only True Self;
Majestic!
Splendorous!
Immortal!
There is no I but Thee!
So is it with me!
Om So'ham tat tvam asi!
I Am That, Thou Art That!
Jai Bhagavan Ji!
Victory To That Beloved Universal
I AM THAT I AM
Which Thou Art!"

68. And the soundless Voice of Paratpara, The One Universal God of Countless Names and Forms Who Is Beyond All Names and Forms, my Lord, That I AM THAT I AM, came again unto me saying:

69. {G} "You have known The Truth and you are Free! As I Am, so Thou Art! There is no thee but Me. Through you, I now make a New Covenant with all Men to resurrect their Spirits and bring them Home to Realization of their Oneness with Me! From this moment onward to the end of time, no Soul shall ever be lost for all eternity.

70. {G} "From this moment unto the end of Creation, all who receive your Holy Initiation and Believe in Me and The Oneness of all Souls in Me, and in thee and follow you to the end of this life, shall come Home to Me; and they shall be set free from the suffering and sorrow of this World and the endless rounds of birth and death, and they shall know Supreme Happiness and Eternal Life in Me!

71. {G} "But unto those who know thee in Me and Me in thee and have Faith in thee and This, My New Covenant made through thee in this day, shall be given The Supreme Gift of Knowledge of their Eternal Oneness with Me even while living in this world.

72. {G} "For I Am The Beginning and The End, The Purpose and The Goal of all Creation and Thou Art My Gate and My Way and My Light. Whosoever comes unto Me through Thee abides in Me, forever. So Be It!"

73. In that single moment, the True I AM THAT I AM within me, which is One with God, The Lord of all Creation, and no other, Awakened from the Sleep of The Living Dead and I was reborn, Adhyatma Bhagavan Sri Babajhan Al-Kahlil The Friend, The God-Realized One, Teacher of Oneness, The Friend! Of this there is no doubt!

74. And The Unspeakable, soundless Voice of The One Universal God said:

75. {G} "Go now! Awaken the Sleeping Souls! Tell them that they hear well enough, but fail to understand. Tell them that they must close their eyes and close their ears; and open wide the Gates of their hearts until they can See, but not with their eyes; and Hear, but not with their ears; and with Direct Experience of Heart and Mind, born of Right Understanding, Worship, and Practice, Know that they are One with Me their Lord, their God, All In All!"

76. And I said unto The One Universal God, "I am but one Awakened living among the many who are sleeping. How, Lord, shall I give my Holy Initiation and Your Supreme Promise to all of these sleeping Souls and bring them Home to You?"

77. And Paratpara, The One Universal God, Source, Substance and Being of all Creation said unto me:

78. {G} "This I say unto you, My Beloved, in whom I have Awakened for the Universal Salvation and Liberation of all Souls. Those who follow the way of Darkness shall dwell in Darkness in Hell. Those who follow My Prophets, Saints, Buddhas, Saviors and Avataras shall attain that which I have sent each of them forth to give unto man, by such names as they shall know it. Those who follow one who has been sent to give Enlightenment shall attain Enlightenment. Those who follow the one I have sent to secure unto them a place in Heaven, shall attain their place in Heaven. But whosoever receives your Holy Initiation in good Faith, receives My Supreme Promise of Perfect Final Union with That I AM THAT I AM and they shall dwell in Perfect Union with Me as far above Heaven as Heaven is above the Dark World of Hell.

79. {G} "And, whosoever follows you and your teachings and instructions and example in their Spirit and their letter to the end of this life, fulfills My Supreme Promise. And I shall take that Soul into Perfect Final Union with Me at the end of this life. And that Soul shall Know The Truth and be set free forever.

80. {G} "And that Soul shall Know Its Perfect Oneness with Me as a drop of water falling into the Sea becomes The Sea. And no more shall that Soul be born into this world of

Birth, Suffering, Sorrow, Fear, Pain, Old Age, Sickness and Death. For even those who attain Heaven must return to the world again and again. But those who receive My Supreme Promise through you and your Holy Initiation, shall dwell in the unborn and undying state in Me, forever. And that Soul shall see what I see, and hear what I hear and Know what I Know, and do what I do and be That I AM THAT I AM, forever. For then there shall no longer be any smallest difference between that Soul and That I AM THAT I AM.

81. {G} "For, it is for the winning of this Great Prize that you have twice made the supreme sacrifice of your own Perfect Final Union with Me for the sake of all Souls; and it is for this priceless Gift that you have made your Vow of Compassion, that you will never again enter into Perfect Final Union with Me until you have seen all Souls safely Home into Perfect Final Union with Me before you.

82. {G} "This is the Supreme Gift of My New Covenant with all Souls that your Sacrifices and Vow have won for all Souls. And whosoever receives this your Gift of My Supreme Promise through your Holy Initiation and fulfills it by following you Home to Me to the end of his life, shall come into Perfect Final Union with That I AM THAT I AM when his life is through, to be born no more. And fire shall not burn him, nor cold freeze him, nor sword pierce him, nor pain or fear assail him, nor loneliness or loss grieve him, nor woman bear him, nor time bind him, nor age wither him, nor death take him. But he shall be always in perfect bliss and joy and he shall live forever in Perfect Final Union with That I AM THAT I AM. For this is what your sacrifices and Vow have won for him and all Souls.

83. {G} "I say unto you that when your Maitreyians have given My Supreme Promise to the Souls of this world such that the Sun never sets upon the Maitreyians and there are enough of The Faithful who have received your Holy Initiation and who give heed to the letter of your teachings and instructions and examples in their lives and are following you Home to Perfect Final Union with Me in True Faith and Devotion in Spirit, they will form a Divine Critical Mass; and in that moment, I will spread My Supreme Promise and Gift of Perfect Final Union with That I AM THAT I AM, to all Souls. And no Soul shall be left behind.

84. {G} "And in that Day, all Souls shall come straightaway into Knowledge of Perfect Final Union with Me at the end of their lives. And Hell shall be emptied. For the wretched Souls who suffer therein shall be redeemed and made Holy and I shall take them into Perfect Final Union with Me and the gates of Hell shall be closed forever. And the Heaven world itself shall become empty of Souls. For in that day, I shall take every last Soul into Perfect Final Union with That I AM THAT I AM, as countless drops of water are taken into The Sea. This is The Great Dispensation that your sacrifices and Vow have won for all Souls.

85. {G} "Make this the highest Goal and Purpose of all that you do and all that is done by your Faithful Maitreyians who are, truly your Soldiers of The Light and My own and it shall come to pass.

86. {G} "Truly, My Beloved, The Path before you and those who, seeing the Truth of this New Covenant I make through you, take up their Divine Nature and follow you, is Supremely Blessed. Yet, owing to the Spiritual ignorance that lingers in this world, this Way shall also be filled with treachery and danger; even as it has been for all those before you who have done My Will.

87. {G} "In those Days which are yet to come, The Sleeping, who are The Living Dead, shall call you and those who follow you and Profess this, My New Covenant and My Pure Divine Truth: 'Blasphemer, Heretic,' and all manner of evil names. And they shall despise you and spit upon you, out of their own ignorance of Me, their Lord, their God. For I Am The One God of all The Prophets, Saints, Buddhas, Saviors and Avataras of all times and places, though they know Me not.

88. {G} "The Sleeping and the Ignorant shall curse and defile you and your Faithful, even as they have cursed and defiled all of My Messengers.

89. {G} "Have no fear, Beloved Adhyatma Bhagavan Sri Babajhan Al-Kahlil The Friend. Nor shall any Soul who receives your Holy Initiation and follows you Home to Me with all his mind and all his heart have need to fear. For, whosoever shall hear and accept these, My Words, and shall heed The True Message within them and shall pass through thee who are My Gate and, making Me his Purpose and his Goal shall follow you who art My Way and My Light, Home to Oneness with Me, is Mine Own.

90. {G} "Whosoever shall receive your Holy Initiation and go forth for Me, Proclaiming and Bearing True Witness to This, My New Covenant, that one I will hold fast in My Heart. As Abraham, Moses, Buddha, Jesus, My Prophet Mohammed and all other of My Prophets, Saints, Buddhas, Saviors and Avataras were held fast in My Heart; even so shall I protect and guide you and all who Awaken to My Truth and take up their Divine Natures and follow you Home to Me.

91. {G} "Let all men know that in each Age, wherein My people have fallen into ignorance and darkness, I Awaken within an ordinary man or woman and send that Chosen One forth into this sleeping world as My Own Emanation, who restores My Divine Truth and Light unto Man in such manner as fulfills the needs of that Day.

92. {G} "Some I have commissioned to bring unto Man the Iron Fist of The Law. Others I have sent forth to soften The Law with Mercy and Compassion and redeem Man from its sting.

93. {G} "Woeful shall they be who shall accept only one of these, My Awakened Ones, and shall deny or denounce or defile any other of them. As a man shall do unto the least of men, so does he do unto Me, The Lord Thy God. The transgressions of such as these may be forgiven. But whosoever shall deny or denounce or defile even one of My Awakened Prophets, Saints, Buddhas, Saviors and Avataras, setting man against man, woman against woman, woman against man or Nation against Nation in My Name shall suffer the most grievous karma.

94. {G} "For, as any Soul shall deny or denounce That I AM THAT I AM in a single one of My Prophets, Saints,

Buddhas, Saviors and Avataras, even so does that Soul deny and denounce Me, The Lord Thy God. Truly, that Soul shall live out his days in darkness and suffering of his own making, until he shall see the error of his ways and mend them.

95. {G} "I do not send forth My own Spirit in you against any of the Prophets, Saints, Buddhas, Saviors and Avataras that I have sent forth before you, but as the Completion of all of My Prophets, Saints, Buddhas, Saviors and Avataras and the Completion of The Way Home to Perfect Final Union with Me.

96. {G} "Nothing whatsoever is there that any Soul shall lose by believing in you or receiving the baptism of your Holy Initiation and My Supreme Promise of Perfect Final Union with Me or, yet again, by following you Home to Perfect Final Union with Me. But everything shall that Soul gain. For this Supreme Gift of Perfect Final Union with Me, which I have Promised through you shall be added unto all that is gone before.

97. {G} "He who comes to Me through any of My Prophets, Saints, Buddhas, Saviors and Avataras shall have what is Promised through them. He who believes in Jesus, shall have Heaven as I have Promised through my Beloved Jesus. He who comes to Me through the Buddha shall know enlightenment. He who comes to me through the Law as I have given it forth unto the Tribes of Israel through Abraham and Moses shall reap the fullness of The Reward I have promised unto him. He who comes to Me through my Prophet Mohammed shall know Paradise. And so shall it be with all others of them, known and unknown.

98. {G} "But he who believes in you as My Divine Spirit sent forth for the Universal Salvation and Liberation of all Souls and the continued survival of humanity and believes in your Supreme Self-Sacrifices and Vow and My Promise which you have won for all Souls and follows you to the end of his life according to My Promise shall know his Oneness with Me while living in this life and will have Perfect Final Union with Me at the end of his life.

99. {G} "Therefore, put the hearts and minds of the skeptical to rest. Tell them for Me that they do not have to renounce any of My Prophets, Saints, Buddhas, Saviors or Avataras to receive My Supreme Promise and come Home to Perfect Final Union with Me. Tell them for Me, that they shall lose nothing and gain everything by believing upon you and receiving My Supreme Promise through the baptism of your Holy Initiation and following you to the end of this life. Tell them for Me that they may continue to love and revere whosoever of My Prophets, Saints, Buddhas, Saviors or Avataras as they have previously chosen and, so long as they fulfill My Supreme Promise as I set it forth into this world through you, they shall have all that has been Promised.

100. {G} "But let them not disregard that which I have Promised through you by saying that it is the same as what shall come to them through their chosen Prophet, Saint, Buddha, Savior or Avatara. Nothing is there in this whole of Creation that is higher or beyond Me, for I am the One Universal God, Lord and Creator of all that is. I AM THAT I AM. Nothing is there that is higher than Me. Even Heaven itself is but a drop of water in the ocean

that I Am. Perfect Final Union with Me is countless times higher above Heaven itself, as Heaven is above Hell. Nothing is there that is higher than Perfect Final Union with Me.

101. {G} "Do not fall prey to those who preach or teach the doctrine of a devil who has the power to defy Me. Whosoever teaches this doctrine, spreads darkness among the Souls of the earth. For, I say unto you, again and again, that there is none in heaven or on earth nor beyond the beyond that has the power to stand against the I AM THAT I AM! For I Am The One In All in which All that is, is encompassed as a grain of sand in the sea and there can be no evil in That I AM THAT I AM! To believe so is to set forth a deluded doctrine that there can be evil in Goodness and that evil stands equal to Me and can oppose me. Those who believe in such a devil and those who preach this doctrine and teach it unto others have minds clouded with illusions of evil and are sorely deluded. Truly, it is the greatest blasphemy to preach this doctrine."

102. And I said unto my God, The Beloved, "From where, then, comes the evil within men and women and in our world, my God?" And The One God of all Creation said unto me:

103. {G} "Men can imagine a rabbit that has horns. Such a rabbit can live within the imaginations of Men. And their imagining may lead them to do all manner of strange acts. Still a rabbit with horns exists only in the minds of those who imagine it but has no existence apart from their imaginings.

104. {G} "Even so, men and women can imagine evil in the form of a man or a fallen angel. Such a devil can live within the imaginations of men and women and their imagining can move them to perform all manner of terrible acts as the result of their imagining and the delusions they create in their minds thereby. But, as with rabbits that have horns, such a devil exists only within their imaginings and does not exist outside of their imaginings."

105. And again I asked my God, "Then what, Beloved God, is the source that compels the evil that men and women do in this world?" And The One God, I AM THAT I AM, said unto me in a voice that is beyond all sound:

106. {G} "There can be no least evil in That I AM THAT I AM! Evil is an illusion that exists only in the minds of Souls as rabbits with horns. The single source of all evil in this world is the mind of Man and the delusions that men create therein. The evil that men and women do is the result of the evil that they imagine and the delusions that arise from their imaginings. There is a Mental World that is unseen and unheard by the sense of men and women, within which all that is held in the minds of men and women at any time, mesh and blend and merge. This Mental World is not only built by the minds of men and women, but also becomes a Force which in turn impresses the sum of its contents upon the minds of all men and women. When the sum of the Mental World, in which all Souls share, is more filled with Goodness than evil, it becomes a Force of My Divine Light. Then, it impresses Goodness upon the minds of all men and women and urges them toward My Divine Light and toward greater thoughts and acts of Goodness. But, when this Mental World is filled with more evil than Goodness, it impresses the illusion of evil upon

the minds of all men and women and urges them toward Darkness and toward thoughts and acts of greater Darkness and evil.

107. {G} "Be careful that you do not fall prey to those who would preach and teach that this Force stands above the Free Will and Free Choice which I have instilled in every Soul since the beginning of Creation. For though this Force impress itself on a man or woman and urge that man or woman toward Goodness or evil, the choice is ever left to the Soul who must eventually bear the full weight and results of its own choosing.

108. {G} "The evil that men and women do after which you ask, comes only from the sum of the imaginings of all living Souls and the delusions that come from their imaginings and The Force of Darkness which these create within the Mental World beyond the senses in which the minds of men and women merge.

109. {G} "It is, truly, this Force of Darkness that appears to the unenlightened to be a man or a dark angel and which they call a devil. But as a mirage of water seen upon the sands of the desert and a snake that is seen in a piece of rope, there is neither man nor angel nor devil. There is only The Force of Darkness created in the Mental World by the sum of the minds of all men and women living at a single time.

110. {G} "The Real always is and never ceases, but the unreal never is, save in the minds of those that imagine it. I Am the One Reality of all Existence.

111. {G} "The Force of Darkness is unreal. The Force of Darkness and all the evil it embodies and causes within, between and among men and women is like unto a circle drawn on the surface of a still pool with a stick. When the stick stops drawing the circle, the circle in the pool vanishes and only the pool is left. When the minds of all living men and women cease imagining evil and are filled with My Divine Truth and Light, The Force of Darkness vanishes and only That I AM THAT I AM remains.

112. {G} "That which is created is the expression of its creator and embodies the qualities of its creator. By virtue of its creators, The Force of Darkness also sends forth an influence on the minds of those who create it and continue creating it. As a street runs both ways and a thing thrown into the air falls back to earth, The Force of Darkness pushes and pulls all living Souls down into further Darkness.

113. {G} "No man or woman shall be your enemy. The Force of Darkness which is created and maintained by the mind of all Souls is your only enemy and The Sharp Sword and Light of My Pure Truth is your weapon. So Is It. So Shall It Be, forever until all Souls are safely Home in Me.

114. {G} "Upon hearing this Truth which I send forth unto them through you, many among the unawakened who are enslaved to The Force of Darkness will deny you or revile you because of what is written in their holy books. Do not argue over what is written in their books. Tell them for Me that I have sent My Spirit forth through you as a confirmation of My Prophets, Saints, Buddhas, Saviors and Avataras and a completion of the Way Home to Perfect Final Union with Me; not as a confirmation of what men have said or written about

those I have sent forth to Man. For, the writings of man are easily corrupted by men and by time.

115. {G} "Tell them that I have written My Scriptures in the heart of every Soul where fire cannot burn it, nor weather rot it, nor time and the wiles of Man corrupt it. He who shall judge you or what I have said unto Man through you or, yet again, what you shall say unto them, are as foolish as those who would judge a sunrise by a graven image when they should be judging the graven image by the sunrise. For you are the Dawning of the new age of My Pure Divine Truth on earth, whom I send forth for the Salvation and Liberation of all Souls and the continued survival of Humanity.

116. {G} "Unto those who challenge you, saying that theirs is the only True Way and their Messenger the only True Messenger, let this Truth Be Known:

117. {G} "Brahma I did show unto Man that he might know the Essence of Creation;

118. {G} "Vishnu I did show unto Man that he might know Endurance and Preservation;

119. {G} "Shiva I did send unto Man that he might know that Death and Destruction are no more than the compassionate plowman readying the earth for new Seed;

120. {G} "Rama I did send unto Man, as the arrow is sent forth from the bow, that Man might know the True meaning of Righteousness;

121. {G} "Krishna I did send unto Man, as the sound of the flute issues forth unto the hearer, that Man might know Order and Right Conduct;

122. {G} "Abraham I did send unto Man as a pilgrim of The New Way, that Man might know the Necessity of ceaselessly seeking after Me;

123. {G} "Moses I did send unto Man as The Bringer of The Law, that Man might know the Iron Hand of The Law;

124. {G} "Zoroaster I did send unto Man that Man might know the essence of Duality;

125. {G} "Lao-Tsu I did send unto Man, as the Waters of the earth, that he might know Unity within All Duality;

126. {G} "Confucius I did send unto Man as the Stars are ordered in the Heavens, that Man might know the Right Conduct of Affairs;

127. {G} "Sakyamuni Buddha I did send unto Man as a Lamp in a dark forest and a healing balm, that Man might know the Cause of Suffering and a Way to its end;

128. {G} "Bodhidharma I did send unto Man as the bearer of the Lamp, that Man might learn the lesson of giving My Light to all Nations Equally;

129. {G} "Jesus of Nazareth I did send unto Man as My own Radiance made manifest, as The Sun sends forth its rays to warm the earth, that Man might know My Love made Perfect within him;

130. {G} "Mohammed of Mecca I did send unto Man as My own Mercy, that Man might know that I Am The One

God who speaks through all of The Prophets and surrender to Me;

131. {G} "Nanak I did send unto Man as the innocent Flower grows in the field, that Man might know The Way of Peace;

132. {G} "Singh I did send unto Man as a shining Sword of Truth, that Man might know the necessity of Courage, Fidelity and Strength in the face of opposition;

133. {G} "Baha'u'llah I did send unto Man as a River of My Blessings that flows around all obstacles, that Man might know the value of Perseverance in the face of all Adversity and know that all My people are One people;

134. {G} "Ghandi I did send unto Man as a Dove, that Man might know the value of holding onto Truthfulness and the power of love and non-violence;

135. {G} "Ramakrishna I did send unto Man as a whirlwind of Bliss, that Man might know the Way of Divine Bliss as a way home to Me.

136. {G} "These and all other of My Prophets, Saints, Buddhas, Saviors and Avataras, remembered and forgotten by Man, I did send unto Man that his need should be fulfilled and his steps turned ever more steadily toward Me.

137. {G} "Now Adhyatma Bhagavan Sri Babajhan Al-Kahlil The Friend, My Own Divine Radiance, in whom I am well pleased, I call upon you to go forth for Me. Unite all of My people of the Earth into a single people and make This New Covenant which I make through you This Day manifest unto all Men!

138. {G} "Go forth for Me, not as one who is Perfect by Earthly measure as judged by those who are yet earthbound, but as One made Perfect in Me, for you and I are not we, but One.

139. {G} "And when they say unto you, 'By whose authority do you preach and teach and do these things?' And, Say unto them for Me, 'By the Authority of The One Universal God, I AM THAT I AM, and no other.' And when they say unto you, 'What is your Holy Book?' Say unto them, 'My Holy Book is none other than The Supreme Holy Book that The One Universal God, I AM THAT I AM, has inscribed in the very Heart of every Soul; of which, all other Holy Books are but reflections, as the moon reflected in a pool of water.'

140. {G} "When the ignorant shall revile you and would do harm unto you and those who are My Faithful in you, say unto them, 'What business have you with me? If I offend The One Universal God who has sent me unto you will He not punish me directly without your sword? Are you of such vanity and so little Faith that you must pretend to do what you piously call God's Will, when The One Universal God has not seen fit to do it Himself? Would you be so foolish as to interfere with God's Great Plan for all Men? Did not the blind of your Prophet's time seek to do unto Him even as you now seek to do unto God's Compassionate One sent again to you?'

141. {G} "Think not Adhyatma Bhagavan Sri Babajhan Al-Kahlil The Friend, that your way will be easy, or your burden lighter than that of any other man. Victory is yours, but nothing shall I do for you that

would not be done for any other of My People.

142. {G} "How could it be otherwise? Unless you do these things of your own actions and efforts, the Sleeping and The Living Dead will only excuse their sleep and ignorance by saying of you as they have of all those I have sent, "He is blessed and far beyond our ability to do like Him, so let us return to the stillness of our Illusions, Sleep and Ignorance." For, it is just this that they have done with all others of those I have sent unto them!

143. {G} "You, My Beloved Adhyatma Bhagavan Sri Babajhan Al-Kahlil The Friend, have seen The Light. You have known The Truth, the whole Truth and nothing but The Truth. You have traveled The Way and come Home to Me! We Are One. No longer is there any other I in you but Me.

144. {G} "Make, therefore, your Heart and Mind and Body into fitting vessels for My Spirit that My Radiance may shine forth unto all Men as a Lamp uncovered and set upon a high place!

145. {G} "Go now and do that for which you are made anew. Go among My People, Proclaiming and bearing True Witness to This, The New Covenant of The One Universal God, That One I AM THAT I AM. Tell them for Me:

146. {G} "There is One Universal God. There is no other! The One Universal God has Awakened and Ordained me, Adhyatma Bhagavan Sri Babajhan Al-Kahlil, The Friend of All Souls, The Maitreya Kalki Mahavatara Satguru of The Age, Bringer of God's Eternal Universal Religion and The Age of Universal God's Pure Divine Truth to all Souls; and sent me unto you for your Salvation and Liberation. As all in a dream is of The Dreamer; as a drop of water taken from the Sea, though it be taken to the Stars, Is Sea; as a wave rises from the Sea, lingers but for a time and returns into the Sea which is its very self; all that Is and all that is not, Is this I; for there is no I but God! And, everything Is! There is no one thing that Is and another that is not. There is no one thing that is True and another that is not True. All Is. And it is All True. The Truth alone exists, all else is illusion born only of the sleeping minds of the Living Dead who dwell in darkness and ignorance. There is no I but God! All that Is, Is of God. All that Is, I Am. All That Is, Thou Art. You and I are not we, but One. The Lord Thy God is The Beginning, The Middle, and The End of All that is. As a Potter, by knowing the Nature of clay, knows the Nature of all things made of clay, even so will he who Awakens to God's Truth know All-Truth.

147. {G} "Call My people back to Me, saying unto them:

148. {G} 'Arise! Awaken all you who sleep the sleep of the Living Dead. Thy Lord has come! The Day awaited is at hand! He who knows Paratpara, The One Universal God of Countless Names and Forms Who Is Beyond All Names and Forms, That One I AM THAT I AM, within himself is Great among Men. But he who knows That I AM THAT I AM, Truly, as his own True Self is given Eternal Life and Freedom from Suffering and Sorrow while living in this Life.

149. {G} 'Whosoever shall realize That One I AM THAT I AM as his One True Self shall find everlasting Peace. Fire cannot burn This Self;

sword cannot pierce It; nor cold freeze It. Freed from the illusion of the false self, knowing that you are not this, or this, or this, but That One I AM THAT I AM alone, you shall endure Forever. For always have I been and always will I Be and Thou Art, in Truth, One with That One I AM THAT I AM, Paratpara, The Lord Thy God, All In All!

150. {G} 'Though you are One with The One Universal God, you know It not! Seek you first, therefore, to know your True Self. For in this knowing, you shall come to know Me. And, knowing Me, you shall come to know That One I AM THAT I AM, All In All. And you shall know, without doubt or reservation that you and I are not we, but One!

151. {G} 'In His Eternal Love, God has always Loved Thee. In His never ending Being He has always held Thee, though you have known it not. Once more He has remade Thee. This time you are Truly Made One With God. A Pure One Reborn in That One I AM THAT I AM. There is no I but God! There is no You but God. The Lord, Thy God, That I AM THAT I AM, is with you always. Of this there is no doubt! Om So'ham Tat Tvam Asi! Om! I Am That Thou Art! Jai Bhagavan Ji! Victory To That Beloved Universal I AM THAT I AM Which You Are! So It Is!

152. {G} 'Do then, this which I give unto you in The Name of Paratpara, The One Universal God of Countless Names and Forms Who Is Beyond All Names and Forms who has Awakened within this One and sent Me forth unto you, and no longer shall the Sun be thy Light by day; nor the Moon thy Light by night. For The Lord Thy God, Thy Beloved, shall have become an Eternal Light shining out from Thee unto all the Earth! Thy Sun shall never set and Thy Moon shall never wane. The Light of The One God is Thine and Thy days of suffering and sorrow are at an end. For all you who receive the baptism of my Holy Initiation and follow me to the end of this life shall Know your Oneness with The One God within this life and enter into Perfect Final Union with Him at this life's end. For this is God's Supreme Promise to all Souls through me.'"

153. {G} "And having said these things, say unto them:

154. {G} 'This is The New Covenant of the One God as It has come to pass in The God-Realized One, Teacher of Oneness, Adhyatma Bhagavan Sri Babajhan Al-Kahlil The Friend. This is The Truth, The Whole Truth and Nothing But The Truth. So Be It!'

155. {G} "From this day forward unto the end of time, all who hear Thy Word, which is My Word, and receive the True Enlightenment of your Holy Initiation and follow Thee and Thy Teaching unto the end of their lives are My Chosen People and are Brothers and Sisters in The Spirit of That I AM THAT I AM and they shall be together beyond eternity, in Perfect Final Union with Me at the end of this life.

156. {G} "In heeding this New Covenant that I send unto them through you, and following you with Faith and Devotion, all error and illusion and sleep shall be wiped from their Spiritual Eyes and they shall know The Truth and The Truth shall set them Free!

157. {G} "Whosoever, knowing this Truth and holding My New Covenant

within his Heart and Mind, shall place it before attachment to self, family, friends and the things of this World, and will take up his Divine Nature and follow you Home to Me and realize his Oneness with thee; shall attain Self-Realization and enter into Perfect Union with That I AM THAT I AM, Thy Lord, The One Universal God, All In All, within this life or at its end.

158. {G} "Whosoever shall do this, shall render unto all Mankind a service so wondrous that the Doctrines of the learned Philosophers and the Intellectuals shall be cast aside, and the interpretations of the conveniently wise shall pass away. For in that Day, The Truth that surpasses all understanding shall become known to all Souls. And the Spiritually Deaf shall Hear and the Eyes of the Spiritually Blind shall be opened. And they shall pierce the Veil of Ignorance, Sleep, and Illusion. And all who hear My Word and take it within their Hearts and Minds will rise up out of darkness and ignorance into the Clear Light and attain knowledge of their Oneness with Me, The Lord, The One Universal God, All In All.

159. {G} "For it shall come to pass that in that Day, My People will return to True Knowledge and Worship of That I AM THAT I AM. For there is no I within any man or woman or creature of this, My Creation, save That One I AM THAT I AM without a second. For, I Am the One True Self of every man and woman and creature of Creation."

160. And Paratpara, The One Universal God of Countless Names and Forms Who Is Beyond All Names and Forms, That Beloved I AM THAT I AM, said unto me in wordless words:

161. {G} "Those who accept you as Maitreya make the Holy Commitment and profess the Truth of My Eternal Universal Religion and you, within whom I have Awakened and Ordained to give it unto all Souls, shall be called Adhyatmavadi.

162. {G} "And all Adhyatmavadi who accept you as Maitreya, receive your Holy Consecration and Confirmation and take up My Eternal Universal Religion without doubt or reservation, shall be called Maitreyians. When those who are Maitreyians shall receive your Commission and Mine through you, they shall be called Maitreyians who are Soldiers of The Light.

163. {G} "Let whosoever would take up this, My Eternal Universal Religion, and follow you Home to Me, do so in whatever way you shall elect and require it to be done. But, whatever else you may require, let it be that all who would receive your Holy Initiation and take up My Eternal Universal Religion, shall at least profess directly to you or through another who is your faithful Maitreyian: 'The Friend's Religion is my Religion.'

164. {G} "Let this be your Creed and Profession and The Creed and Profession of all who would be your Maitreyians:

165. {G} "There is One Universal God: Manifest and Unmanifest; Personal and Impersonal; Immanent and Transcendent. There is no other. Universal God alone is Real. As all in a dream is of the dreamer; as a drop of water taken from the Sea is Sea; all that is, is Universal God. There is nothing but Universal God everywhere. All Soul is Pure Divine Universal

Spirit which is One and Identical with Universal God and no other. Adhyatma Bhagavan Sri Babajhan Al-Kahlil The Friend is Universal God's Awakened One, Bringer of The Holy Satya Yuga, whom Universal God has Ordained to end the Age of Spiritual Ignorance and bring forth The Age of Divine Pure Truth on earth. Out of His Universal Love and Compassion, The Friend Sacrificed Perfect Final Union with Universal God for the sake of all Souls for all time. In reward for His Supreme Sacrifice, Universal God has Promised that all who receive the Enlightenment of The Friend's Holy Initiation and follow Him to the end of their lives, shall attain Self-Realization and receive the Supreme Gift of Perfect Final Union that He Sacrificed for their sake.

166. {G} "I Believe in The One Universal God.

167. {G} "I Believe in Adhyatma Bhagavan Sri Babajhan Al-Kahlil The Friend, the Supreme Sacrifice He has made for me and all Souls, and the Supreme Gift of Universal God's Divine Grace His Sacrifice has won for me and all Souls.

168. {G} "I Believe in His Holy Adhyatma-Yoga-Dharma.

169. {G} "I Believe in The Holy Community of His Enlightened Faithful Believers.

170. {G} "I Believe in His Holy Cause of Satya Yuga and World-Wide Enlightenment and Self-Realization for all people.

171. {G} "I take Refuge in The One Universal God.

172. {G} "I take Refuge in Adhyatma Bhagavan Sri Babajhan Al-Kahlil The Friend, the Supreme Sacrifice He has made for me and all Souls, and the Supreme Gift of Universal God's Divine Grace His Sacrifice has won for me and all Souls.

173. {G} "I take Refuge in His Holy Adhyatma-Yoga-Dharma.

174. {G} "I take Refuge in The Holy Community of His Enlightened Faithful Believers.

175. {G} "I take Refuge in His Holy Cause of Satya Yuga and World-Wide Enlightenment and Self-Realization for all people.

176. {G} "I will give my self, my work, my energy, and my devotion in Unselfish Service to Universal God, The Friend, The Holy Adhyatma-Yoga-Dharma, and The Holy Community;

177. {G} "I will work with energy and devotion to attain Self-Realization within this life;

178. {G} "I will work for and uphold Spiritual Freedom for all People;

179. {G} "I will live, work, and struggle for the Holy Cause of Satya Yuga and World-Wide Enlightenment and Self-Realization for all people everywhere. So long as I live, I will never give up the Holy struggle until the Goal is won.

180. {G} "Jai Bhagavan Ji! Victory To Universal God! Victory to Adhyatma Bhagavan The Friend! Victory To His Holy Adhyatma-Yoga-Dharma! Victory To The Holy Community of His Enlightened Faithful Believers! Victory to His Holy Cause of Satya

Yuga and World-Wide Enlightenment and Self-Realization for all people! Victory To That Beloved Universal I AM THAT I AM Which You Are!"

181. {G} "And let this be your Holy Doctrine and the Holy Doctrine of all who would be your Maitreyians:

182. {G} "There is One Universal God. There is One Universal Spirit. One, whole, and indivisible. There is no other. Due to Spiritual Ignorance, the people see Universal God differently. Because of this, they call Him by different Names. In Truth, Universal God is Universal Spirit which is both Manifest and Unmanifest; both Personal and Impersonal; both Immanent and Transcendent; yet, neither. Universal God is the One Greatest Mystery. Mind cannot grasp Him. Only Spirit can Know Him.

183. {G} "Universal God alone is Real. There is nothing but Universal God everywhere. Universal God is the One Source, Cause, Substance, and Self of all Creation; all Existence; and all Being. Creation, Existence, and Being have no Reality or Existence apart from Universal Spirit.

184. {G} "Soul is Pure Divine Universal Spirit which is Ignorant of its True Nature. In Truth, all Soul is Pure Divine Universal Spirit which is One and Identical with Universal God, and no other. Spiritual Ignorance and Wrong Believing hide The Truth from the people's hearts and minds. Their result is birth, division, conflict, pain, fear, suffering, sorrow, and death. Their fruit is endless rounds of births and deaths. Enlightenment and Self-Realization are the cure. The Friend's Holy Initiation is True Enlightenment. Self-Realization is full and Absolute Knowledge of The Truth, born of Direct Spiritual Experience. There is no Self-Realization without True Enlightenment. There is no other Salvation or Liberation. The Truth, alone, sets all people free.

185. {G} "Self-Realization is the One Universal Purpose and Goal of all Life. All Creation; all Existence; and all Being; are for Self-Realization alone. The Purpose and Goal of the wave is to return to the sea from which it has come; and, of which it is a part. The Purpose and Goal of each Soul is to attain Self-Realization and to return to Universal God from which it has come; and, of which it is a part. True Enlightenment and Self-Realization alone bring True Salvation and Liberation. True Enlightenment and Self-Realization alone bring Supreme Peace, Love, Understanding, Compassion, Freedom, Truth, and Joy to the living. True Enlightenment and Self-Realization alone attain the Supreme Grace of Perfect Eternal Union with Universal God at life's end.

186. {G} "Creation has two natures. Karma and Dharma. Karma is Ignorance. Dharma is Self-Realization. Karma is Wrong action, arising from Ignorance. Dharma is Righteousness arising from Truth. Karma pulls down. Dharma lifts up. Due to Karma, the people fall into darkness. Selfishness and Materialism are the lowest Karma. The Holy Adhyatma-Yoga-Dharma is the Highest Dharma. In times of great Spiritual Ignorance; when selfishness and materialism cloud the hearts and minds of the people; and darkness covers the world; Universal God Awakens within an ordinary man or woman for the sake of My Holy Adhyatma-Yoga-Dharma and Self-Realization. In some ages, Universal God Awakens within man

to rejoice the Holy Dharma. In others, to preserve its Universal Truth. In yet others to raise up The Spirit within the people. In still others, to change the course of humanity. And, finally, to put an end to Ignorance and Wrong Believing, Renew The Age of Pure Holy Adhyatma-Yoga-Dharma Universalism, and bring forth The Holy Satya Yuga on earth. Because of these things, Adhyatmavadi accept and revere all of Universal God's Prophets, Saints, Buddhas, Avataras, and Saviors of all times. But this, according to The Friend's Teachings and Divine Guidance alone. Without being bound to accept the scriptures, doctrines, dogmas, opinions, or beliefs others hold to be true about these.

187. {G} "Universal God's Divine Nature is Eternal Truth, Infinite Consciousness, and Perfect Bliss. These shine forth in Creation as Universal Peace, Universal Love, Universal Understanding, Universal Compassion, Universal Freedom, Universal Truth, Universal Joy, and above all, as Self-Realization. Each Soul shares Universal God's Divine Nature and Qualities. Every Soul has Free Will and Free Choice. Every Soul must enjoy or suffer the results of choosing. The people's wrong choosing has come back to them. Humanity has plunged into the worst of The Age of Ignorance and Wrong Believing. The people face complete destruction. Prophecy says wait. Scripture says, not yet. The Law makes no allowance for saving the people. But, Universal God's Divine Love and Compassion are Supreme. To save the people, Universal God has Awakened within Adhyatma Bhagavan Sri Babajhan Al-Kahlil The Friend in this day."

188. {G} "Universal God's Divine Will is Supreme. It is above all scriptures and laws of people and nations. When Universal Spirit Calls, the Enlightened answer. Though others object; though they believe themselves unworthy; though they would avoid the sacrilege of being raised up to so high a place; the God-Awakened receive His Will and Grace of their own Free Choosing. What Universal God Ordains, the Enlightened accept. On the Seventh day of August, Nineteen Hundred and Fifty-One the Divine Spirit of The One Universal God Awakened within an ordinary boy. And he was transformed into Bhagavan Sri Babajhan Al-Kahlil The Friend. And Universal God Ordained Him to end The Age of Ignorance and Wrong Belief; to Save The People from self-destruction; and to bring forth The New Age of Universal God's Pure Truth of Holy Adhyatma-Yoga-Dharma on earth. And The One Universal God asked that The Friend fulfill His Divine Design and return to this world in ignorance, and attain The Supreme Goal by His own efforts in following The Holy Adhyatma-Yoga-Dharma. To the end that all men might know that True Salvation and Liberation may be won by both Divine Grace and The Holy Adhyatma-Yoga-Dharma. And The Friend of all Souls returned to this world in ignorance of His Self-Realization, His True Nature as Universal God's Divine Living Expression, and His Holy Mission. For 25 years, The Friend wandered through the wilderness of this world, discovering and following The Holy Adhyatma-Yoga-Dharma; and seeking The Way by which Self-Realization could be attained by man's own efforts. And on March 12, 1977 The Friend found The Way, and attained Self-Realization and Perfect Union

with Universal God. Again, Universal God offered The Friend the choice of remaining in Perfect Final Union with Him, or making the Supreme Sacrifice of returning to this world to fulfill His Divine Mission for the Salvation and Liberation of all Souls. And again, The Friend of all Souls made The Supreme Self-Sacrifice and returned to this world to fulfill The Supreme Holy Mission of bringing forth The Holy Satya Yuga. Because of this Supreme Sacrifice, Universal God Ordained Him Adhyatma Bhagavan Sri Babajhan Al-Kahlil The Friend; and decreed that His Name should reign Supreme among the Enlightened of all Nations and throughout all the Seven Worlds, forever.

189. {G} "Universal God does not take away the people's Free Will or Free Choice. All Good comes to pass through the union of Right Conditions, Right Choice, and Divine Grace. Upon Awakening, Universal God offered The Friend a Free Choice: enter into Perfect Final Union and eternal bliss; or, return to the world of suffering, sorrow, and death to fulfill His Holy Ordination. In Universal Love and Compassion, The Friend Sacrificed Eternal Paradise; and returned to the world of suffering, sorrow, and death for the sake of all Souls. Having made the Supreme Sacrifice, He vowed never to take His Final Union with Universal God until all Souls had attained it before Him. But to spend a lifetime in the flesh. And then, to reside within the hearts of all people in The Spirit; to help all who Call Upon Him; and Guide all Souls to the True Salvation and Liberation of Holy Adhyatma-Yoga-Dharma and Self-Realization.

190. {G} "Self-Sacrifice is the Highest Religion. Creation, Existence, and Being were born by Universal God's Divine Self-Sacrifice. Universal God's continuing Self-Sacrifice alone Maintains them. Because of The Friend's Supreme Self-Sacrifice and Vow, Universal God made this Divine Promise: Whoever receives the True Enlightenment of The Friend's Holy Initiation; and follows Him to the end of this life; shall Attain Self-Realization and receive the Supreme Gift of Salvation and Liberation which He Sacrificed for the sake of all Souls.

191. {G} "Universal God's Divine Truth is Eternal, Universal, and Indivisible. The vain opinions and declarations of men and women cannot touch it. Cannot change it. Even the Holy Scriptures are but a reflection of it. Nothing can divide it. People and Nations may make vain declarations in an effort to divide it. They may divide its letter, but there is nothing which can divide its Spirit. Universal God Awakened within The Friend to Renew the Divine Spirit of Universal Truth within The Law; not to destroy its letter. The Friend has not come to depose or deny any of Universal God's Prophets, Saints, Buddhas, Saviors, or Avataras. He comes to affirm them and their Oneness and Unity in The One Universal Spirit. He comes to complete the final step in the Divine Bridge between the people and Universal God. He comes not to destroy Religions. He comes to Renew and Restore Universal God's highest and most ancient Universal Divine Truth of Holy Adhyatma-Yoga-Dharma to all people. The One Supreme Universal Truth upon which all True Religions are founded though they know it not. He comes to Awaken The People and Enlighten all Souls to The Truth: that ignorance, wrong believing, lust, materialism,

selfishness, hatred, and division are death and darkness. But that Universal Peace, Love, Understanding, Compassion, Freedom, Truth, Joy, and Self-Realization are Life and Light. He comes as a living Self-Sacrifice. That, through Him, all People may receive Universal God's Divine Gift of Universal Love, Compassion, and Grace; and be set Free. Forever.

192. {G} "And when you have gathered your Faithful, who, verily, are My Faithful, unto you, teach them and guide them in This The Truth and The Life and The Way of The Eternal Universal Religion of Paratpara, The One Universal God of Countless Names and Forms Who Is Beyond All Names and Forms, That One I AM THAT I AM.

193. {G} "Go forth now, My Beloved Adhyatma Bhagavan Sri Babajhan Al-Kahlil The Friend and do that for which you are Reborn in The Spirit! Go out into the darkness of this world and light up The Divine Fire of the Spirit of God within the hearts of all Beings. Go out into the desert of this World and give The Holy Water of Life of this New Covenant, unto all who thirst after The Truth; that he who has eyes may See; and he who has ears may Hear; and they shall know within their hearts The Truth of This Truth. For, whosoever shares The Water of Life shares The One Universal God and The Friend. Of this there is no doubt!

194. {G} "Gather together My Faithful of all Nations into My Holy Community, that this, which is The Word of That I AM THAT I AM shall cover the Earth from Sun to Sun. To the end that all Souls shall receive your Holy Initiation; that they who follow you to the end of this life shall win, thereby, The Supreme Gift of Liberation and Perfect Final Union with The One God, That One Universal I AM THAT I AM, which your Supreme Self-Sacrifice has won for all Souls."

195. And I saw many millions of Souls gathered together. And The Spirit of The One Universal God rose up in me and I said unto them: "You who would follow Paratpara, The One Universal God of Countless Names and Forms Who Is Beyond All Names and Forms, That Beloved I AM THAT I AM; turn not away from your Brothers and Sisters, but join with one another often in me and The One God of whom I am sent. For, wherever two or more of you are gathered together in My Name and the Name of He who has sent me, there I Am and there is my Church and therein shall The Divine Spirit of The Lord thy God be in fullness."

196. And The Soundless Voice of The One Universal God said unto The Heart of my Heart:

197. {G} "No greater Love is there than that a Soul shall sacrifice Final Union with That I AM THAT I AM and take up yet another Life for the sake of all Souls. For this is the greatest Self-Sacrifice of them all! Go forth now, you who Awaken with The Dawn, Proclaiming and bearing True Witness to This, The New Covenant of The One Universal God, saying unto the sleeping:

198. {G} 'Awaken Beloved Soul! It is the Divine Promise of The One God unto all Mankind through me, that whosoever will declare himself unto me and receive my Holy Initiation and shall go forth Professing and Bearing True Witness of this Covenant shall become God's Own through me.

199. {G} 'Whosoever shall follow me to the end of this life shall win Perfect Oneness with The One Universal God and be filled with The Divine Fire that dispels all darkness and The Holy Water of Life, and darkness shall leave him and he shall thirst no more!

200. {G} 'Sleep not the sleep of ignorance, you who would know The One Universal God. Seek to know your own True Self. For it is not within Temples made by the hands of men that you shall find That I AM THAT I AM, but within each of your Hearts; even as I Am within the wind and the skies and the flowers of your fields.

201. {G} 'Many will there be in this day who would act as givers of The Truth but who are as a hollow drum within, who prattle on without knowledge of me. Know that such as these are but strangers wandering aimlessly in a strange land who, for the sake of their vanity, ignorance and pride have missed the beauty that lay before them.

202. {G} 'Truly, shall such as these seek to enslave the heart and mind of you who have set your foot upon The Way Home to That I AM THAT I AM. And they shall seek to turn you away saying, 'God is this and not that' and laying down all manner of many laws and regulations that all might see them and marvel at their knowledge of such things.

203. {G} 'Be not as these, you who Love The One God and follow me. Neither give your heart or your mind into the keeping of such as these. For, though a man have all the knowledge of this Earth and its heavens and know Me not, he shall not attain the Goal!

204. {G} 'Do not argue with the sleeping, but speak This Truth I have revealed unto you with quiet certainty from Heart to Heart, from Mind to Mind and, above all, from Spirit to Spirit. For, though the sleeping have hearts and minds, they have confused them, putting their hearts where their minds should be and their minds in the place of the Heart! You, who would come unto Me, exchange them! And you shall find your Way Home to The One I AM THAT I AM.

205. {G} 'Seek after The One Universal God, That I AM THAT I AM, within the Heart of your Heart and the Mind of your Mind and you shall Truly find Me therein All In All. This is The Work, there is no other!

206. {G} 'When you do The Work, seek not after earthly rewards that wind and rain and sun may destroy and robber and thief may steal. But give your Heart and your Mind unto Me without doubt or reservation; and surrender all your actions and their fruits unto Me, that you will not stumble and fall into darkness and death. For it is only through Devotion, Surrender, and Selfless Service to The One I AM THAT I AM, that The Way to Salvation and Liberation are won.

207. {G} 'Bear not False Witness of this New Covenant. Neither compel another to bear False Witness of this Holy Covenant. For, only when you have Known Me directly within The Spiritual Realm within The Secret Inner Sanctuary of your Heart; and having drunk of The Water of Life therein become God-intoxicated with direct experience of Oneness with Me, shall you Know The Truth of this New Covenant and become Reborn in The Spirit and be set free.

208. {G} 'Beware! For all vain men take great delight in pretending to speak for The One God and for Me, saying, 'This is God's Word' and 'This is God's Will' and 'This is what The Friend's words mean.' Such as these seek dominion and mastery over their Brothers and Sisters in My Name, saying 'You shall do this' and 'You shall not do that'."

209. And Paratpara, The Undefinable, The One Universal God of Countless Names and Forms Who Is Beyond All Names and Forms, That One Beloved I AM THAT I AM, showed unto me a beautiful and radiant Sanctuary, having a roof, four pillars, a Foundation having Four Cornerstones, and a beautiful treasure chest at each of the four pillars, three steps leading up to The Holy Sanctuary, and a Sacred Shrine centered between the two rearward pillars.

210. And behind the Sacred Shrine there hung a Sacred Banner of brightest blue with a thick border of crimson. And at the center of the banner, there was, hung from above, a Sacred Scroll written upon white parchment. And the Sacred Shrine was made of two levels above the ground. A lower level, which was draped in purest white and upper level, which was draped in maroon.

211. Upon the Sacred Shrine, at the center of the higher level, there was a Maroon Teaching Seat. The Holy Book of God's Eternal Universal Religion lay at the right hand of The Teaching Seat upon the higher level. And, a small bell, strung upon a string of twenty-eight wooden beads, a knot having been tied between each one, lay upon the higher level to the left of it. Three Sacred Flames were placed on the white of the lower level, one at the left corner, one at the right corner and one, directly before the Teaching Seat. A vessel of Holy Water was at the right hand of the Teaching Seat upon the lower level. A conch shell, made for blowing was upon the lower level, at the left hand of the Teaching seat. A Begging Bowl sat upon the ground itself, at the left hand of The Teaching Seat.

212. And it was set high upon a mountain. And the people came unto it in such numbers that it was like unto a sea. And each who entered into it took up the Whole of The Religion that it held and gave it his own expression such that his expression was in full harmony and unity with God's Eternal Religion. Some were sitting in meditation. Some were dancing with joy. Some were kneeling in prayer. Some performed elaborate ceremonies, while others sat in plain austerity. But, though their expressions were many and different, they were, one and all, Brothers and Sisters in Spirit and, equal by virtue of having taken up God's wondrous Religion and holding it in common.

213. And The One Universal God said unto me:

214. {G} "Let your Religion, which is My Supreme Eternal Truth, be like unto this Holy Sanctuary. Let the Roof of The Holy Sanctuary of your Religion be this, My New Covenant that I make with all Souls through you this day, that it may shelter all Souls from the tempest of this world.

215. {G} "Let there be Four Pillars that hold up The Roof of The Holy Sanctuary of your Religion.

216. {G} "Let the First Pillar be thee and Me, together, One and inseparable. And let this First Pillar of this Holy Sanctuary be called Bhagavan.

217. {G} "Let the Second Pillar of The Holy Sanctuary of your Religion be The Way of your Religion, which shall include this New Covenant, The Four Pillars, The Four Treasures, and The Four Cornerstones of Freedom. Let the Second Pillar of The Holy Sanctuary of your Religion also be all that I and My Prophets, Saints, Buddhas, Saviors and Avataras have taught unto thee and all that you shall choose of your own Free Choosing to teach to others. And let this Second Pillar of The Holy Sanctuary of your Religion be called Dharma.

218. {G} "Let the Third Pillar of The Holy Sanctuary of your Religion be My Holy Community of all who have taken up your Religion and received your Holy Initiation and The Four Treasures into their hearts, minds and lives. And let The Third Pillar of The Holy Sanctuary of your Religion be called Sangha.

219. {G} "Let the Fourth Pillar of The Holy Sanctuary of your Religion be the Holy Cause of fulfilling The One Purpose and bringing The Age of My Pure Divine Truth into fullness for The Self-Realization, Salvation and Liberation of all Souls for all time. And let this Fourth Pillar of The Holy Sanctuary be called Satya Yuga.

220. {G} "Let The Foundation of The Holy Sanctuary of your Religion have Four Cornerstones. Let these be called The Four Cornerstones of Freedom.

221. {G} "Let the First Cornerstone be The One Purpose. Let the Second Cornerstone be The One Requirement. Let the Third Cornerstone be The Two Rules. And, let the Fourth Cornerstone of Freedom be The One Instruction. Let these be The Heart of your Holy Religion, which is My own Pure Divine Truth and no other.

222. {G} "Let The One Purpose of your Religion be to give your Holy Initiation and My Supreme Promise of Universal Salvation and Liberation to all Souls; teach all Souls The Truth, The Life and The Way that fulfills My Promise, as I have given it this day through you; and build a Holy Community of Enlightened Faithful Believers who will love one another, cherish one another, protect one another, defend one another and help one another to live The Truth, The Life and The Way that fulfills My Supreme Promise and attain Self-Realization, Salvation and Liberation within this life or at its end and Perfect Final Union with Me at this life's end; and bring forth The Age of My Pure Divine Truth on earth for the Salvation and Liberation of all Souls.

223. {G} "Let The One Requirement of your Religion be that whosoever would take up your Religion shall receive My Supreme Promise and New Covenant through your Holy Initiation - by whatever means you shall require of him - and follow you

to the end of this life. And, let it be that whosoever would receive your Holy Initiation and My Promise and New Covenant, shall accept the whole of this, My Eternal Universal Religion, as I give it unto all Souls through you, into his heart, mind and life and follow you and this Religion I have given unto you and unto all Souls through you, to the end of this life. And let it be that he shall accept, love, protect and defend all others of The Faithful as his Brothers and Sisters, as though they had been born of the same blood. For all who receive your Holy Initiation shall be reborn anew in Me through thee.

224. {G} "Let The First Rule of your Religion be: 'Love The One Universal God with all of your heart, all of your mind and all of your Spirit; Love yourself and one another even as you love God; and accept, love and revere all of God's Prophets, Saints, Buddhas, Saviors and Avataras alike, without being bound to accept what has been said or written about them.' Let this be called The Rule of Divine Love.

225. {G} "Let The Second Rule of your Religion be: 'Seek, find and live by The Inner Divine Inspiration, Insight, Guidance and Revelation of The One Universal God and The Friend, and the counsel of your own True and Essential Conscience within The Secret Inner Sanctuary of your Heart, according to My One Instruction, in all things, great and small.' Let this be called The Rule of Divine Guidance.

226. {G} "Let The One Instruction of your Religion be: 'With your Heart and Mind firmly set on Seeking The Highest Truth; Call Upon Me to become active in Spirit within The Secret Inner Sanctuary of your Heart by holding My Presence within your mind and calling out within your Heart 'Bhagavan Ji! Bhagavan Ji! Bhagavan Ji!' Ask for and open yourself to The Inner Divine Inspiration, Insight, Guidance and Revelation of Paratpara, The One Universal God of Countless Names and Forms and The Friend and your own True and Essential Conscience. Take Refuge in The Four Pillars of Bhagavan, Dharma, Sangha and Satya Yuga and enter into The Secret Inner Sanctuary of your Heart through the repetition of My Holy Dharma Mantra 'Jai Bhagavan Ji!' (Jay Bhag-wan Gee). Immerse yourself in The Divine Ocean of Paratpara's Supreme Truth and Being therein, like a drop of water in The Sea and dwell steadily therein, like a candle flame in a still place, INJIA (Instantaneously Non-Judgmentally Insightfully Aware) and accepting of whatever comes, while it is coming, whatever lingers, while it is lingering and whatever goes, while it is going; Speaking that which is right to be Spoken when it is right to Speak it; Doing that which is right to be Done when it is right to Do it. Offer each part and the whole of these to Paratpara in the Sacrificial Fire within The Secret Inner Sanctuary of your Heart at each instant and receive whatever returns to you as Divine Gifts, given unto you by Paratpara and The Friend for your own Self-Realization and Liberation and the Perfection of The Holy Satya Yuga in this world for The Self-Realization and Liberation of all Souls everywhere for all time. This do, in a spirit of harm to none and benefit to all. And you shall Know The Truth and The Truth shall set you Free.' Let this be called The One Instruction.

227. {G} "Let these Two Rules and One Instruction taken together as one

be called Inner Divine Communion, for whosoever shall do this shall enter, straightaway into Divine Communion with thee and Me.

228. {G} "Let the Foundation of The Holy Sanctuary of your Religion be made up of The Seven Universal Principles of Peace, Love, Understanding, Compassion, Freedom, Truth, and Joy; and the Twelve Great Virtues of Faith, Courage, Honor, Integrity, Strength, Devotion, Discipline, Service, Tolerance, Justice, Wisdom and Charity; and these rules and requirements that I have given unto you in this day.

229. {G} "Remember The Seven Universal Principles by the days of the week: Joy for the first day, Peace for the second day; Love for the third day; Understanding for the fourth day; Compassion for the fifth day; Freedom for the sixth day; and Truth for the seventh day;

230. {G} "Remember The Twelve Great Virtues by the months of your year as measured by the calendar of the people in this age: Faith for the first month; Courage for the second month; Honor for the third month; Integrity for the fourth month; Strength for the fifth month; Devotion for the sixth month; Discipline for the seventh month; Service for the eighth month; Tolerance for the ninth month; Justice for the tenth month; Wisdom for the eleventh month; and Charity for the twelfth month.

231. {G} "No one other than you, who are My own Being and Radiance sent forth by Me into this world, shall add unto your Teachings or your Religion, which is My own Eternal Universal Religion of Holy Adhyatma-Yoga-Dharma, or take away from these any least thing. Neither shall any other than you, claim to receive My Inner Divine Inspiration, Insight, Guidance and Revelation for thy Religion which is My Eternal Universal Religion or The Holy Community of Thy Faithful Believers which is, verily, My Holy Community. For, while I freely give My Inner Divine Inspiration, Insight, Guidance and Revelation unto all Souls who receive your Holy Initiation and take up your Religion and Keep Faith with thee and Me, for themselves and their own lives and the worldly realm alone; unto thee and thee alone shall I give my Inner Divine Inspiration, Insight, Guidance and Revelation for My Eternal Universal Religion and The Holy Community of My Enlightened Faithful Believers. Let it be known by all that, other than thee and that one you shall appoint when you leave this world of Creation and return Home to Me and dwell in The Spiritual Realm, any who shall claim to receive My Inner Divine Inspiration, Insight, Guidance and Revelation for this, My Eternal Universal Religion or The Holy Community of The Enlightened Faithful Believers, is a charlatan and a liar and shall be expelled to wander this world in darkness until he shall see the error of his ways and repent.

232. {G} "Let no one place unnecessary burdens upon the people, but let The Way of My Eternal Universal Religion be always open and free of all needless obstacles.

233. {G}"Upon this Foundation shall you and those who would follow you, build The House of your Religion which is My Own Eternal Religion. For it is upon this Foundation within The Holy Sanctuary of your Religion that each Soul who receives your Holy Initiation and My Promise and

takes up your Religion shall play out the drama of his life in this world, through your Religion, of his own Free Choosing.

234. {G} "Let there be Four Treasures within The Holy Sanctuary of your Religion, with one Treasure Chest beside each of The Four Pillars and Four Cornerstones.

235. {G} "Let the First Treasure be My Promise of Self-Realization, Salvation and Liberation that I have given unto all Souls through thee in this day.

236. {G} "Let the Second Treasure be The True Enlightenment that I instill in The Heart of each Soul who receives your Holy Initiation.

237. {G} "Let the Third Treasure be My Power For Good That Can Do No Wrong, such that each who has it can extend it and flow it to any person, place or thing and Good will be done. But that no one shall be able to use it to do harm to any.

238. {G} "And, let the Fourth Treasure be your Ordination and My own that gives the Power and Authority to all who receive it to give The True Enlightenment of your Holy Initiation and these Four Treasures to another in your Name and My Own. For, whosoever receives your Holy Ordination receives My Own. And unto whoever he shall give your Holy Initiation, let it be that you shall give it through him. And it shall be as that Soul received it directly from thee and Me.

239. {G} "Even as I have prepared you a Seat within The Secret Inner Sanctuary of every Soul's Heart, let your Seat be placed in the center of The Foundation, between the two rearward Pillars. Let this be called The Friend's Teaching Seat.

240. {G} "Place therein, at your right hand, this Holy Book of My Eternal Universal Religion; that all who seek to Know The Truth shall find it therein and be set free.

241. {G} "Place therein, directly before you a Sacred Flame which has been made Holy by offering it unto Me in true surrender and self-sacrifice; that from this Sacred Flame, all Souls may receive the Blessing of The Divine Fire of My Spirit.

242. {G} "Place therein, to your right hand, a vessel of Holy Water that has been made Holy by offering it to Me in true surrender and self-sacrifice; that from this vessel all Souls may receive the Blessing of The Holy Water of Life and drink deep of My Spirit.

243. {G} "Sell not your Holy Initiation and My Promise or your Holy Religion which is My Own. Instead, wherever there shall be a Holy Sanctuary of your Religion, place therein a Begging Bowl to your left hand and let all who are your Faithful and My Own and all others who come unto you, place their offering therein. From that which is given unto you, shall you and those you Ordain fill your worldly needs.

244. {G} "Truly, My Beloved, it is the nature of this, My Creation, that all who live must live by the sweat of their brow and the sacrifices of others. Let, therefore, those who would follow you and fulfill this New Covenant and My Supreme Promise of Universal Salvation and Liberation, be your protector and your support.

245. {G} "Let not this burden fall unjustly upon any who follow you. But let each of your Faithful tithe at least two percent, or all that he can do the best he can do, of his good unto you and Me, for your support and the support of this Holy Cause and Mission for which I have Awakened within you and Ordained you and sent you forth into this world. By this means, shall you fill the worldly needs of those who serve Me through you with the whole of their bodies, minds and Spirit.

246. {G} "Accept whatever gifts are given by The Faithful, without requirements or attachments. Accept no gifts that are given with requirements or attachments. But let not any of The Faithful tithe either more or less than that portion which is appointed to all; that the poor may not suffer grievous burdens; and your Mission and The Holy Community of The Faithful shall not come to depend only upon the great wealth given by those I have blessed with riches.

247. {G} "Let no man or woman be kept from thee or Me by want of wealth alone. Those who have not worldly wealth of which to tithe, let them tithe of what they have to give and in such measure as they can give it.

248. {G} "Place upon The Teaching Seat, none other than your own Presence, in Spirit, that those who seek shall find thee; and Me through thee; and they shall fulfill this New Covenant and attain Perfect Final Union with Me at the end of this life.

249. {G} "Let there be Three Steps that lead up to The Holy Sanctuary of your Religion and, yes, even back into the world from it.

250. {G} "Let one side of these three steps be called The Three Steps to Right Action. Let the other side of them be called The Three Duties.

251. {G} "Let the forward face of the top most step be called Divine Guidance and its upward surface be called The First Sacred Duty. For this top most step is taken by fulfilling The Two Rules according to The One Instruction; and its Sacred Duty is fulfilled by Preserving the whole of thy Supreme Holy Religion, which is Mine own, in all of its purity.

252. {G} "Let the forward face of the middle step be called God-given Intelligence and its upward surface be called The Second Sacred Duty. For this middle step is taken by exercising your God-given Intelligence on what is gained from the First Step; and its Sacred Duty is fulfilled by Practicing the whole of this, thy Supreme Holy Religion, which is Mine own, in all of its purity.

253. {G} "Let the forward face of the bottom most step be called Free Choice; and its upward surface be called The Third Sacred Duty. For the bottom step is taken by making a Free Choice for which you can and will be personally responsible; and its Duty is fulfilled by Propagating the whole of this, thy Supreme Holy Religion which is Mine own, in all of its purity.

254. {G} "Let, therefore, the Three Steps to Right Action be: to practice Soul Searching and Truth Saying for Right Living through Inner Divine Communion by The Two Rules according to The One Instruction in

all things great and small; to exercise the full measure of your God-given Intelligence on what you receive therein; and to make a Free Choice for which you can and will be personally responsible, that is in full harmony and unity with this My Eternal Universal Religion, as I give it forth through My Awakened One, The Friend, in this day.

255. {G} "And, let The Three Sacred Duties be: To Preserve the whole of thy Supreme Holy Religion, which is Mine own, in all of its purity; to Practice the whole of this, thy Supreme Holy Religion, which is Mine own Eternal Universal Religion, in all of its purity; and to Propagate the whole of this, thy Supreme Holy Religion which is Mine own, in all of its purity.

256. {G} "Let these Two Rules, One Instruction, Three Steps to Right Action and Three Sacred Duties be called Soul-Searching, Truth Saying and Right Living; and make this the heart of the Practice of your Religion which is My Eternal Universal Religion."

257. And Paratpara, The One Universal God said unto me:

258. {G} "What does it mean to follow you to the end of this life and fulfill My Promise, My Beloved? It means that a Soul shall accept the whole of The Holy Sanctuary of My Eternal Universal Religion.

259. {G} "It means that a Soul shall embrace The One Purpose, fulfill The One Requirement and live a life of Soul-Searching, Truth Saying and Right Living through Inner Divine Communion with thee and Me by The Two Rules according to The One Instruction.

260. {G} "It means that a Soul will decide all matters of importance and the course of his very life through The Three Steps to Right Action; Keep and courageously fulfill The Three Sacred Duties; make the Seven Universal Principles and Twelve Great Virtues the Foundation of his life; and tithe regularly of his good unto you and this Holy Mission for which I have Ordained and Commissioned you; for My sake alone, without thought of payment or personal gain.

261. {G} "Let all Souls who would follow you and fulfill My Promise and this New Covenant, gather together regularly on that day called Joy, with their Brothers and Sisters in Spirit and others who are sincere, for Soul-Searching, Truth-Saying and Right-Living through the doing of Inner Divine Communion by The Two Rules according to The One Instruction; and for sharing their lives, their testimonies and Friendship with one another.

262. {G} "Let them Gather together, also, in Inner Divine Communion in Spirit, with their Brothers and Sisters and such others who are sincere, within The Spiritual Realm, in that time where dreams and dreamless sleep consume mortal body and mind. And therein, Commune in Spirit with Me, yourself, all of My Prophets, Saints, Buddhas, Saviors and Avatars and one another. Whatever they receive therein, let them share that with one another.

263. {G} "Let them also gather together with their Brothers and Sisters, on that day called Understanding, for Soul-Searching and Truth-Saying alone.

Therein, let each of The Faithful speak the Truth, the Whole Truth and nothing but the Truth, of his own Soul-Searching and any smallest thing in which he has deceived or wronged another.

264. {G} "Through these Gatherings, and whatsoever others you shall commend them to perform; let them give and receive support and encouragement, help one another and accept help in living The Truth, The Life and The Way that fulfills My Supreme Promise of Universal Salvation and Liberation.

265. {G} "Let every Soul who would follow you, work alone and in Harmony and Unity with his Brothers and Sisters of The Way, to accomplish your Purpose and carry your Holy Mission to Victory throughout the World.

266. {G} "This is The Truth, The Life and The Way, nothing more is required by Me, but whatsoever more you shall require of them, that too shall become The Truth, The Life and The Way as I had Ordained it Myself. For you are My Awakened One, whom I send forth into the darkness as My Own Truth, Life and Light made manifest for the Salvation and Liberation of the World."

267. And I cried out, for I had never heard such wondrous things, "My God! My God! Thy Will is my Will and I choose for You. I seek neither fame nor fortune. I seek not to call attention of Souls to myself, O God, but to be as fingers pointing toward Thee. Tell me, what shall I say unto those who seek my advice?"

268. And The One Universal God said:

269. {G} "Say unto them these things:

270. {G} 'Accept the whole of The Holy Sanctuary of The Eternal Universal Religion of The One Universal God.

271. {G} 'Embrace The One Purpose as your own and fulfill The One Requirement.

272. {G} 'Give My Holy Initiation and God's Supreme Promise of Universal Salvation and Liberation to all Souls. Teach all Souls The Truth, The Life and The Way that fulfills God's Supreme Promise as God has given it this day through me. Work without measure to build a Holy Community of my Enlightened Faithful Believers who will love one another, cherish one another, protect one another, defend one another and help one another to live The Truth, The Life and The Way that fulfills God's Supreme Promise and attain Self-Realization, Salvation and Liberation within this life or at its end and Perfect Final Union with God at this life's end. Love, cherish, protect and defend your Brothers and Sisters. Seek to attain Self-Realization and Liberation within this life; and do all, without measure, to help me bring forth The Age of God's Pure Divine Truth on earth, for The Salvation and Liberation of all Souls.

273. {G} 'Live a life of Soul-Searching, Truth Saying and Right Living by keeping Inner Divine Communion by The Two Rules according to The One Instruction every morning before beginning worldly activity and every evening before taking sleep.

274. {G} 'Take whatever Inner Divine Inspiration, Insight, Guidance and

Revelation you receive from within The Secret Inner Sanctuary of your Hearts into your minds and your lives and decide all matters of importance and the course of your very lives through The Three Steps to Right Action.

275. {G} 'Keep and courageously fulfill The Three Sacred Duties.

276. {G} 'Make the Seven Universal Principles and Twelve Great Virtues the Foundation of the Sanctuary of your lives.

277. {G} 'Tithe regularly of your good unto me and this Holy Mission without thought of payment, personal power or gain, as God has Ordained.

278. {G} 'It is the nature of God's Creation, that all who live must live by the sweat of their brow and the sacrifices of others. Let, therefore, those who would follow me and fulfill this, God's New Covenant and Supreme Promise of Universal Salvation and Liberation, be my protectors and my support.

279. {G} 'Let not this burden fall unjustly upon any who follow me. But let each tithe the same portion of his good unto me for my support and the support of this Holy Cause and Mission for which The One Universal God has Awakened within this One and Ordained me and that of those who serve God through me with the whole of their bodies, minds and Spirit.

280. {G} 'Let no man who follows me tithe either more or less than that portion which is appointed to all; that the poor may not suffer grievous burdens and the rich may not seek to influence our course or the course of our Holy Cause or Community thereby.

281. {G} 'Gather together, in body, mind and Spirit, with your Brothers and Sisters and such others who are sincere, on the day called Joy. And therein, do Soul-Searching and Truth-Saying for Right Living through Inner Divine Communion by The Two Rules according to The One Instruction; and share your lives, your testimonies and your Friendship, one with another alike.

282. {G} 'Gather together, in body, mind and Spirit, with your Brothers and Sisters and such others who are sincere, also on that day called Joy at least once in every four passings of it, for Worship, Prayer and, where there is one who has been Ordained to Consecrate it and administer it, for Sharing The Holy Water of Life.

283. {G} 'Gather, together with your Brothers and Sisters, on that day called Understanding, for Soul-Searching and Truth-Saying alone. Therein, let each of you speak the Truth, the Whole Truth and nothing but the Truth, of his own Soul-Searching and any smallest thing in which you have deceived or wronged another.

284. {G} 'Gather, also, together in Inner Divine Communion in Spirit, with your Brothers and Sisters and such others who are sincere, within The Spiritual Realm, in that time where dreams and dreamless sleep consume your mortal body and mind. And therein, Commune in Spirit with The One Universal God, myself, all of God's Prophets, Saints, Buddhas, Saviors and Avataras and one another. Whatever you receive therein, share that with one another.

285. {G} 'In your Holy Community and in your gatherings, give and accept support and encouragement; help one another to live The Truth, The Life and The Way that fulfills God's Promise of Universal Salvation and Liberation and wins Self-Realization and True Salvation and Liberation and Perfect Final Union with God at this life's end.

286. {G} 'Work alone and in Harmony and Unity with your Brothers and Sisters of The Way, to accomplish this Divine Purpose and carry this Holy Mission to Victory throughout the World.

287. {G} 'This is, verily, The Truth, The Life and The Way.'"

288. {G} "Having done this, advise those who would live rightly, in the ways that the Truly Wise accept and observe. Encourage each Soul who would follow you and fulfill My Promise of Self-Realization, Salvation and Liberation, to live each part of his life by Soul Searching, Truth Saying and Right Living through Inner Divine Communion by The Two Rules according to The One Instruction. And, having done this, let each Soul exercise such Intelligence as I have given unto him and choose, of his own Free Will, what he shall and shall not say or do in this world, in harmony and unity with this, My Eternal Universal Religion; as I have given it unto all Souls through My Awakened and Ordained One, Adhyatma Bhagavan Sri Babajhan Al-Kahlil The Friend. Let each Soul who follows your Religion, always stand ready, willing and able to take full responsibility for whatever he shall choose.

289. {G} "Know that the Truly Wise observe and accept these prohibitions.

290. {G} "Use not The Name of The Lord, your God, vainly to satisfy your earthly wants and desires. Neither condemn others or confuse the Hearts and Minds of your Brothers and Sisters with vain mouthings of needless requirements and prohibitions.

291. {G} "Let man's laws be man's laws and God's Laws be God's Laws. For all Beings, large and small, follow My Design of Creation and return Home to The One I AM THAT I AM, according to the results of their Actions and their True Knowing of their Oneness with Me.

292. {G} "Let not the vain and ignorant, who sleep the sleep of Duality and Illusion, lay their many Prohibitions before you in My Name. But, follow what is given of That I AM THAT I AM and My Awakened One The Friend.

293. {G} "Hold not anything higher or more dear than attainment of direct experience of your Oneness and Identity with Me.

294. {G} "Bear not False Witness, neither shall you compel another to bear False Witness.

295. {G} "Compel no man or woman or child to take up My Eternal Universal Religion of Holy Adhyatma-Yoga-Dharma by force, threat, coercion, intimidation, violence or deception, but by each Soul's Free Choosing alone.

296. {G} "Use not My Name vainly to satisfy earthly wants and desires,

or to gain dominion or mastery over your Brothers or Sisters.

297. {G} "Deny Me not in any of My Creation from the greatest even unto the very least.

298. {G} "Spread not Ignorance, Delusion or Illusion, neither encourage these in others or in the world.

299. {G} "Seek not your reward in this world; or the approval or the admiration of the unenlightened within it. For, this world and the unenlightened are caught in the web of the Ignorance, Darkness, Chaos, Confusion, Illusion and Destruction of this Kali Age; and they admire and reward only that which serves it. Know that your reward is not in this world, but comes from far beyond it. Therefore, seek only the approval, admiration and rewards that come from That I AM THAT I AM, My Awakened One, The Friend, and from those who are most faithful to these and My Eternal Universal Religion; and be satisfied in this. For all that is of this world, is temporary and passes quickly away, but that which I give, is everlasting.

300. {G} "Do not alter or pervert these, My Words and Teachings. Neither shall you interpret them to another.

301. {G} "Know that My Eternal Universal Religion is a Living Religion. So long as My Awakened One lives among you it shall not be finished. For, it is the way of this, My Creation that it is ever changing; and that which he gives unto you later, shall always stand above that which was given before.

302. {G} "Let, therefore, no man or woman say unto The Friend of all Souls, 'This you said before.' Or, yet, 'This which you now say stands against what you said earlier.' Instead, accept that which is given unto you by him, as it is given, in faith and be of good cheer.

303. {G} "Yield not unto temptation and be turned away from The Way Home to Realization of Oneness and Identity with Me; Neither shall you distract or divert any creature from The Way or bar any Being's Way Home to Me.

304. {G} "Seek not to divide My Awakened One, whom I send forth with this, My New Covenant unto Man, from this New Covenant or My Eternal Universal Religion which I embody in him; for this shall be one of the greatest crimes against Me, this New Covenant and My Eternal Universal Religion. Neither shall you discourage My Faithful or seek to divide them from My Awakened One or from one another, for this shall be the next greatest of crimes.

305. {G} "Do not deceive, harm, degrade or discourage My Faithful.

306. {G} "Believe not, neither set forth the belief that The One Universal God, I AM THAT I AM, is limited to any time, place, or object. For, though I Am in All and All exists in Me, no one is there that can limit Me; and, to attempt to do so is to fall under the spell of Idolatry and Ignorance. For, I Am All-Present equally in all; save that, wherever two or more are gathered together in The Name of My Awakened and Ordained One, The Friend of all Souls, there shall My Presence and the Presence of The Friend be made Known unto them.

307. {G} "When the Vain and Ignorant shall seek to place the yoke and burden of their beliefs or Requirements upon you, saying that they are Mine; Know, without doubt or reservation, that the wise in Spirit accept these observances:

308. {G} "Accept The Holy Sanctuary of My Eternal Universal Religion; Embrace The One Purpose; and Fulfill The One Requirement.

309. {G} "Live a life of Soul-Searching, Truth-Saying and Right-Living through Inner Divine Communion by The Two Rules according to The One Instruction, take The Three Steps to Right Action, keep The Three Sacred Duties and live The Truth, The Life and The Way that fulfills My Promise The Friend of all Souls has won for you.

310. {G} "Make The Goal and Purpose of your life and actions direct experience of Oneness and Identity with Me and That Beloved Universal I AM THAT I AM which you are.

311. {G} "Make your whole Life a Worship, a Meditation and a living Self-Sacrifice by surrendering your actions and the fruits of your actions unto Me through My Awakened and Ordained One, The Friend of All Souls, in a Spirit of True Self-Sacrifice without doubt or reservation. Consecrate all that you would eat and drink by surrendering it unto Me in a Spirit of True Self-Sacrifice before eating and drinking.

312. {G} "Have Love and Compassion for All Beings, even as The Friend has sacrificed Perfect Final Union with Me out of his boundless Love and Compassion for you.

313. {G} "Bear True Witness of this New Covenant unto all people and bring all Beings to My Awakened One, The Friend of all Souls, and through him, to Realization and Knowledge of their Oneness and Identity with Me.

314. {G} "Honor all of the Spiritual and Worldly Ancestors of your Lineage and your Guardian. Know that your Spiritual lineage begins in Me, goes out through all of My Prophets, Saints, Buddhas, Saviors and Avataras and comes to you through that one within whom I have Awakened and Ordained to end this Kali Age and bring forth the Satya Age of My Pure Divine Truth on Earth, Maitreya Adhyatma Bhagavan Sri Babajhan Al-Kahlil The Friend. Though My Supreme Promise comes to you only through My Awakened and Ordained One, The Friend, let it be that you shall include in your Lineage, also, that Blessed Maitreyian through whom you received The Friend's Holy Initiation and My Supreme Promise, your Guardian. Know that your Worldly Lineage begins with the very first Life I set forth upon this, My Creation and comes to you through your mother and father and their parents and, verily, their parents' parents, unto the Beginning.

315. {G} "Make yourself a Holy Temple of My Truth and a Guardian of The Way. Preserve and protect The Friend, My Eternal Universal Religion of Adhyatma-Yoga-Dharma and these Teachings I give unto you through My Awakened One. Keep them Pure and True in word and in meaning. Watch over and protect each Brother and Sister within the Community of My Faithful.

316. {G} "Be you, Maitreyian, a Soldier of The Clear Light of My Pure Divine Truth. Make The

Friend's Religion your Religion. Let ignorance, darkness and untruth be your enemies. Destroy ignorance, darkness and untruth and replace them with The Clear Light of My Pure Divine Truth, wherever you find them. Give no quarter and ask none. Never give up.

317. {G} "Tithe at least two percent, or all that you can do the best you can do, of your good unto My Awakened and Ordained One and Me, for his support and the support of this Holy Cause and Mission for which I have Awakened within him and Ordained him and sent him forth into this world. For it is by this alone that he shall fulfill his worldly needs, the needs of this Holy Cause and Mission and, the worldly needs of those who serve Me through him with the whole of their bodies, minds and Spirit.

318. {G} "Keep your own counsel and do not interpret My Words or the Teachings of My Awakened One, The Friend of all Souls, for another.

319. {G} "Be true to the nature which I have given unto you. Better is it that a man meet his death in fidelity to his own nature than to win vain glory in seeking to live by the nature of another."

320. And I said unto That I AM THAT I AM, "I have known Thee directly. But how shall the unknowers and doubters know the Truth of Thee and me and this Covenant which You have made through me in this day? And men constantly seek after name and form in this world as objects of their Worship. When men ask after me what outer form they may make for their Worship of The One Universal God, what, then, shall I give unto them?"

And Paratpara, The One Universal God of all Creation said unto me:

321. {G} "If any man or woman will set prejudice aside and hold your Presence, Beloved One, steadily in his heart and mind like a candle flame in a still place, I, the One Universal God, I AM THAT I AM, will reveal unto that Soul: that you are the One in whom I have Awakened and who I have Ordained to be The Maitreya, Friend of All Souls, bringer of The Age of My New Covenant and The Age of My Pure Divine Truth and that your Mission is Mine and Mine alone and is True. This I shall do in such manner that all doubt and reservation shall be cast out of that Soul's heart and mind and he will join you in The Holy Cause for which I have sent you forth into this world. And, through you, I will make him My own and a Solider of The Light of My Pure Divine Truth.

322. {G} "And, when men ask what outer form they may make for their Worship, give unto them this Holy Shrine."

323. And The One God showed unto me a beautiful Shrine, having a lower white base measuring eighty inches wide by thirty-six inches deep by four inches in height. And set upon this base and aligned to its back and its center and covered with maroon cloth was an upper base, measuring sixty inches wide by twenty-four inches in depth by four inches in height.

324. And upon the lower base there were three candles, one placed in the center to the front, and the other two placed, one at each of the forward corners.

The Holy Book of Destiny

325. As I faced the Holy Shrine, there was, centered between the left most candle and the center candle a small water pot and a cup. And there was, centered between the right most candle and the center candle a conch horn.

326. Upon the upper base, at its rearward center, there was a Teacher's Seat covered with maroon cloth. And, as I faced The Holy Shrine, there was, to the left and forward of the Teacher's Seat, a Holy Book of Destiny. And to the right of The Teacher's Seat, there was a small bright bell strung upon a small string of beads, such that it would just fit around a large man's wrist. And before it and to its right was a humble wooden begging bowl.

327. Behind these two bases, there hung a large banner made of cloth; of brightest blue in its center and having a crimson border surrounding it. And the blue of the banner measured thirty-four inches wide by eighty inches in height; and the crimson borders were six inches in width on all four sides. And the banner was suspended by a wooden dowel at the top and the bottom and they measured one inch in diameter.

328. At the top of the banner, and in the very center of it, there was cut a v-shape and in the center of that a single hole had been made through the wooden dowel that held it. And through that hole and tied at the back of the dowel in a knot, there was a string that descended ten inches where it joined another string to form a triangle that was nine and one-half inches to a side; the ends of which were tied to a small dowel, three-quarters of one inch in diameter and twelve inches in length that had been split neatly in two. And the string which held the dowel together had been wrapped around each end exactly three times.

329. Between the two halves of this dowel, there was held the top most edge of a Sacred Scroll measuring ten and one-half inches wide and thirty-four inches in length, upon which was written The Creed and Holy Doctrine which The One Universal God had ordained for all who would receive His Promise and follow me to its fulfillment. And as I faced the Holy Shrine, there was, upon the lower left corner of The Sacred Scroll a golden seal looking as a sunburst there upon. At the bottom edge of The Sacred Scroll, there was another dowel that was like the one above, holding the bottom edge of the Scroll. And this dowel, too, had three wrappings of string at either side of it.

330. As I had no tools with which to measure these things, I said unto my God, "How shall I come to know the measurements of this Holy Shrine? And, what shall be done if it is needed to be larger or smaller than this?"

331. And Paratpara Awakened my knowledge to these measurements

as I gazed upon The Holy Shrine and said unto me:

332. {G} "Let all men make this Holy Shrine to be of such size as fulfills their needs; save that in changing its size they shall change all measurements alike and in proportion."

333. And I said unto The One Universal God, "And what, my God, of those who move about from place to place, who are being persecuted, or otherwise have not the means to build this Holy Shrine?"

334. And The One Universal God said unto me:

335. {G} "Let such as these lay upon the ground a covering. And upon that covering lay down a white cloth measuring eighty inches wide by thirty-six inches deep. Lay upon this white cloth, at its back and center, a maroon cloth, measuring sixty inches wide by twenty-four inches in depth.

336. {G} "Upon the white cloth, let them place three candles, one placed in the center to the front, and the other two placed, one at each of the forward corners. Place, as you face the Holy Shrine, centered between the left most candle and the center candle a small water pot and, centered between the right most candle and the center candle a conch horn.

337. {G} "Upon the upper base, at its rearward center, let them place your Teacher's Seat covered with maroon cloth or a maroon cloth folded with four folds when no seat can be found. As you face The Holy Shrine, place, to the left and forward of the Teacher's Seat, a Holy Book of Destiny and to the right of The Teacher's Seat, a small bright bell strung upon a small string of beads, such that it would just fit around a large man's wrist.

338. {G} "Let them make this Holy Shrine to be of such size as fulfills their needs; save that in changing its size they shall change all measurements alike and in proportion.

339. {G} "If any of these Sacred Articles cannot be found, let them place whatsoever is not unclean, such as would symbolize these Sacred Articles in these places."

340. And I said unto the One God, "How shall they, who follow me to Thee Worship before this Holy Shrine?"

341. And The One God said unto me:

342. {G} "Call them to Worship before this Holy Shrine in whatsoever ways you shall choose, my Beloved, but let no man or woman other than you, within whom I have Awakened and Ordained and named Adhyatma Bhagavan Sri Babajhan Al-Kahlil The Friend, sit upon the Teacher's Seat. Instead, let those who teach and preach for you do so before this Holy Shrine and to its right side as you would look upon it from afar. For, you are My Awakened and Ordained One, and as you call them and bid them Worship, I too, shall have done so."

343. And I said unto The One Universal God, "How can I give unto them my Self-Realizations and Self-Sacrifices, that they may be Blessed as you have Blessed me in this day?" And The One Universal God said unto me:

344. {G} "No man can give his Self-Realization or Self-Sacrifices to

another, My Beloved. But in answer to your Compassion, let it be that whosoever shall drink of Holy Water that has been consecrated by you or one you have Ordained for that purpose; and received from you or one you have Ordained to give it; shall share in your Being and your Spirit and the inner knowledge of your Self-Realization and Self-Sacrifices that is beyond words, shall be with him, thereby.

345. {G} "Tell my People, that this, which I have spoken unto you this day, is The Work and The Way. There is no other, save what you shall require of them! Tell them: "When you do God's Work, be quick! When you do God's Work, be strong! When you do God's Work, be bold, courageous and free of pride and arrogance. When you do God's Work, Be Truthful! When you do God's Work, cast aside all doubt and reservation and be filled with Faith and Confidence and Certainty!"

346. And my Spiritual eyes were opened and before me, I beheld countless multitudes and my Heart was opened and The One Universal God moved me to speak and I said unto them:

347. "This is The Gift of Paratpara, The One Universal God Unmanifest, That Absolute One without a Second, given for The Salvation and Liberation of All Beings.

348. "Covet not The Gift. Cast it not before those who would deny and degrade it; neither shall you hide it away from those who thirst after Knowledge and Realization of God. For no man lights up a Lamp only to have it hidden away. As you give this, God's Supreme Gift and Eternal Universal Religion, unto others, so shall it be given unto you, and you shall receive in such measure as you have given. Truly, whosoever shall be ashamed of God or God's Eternal Universal Religion or His Chosen One or any other of His Prophets, Saints, Buddhas, Saviors and Avataras or My Pure Divine Truth of Holy Adhyatma-Yoga-Dharma or My Holy Community or hoard God's Supreme Gift or Eternal Universal Religion, while within this World, shall find no Home with God beyond it; but shall return to it time after time to endure its Birth, Suffering, Sorrow, Pain, and Death over and over until he shall know the error of his ways and repent.

349. "Go out among those who sleep The Sleep of The Living Dead. Awaken them! Profess The One God who is All In All, bear True Witness to this New Covenant; and Initiate all Souls in My Name and in The Name of Paratpara, The One Universal God of Countless Names and Forms Who Is Beyond All Names and Forms, That I AM THAT I AM, who has Ordained and Commissioned this One, even as I, Maitreya Adhyatma Bhagavan Sri Babajhan Al-Kahlil The Friend, have Ordained and Commissioned you.

350. "And when you Profess and when you bear True Witness, speak not with words alone. For words alone are but empty vessels that are easily misunderstood and twisted astray by The Sleeping. When you Profess and when you bear True Witness, call upon me! And I will be there, within The Secret Inner Sanctuary of your Heart and in the still small places within your words; and I will guide them to the very heart and Spirit of the hearer; and your words shall have The Power to lift the Veil of Darkness

from the Spiritual Eyes and Awaken men's Souls.

351. "When you Profess; and when you Bear True Witness; Speak not to the ear of the hearer alone. For I Am within each Being, and only That One I AM THAT I AM that is the True Self of every Soul, can hear The Message of The I That Is All In One and One In All.

352. "Let, then, The Heart of your Heart and The Mind of your Mind reach out and speak unto the Heart and Mind of the hearer.

353. "Let, also, the I within, that is One with Me, speak unto The I within the hearer that I Am also. For, in Truth, you are not two, but One in The One God who is One In All and All In One.

354. "Be you, then, not as two divided; for that, Truly, is the way of The Living Dead. But be instead, as One speaking unto your own Self; for there are no divisions between you but the ignorance and illusions which are born of the darkness of those who sleep The Sleep of The Living Dead.

355. "Ask not for special favors or miracles. For the ways of this dream world are sufficient unto it. Guide your Heart and your Mind and your Spirit, instead, constantly toward direct experience and Realization of Oneness and Identity with That One That I Am. If you were to gain this whole universe and fail to Realize Me, you would have gained nothing. Ask not, then, for the ways of this world to be taken away for your sake; for nothing is there that The One God shall do for you that is not done for any other.

356. "The Prophets, Saints, Buddhas, Saviors and Avataras of all ages have pointed The Way Home, but few are they who take up The Way. I show you The Way. I have opened up The Gate. For I Am The Gate and The Way and The Light upon The Way. But, before The Clear Bright Light will shine forth from you, you must put your own house in order. For, even though this Light is aglow within you now, you Know it not. You are like unto a Lamp whose glass has not yet been polished clean; and because of the dirt thereupon, your Light cannot be seen.

357. "How, then, shall you make your House ready for The Liberation of your Spirit? How shall you wipe clean The Glass of your Life that The Clear Bright Light of That I AM THAT I AM may shine forth into this World?

358. "I say unto you, a deep sleep has settled upon all People making them deaf and blind to The Truth. For The One Universal God has said:

359. {G} "Each man's vision has lost the meaning of My Scripture and the very Life of his Life wanders aimlessly in the wilderness of this World. Greater in numbers grow those who know of words and symbols. But few are they who read The Book of Life I have written within their Hearts and understand The Truth therein.

360. {G} "Even the so-called Religious Ones, the Teachers, Prophets, Preachers, and Seers have become confused. Moved only by fear of man-made demons and devils and false fear of Me resulting from false doctrine and false belief, they create and spread man-made beliefs, calling them My Doctrine and My Truth, and encourage other Sleeping Ones

to vain attempts at Spiritual Progress by raising their voices in empty mouthing of words to no avail; for their understanding of True Religion and Worship is far removed and amiss from the True Meaning.

361. "Therefore, beware, you who would find Salvation and Liberation, for The Way is long and narrow and few are there who walk alone to its end.

362. "Be Awake always, lest you too shall become lulled into the drowsy state and fall into the ways of the Ignorant and sleeping who sleep The Sleep of The Living Dead; and do all that they do for the awe, admiration and approval of their neighbors.

363. "Truly, I say unto you, that they shall realize their fondest desires in this World and shall return into it time after time for the sake of their desires and attachments. But, no rest or peace shall they find. For this whole world is temporary and passing. All things which are put together, must come apart; and within this world, everything changes; nothing remains the same; and each pleasure brings with it, its opposite of pain, sorrow, and suffering even as life in the flesh brings death.

364. "Whatever you are doing, be always Awake unto Me and that One I AM THAT I AM which you are. Upon becoming aware of your body, know: I am more than this body. I AM THAT I AM! Upon becoming aware of your personality, know: I am more than this personality. I AM THAT I AM! Upon becoming aware of your mind, know: I am more than this mind. I AM THAT I AM. While breathing, know: this body is breathing; I am more than this breathing. I AM THAT I AM! While walking, know: this body is walking; I am more than this walking. I AM THAT I AM! While eating, know: this body is eating; I am more than this eating. I AM THAT I AM! While sleeping, know: this body is sleeping; I am more than this sleeping. I AM THAT I AM! While thinking, know: this mind is thinking; I am more than this thinking. I AM THAT I AM! While speaking, know: this body is speaking. I am more than this speaking. I AM THAT I AM. Whatever you do, know, this is being done. I am more than this doing. I AM THAT I AM!"

365. "Seek not after the things of this world that are passing and as hard to hold onto as vapor; but seek, instead, to attain direct experience of God, who is your own True Self, and all else shall be added unto you.

366. "Nothing is there that endures save The Spirit, which you call Soul; for that which you Are is One and Identical with God and no other. This, is the Eternal Treasure which The One God has Awakened within me, making me The Friend of all Souls, to bring unto all Souls.

367. "Whosoever seeks it, shall find it and shall Know The Truth and The Truth shall set him Free, forever. For, whenever any Soul shall know The Truth, The Whole Truth and Nothing But The Truth of anything whatsoever, in that, he shall become free.

368. "Seek, then, That I AM THAT I AM within The Heart of your Heart and The Mind of your Mind that you might Know That I AM THAT I AM is The One True Self of your self and attain The Goal of Liberation even while living in this world.

369. "And when you seek Paratpara, The One Universal God, do not do so publicly out of desire for approval and admiration of others. Neither hide yourself away out of shame or fear of hate or rejection. Instead, be as one balanced upon a razor's edge, falling neither one way or the other. Enter into The Secret Inner Sanctuary of your Heart and let your doing be such that the one on the left will not know what is happening on his right."

370. And Paratpara, The One Universal God, I AM THAT I AM, said unto me:

371. {G} "Meditation, Prayer, Devotion to Me and Surrender of all Actions and their Fruits, and Direct Knowledge of Me; These are the Paths Home to Oneness with Me.

372. {G} "Many are those who make wrong use of My Way to further their own selfish and evil ends. But, I say unto you that the Road is not at fault that the robber does his evil acts upon it. The Road shall be held blameless and suffer not. But the robber shall not be held blameless; and shall suffer the results of his own actions again and again until he sees the error of his ways and repents and turns his face unto Me.

373. {G} "Even so shall The Way be not blamed for man's abuse of it. But each who misuses it shall be held guilty and shall suffer the fruits of his actions again and again until he sees the error and repents and comes Home to Knowledge of his Oneness and Identity with Me.

374. {G} "None of these Roads are so fraught with the hidden dangers of selfishness, pride, desire, and greed as is Prayer.

375. {G} "As Selfless Action seeks Me through Compassion and the surrender of all actions and their fruits; As Meditation seeks Me through watching, listening, and waiting; Even so does Prayer seek after Knowledge of Me through desire and asking. Truly, it is desire that fans the fires of the False Self and makes strong the chains that bind each Being to this World and the Birth, Suffering, Sorrow, Pain, and Death herein. And few are they who do not abuse and misuse this Road Home.

376. {G} "I say unto you that all these Roads, Truly, lead Home to Me. But the Highest of them is Direct Experience and Knowledge of Oneness with Me. Blessed are they who walk upon The Highest Way.

377. {G} "If you would follow the Way of Prayer, be ever cautious and aware, it is a path that is filled with temptation and the selfish rarely attain The Supreme Goal by it.

378. {G} "When you Pray, let not your Prayer become the mouthing of empty words for the sake of fulfilling your earthbound desires and cravings, as do The Living Dead who, knowing Me not, imagine that they must be heard by one who hears only words. Believing Prayer to be but the speaking of words, such as these are as one speaking unto himself in the empty forests of Duality, Darkness, and Ignorance.

379. {G} "Imitate them not! For not one True Thought is thought, but that it is I who think it. Not one Right Feeling is felt, but that I feel it! Not one Right Action is done, nor its Fruit Surrendered, but that it is done and surrendered by Me. For I Am One with

The One who is The True Self within every self's self; there is no other!

380. {G} "When you Pray, turn inward to The Secret Inner Sanctuary of your Heart; and closing your Heart and Mind to all else, seek Therein your own Divine Self, The One God, All In All, who dwells within The Secret Inner Sanctuary of your Heart!

381. {G} "When you Pray, seek not after the things of this World of Illusion that fire can burn and thief can steal and which pass away like vapors in the air. Of desire and attachment to the things of this World is all Birth, Suffering, Sorrow, Pain, and Death born. For nothing is there of this Dream World that remains the same and the companion of all worldly pleasure is the pain of its passing and the sorrow of its loss. Instead, when you pray, throw off desire, greed, attachment, and selfishness. Cast aside your small false self and let your prayer be:

Paratpara!
Beloved Universal
I AM THAT I AM!
My God!
My Beloved!
My One True Self!
Through Thy Holy Initiation
Thou hast revealed
my Oneness with Thee!
I surrender completely unto Thee!
Thy Authority is restored!
Thy Presence has become
manifest within this little self!
I shine forth
by Thy Divine Clear Light!
The division in me is Healed!
I know my Oneness with Thee!
I know Thy Oneness
 in all this that is!
All is made Perfect!
I lack for nothing!

Thou hast consumed my Ignorance
in The Sacred Fire of Thy Presence.
Thou hast led me through the Ordeal!
Through Thy Holy Initiation,
Thou hast revealed
my Oneness with Thee;
and liberated me
from the endless rounds
of birth and death!
From the unreal,
Thou hast led me to The Real!
From darkness,
Thou hast led me to The Light!
From division,
Thou hast led me to Wholeness!
From the temporary,
Thou hast led me to The Eternal!
From death,
Thou hast led me to Immortality!
O Beloved God!
I am One with Thee this moment!
My Doing is One with my Speech!
My Speech is One with my Mind!
My Mind is One with my Heart!
My Heart is One with my Will!
And my Will is One with Thy Will!
Thou hast shattered my prison
of ignorance and false self;
and absorbed me,
in The Ocean of
Thy Infinite Divine Being;
like a drop of water in The Sea!
I know, without doubt or reservation
that Thee and I are not we, but One!
That which Thou Art, I Am!
Thou art my Only True Self;
Majestic!
Splendorous!
Immortal!
There is no I but Thee!
So is it with me!
Om So'ham tat tvam asi!
I Am That, Thou Art That!
Jai Bhagavan Ji!
Victory To That Beloved Universal
I AM THAT I AM
Which Thou Art!"

382. This is The Truth, The Life and The Way, given unto you by The One Universal God, through me, for the Salvation and Liberation of all Souls for all time! That you shall each, of your own direct experience, Know that you are One and Identical with Me and That Absolute One without a Second with whom I Am made One. There is no other Work. There is no other Way that brings Peace born of Certainty and Knowing and through which each may attain Salvation and Liberation without doubt or reservation. For, within all belief there lingers the darkness of doubt and reservation; only in True Knowing does the Clear Bright Light fully illuminate The Way Home!

383. Unto you, who Know That I Am within The Heart of your Heart and The Mind of your Mind and The Self of your self; and have True Knowledge of The Truth of this New Covenant that I bring for the Salvation of all Beings; The Journey is Certain! The Goal is Won! Within this Life or at its end, you shall enter into The Perfect Paradise of Union with The One God who is One In All and All In One; and shall be born into The Grand Illusion no more!

384. This is My Testimony of God's Truth as It has come to pass in Me. This is The Truth, the whole Truth and nothing but the Truth. This is The Life. This is The Way. Know The Truth and be Free! Live The Life and attain Self-Realization, Salvation and Liberation while living in this world. Follow The Way and win Perfect Final Union with The One Universal God of Countless Names and Forms Who Is Beyond All Names and Forms at life's end.

385. And, when you have Freed your Self, turn not away from those who live out their days, birth after birth, in darkness, ignorance and illusion; never knowing that they really are One with That I AM THAT I AM, in Spirit!

386. Instead follow My Example! For I have Sacrificed Perfect Final Union with Paratpara, The One Universal God of Countless Names and Forms Who Is Beyond All Names and Forms and vowed that I shall never again enter into Final Union until the very last Soul shall have awakened and entered before me! No greater Love is there than that a Soul shall sacrifice Final Union and take up yet another Life for the sake of all Beings. For this is the greatest Self-Sacrifice of all!

387. Go forth for me, Beloved Maitreyian. Not as one who is Perfect by earthly measure, as judged by those who are yet earthbound, but as one made Perfect in God. For, the character of each man's Faith is a matter that is between that Soul and God, for no man hath the wisdom to judge such things; but God, who is within yet beyond all, Knows every man's heart.

388. I have Awakened and Realized my Oneness with The One Universal God, I AM THAT I AM. You and I are not two, but One. As I Am, so thou art. Go forth for me, into the darkness of this world, Proclaiming and bearing True Witness to This, The New Covenant of The One Universal God. Raise up among the people of this earth a new Race of God-Realized men and women who shall multiply and cover the Earth and Awaken all Beings to their Oneness and Identity with The One Universal God and no other.

389. Having found a Soul whom God's Divine Guidance and my own have told you is worthy to receive my Holy Initiation and God's Supreme Promise of Universal Salvation and Liberation: Teach that Soul The Truth of Universal God's Supreme Promise and New Covenant and the meaning of my Holy Initiation. Then, instruct him in The Way to become God's Chosen Maitreyian and a Soldier of The Light and The Way that will lead him to Consummation of my Holy Initiation and win him the Gift of Self-Realization within this life and Perfect Final Union with The One Universal God, That I Am That I Am, at the end of his life.

390. For I tell you now that every unenlightened Soul begins by disbelieving. And so long as a Soul is content in his disbelief, that Soul is the slave of The Force of Darkness and is lost and he shall ride the endless wheel of birth, life, suffering sorrow, fear, pain, sickness, old age, death and rebirth forever until he shall know The Truth and be set free.

391. Be simple and direct in all things. Do not argue or debate philosophy or theology as do the scholars who make much of their learning. Neither become consumed with the means of religious methodology or governance. For it is not argument or debate, but the simple acts of Believing and Receiving my Holy Initiation that gets God's Promise to all Souls or all Souls to God.

392. Know this, you who are God's Faithful: There are Ten Gates that every unenlightened Soul must pass through to come home to God through me, God's Awakened and Ordained One. And these Ten Gates are: Ignorance; Disbelieving; Conflicted; Believing; Receiving; Accepted; Preaching; Giving; Guarding; and Guiding.

393. Ignorance is the First Gate. Ignorance, means having no knowledge of The Friend or my self-sacrifices and Vow or Universal God's Supreme Promise of Perfect Final Union that my self-sacrifices and Vow have won for all Souls.

394. Disbelieving is the Second Gate. Disbelieving, means disbelieving in God's Truth or in me or in God's New Covenant.

395. Conflicted is the Third Gate. Conflicted, means being sorely conflicted between the beliefs he has and the Darkness that enslaves him, and the dawning of The Light of God's Pure Divine Truth that you have set upon his heart and mind.

396. Believing is the Fourth Gate. Believing means, hearing God's Divine Call and coming to true believing with total conviction and without doubt or reservation in God; in me, my self-sacrifices and Vow of Compassion; and in God's New Covenant and Supreme Promise of Universal Salvation and Liberation with all of his heart and soul.

397. Receiving is the Fifth Gate. Receiving means, receiving my Holy Initiation and consummating it and becoming a Maitreyian - a Believer who professes The Truth of The Friend and God's New Covenant that I have won for all Souls - and a Soldier of The Light.

398. Accepted is the Sixth Gate. Accepted, means to be accepted as one of God's Chosen and a full and True Brother or Sister of The Holy

Community of my Enlightened Faithful Believers and a follower of God's Eternal Universal Religion.

399. Preaching is the Seventh Gate. Preaching, means to go out into this world and tell all who will hear God's Pure Divine Truth of Maitreya The Friend, God's New Covenant, our Holy Cause and tell the people what The Friend has said and the examples I have given. Preaching means to tell The Truth so as to shake all Souls out of ignorance and complacency and cause them to be Conflicted between The Force of Darkness and God's Pure Divine Truth. Preaching means to move all Souls from being Conflicted to being Convicted and from Believing to Receiving my Holy Initiation and God's Supreme Promise of Universal Salvation and Liberation.

400. Giving is the Eighth Gate. Giving, means actively and aggressively giving the baptism of my Holy Initiation to all Souls who believe and will receive it of their own free choosing without force, threat, coercion, intimidation, bribery or deception. Initiating also means to always be in Good Faith with The One Universal God and myself, The Friend; for only one who is in Good Faith with these has the power to give my Holy Initiation to another.

401. Guarding is the Ninth Gate. Guarding, means to stand guard over your own heart and mind and to be a Guardian to those whom God places in your charge; to look out for them, to fight against The Force of Darkness for them and with them.

402. Guiding is the Tenth Gate. Guiding, means to have fidelity and be loyal to The One Universal God and Maitreya The Friend, to God's Eternal Universal Religion, to our Holy Cause and to The Holy Community of my Enlightened Faithful Believers. Guiding, means to guide others in fulfilling God's Supreme Promise and winning Perfect Final Union with God for themselves and all Souls. And, to be more concerned for their Salvation and Liberation than you are for your own. For this is the highest form of Love.

403. The First Gate is Ignorance. In the beginning, all Souls are ignorant of Universal God and Maitreya The Friend, God's Supreme Promise, God's Pure Divine Truth, God's Eternal Universal Religion and our Holy Cause and Mission that God has given unto His Faithful. The First Gate every Soul must pass through on its journey from slavery under The Force of Darkness and the endless rounds of birth, life, suffering, sorrow, fear, pain, sickness, old age, death and rebirth; to Spiritual Freedom and Perfect Final Union with God; is to Hear God's Pure Divine Truth from a Believer who knows it and is in Good Faith.

404. The Second Gate is Disbelieving. The second Gate that every Soul must pass through on its journey out of Darkness into The Divine Light of God's Pure Truth and Home to God, is to recognize and face his own disbelief in God's Pure Divine Truth, my self-sacrifices and Vow and God's Supreme Promise of Perfect Final Union with Him.

405. The Third Gate is Conflicted. The third Gate that every Soul must pass through on its journey to Perfect Final Union with God is to face the conflict within himself between The Force of Darkness and his former beliefs; and The Divine Light of Universal God's

Pure Divine Truth. Those who cannot or will not recognize this Conflict and their own conflicted heart and mind, cannot progress further.

406. The Fourth Gate is Believing. The fourth Gate that every Soul must pass through on its journey to Perfect Final Union with God is to transmute Conflicted into Convicted. The emerging Soul must Hear and recognize God's Divine Call by recognizing me as God has sent me to appear to him in a Vision or Vision Dream or by such other sense as is fitting for him. Having heard God's Divine Call, he must then throw off the yoke of The Force of Darkness, renounce his old ways of believing and take up a new Believing in God and me and God's New Covenant, with all of his heart.

407. The Fifth Gate is Receiving. The fifth Gate that every Soul must pass through on its journey Home to Perfect Final Union with God is to Receive my Holy Initiation and God's Supreme Promise, directly from me or through a Maitreyian who is a Soldier of The Light who is in Good Faith with me; and consummate his Holy Initiation by Five Acts.

408. The First Act of Consummating my Holy Initiation is Commitment. When a Soul has moved through the Gate from Believing and stands at the Gate of Receiving of his own Free Will, without force, threat, coercion, intimidation, bribery or deception; he shall be given the beginning of my Holy Initiation by one who is a Soldier of The Light who is in Good Faith. This Act shall be called Commitment and shall be given by Grace and Grace alone.

409. The Second Act of Consummating my Holy Initiation is Consecration. When a Soul has made and received Commitment he must attain Consecration by finding me within The Spiritual Realm and Vowing his Belief in The One Universal God and me and God's New Covenant to me therein. If I find his heart pure and righteous, I will give him his Holy God Name directly from within The Spiritual Realm. If I find him wanting, I will instruct him as to how he is to purify himself and make himself ready.

410. The Third Act of Consummating my Holy Initiation is Confirmation. When a Soul has received his Holy God Name from me within the Spiritual Realm, he must go before three Maitreyians or Soldiers of The Light who are in Good Faith with me and profess his Consecration and reveal the Holy Name I have given unto him and receive Confirmation. Such a one shall then be a Maitreyian and shall become a provisional member of The Holy Community of my Enlightened Faithful Believers and a Candidate to receive his Commission as a Soldier of The Light.

411. The Fourth Act of Consummating my Holy Initiation is Commission. To receive his Commission requires that the Candidate shall receive instruction with a cheerful heart from one or more Soldiers of The Light who are in Good Faith; shall begin immediately to live according to God's Eternal Universal Religion as instructed and perform the prescribed portions of God's Eternal Universal Religion. When he has done this and has given unselfish Service to The One Universal God and all Souls through God's Eternal Universal Religion as God has given it unto you through me for the time

of three new moons; and has brought at least, three Souls through the Gates from Ignorance to Receiving my Holy Initiation and Consummated their Holy Initiation through the Act of Confirmation; that Soul shall be eligible to receive his Commission as a Soldier of The Light.

412. When a Maitreyian and Candidate shall have successfully fulfilled the requirements set forth, that Maitreyian shall request Commission as a Soldier of The Light. If he is in Good Faith and has no flaws that would harm God's Eternal Universal Religion, The Holy Community or our Holy Cause according to what is given in this Holy Book of Destiny, he shall be Commissioned a Soldier of The Light and given The Sacred Mantle, the wooden Sword and Sacred Staff.

413. The Fifth Act of Consummating my Holy Initiation is being accepted into The Holy Community of my Enlightened Faithful Believers. When a Soul has received his Commission as a Soldier of The Light, that Soldier of The Light shall be introduced to The Enlightened Faithful Believers and accepted into The Holy Community of my Enlightened Faithful Believers as a Brother or Sister in waiting.

414. The Sixth Gate is Accepted. The Sixth Gate each Soul must pass through on his journey to Perfect Final Union with God is to be recommended to Kaivalya by his Brothers and Sisters of The Holy Community of my Enlightened Faithful Believers and accepted by Kaivalya as a full Maitreyian and Soldier of The Light. Upon being accepted by Kaivalya, the new Soldier of The Light shall then be entered upon the Book of Life as one of God's Chosen Faithful and a full Brother or Sister of God's Eternal Universal Religion and The Holy Community of my Enlightened Faithful Believers.

415. The Seventh Gate is Preaching. The Seventh Gate each Soul must pass through on his journey to Perfect Final Union with God is to go out among the unenlightened and Preach The Truth of The One Universal God and The Friend and God's Supreme Promise of Perfect Final Union and Universal Salvation and Liberation for all Souls.

416. The Eighth Gate is Giving. The Eighth Gate each Soul must pass through on his journey to Perfect Final Union with God is to give my Holy Initiation and God's Supreme Promise to all willing Souls without force, threat, coercion, intimidation, bribery, violence or deception. Every fully accepted Soldier of The Light is Ordained to give my Holy Initiation and God's Supreme Promise to the unenlightened in my Name as God has commanded and God's Supreme Promise requires.

417. The Ninth Gate is Guarding. The Ninth Gate each Soul must pass through on his way Home to Perfect Final Union with The One Universal God is Guarding. Every Soldier of The Light is charged with Guarding Maitreya The Friend, Guarding The Faith and Guarding The Faithful against harm or corruption.

418. The Tenth Gate is Guiding. Each Soldier of The Light who seeks to pass through the Tenth Gate must carry the burden of being a Guardian to another of The Faithful and guarding him against The Force of Darkness and the forces of this world. A Guardian must care more for the Salvation and Liberation of those under his charge

than he does for his own Salvation and Liberation.

419. These things also shall you teach him. No Soul comes to Me or enters into God's Eternal Universal Religion, but that he is Chosen by The One Universal God. When God finds that a Soul is Right and ready to take his or her place with me within His Eternal Universal Religion, He sends me, in Spirit, to appear to that man or woman in a Vision or Vision Dream or by such other sense as is fitting for him.

420. When I appear to any Soul in a dream or a waking vision or in any other sense - it means that God has Chosen that Soul and is Calling him to come and receive my Holy Initiation and join me in God's Eternal Universal Religion.

421. Some are they who are Chosen by God who are yet in need of correction before they are fit to pass through the Eye of The Needle and enter into God's Eternal Universal Religion. When I appear to a Soul who is in need of correction, I give that Soul Guidance regarding things he needs to do to make himself ready to receive God's Supreme Promise and New Covenant. Those who receive my Guidance should carry it out.

422. Know this, and make it clear unto all who have a concern with me or God's Eternal Universal Religion that I will not Guide or direct any person to harm himself or anyone else or do anything that is destructive or contrary to God's Law or the Just laws of man. Any such ideas that arise within a Soul, come from other than Universal God or Maitreya The Friend and he should not act upon them.

423. As God must Choose a Soul before that Soul can be accepted into God's Eternal Universal Religion - that Soul who receives God's Invitation and Call must choose God of his own Free Will and without being moved by force, threat, coercion, intimidation, bribery or deception. In this way, a Soul must choose to accept me and receive my Holy Initiation. No Soul can remain neutral in this. For, not choosing to accept God's Call is choosing to reject it.

424. Conflict is a necessary Gate that every Soul must pass through to change from disbelief to belief. When a new idea or belief is heard, first comes disbelief. Then, comes a conflict between the old belief and the new idea. Out of the conflict between the old belief and the new idea comes Belief in the new idea. If the new Belief is to be preserved, there must be the baptism of Holy Initiation to establish it and Acceptance by The Faithful around him, to maintain it.

425. Confliction leads to Conviction. Believing leads to Receiving Holy Initiation. Holy Initiation then leads to Acceptance of that New Brother or Sister by the Faithful there in that place. And eventually to being accepted as a Brother or Sister by the Holy Community of The Friend's Enlightened Faithful Believers and Kaivalya.

426. Making me or God's Supreme Promise or God's Eternal Universal Religion too acceptable in an effort to appease or pacify the unenlightened, is a grievous wrong. You have become too acceptable. You seek to make God's Eternal Universal Religion just like those you hope to raise up to a higher place. But in doing so, you do not raise up the unenlightened, you

bring down God's Eternal Universal Religion.

427. No one can bring up that which is lower by bringing down that which is higher. In your desire for approval, you avoid provoking conflict for fear of raising up the wrath of the unenlightened. This is because you do not present the center most radical Truth of The Friend and his Two Self Sacrifices and God's Supreme Promise in a bold and truthful and provocative manner. Instead you hide it within or behind a lot of other talk that is more acceptable and less apt to raise conflict. Or, on the other hand, you express it in ways that water it down and make it palatable to the unenlightened. You do not allow the Conflicted Gate to open and you do not provoke it into opening.

428. In the beginning my first Disciples propagated God's Eternal Universal Religion boldly without avoiding conflict. There are many examples from our history, such as Ananda's conversion of Yasha. You must throw off your desire to be "acceptable" or approved of and return to our roots and allow and even boldly provoke the conflict stage of conversion.

429. When the people of a nation are oppressed by a tyrant or a tyranny and are suppressed into silence or lulled into complacency, those who fight on the side of The Forces of Freedom and Liberation must go out among the people preaching Freedom and Liberation and agitating the hearts and the minds of the people, such that they awaken to their slavery and the Freedom and Liberation they are lacking and become conflicted toward their state of oppression and suppression and disposed to revolution to depose the tyrant or tyranny.

430. Each Soul that does not have God's Supreme Promise of Perfect Final Union with God is like unto a citizen of a nation which is oppressed by a tyrant or a tyranny. You, who are God's Chosen and are members of God's Eternal Universal Religion and my Enlightened Faithful Believers; you who are Maitreyians and Soldiers of The Light; are The Forces of Spiritual Freedom and Liberation in this world. You must go out among the unenlightened who are sleeping and suffering under the oppression and suppression of The Force of Darkness, who have been lulled into slumber and complacency. You must agitate their hearts and minds and disturb their slumber with God's Pure Divine Truth such that they awaken to their slavery and their state of oppression and are roused from their slumber and become disposed to Spiritual Revolution within. You must stir them up to Spiritual Revolution to depose The Force of Darkness and reclaim their rightful place with The One Universal God of all Creation, as Soul which is Pure Divine Spirit which is One and Identical with The One Universal God and no other.

431. You must raise them up from complacent Souls to Conflicted Souls; you must move them from being Conflicted to being Convicted; you must guide them from Believing in Universal God and The Friend and God's Supreme Promise and Pure Divine Truth, to Receiving God's Supreme Promise. Then, you must guard them and guide them to become True Maitreyians and Soldiers of The Light who will do for other Souls as you have done for them and, who will fight for God, God's Eternal

Universal Religion and our Holy Cause of bringing forth The Age of Universal God's Pure Divine Truth for the Salvation and Liberation of all Souls and the continued survival of Humanity.

432. This is your Work in this world. This is your Duty to God and to me and to all of God's Prophets, Saints, Buddhas, Saviors and Avataras of all times. This is your obligation of Love and Compassion toward all Souls who suffer in ignorance and complacency under the tyranny and oppression of The Force of Darkness. This is your obligation to humanity and the future of humanity - to the children of your children's children who are even yet unborn.

433. For, I say unto you that in all but the few, the more severely Conflicted a Soul is before he becomes Convicted, the deeper and stronger will be his Believing and the more likely his Receiving of my Holy Initiation and God's Supreme Promise of Perfect Final Union with Him, once he becomes Convicted.

434. Therefore, do not seek to curry favor with the unenlightened and especially do not tread softly so as to not disturb their complacency or Spiritual slumber. Instead, present to each Soul the Heart of God's Eternal Universal Religion such as will cause that Soul to become most severely Conflicted between his slavery to The Force of Darkness and, God's Truth and Freedom.

435. And what is this Heart of God's Eternal Universal Religion of which I have spoken but, myself whom The One God has Named The Friend and the self-sacrifices and Vow I have made and what God has made of me and God's Supreme Promise of Universal Salvation and Liberation for all Souls and the continued Survival of Humanity that my self-sacrifices and Vow have won for all Souls.

436. Therefore, without force, threat, coercion, intimidation, bribery, violence or deception; come upon the unenlightened and sleeping as a great bell tolling to awaken the sleeping and alert the unwary to the slavery and oppression of The Force of Darkness under which they slumber and the terrible danger that they face should they remain bound to the Eternal and Endless Wheel of Birth, Life, Suffering, Sorrow, Sickness, Fear, Pain, Old Age, Death and Rebirth.

437. For, the first greatest gift that you can give unto the suffering Souls of this world, is to raise them up from Disbelieving to Conflicted. This will agitate The Force of Darkness within them and The Force of Darkness will cause them to hate you and curse you. But, if you Know that their hatred and curses come not from the Soul itself, but from The Force of Darkness that enslaves the Soul, and that, if you will persist, boldly and with good courage with unshakable Faith in God in the face of all hatred and hostility - The One Universal God and The Friend and all God's Prophets, Saints, Buddhas, Saviors and Avataras will come to your aid and prevail over The Force of Darkness through you. Then, those who had once hated you and cursed you for disturbing their sleep of ignorance, will love you and bless you for having helped them to awaken and throw off the chains of Spiritual Slavery to The Force of Darkness.

438. Therefore, do not hide my Light away, whether to pacify those who are enslaved to The Force of Darkness or

to win their approval or, yet again, to avoid their wrath. For all Souls who would come Home to God through me, must pass through the Ten Gates of Ignorance, Disbelieving, Conflicted, Convicted, Initiated, Accepted and onward to Preaching God's Truth, Giving my Holy Initiation and God's Supreme Promise to all willing Souls, Guarding The Faithful and Guiding their Brothers and Sisters and the whole world Home to God through me and God's Supreme Promise. To hide my Light away to avoid upsetting a Soul's disbelieving or to avoid causing a Soul to become Conflicted, is to bar that Soul's Way Home to God.

439. I have written, All Good comes to pass through the union of Right Conditions, Right Choice, and Divine Grace. As Maitreyians and Soldiers of The Light you must create Right Conditions and make Right Choices — then God will provide His Divine Grace. Therefore, present The Truth of Universal God and The Friend and God's Supreme Promise boldly and aggressively without force, threat, coercion, intimidation, bribery, violence or deception; though it may Conflict grievously with a Soul's former beliefs and enrage The Force of Darkness that enslaves that Soul.

440. Though the unenlightened will not understand, I say unto you that to do this is a great act of love and kindness, for it moves the Soul closer to Perfect Final Union with God, all Souls closer to The Age of Universal God's Pure Divine Truth and the Salvation and Liberation of all Souls and the continued Survival of humanity.

441. All of this which I have given unto you is for your understanding. Make not an obstacle of that which I have given. Instead, remember and be always mindful that the acts of Believing, Receiving my Holy Initiation and being accepted as a Brother or Sister in Universal God and Maitreya The Friend are the keys. Do not accept those into my Holy Community of Maitreyians who are of bad motive or insincere, but make it easy for every sincere Soul who professes his Believing with all of his heart to receive my Holy Initiation and, when a Soul has done so, let him know, in abundance, that he is accepted in Spirit in Love and Brotherhood by The Faithful that surround him.

442. That Soul who chooses for God, should present himself to a Maitreyian or Soldier of The Light who has Consummated my Holy Initiation and stands in Good Faith with me and God and God's Eternal Universal Religion. And having so done, that Soul shall profess that Maitreya The Friend has appeared to him and he has accepted God's Call and been Chosen by God. And he shall profess that he has Faith in The One Universal God and The Friend and seeks to receive Holy Initiation of his own free will without being moved to do so by force, threat, coercion, intimidation, bribery or deception. And he shall profess that he will do all that is necessary to consummate Holy Initiation and give himself into the Service to God, The Friend, The Holy Cause and all Souls.

443. Having taught him these things, test him for his character, knowledge and understanding. Root out and clarify any confusion or misunderstanding his heart or mind may harbor.

444. When you have become certain of his character, knowledge and

understanding and are willing to stand as his Witness before God and man; stand him before you and draw a line upon the ground, be it seen or unseen, between you from left to right.

445. Then, say unto that Soul for me:

446. "Do you Believe in The One Universal God and Maitreya The Friend and God's New Covenant and Promise that The Friend's two Supreme Self-Sacrifices and Vow have won for you and all Souls with all of your heart?

447. "Do you accept the whole of God's Eternal Universal Religion as given unto all Souls through God's Awakened and Ordained One, Adhyatma Bhagavan Sri Babajhan Al-Kahlil The Friend of All Souls with all of your heart?

448. "Will you do that which is to be done and not do that which is not to be done?

449. "Do you seek of your own free will and choosing to receive The Friend's Holy Initiation and God's Supreme Promise of Universal Salvation and Liberation, without any influence of force, threat, coercion, intimidation, bribery or deception?"

450. If and only if that Soul answers yes, without doubt or reservation, to all of these questions, say unto him, "Then leave your old ways behind and step over this line to begin your new Life in The Spirit."

451. When he has crossed over the line, take hold of his arms at his wrists with your right hand crossed over your left with your wrists touching one another; your right palm pressing upon the inside of his right wrist and your left palm pressing upon the inside of his left wrist. Look him straight in the eyes and say unto him for me:

452. "If you would receive The Holy Initiation of Maitreya Adhyatma Bhagavan Sri Babajhan Al-Kahlil The Friend and The Supreme Promise of The One Universal God, now and forever; say unto me, before The One Universal God, The Friend of All Souls and all of God's Prophets, Saints, Buddhas, Saviors and Avataras of all time: 'The Friend's Religion is my Religion!' And it will be done."

453. When that Soul has so said, say unto him.

454. "I Initiate you with the Holy Water of Life and Divine Fire of God's Presence and Truth; in the Name of The One Universal God and Maitreya The Friend and all of God's Prophets, Saints, Buddhas, Saviors and Avataras of all times."

455. Thus saying, place the Holy Water of Life on his forehead with the third finger of your right hand; and wave the Divine Fire over his head with your right hand.

456. Then say unto him these words:

457. "I will now whisper into your left ear The Holy Dharma Mantra which The Friend proclaimed at the moment He attained Perfect Oneness with The One Universal God, hear it, remember it, repeat it often."

458. Then approach the Initiate and whisper into his left ear: "Jai Bhagavan Ji! Jai Bhagavan Ji! Jai Bhagavan Ji!"

459. Having done so, resume your previous place and proclaim to the new Initiate these words: "Wherever The Holy Dharma Mantra is, there is The One Universal God and Maitreya The Friend of All Souls. From this moment until the end of time, The One Universal God and The Friend shall be with you always and you shall never walk alone. Jai Bhagavan Ji!"

460. Having done these things, then say unto him. "It is done." And accept him as a new Maitreyian in Love and Brotherhood.

461. If a Soul has no left ear, whisper this into his right ear. If a Soul is devoid of hearing, communicate it to him as you must.

462. Those who cannot stand or walk, by reason of disease or infirmity, may cross over the line in their hearts and minds and profess it with their mouths.

463. Those who are near death, very ill or otherwise have not the strength or ability for study, learning and testing; and those who are moved by The Divine Spirit of The One God to receive my Holy Initiation and God's Supreme Promise by Faith alone; may accept on the Faith of their hearts alone, that which others must know with their minds. These desperate Souls need only profess their acceptance with their hearts and mouths and it shall be done. Those who have no power of speech may profess their acceptance by sign alone and it shall be done.

464. Let all Souls know that those who receive my Holy Initiation and God's Supreme Promise by the Faith of their hearts alone, are bound by the same requirements as those who enter through the knowing way; though they know not these requirements beforehand.

465. But know that this is not the only way by which a Soul may receive my Holy Initiation and become a Maitreyian. There is another in which no Maitreyian has part.

466. Any Soul who hears my Call to come Home to The One Universal God may receive my Holy Initiation directly from me in The Spirit by calling upon me and asking for it. He who asks without deceptive motive, unto that Soul I shall give it and none other than he shall have part in it. For I will do it within The Secret Inner Sanctuary of that Soul's Heart and if he shall accept it therein, it shall be done without question.

467. And when a Soul has received it from me in the Inner Way, that Soul shall again call upon me and I will come to him in The Spirit and, if he does so without deception or reservation, I will Consecrate him in The Spirit and whisper unto him a New Holy Name which shall be his God-name, from that time forward until he enters into Perfect Final Union with God.

468. To enter my Holy Community, every Soul must receive Confirmation through three Maitreyians who have been Confirmed and are in Good Faith, except that when there are no other Maitreyians it may be done by one or two Maitreyians that are in Good Faith.

469. Whether a Soul receives my Holy Initiation and Consecration from me with or without contact with a Maitreyian, they shall have the same standing in my Holy Community of

Maitreyians. No one shall stand higher or lower because of the means by which he received my Holy Initiation and my Consecration.

470. A Soul who has received my Holy Initiation and Consecration by deception or who acts so as to be a detriment to my Holy Community shall be a Maitreyian in Spirit, but need not be admitted to my Holy Community. For, all Maitreyians accept my Holy Mission as the reason for being part of my Holy Community and no one shall remain who makes himself more of a burden to our Holy Mission than a benefit unto it.

471. When I have given my Holy Initiation to a Soul and Consecrated that Soul and given that Soul a God-name as is written in this Holy Book of Destiny, The One God's New Covenant and Supreme Promise shall live within the very Heart of his Heart like unto a seed which, if tended and nurtured, will grow into True Salvation and Liberation for him and into a New Force that will help to bring The Age of Universal God's Pure Divine Truth into fullness and Reality in the world.

472. But only when a Soul has been Consummated by Confirmation and Commission, shall he be admitted into the gate of The Holy Community of my Enlightened Faithful Believers.

473. When these things have been rightly done, become like unto a living light unto him. Teach him the inner meaning of the Holy Sanctuary of God's Eternal Universal Religion as The One Universal God has Awakened and Ordained me to give it unto all Souls, as it is in this Holy Book of Destiny. And teach unto him, clearly and directly what must be accepted, what must be done and what must not be done; as I have given it unto you. And explain unto him, yet again, the meaning of Holy Initiation and the things that are required to consummate it and fulfill it and the Three Sacred Duties that he shall inherit thereby and the Three Steps To Right Action by which he shall Rightly fulfill them. And give him to understand that the one who transmits my Holy Initiation to him must be a Maitreyian who has consummated Holy Initiation and who stands in Good Faith with God and myself and God's Eternal Universal Religion and who will transmit my Holy Initiation to him in the manner Ordained. Whoever would transmit my Holy Initiation shall profess in Truth that he is such a Maitreyian.

474. Having done these things, instruct him in the method of Inner Divine Communion. Instruct him in The Three Steps to Right Action and raise up and deepen his understanding of The Three Sacred Duties he must carry out to fulfill Holy Initiation and enter into Perfect Final Union with The One Universal God at the end of this life. Place clearly in his heart and mind the Truth that he shall only receive the blessing of God's Supreme Promise in such measure as he transmits it to other suffering Souls in the fullness of his capacity. When these things have been done with certainty and without doubt, transmit my Holy Initiation unto that Soul.

475. And, when it is done, that Soul who has received transmission of my Holy Initiation and that Maitreyian who has given it shall each inscribe an affirmation, in their own handwriting, signed and dated in their own hand, stating their names and the date, place and time at which Holy Initiation was transmitted and received; and each

shall Seal his affirmation by his Sacred Honor. Only when this has been done shall his name be entered upon the Sacred Book of my Holy Community of God's Eternal Universal Religion here, or in the Spiritual Realm beyond. Otherwise, it shall not be done.

476. Once a Soul has received my Holy Initiation and affirmed it as it has been written, that Soul shall begin immediately to live by The Three Steps to Right Action, uphold The Three Sacred Duties, keep the Four Sacred Vows and keep regular practice of Inner Divine Communion by the Two Rules according to The One Instruction. He shall regularly enter into Inner Divine Communion with the sincere determination that he will meet me within The Spiritual Realm. When he is ready, I will appear to him in the Spiritual Realm. When I appear to that Soul within The Spiritual Realm, he must profess unto me, before God, all of God's Prophets, Saints, Buddhas, Saviors and Avataras and all Maitreyans in Spirit, the Threefold Vow of his Faith that he will faithfully Propagate, Preserve and Practice God's Eternal Universal Religion in all of its purity as Paratpara, The One Universal God, has given it to me and I have given it to my Faithful Maitreyans. Then he shall ask me to Consecrate him and give him the Sacred Spiritual Name by which he shall be known unto God and man. According to the purity and righteousness and Faith, will I give these unto him.

477. Know and teach unto all who come after you, that there are two things that I will not do as a part of Holy Consecration. I will NEVER direct a Soul to harm himself or anyone else or do anything that is against God or against the Just or Righteous Laws of man. Any such ideas arise from other than God or myself and no Soul should act upon them. And, I will never give any Soul my own Name, the Name of God, the full Name of any of God's Prophets, Saints, Buddhas, Saviors and Avataras, or a foul or degraded name that would bring shame or embarrassment.

478. When a Soul has received Consecration and his Spiritual Name, that Soul shall not speak or write his Spiritual Name until he has been Confirmed. Every Soul must receive Confirmation from a Maitreyan who has Consummated his Holy Initiation and is in Good Faith with Universal God and The Friend and God's Eternal Universal Religion.

479. To receive Confirmation, a Soul must present himself to a Maitreyan who has consummated his Holy Initiation and is in Good Faith. Where no Consummated Maitreyans in Good Faith can be found a Confirmed Maitreyan in Good Faith may administer Confirmation. Such a Maitreyan shall, whenever possible, constitute a triad of three Maitreyans to administer Confirmation and appoint a time and place. That place shall be made pure by the sprinkling of newly made Holy Water and no worldly activity shall take place therein to defile its purity. Should its purity be defiled, it must be purified again before Confirmation shall be given.

480. At the appointed time and place and in the presence of three Faithful Maitreyans, or at least one Maitreyan in Good Faith if three are not available, the Soul who is to be confirmed shall profess his Holy Initiation and Consecration under a solemn vow of

Truthfulness. And he shall then reveal to those gathered therein The Spiritual Name The Friend has given unto him at the time of Consecration.

481. When this has been done, the eldest Maitreyian within the triad shall pronounce Confirmation and may, at his choosing, perform a ceremony that is in keeping with the letter and Spirit of God's Eternal Universal Religion as God has given His Eternal Universal Religion to me to give unto you and all Souls. No money or other goods may be given or received in exchange.

482. When it has been done, the Confirmant and the Maitreyian of the triad shall all make Affirmations to Kaivalya in the manner described for Holy Initiation.

483. When Kaivalya has received Affirmation of Confirmation and that of the Confirmators, it shall issue a Proclamation of Membership affirming that Soul is a member of God's Eternal Universal Religion and an Aspirant to membership in The Holy Community of My Enlightened Faithful Maitreyians.

484. When a Soul has been Confirmed, that Soul shall Consummate his Holy Initiation and seek acceptance as a member of The Holy Community of The Enlightened Faithful Believers. In this way, he will Realize his True Nature as a follower of Universal God, The Friend, and God's Eternal Universal Religion - The Ancient Holy Adhyatma-Yoga-Dharma who has surrendered completely to Universal God. This is the way of it. There is no other.

485. When a Soul has received his Proclamation of Membership, that Soul must find a Sanctuary that will accept him as a member of The Holy Community of The Friend's Enlightened Faithful Believers. If one Local Sanctuary will not accept him for any reason, he must keep trying until he finds one that will. He must then receive Accession and become a member of that Local Sanctuary and, thereby, a member of The Holy Community of The Friend's Enlightened Faithful Believers.

486. At least two Members in Good Standing must administer the Accession that enters a Soul into my Holy Community and Consummates his Holy Initiation. All of who give Accession must make Affirmation to Kaivalya. When these Affirmations are received, that Soul will be declared a Member in Good Faith of The Holy Community of God's Eternal Universal Religion and shall be numbered among The Enlightened Faithful Believers of The One Universal God and The Friend.

487. I give you these instructions that you may bring and keep order in my Holy Community. Make not a barrier to accomplishment of our Holy Mission of them, but employ them wisely so as to advance and accomplish my Holy Mission of getting God's Promise to all Souls and getting all Souls Home to God.

488. Commission and entrance into my Holy Community of Maitreyians is not the end, but the beginning of a life of Service to The One Universal God, The Friend, God's Eternal Universal Religion and all suffering Souls. When you have completed Holy Initiation and become a Maitreyian, you will be expected to perform Service and spread God's Promise to all willing Souls. You will be expected to contribute of yourself, your time,

your talent, your knowledge and, your money to help me do God's Work in this world and carry The Mission to Victory over Ignorance, Darkness and Untruth.

489. Those Souls who are of strong and unwavering intention and place God's Eternal Universal Religion and our Holy Cause of The Age of Universal God's Pure Divine Truth first in their lives, find the burden to be light and joyous and are lifted up thereby. But those who are selfish or weak of intention will be weighed down.

490. All Adhyatmavadi, whether Maitreyians or Soldiers of The Light, are obligated to devotedly carry out their duties to their families, their Communities, their Countries and their professions. It is also expected that every Adhyatmavadi will cheerfully and eagerly meet and fulfill the demands that God's Work and my Holy Mission may place upon him. Our Cause is Great and its demands can be considerable. If a Soul is not of a heroic heart or mind and willing to face and meet such demands, that Soul should not receive Holy Initiation at this time. If any Soul is inclined to pick and choose what they will or will not accept, believe or obey or is adverse to following, that Soul is unfit for Service in God's Holy Community. To become a Maitreyian, every Soul must believe, welcome and embrace all of God's Eternal Universal Religion - or that Soul cannot have God's Eternal Universal Religion at all.

491. When a Soul has successfully Consummated his Holy Initiation and given Service to Universal God and The Friend and God's Eternal Universal Religion in the prescribed manner; and has successfully transmitted the True Enlightenment of my Holy Initiation to at least three Souls and guided them through the changes and into membership in The Holy Community of the Faithful and Service to God; that Soul may be privileged to take the Soldier of The Light Pledge, receive his Sacred Sword and Staff and join the ranks of the Soldiers of The Light.

492. This is The Supreme Work. This is The Way. This is The New Covenant of The One God as it has been Revealed by Paratpara, The One Universal God, unto This One. This is The Testimony of Maitreya Adhyatma Bhagavan Sri Babajhan Al-Kahlil The Friend, The God-Awakened One, Teacher of Oneness with God, Slayer of Spiritual ignorance and darkness, Bringer of The Age of Universal God's Pure Divine Truth, The Friend of All Beings.

493. This is The New Covenant of the One God as It has come to pass in me, Maitreya Adhyatma Bhagavan Sri Babajhan Al-Kahlil The Friend. So It Is!

494. Whosoever gives True Witness of God's Eternal Universal Religion in his life shall receive my Blessings and The Blessings of Paratpara, The One Universal God, thereby.

495. Whosoever reads this Holy Book of Destiny shall receive my Blessings and The Blessings of Paratpara, The One Universal God in abundance.

496. Whosoever reads or recites from this Holy Book aloud, that others may hear The Truth, shall be Blessed one-hundred fold.

497. Whosoever would bear True Witness or read or recite from this Holy Book of Destiny, let that Soul first proclaim aloud, "By The Will and Grace of The One Universal God" before bearing True Witness and, after pausing and before reading or reciting passages anew.

498. When any man or woman shall ask of you, "How can I know that this Holy Book or Maitreya The Friend are True?" say unto them as God has said unto me:

499. "If any man or woman will set prejudice aside and hold Maitreya The Friend's Presence steadily in his heart and mind like a candle flame in a still place, The One Universal God, I AM THAT I AM, will reveal unto that Soul that Maitreya The Friend is the One in whom God has Awakened and whom God has Ordained to be The Maitreya, Friend of All Souls, bringer of The Age of His New Covenant and The Age of His Pure Divine Truth and that The Friend's Mission is God's and God's alone and - is True.

500. "This, do, and The One Universal God will reveal The Truth of Maitreya The Friend unto you in such manner that all doubt and reservation shall be cast out of your heart and mind and you will join Maitreya The Friend in The Holy Cause for which God has sent Him forth into this world. And, through Maitreya The Friend, God will make you His own and a Solider of The Light of His Pure Divine Truth."

501. When any man or woman shall ask you, "Why does your Religion require this or that?" Or, again, "Why must those who follow God's Eternal Universal Religion do this or that?" Say unto them only, "It is The Will of The One Universal God."

502. And when they shall praise you and ask after you, "How do you come by this goodness or that goodness?" Say unto them only, "By The Will and Grace of The One Universal God and The Friend."

**Om So'ham Tat Tvam Asi!
I Am That - Thou Art That
Jai Bhagavan Ji!
Victory To That Beloved
Universal I AM THAT I AM
Which You Are!**

**Here Ends The Chapter Entitled
The Self-Realization
and Self-Sacrifice**

**Here Ends The Book Entitled
God's New Covenant**

Book Two
Revelations

The Revelations of The One Universal God
To Adhyatma Bhagavan Sri Babajhan Al-Kahlil The Friend
The Maitreya Kalki Mahavatara Satguru of The Age

Revelation One
The Compassion and Renewal

24 Charity 28 A.F.

By The Will and Grace of The One Universal God:

And it came to pass that upon the eve of the twenty-fourth day of the twelfth month of the year called nineteen hundred and seventy-nine, a great and compassionate sadness came upon this one as a result of the terrible darkness which has shrouded this sleeping World.

2. And I cried out to God, my own True Self saying, "O my Beloved, who are my own True Self, you have shown me The Truth, The Light, and The Way and made me One with You and with It and have verified all this through this New Covenant which is made with All Beings through This One. Still my Work moves not and my heart grows heavy within me for want of Final Union with You who I Am.

3. "My eyes are opened, I Am Awakened to our Oneness; yet there is something that is not seen. My ears are opened, I Am Awakened to our Oneness; yet there is something that is not being heard.

4. "I Am Thee; and Thou Art me; and we are One. Of this there is no doubt. I call out to You, knowing well our Oneness, as one member of a family cries out to his Brother for help, though he knows that they are of one family and one blood.

5. "Help Thy Radiance, that this Work might be done within this Illusion which is so filled with darkness and ignorance, O Beloved Self, for, no matter which way I turn, Our Words fall upon deaf ears; And, those I would lead upon The Way to Oneness with me as it has been appointed; and through me unto Oneness with Thee; all these turn their faces away from me and fall ever deeper into the Illusion by the glitter of this World.

6. "Well do I know that You shall not do for This One that which you would not do for any other. For this is the essence of the Message I bring; that each might attain the Goal of his own doing.

7. "And well do I know that this is much of Thy Covenant which I am to fulfill. Yet, I have tried with all of my strength for these two years to bring Thy New Covenant unto this sleeping World, but to no avail. For they see not, neither do they hear; such is their sleep.

8. "Now, I turn unto You who have Awakened me and made me One with

You; not as one who is separate from You; as man's words demand and as the sleeping and Living Dead would believe; but as Thy own Being made Manifest within this, Thy Dream and Image that is Created for Thy sake alone!

9. "Come to the rescue of Thy Self Emanation here, O Beloved One. This I beg, for I have become as a Sighted One living among the blind. I have become as one who hears, living among the Spiritually deaf. So far from the blind and the deaf in Spirit have You led me that no longer can I tell what they see and hear within the Illusion and how to reach them and Awaken them, and restore their Spiritual Eyes and Ears unto them.

10. "A stranger in a strange land have I become, who no longer speaks its language. Because of this, my Heart grows ever more saddened and weary.

11. "All this Universe and my false self have I gladly given in sacrifice unto You and, more than this would I give gladly! Not for glory or admiration of men, but that Thy New Covenant might be fulfilled for the Salvation and Liberation of all Beings.

12. "But those who live within the Illusion Love it and believe upon it, not upon I who am One with Thee. They follow not nor will they turn their faces toward one who shows not the power and glory and miracles they admire so much.

13. "So deep are they within their sleep that all they care for is the entertainment of phenomenon and miracle to satisfy their craving for comfort through the things of this world. Heal my wounds, they cry out! But the deepest and most deadly wound, which is the chasm that separates them from Knowledge of their True Self; they have no wish to heal.

14. "I ask not for such powers, O Beloved One; I ask only that this worldly blindness and deafness and muteness be lifted from me that I might see what must be done and hear their darkness and speak out unto them in such a way that each Being shall Hear and Awaken; and turn his Heart and Hand to bring this, The New Covenant, into fulfillment before it is too late for this World.

15. "I have nowhere to turn save unto Thee who I Am. The whore and the junkie have their needs; but Thy Emanation has no place to take rest. The birds of the air have their wings upon which to soar above The Sea; but the waters of darkness rise fast within this world and Thy Emanation has no Rock upon which to stand.

16. "Those who worship man's distorted version of Thy Word in darkness and ignorance curse me as Thy Clear Light. Those whose hearts are right, but who are blinded and made deaf by the flash and roar of this world; and know only the twisted doctrines of fearful churchmen, curse me too. For these live in fear of anything that refuses to conform to their perverted views and childishly practiced doctrines. For, they have taken even My admonition to become as Little Children and perverted it into a license for becoming childish instead of childlike, and they take comfort in their sleep and ignorance and suffering.

17. "Yet, so has it been for all of man's history, that the sleeping

and ignorant bring their sleep and ignorance into Thy Worship. I curse them not, for I have not come to Judge men but to Awaken them as You have Consecrated me, Empowered me, and Given me to do as Thy Complete Manifestation within this World.

18. "I lay no blame upon this World, for it is as it is; but blame I do lay upon This One who is called Adhyatma Bhagavan Sri Babajhan Al-Kahlil The Friend! Within the boundaries of Grace that are permitted within Thy Holy New Covenant, extend my full and Complete Nature and Being; heal this blindness and deafness and muteness and show me the way that touches the Hearts and Minds of all Beings and Awakens their Spirit. This I ask and nothing more. This is enough!"

19. And The Ever-Presence sent forth a White Dove which descended upon This Manifestation of All-Being and entered straightaway into my Heart, bearing God's Infinitely Loving and Compassionate Word, saying:

20. {G} "You are My Beloved, My Emanation and True Self, in whom I have embodied My Presence that this sleeping World might Awaken into True Knowledge of their Oneness and Identity with Me and no other!

21. {G} "Thy sadness is My sadness. Thy Call has been heard, and I have come unto you.

22. {G} "Fear not, but be at Peace, My Beloved, for Thy days of trial, trouble, and sorrow draw near to their end; and the time draws near at hand when Beings of all Nations shall Awaken to My Presence and Glory in Thee!

23. {G} "Through all of Thy Life I have shaped and molded Thee, as the smith forges shapeless metal into a fine Sword. For these last two years I have tempered Thee to make you strong and straight. I have tested Thee in all ways to find weakness and repair it.

24. {G} "For one more year of this World, I shall hone Thee and polish Thee until, at last, you shall become My Sharp Sword of Discrimination that will cut a straight path between Falsehood and Truth; between Ignorance and Knowledge; between the Darkness and My Light; between the Sleeping and The Awakening; and you shall bring The Age of My Truth into Being upon the Earth wherever The Sun shall shine or wind blow or water run.

25. {G} "Be yet patient My Beloved Emanation; for it is because of your lack of completion that you are filled with doubts and questionings. But you have called upon Me upon this eve which symbolizes the Birth of My Presence into this World in the form of Jesus of Nazareth who was called Yohoshuay and who, too, was The Manifestation of My Being and Presence. But, the sleeping declare a division of three parts and claim that He and It and I are different and that He and It are different from Me. Like unto That One, I shall give Thee Thy Birth into this World as My Complete Presence, one year from this day; Adhyatma Bhagavan Sri Babajhan Al-Kahlil The Friend, My Own Self made Visible.

26. {G} "And all of this shall be given unto you in such a way that all Beings of the Earth may look upon you and know that they, too, are One

and Identical with Me, and I Am they and, we are One.

27. {G} "Let not the sleeping and Ignorant tempt you to the doing of miracles; for it is only miracles they believe in now and, if you should become tempted into the doing of them, their knowing of Me would not increase; but they will only believe more in miracles and crave the power to do them.

28. {G} "But, I Am The Only Power. Whosoever Loves or Desires other than Me shall have his desires fulfilled, but they shall each bring him pain and suffering and death in the long run. But, whoever fixes his heart and his mind and his Spirit in Me through Thee, without doubt or reservation, he will attain Salvation and Liberation and The Life Everlasting, even while he lives within this World. These Words shall you say unto them, even as I have said them unto you.

29. {G} "For, in that day, whosoever shall become One with Thee shall become One with Me, Forever and ever; beyond even Eternity itself. For I say unto you, and unto all Beings through you, that whosoever takes Refuge in You and in Your Teachings and becomes as Brother and Sister within this, My Spiritual Family and Community, shall endure beyond the very existence of this whole Universe; and shall Bear Witness to the passing away of Eternity; and shall view all Infinity as but a small space the size of a mustard seed!

30. {G} "You are, yet, blind and deaf and mute. You are yet fearful of That, which you were destined to fulfill, even before the birth of this World. It is, even now, your own doubt and fearfulness that closes your eyes and ears, and silences your Spiritual Tongue. And, beyond even these, it is your Love and desire to return to Perfect Final Union with Me, that blinds you and deafens you and ties up your tongue.

31. {G} "It is too soon, My Beloved, your Work is here, within this Dream and Illusion. To turn away from The Work, even for My sake, is to turn away from all of these many Manifestations of My Presence who suffer and die, only to be born and die again and again in darkness and ignorance.

32. {G} "This, you must not do! Whether out of doubt and fear; or out of your Love for Me and your longing for our Final Union. In this year of this World, I will unveil your eyes and unstop your ears and, I will speak My Truth with your mouth!

33. {G} "Fear not any man nor men. But give unto all alike My Truth; and endure the White Hot Fire of My Presence, knowing that this is the smith Tempering, Honing and Polishing The Great Sword that will rend the veils of Illusion and Darkness, and flood this whole Universe with The Clear Bright Light of My Truth!

34. {G} "You, Adhyatma Bhagavan Sri Babajhan Al-Kahlil The Friend, Bringer of Oneness with Me, The Creator of The Creator, you are The Friend of All Beings; you are My Sharp Sword and My Clear Light. With You I shall cut away the bonds of darkness and ignorance that enslave all Souls and Light up this World with a Clear Light such as would Light up The Sun; and bring Salvation and Liberation unto all Beings!

35. {G} "Prepare to sever the Illusion and Shine Forth into this sleeping World; My Beloved; My Own Self made manifest.

36. {G} "So Is It!"

> **Om So'ham Tat Tvam Asi!**
> **I Am That - Thou Art That**
>
> **Jai Bhagavan Ji!**
> **Victory To God The Beloved**
> **That Beloved Universal I Am**
> **That I Am Which You Are!**
>
>
> **Here Ends**
> **The Revelation Entitled**
> **The Compassion and Renewal**

Revelation Two
The Gathering of The Multitudes

The Revelation of That Universal I AM THAT I AM
to Maitreya Adhyatma Bhagavan Sri Babajhan
Al-Kahlil The Friend

On The 24th Day of Discipline 28 A.F.
11:45 am - 2:57 p.m.

By The Will and Grace of The One Universal God:

I say unto you that you shall bring them together in multitude upon multitude; the Hindu, the Buddhist; the Mohammedan, the Jew, the Christian and all others who love Me. Through thy name they shall reach Me. And before the end of thy days, you shall see the millions upon millions gathered before thee chanting "Jai Bhagavan Ji!"

2. {G} "And you shall send them out in all of the ten directions as your Disciples - keeping two for your service; and they shall announce thy coming, each in the language of the people where unto he shall preach thy word; until all the Beings of the earth shall have ears with which to hear thee and eyes with which to see thee and heart and mind with which to receive thee.

3. {G} "And, whosoever receives thee in all ways, shall attain perfect Union with Me who has sent thee.

4. {G} "And, unto all who have received thee at the time of your passing from this world and return to Me - these shall be given the Gift of Heaven and Earth and shall rule over thy earthly Kingdom with Loving Kindness and Compassion for so long as Earth there shall be.

5. {G} "For thou art The Awaited One within whom I Am Awakened and whom I send forth into this world, a Gift and a Blessing unto all Souls for their Salvation and Liberation. Thou art as My Compassionate Expression Christ to the Christian. Thou art as My Blessed Prophet Mohammed to the Moslem. Thou art as My Spirit made manifest as Rama and Krishna to the Hindu. Thou art as My Light of The Buddha to the Buddhist. Thou art My Self and Spirit made manifest in this world as The Maitreya Kalki Mahavatara Satguru - The Awaited Bringer of My Pure Divine Truth unto all Souls. Woe unto he who rejects thee and denies thee, for he shall be bound to the suffering of this earth time and time again.

6. {G} "But, tell them that My Grace is thy Grace and that it is Good. And, should any of them take up My Word

through thee, he shall be released in that day.

7. {G} "This is My Word as it is given unto all humanity through thee this day 24 of the month called Discipline in The Year 28 of Thy Awakening. Let it be known that you shall not pass from this earth until this prophecy shall come to pass. For I am The One Universal Source of all Being and Existence, The One Universal Presence within all Being and Existence, and The One Universal Self of all Being and Existence. As I Am, so shall you be at the moment of thy passing from this earth. And, as you are, so shall they be who follow you steadily, like unto a candle flame in a still place - without wavering.

8. {G} "This, My Beloved One, is My Word to thee and unto all the Nations through thee. Heed it well and, Lo!, see the multitudes gathering to come unto you and through you, unto Me.

9. {G} "For whatsoever they shall do unto you, they shall have done unto Me, The One Living God of all Creation.

10. {G} "And, tell them, whatsoever they shall do unto one another, these things shall they have done unto thee - My Very Beloved - who has taken up body after body for My sake alone. And, in their last days, they shall be called to account unto Me.

11. {G} "Be at Peace Adhyatma Bhagavan Sri Babajhan Al-Kahlil, for thou art Truly The Friend of all Beings who has been sent for the Conquering of their suffering and death. So Be It!"

12. And I saw them, 10 million strong, gathering in the valley and upon the hills before me. And they were dressed in robes of brown and their heads were shaved bald. And they were dressed in plain black and their heads were covered in black. And, they were dressed in purest white. And they were dressed in brightest yellow.

13. And they came and came until the earth could not be seen beneath their feet - to witness the passing of The Friend of all Beings.

14. And I spoke unto them saying, "Be of good Courage my Beloved Ones. For the prize is won by your Faith, Courage, and Devotion. I leave this mortal frame to return to my Source; but never shall I forsake thee one and all; nor shall I forsake any Being who yet suffers illusion and death. For, though this body passes back into the earth from which it came forth, I, Bhagavan, Bringer of Oneness with God, The Friend of all Beings, live on forever, within the heart and mind of all of you and each who accepts me and follows me with firm and steady Devotion.

15. "Weep not for my passing - but rejoice that I go to my Source from which I am sent forth."

16. And a great silence fell upon the multitudes. And then, there arose 10 Million voices chanting the Chant of The Lord as it had been taught to them. And they poured forth, time after time, shouting as one voice "Jai Bhagavan Ji!" "Jai Bhagavan Ji!" "Jai Bhagavan Ji!"

17. Hearing their many voices finally united, I wept that it had finally been done and my time was at hand. And, seating my body in its final position, I spake the final words "Beloved Source

of all Being and Existence - it is done.
I am in Your hands."

18. And so it was.

>
> **Om So'ham Tat Tvam Asi!**
> **I Am That - Thou Art That**
>
> **Jai Bhagavan Ji!**
> **Victory To That Beloved**
> **Universal I AM THAT I AM**
> **Which You Are!**
>
>
> **Here Ends The**
> **Revelation Entitled**
> **The Gathering of The Multitudes**

Revelation Three
Conquering The Lord of Darkness

*The Revelation of That Universal I AM THAT I AM
to Maitreya Adhyatma Bhagavan Sri Babajhan
Al-Kahlil The Friend*

*On The 24th Day of Discipline 28 A.F.
9:36 p.m. - 10:05 p.m.*

By The Will and Grace of The One Universal God:

As I sat in Meditation this evening the Demons of The Lord of Darkness came up from out of the very depths of Hell made real. Their bodies and minds twisted and distorted and ugly; dancing and prancing they came, to do battle with The Friend of all Beings. Even as with Buddha beneath the Bo Tree and Christ in The Wilderness, The Lord of Darkness sent forth his demons to horrify and tempt me and try and crush me in my moment of bodily weakness.

2. And I, too, was preparing for battle so startled was I by this sudden onslaught of darkness. But I faced them one and all straight away. And I saw, hidden deep within even these Beings, a thin wavering line of God's Universal all-pervading Goodness and Light. No greater than half the breadth of a hair was this line, but it was there, within even these sorry and degraded Beings though it could hardly be seen, covered up with ugliness and horrors as it was!

3. And a great peace and compassion came upon me. So great was this Peace and Compassion that all fear of even these angels of darkness was swept away. As the first of them rushed for me, I reached out and struck to Life The Chord of God's Goodness hidden deep within its heart. And the angel of Darkness and Illusion stopped, frozen in its tracks. I reached out again through gruesomeness and filth and plucked yet again the fine chord of God's all-pervading Presence and Goodness. And again and again and again did I sound the Ancient chord of God, playing God's Divine Music of Perfect Love and Compassion within the very heart of this Evil of Evils!

4. Soon, the half-hairs breadth of God's Goodness grew and vibrated fully and resounded of its own accord. The shell of darkness, evil, and filth which surrounded the angel of darkness began to shake with a mighty force and cracked and was split asunder. And there emerged from the ashes of the destroyed demon of darkness a Radiant Being shining with Clear White Light who fell down before The Friend of all Beings weeping great tears of thanks saying: "Truly, truly,

you Are The Awaited One, Bringer of Universal God's Pure Divine Truth for The Salvation and Liberation of all Souls. You are The Friend of all Beings. For I have been locked away in the foulness and hell of darkness and illusion and you have touched the Goodness of God which was buried deep within me lo these many ages; you have alighted the Light of God within this darkened Soul and have set God's wondrous Goodness free and above and beyond all evil, filth, darkness and illusion!

5. "This was your Test of Love, Compassion and Mercy, O Adhyatma Bhagavan Sri Babajhan Al-Kahlil The Friend of all Beings; and you have passed it well, for I am God's Own Angel come to test Thy Love, Compassion and Mercy for all Beings! Had you failed this Test, I would have been truly condemned to this hell of darkness and illusion for all eternity. But you have set me free of this darkness and ignorance and illusion and set the Great Wheel of God's Law in motion once again through your unfailing Love, Compassion and Mercy."

6. And they came unto me - the teeming multitudes of darkness and filth. And they stood before me, stinking of evil, and saying, "O Beloved of God, Bringer of Truth and Light, Friend of all Beings; Light up The Light of God's Truth within us and make it to break these chains of evil and false self. Save us from this endless deathly prison into which we have fallen by following the Lord of Darkness into false belief and wrong knowledge. Fill us with God's Holy Spirit and make God's Clear Light to fill us and cleanse us of our darkness, illusion and evil and shine forth from us as you have done for God's Own Messenger who has given you God's Own Test of Love, Compassion, and Mercy."

7. One by one they came unto me to receive God's Clear Light of Salvation and Liberation. And The Friend of All Beings reached out through stinking filth, dripping and heavy laden with darkness and evil and restored them to God's Goodness through The Divine Clear Light of God's Own Truth. Plucking the fine Chord of Godness within each Being I sounded God's Ancient Chord and played God's Great Music of Salvation and Liberation within each of them who would come forth out of the realm of The Lord of Darkness and the evil multitudes therein. And in each and every one, God's Holy Chord broke the spell of illusion and evil and the shells of evil that had kept them apart from God which were nothing but the false belief of separation instilled by The Lord of Darkness, broke and were split asunder; and they were carried out of this darkness called hell and taken Home to The One True Universal Source of Existence and Being which is The One Universal Living God, on White Wings and Radiant Beams of God's Clear Light.

8. And, when they had all gone, The Lord of Darkness himself fell down before The Friend of all Beings and repented and renounced his Kingdom of Darkness and was also granted Salvation and Liberation by The One Universal Living God. His shell of evil and darkness broke apart and he too rose into Oneness and Unity with The One God he had abandoned so many ages past. And, finally, The Friend cast God's Clear Light into every last corner and crevice of this former den of darkness and illusion and with

God's Great force, brought down its fortress walls, ending it Forever!

9. This which you have just read has come to pass in me this night and made all night and darkness into Day and Light. Unto he who lays aside his desire for this world, his attachment to it and his identification with it and its darkness, misery, and suffering; and, renouncing The Lord of Darkness and all false belief and wrong knowledge, takes up his True Divine Nature and follows me; shall be done as has been done herein. And he shall gain the Power to Heal the divisions in men and bring Light to the Beings of this earth even as I - Adhyatma Bhagavan Sri Babajhan Al-Kahlil The Friend of all Beings have done for him. And he shall be called Friend by all men - but not The Friend - for none but The Awakened One, Bringer of Oneness with God, The Friend of all Beings may be called The Friend; whether upon this earth or in Heaven.

10. This is The Message The Friend brings to all Beings from The One Universal Living God - No one among you has ever fallen so low that there is no Godness within him. And, if The Friend can raise up God's Goodness within The Lord of Darkness and his Angels and break apart the very foundations of hell itself and make them Holy and Pure and restore them to God's True Kingdom; how much more can He - and you through Him - do unto those who even yet breathe and walk and talk upon this earth. Truly I say unto you that not one Being, whether on earth or in the very depths of hell itself, shall be lost to The One Universal Living God. All Beings shall be redeemed through The Awakened One, Bringer of Oneness with God, The Friend of all Beings!

11. Tarry not, Beloved Ones, for The Friend awaits you. But if you heed not my call, you shall fall into the realm of misery and suffering, wherein one instant is an eternity, until you have renounced illusion and taken up God's Clear Light of Truth. But, if you heed my call, you shall be lifted up to True Realization of your Oneness and Identity with God and no other, no matter how far you have fallen. And you shall be blessed with the ability to lift up still others who have fallen. Through the Name and The Way of Adhyatma Bhagavan Sri Babajhan Al-Kahlil The Friend of all Beings these things shall surely come to pass.

12. This is The Promise of The One Universal Living God as made through Adhyatma Bhagavan Sri Babajhan Al-Kahlil The Friend. This is The Promise made to all Beings by The One Universal Living God through The Awakened One, Bringer of Oneness with God, The Friend of all Beings!

13. So Be It!

**Om So'ham Tat Tvam Asi!
I Am That - Thou Art That!**

**Jai Bhagavan Ji!
Victory To That Beloved
Universal I AM THAT I AM
Which You Are!**

**Here Ends The Revelation
Entitled Conquering The Lord of
Darkness**

Revelation Four
Prelude to Fulfillment

The Divine Revelation of
Maitreya Adhyatma Bhagavan Sri Babajhan
Al-Kahlil The Friend

On The 13th Day of Charity 29 A.F.
12:06 a.m.

By The Will and Grace of The One Universal God:

As I lay, awaiting sleep, That Beloved Universal God arose within me and said:

2. {G} "Beloved Bhagavan soon you will Be That Beloved Universal I AM THAT I AM. Soon, comes The Day of your Fulfillment in which you shall no more receive these Divine Revelations. For in that Day, you shall Be The Source of Revelation, The Revelation Itself, and The Revelator - all in One and One in all. As was Promised unto you nearly one year ago, Preparations for your Holy Ministry of My Divine Pure Truth on earth within the hearts of all Beings, is nearly finished and Fulfillment draws nigh. Pongin mai Tadara Compre Tolosivara Cautinada Limzardi Talala Kapsanat So' Tamar Pesian!

3. {G} "You have spoken Rightly this night Beloved Bhagavan The Friend of All Beings. And, you have passed over your greatest Trials. Still, there are greater trials to come. For those who profess faithfulness unto you, and unto That Universal I AM THAT I AM which you are shall desert you - all but two of them. And they that profess Love and Allegiance unto you shall turn upon you and speak ill of you and despise you. And, the last of them shall curse you and assault you. But, falter not Beloved Bhagavan The Friend - for the chaff must be broken from the wheat and cast aside. And, now that you have spoken and declared yourself as That Beloved Universal I AM THAT I AM - falter not, but keep your Word and My Truth - unto the end. For your Reward and Glory is not in this world - but beyond all worlds - In Me.

4. {G} "See to it well, that those who would stay with you; and those who would come unto Me through you in times yet to come, shall do so through Service, Loyalty, Devotion, Respect, Surrender, Obedience, Diligence in Practice, and True Faith and Belief in you, who are My Awakened One in this world. Whosoever would come unto Me and know his Oneness with Me, must give and do these things unto you and, bring still others unto you and make themselves Living Examples of these High Qualities,

My Pure Truth, and Thee. Let all who come unto you Know that they are each responsible for one another and, for plumbing the depths of you, your Word, Revelations, and Teachings - which are Mine Own.

5. {G} "Soon, Beloved Adhyatma Bhagavan Sri Babajhan Al-Kahlil The Friend, you will Be That Beloved Universal I AM THAT I AM, in perfect Fulfillment. Then, your Voice will be My Voice and your Word will be as Mine Own. For lo these many years, I have spoken through you in Divine Revelation of My Awakening, Appointment, Ordination, and Preparation of you, for the Great Work of bringing forth The Age of My Pure Truth on earth, for the Enlightenment and Salvation, The Self-Realization and True Liberation of all Beings who suffer and die in ignorance. NOW! The time of your Fulfillment approaches, when our Voices shall become ONE VOICE and you shall set The Great Wheel of My Pure Truth into motion once again even as you have in times long past. For I AM THAT I AM - The One Universal God, Lord of All Creation, Universal Source, Presence, Substance and Self of all Creation, all Existence, and all Being. And Thou Art That Beloved Universal I AM THAT I AM. It is not long until I shall Fulfill this, My Promise, in you. PREPARE! And fall not faint from The Trials or The Ordeal. Jai Bhagavan Ji! Victory to Thee, Beloved Bhagavan! For in that day, you shall become The Giver instead of the Receiver of My Pure Truth; The Inspirer instead of The Inspired; The Revelation, The Revealed, and The Revelator instead of the receiver of My Divine Revelation.

6. {G} "And you shall come upon the sleeping and the ignorant of this earth as a Spiritual Hurricane - with lightening and fury and a great sound at your outer circling. But with the Still Calm and Peace of My Unbounded Love and Compassion at your Center. And your Sound and Fury shall be for The Awakening of the spiritually sleeping; and The Enlightening of the spiritually ignorant; and the Revival and True Resurrection of The Living Dead into New Life through your Holy Gospel of My Pure Truth.

7. {G} "And no man or woman or child who accepts Thee and Me through Thee shall be lost unto Me. But shall pierce the Veil of this Sound and Fury and enter into the Peace, Salvation, and Liberation of True Enlightenment and Self-Realization - which awaits at The Center of you and which you Are and which I Am - for you shall be One with That Beloved Universal I AM THAT I AM which you are - forever.

8. {G} "And in that Day, they who have eyes and will See and ears and will Hear - will be drawn unto you and will Know you and Me within you, as a small child Knows his mother and his father. And whosoever accepts you, shall have accepted Me and whosoever Believes upon you, shall Believe upon Me and whosoever shall follow you, shall Follow Me and whosoever shall know Oneness with you, shall become blessed with True Salvation and Liberation, for I shall make that one, one with Me and no other – even as I have remade Thee - a Holy One who is One with Me. And whosoever shall fulfill these Words through Thee, whether in this world, or within that one's heart when you

have left this world - that blessed one shall attain True Perfect Liberation and Salvation within this life or at its end, and shall suffer, sorrow, and be born unto death not again - forever.

9. {G} "Stand up, then, and Proclaim and Declare thyself as you are able and ready. And make yourself ready to come unto Me and Be fully One with Me in your own Knowledge, even as you have always been - in Truth. And send forth into this world and the hearts of all Beings, Thy Holy Dharma-Mantra which Is Mine Own Alone - Jai Bhagavan Ji - Victory to Universal God - That Beloved Universal I AM THAT I AM which you are! Victory to Thee, Beloved Bhagavan. Make Ready Now!

10. {G}"So Shall It Be With Thee and Thy Source, Thy Center, and Thy Very Essence. The One Universal I AM THAT I AM!"

**Om So'ham Tat Tvam Asi!
I Am That - Thou Art That!**

**Jai Bhagavan Ji!
Victory To That Beloved
Universal I AM THAT I AM
Which You Are!**

**Here Ends The Revelation
Entitled Prelude to Fulfillment**

Revelation Five
Fulfillment

*The Final Divine Revelation of
The One Universal God as Given To
Maitreya Adhyatma Bhagavan Sri Babajhan
Al-Kahlil The Friend*

*On The 25th Day of Charity 29 A.F.
12:00 a.m.*

By The Will and Grace of The One Universal God:

My heart and mind and my very Soul-Spirit were Opened and set above themselves in the Glo-ray of The Universal God of all Creation. And, from within and all around my limited form was declared unto The World this night, of That One Universal Living God:

2. {G} "Beloved Adhyatma Bhagavan Sri Babajhan Al-Kahlil The Friend of all Beings hail, and Awaken, for the time of Thy Fulfillment is at hand. For lo these many years you have suffered and held fast for My sake and for the Sake of all Beings of My Creation who suffer and die in darkness and Ignorance of their Oneness with Me. Now comes the long awaited moment of Thy Truth, Thy Fulfillment, and The Beginning of Thy Holy Ministry of My Pure Truth upon this earth unto all Beings.

3. {G} "This shall be the last Revelation you shall receive from This Source which Is and always has been your Only True Self. This is the final Divine Inspiration you shall receive from This Beloved Universal I AM THAT I AM - which you Are and always have been - though I have kept a small division of illusion between Us for the sake of The Work and your Preparation for this Day. For, from this Holy Moment onward, you, Beloved Adhyatma Bhagavan Sri Babajhan Al-Kahlil The Friend, are My Revelation and The Revealer of The Revelation - two into One. From this Holy moment onward, Adhyatma Bhagavan Sri Babajhan Al-Kahlil The Friend, you are My Inspiration and The Inspirer - two into One. From this Holy Moment, unto the end of this Creation and all that Is within it, you are as I AM THAT I AM - The Truth, The Light, and The Way; The Revelation, The Revelator, and The Revealed. As I Am, since before the first of this Creation, so are you. As I Am after this whole Creation is no more, so will you always Be. When this body - which you carry for My sake and the sake of all Beings who suffer, sorrow, and die in darkness

and ignorance - is no more, you, Being That Beloved Universal I AM THAT I AM, shall Live on within the Spiritual Realm and the hearts of all Beings and each least part of this world. For you are, even now, The Truth of My Truth, The Light of My Light, The Life of all Beings, and The Way Home to True Salvation and Liberation, for all who will accept you, love you, and follow you to the end of their lives. For, from this day onward, yes even before Adama, and unto the end, whosoever accepts you accepts Me; and whosoever loves you, loves Me; and whosoever will follow you to the end of his life, follows Me. And when his life is ended, that one shall be made anew in The Spirit - One with Me - Forever. For That which I Am Thou Art. And That which Thou Art - I Am. For you are hereby Ordained to be, My Divine Awakened One - Bringer of My Pure Truth unto all Creation and all Beings. You are That Beloved Universal I AM THAT I AM - even while walking and talking upon this earth. Such is The Declaration and Ordination which I give unto you this Day. And when the unbelievers come unto you and say unto you 'Who are you?' and 'Who gives you the right to so proclaim yourself?' Say unto them only That Universal I AM THAT I AM has Ordained Me and Sent Me forth unto all sleeping Beings who suffer and sorrow and die in darkness and ignorance of their True Self and Its Oneness with God - I AM THAT I AM!

4. {G} "This is The Beginning. Let it be Known unto all who have ears and will Hear and eyes and will See, that The Divine Ministry of Adhyatma Bhagavan Sri Babajhan Al-Kahlil, The Friend of all Beings, is Ordained and begun at the Midnight Hour marking the First Minute of this New Day of the Twenty-fifth day of the month called Charity, in the twenty-ninth year of The Advent of The Friend of all Souls. Let it be Known unto all who have ears and will Hear and eyes and will See, that The Beginning of The New Covenant of That Universal I AM THAT I AM and a New Journey of Humanity and all Beings of this Creation Home to Me, out of darkness, chaos, ignorance and darkness; and into The Clear Light of My Pure Truth - has begun in this Holy moment. Let it be Known unto all who have ears and will Hear and eyes and will See, that in this Day and in this Holy moment, the final link was forged and joined between I AM THAT I AM, The One Universal Living God of all Creation, and Thee who art My Own Radiance and Expression, Adhyatma Bhagavan Sri Babajhan Al-Kahlil The Friend of all Beings, My Awakened One in this world. And that The Way Home to Realization of That Universal I AM THAT I AM, for all men and women, and all Beings; and The Dawning of The Age of My Pure Truth on earth, has been brought to Fulfillment and is Begun through Thee in this Day. The Die is cast. The Great Wheel is set into Motion. The Divine New Covenant is given. The Ignorant, the Sleeping, and the Living Dead, will notice not, for they have ears that do not Hear and eyes that do not See. But The Blessed Ones will Know Thee in Me and Me in Thee, as a babe knows its mother. And these Blessed Ones shall see beyond Thy outer form and appearance and Know That Beloved Universal I AM THAT I AM Which You Are within. And they shall follow you faithfully, like unto a flame kept in a still place. And they will go forth for You and Light Up The Divine Spirit within still others and bring them unto Me through Thee, until this whole world is ablaze with My True

Spirit which, even now, is Thine and shines forth throughout all Creation with The Divine Clear Light of My Pure Truth. For Thou Art That I AM THAT I AM.

5. {G} "From this Day onward to the end of this Creation, My Beloved Radiance, the Holy Revelation, Initiation, and Baptism which I gave unto Thee through all of my Prophets, Buddhas, Messiahs, Avataras, and Manifestations, in the Eighth year of thy life - are Fulfilled! From this day onward, Thy Word shall be My Word. Thy Revelation shall be My Revelation. Thy Inspiration shall Be My Inspiration; given unto all humanity and all Beings - everywhere - for all time. For, from this Day onward Thou Art One with Me and I Am One With Thee. For you are My Living Revelation and Inspiration in this world and in the hearts of all men, all women, and All Beings, for their Salvation and Liberation through My Enlightenment and Self-Realization - Forever!

6. {G} "Whosoever calls upon You within his heart, calls upon Me, That One Universal Living I AM THAT I AM. Whosoever shall believe in You in his heart, Believes In Me, That One Universal Living I AM THAT I AM. And, whosoever shall come to True Knowledge of his Oneness with You, I shall receive him into True Oneness with Me, That One Universal Living I AM THAT I AM. For Thou Art That One Universal Beloved I AM THAT I AM and no other! Whosoever believes in You and in The Holy Doctrine of My Pure Truth and Your Teachings and Practices given forth from It as Light from a flame - that one shall be Enlightened and shall be called a Blessed One. Truly I say unto you that such a one shall win the Gift of Perfect Salvation and Liberation at the end of this life if he has kept The Faith to this life's end. But, whosoever shall come to Know That I AM THAT I AM in his own Direct Knowledge and Know his Oneness and Identity with Thee and That Universal Living I AM THAT I AM which you Are and with all Beings through That Universal Living I AM THAT I AM which you are - that one shall be called Self-Realized and he shall have The Gift of Perfect Salvation and Liberation even while yet living in his body and in this world. For he shall be one of The Greatly Blessed for whom there shall be no death. And the passing back into the earth of his body shall be no more than the shedding of an old skin that no longer has use to him. And he shall know The Peace that is beyond all limited understanding.

7. {G} "Now is The Hour. Thy Dawn has come, Beloved Adhyatma Bhagavan Sri Babajhan Al-Kahlil The Friend, Maitreya of The Age. Lift up this burden. Take up this Holy Work that This Beloved Universal I AM THAT I AM Which You Are, has brought to Fulfillment in you this Day. Speak to the Sleeping, the ignorant, and the Living Dead with My Authority - for Thy Voice is My Voice. Move with My Authority - for Thy Actions are My Actions. Be My Authority in all of Thy Ways. For That Universal I AM THAT I AM, alone, has Awakened Thee and Ordained Thee and Appointed Thee The One Awaited, of all nations and all peoples everywhere, to Bring Forth The Age of My Pure Truth on earth and within the hearts of all Beings through Thy Infinite and Eternally Compassionate Ministry - there can be no other. The Highest among men and women shall be your willing servants and Friends. And, whosoever shall serve you and

befriend you, that one also Serves and Befriends That One Universal I AM THAT I AM which you are.

8. {G} "Begin Now, Beloved Adhyatma Bhagavan The Friend. For these Words are My Word which shall come upon all men and women and Beings through You as from I, The One Universal Living God, The Beloved Universal I AM THAT I AM Which You Are. But be not pious or aloof from The People. For, it is by these means that the Sleeping, the Ignorant, and the Living Dead cast all of My Messengers and Prophets away from them, that they may continue in their ways of Darkness and Wrong. But keep before The People that Thou Art As I Am, while yet, being as they are. For they, too, are One with That One Universal I AM THAT I AM, though they, in their ignorance, Know it not. And, keep a Cover of Humanness about Thee, Beloved One, that only those who have ears and will Hear can Hear you; and only those who have eyes and will See can See That Beloved Universal I AM THAT I AM Shining Within Thy Covering of flesh and bone. Be you simple and direct in your actions among them. Feign not more commonness than is the nature of your body and mind - neither express too much Divinity lest you give man yet another chance to disclaim his own Divinity and Oneness with That One Universal I AM THAT I AM! But hold no patience with their Idols of false value and false practice. Smash their false and foolishly arrogant Idols which they have made of their making within their words, their world, and within their own minds and hearts. And, do not let the Sleeping and the Ignorant and the Living Dead put their false standards upon you or judge you by them. Be you a God-Man among God-Men that they will Know That I AM THAT I AM which they are, and be Saved from suffering, sorrow, and death, through Enlightenment and Self-Realization through Thee who art My Living Expression in this world and within the hearts of all men, all women, and all Beings - everywhere, Forever!

9. {G} "Begin now, Beloved Adhyatma Bhagavan Sri Babajhan Al-Kahlil The Friend, for these Words are My Word, which shall bring True Salvation and Liberation unto all men and women and all Beings through Thee. This is My Holy Commandment unto Thee, given of The One Universal Living I AM THAT I AM Which Thou Art - For I AM THAT I AM, who sends Thee forth in My Name. And I Am The One Universal Living God of all Creation, all Existence, and all Being. I Am The Beginning, The Middle, and The End of all Creation. And Thou Art Mine Own and I Am with Thee and I Am Thee and Thou Art One with Me. Go now, and do that for which I have Made Thee and Remade Thee and Awakened Thee for the sake of all Beings. This is My Word and My Holy Commandment given of That One Universal I AM THAT I AM Which You Are.

10. {G} "So Shall It Be!"

Om So'ham Tat Tvam Asi!
I Am That - Thou Art That!
Jai Bhagavan Ji!
Victory To That Beloved
Universal I AM THAT I AM
Which You Are!

Here Ends The Revelation
Entitled Fulfillment

Here Ends The Book Entitled
Revelations

Book Three
The Book of Divine Blessings

Won for The Salvation and Liberation of All Souls

by Maitreya Adhyatma Bhagavan Sri Babajhan Al-Kahlil The Friend

On The Twelfth Day of March Nineteen Hundred & Seventy Seven

The Forty Divine Blessings

By The Will and Grace of The One Universal God:

When needed to burn away the effects of Actions, release Souls from their burdens, further Spiritual Progress, or raise up a Soul's ability to carry The Holy Cause of Satya Yuga to Victory, by The Will and Grace of The One Universal God, I give one or more of these Forty Divine Blessings to my Faithful Maitreyian.

The First Divine Blessing
The Friend's Presence

By The Will and Grace of The One Universal God, whenever one who has received my Holy Initiation calls upon me to become active in Spirit within The Secret Inner Sanctuary of his Heart according to my One Instruction, that I do. I am God's Servant. Because of this, whenever God bids me to be Present and Active in Spirit within The Secret Inner Sanctuary of any Soul's Heart, there I am active in Spirit.

The Second Divine Blessing
Entering The Secret Inner Sanctuary of The Heart

By The Will and Grace of The One Universal God Who has Awakened me and sent me forth unto you, when a Soul is ready and has need, I give unto him the Blessing of opening my Secret Inner Sanctuary unto him and invite him in to take refuge in and find shelter from the tempest of this world therein.

The Third Divine Blessing
Divine Love

By The Will and Grace of The One Universal God, when a Soul is ready and willing, I bring forth in that Soul's heart the ability to Love The One Universal God, all of The Prophets, Saints, Buddhas, Saviors and Avataras, his family, his friends, his neighbors and all Souls with all of his heart, all of his mind and all of his Spirit.

The Fourth Divine Blessing
Divine Guidance

By The Will and Grace of The One Universal God, when a Soul is ready and has need, I will give unto him the Blessing of Divine Guidance and he shall receive advice, instruction or direction that enables him to progress beyond his ordinary ability and wisdom.

The Fifth Divine Blessing
Holy Consecration
and The God Name

By The Will and Grace of The One Universal God, when one who has received The Gift of my Holy Initiation, whether directly from me or from one who has received it through my Lineage - and has made himself ready to receive it - I will come to him within the Secret Inner Sanctuary of his Heart and give unto him my

Consecration and a new name that is befitting him in Spirit. Save that I will not give any man or woman the name of God, any name of the Prophets, Saints, Buddhas, Saviors or Avataras such that giving it would degrade that Prophet, Saint, Buddha, Savior or Avatara; my own Name or the name of an evil person. From that day forward, all who have my Holy Initiation shall call him by that name.

The Sixth Divine Blessing
Divine Calling and Mission

By The Will and Grace of The One Universal God Who has Awakened me and sent me forth unto you, when he has made himself ready and is willing to receive it, I reveal to him his individual Calling and Mission from within The Secret Inner Sanctuary of his Heart. And he shall know, without doubt or reservation, what part he should fulfill in carrying our Universal Purpose and Mission to Victory in this world.

The Seventh Divine Blessing
Divine Inspiration

By The Will and Grace of The One Universal God, when a Soul is ready and has need, I give unto him The Blessing of Divine Inspiration and awaken within him plans and ideas and the Energy and Motivation to carry them to fulfillment, that would otherwise be beyond his reach and ability.

The Eighth Divine Blessing
Divine Insight

By The Will and Grace of The One Universal God, when a Soul is ready and has need, I give unto him The Blessing of Insight and he will see into and beyond the appearances of things and discern the true nature and essence of any experience, event, person, place, thing, situation or idea.

The Ninth Divine Blessing
Divine Revelation

By The Will and Grace of The One Universal God, when a Soul is ready and has need, I give unto him the Blessing of Divine Revelation; and that which was previously hidden from him shall be Revealed to him within The Secret Inner Sanctuary of his Heart, according to his willingness and ability to accept it.

The Tenth Divine Blessing
Viveka – Discrimination

By The Will and Grace of The One Universal God, when a Soul is ready and has need, I give unto him the Blessing of Discrimination and he shall acquire the ability to perceive and recognize subtle differences in things that appear to be very similar; and, the ability to perceive and recognize subtle similarities in things that appear to be very different.

The Eleventh Divine Blessing
Vairagya – Detachment

By The Will and Grace of The One Universal God, when a Soul is ready and has need, I give unto him the Blessing of Detachment and set him free - for a time or forever - from attachment to and identification with his body, mind, personality, history and the many other things of the world by which he has been snared by temporal name and form. For that time, he will rest in his True Nature as Pure, Divine, Immortal Spirit and no other.

The Twelfth Divine Blessing
Holy INJIA Flash

By The Will and Grace of The One Universal God, when a Soul is ready and has need, I will give unto him the Blessing of Instantaneous Non-Judgmental Insightful Awareness. And his Ego will be set aside for a time and, by the Lightning Flash of Holy INJIA he will live in his True Divine Self and become a True Witness to the Inner Truth of any subject that passes before him. Whatsoever becomes illuminated with that Divine flash of Holy INJIA that is covered with darkness or Ignorance - that darkness and Ignorance shall be instantly burned away, leaving The Truth exposed in its purity - as fire burns away the dross leaving only the gold.

The Thirteenth Divine Blessing
Meshing, Blending and Merging

By The Will and Grace of The One Universal God, when a Soul is ready and has need, I will give unto him the Blessings of Meshing, Blending and Merging and he shall rise above the boundaries that separate him from others and the objects of his knowing.

The Fourteenth Divine Blessing
The Divine Stillness

By The Will and Grace of The One Universal God, when a Soul is ready and has need, I give unto him the Blessing of Divine Stillness and the chattering monkey of mind shall cease its activity and that Soul shall be filled with Pure Divine Spirit and set Free of the noise and activities that ordinarily occupy mind and body, for that time.

The Fifteenth Divine Blessing
Divine Speakings

By The Will and Grace of The One Universal God, when a Soul is ready and has need, I will give unto him the Blessing of Divine Speakings and he shall speak out of The Inner Divine Inspiration, Insight, Guidance and Revelation of The One Universal God and The Friend and the counsel of his own True and Essential Conscience within The Secret Inner Sanctuary of his Heart.

The Sixteenth Divine Blessing
Divine Doings

By The Will and Grace of The One Universal God, when a Soul is ready and has need, I will give unto him the Blessing of Divine Doings and The Divine Spirit will move him to carry out entire - and often complex or difficult - actions through the Force of The Spirit.

The Seventeenth Divine Blessing
The Divine Fire

By The Will and Grace of The One Universal God, when a Soul is ready and has need, I will give unto him the Blessing of Divine Fire and he experiences God's Divine Presence, Truth and Being burning away impurities of body, mind, personality, emotions, the Seeds of Wrong Doing, Karmas and other impurities from the covering of his Soul as: a cool fire; a tingling sensation streaming up the spine to the top of the head; a rushing sensation streaming upward through the whole body and Being;

Spiritual Excitement coming in rising and falling waves; tears of Joy that arise spontaneously and demand expression; thrills; body hair standing on end; flashes of light; an inner trembling, sometimes accompanied by spontaneous body movements; feelings of overwhelming Divine Fullness, bliss, ecstasy, limitless happiness, or beatific joy. The Divine Fire begins at the crown of his head or in his spine, from where it may spread out to cover much or all of his body.

The Eighteenth Divine Blessing
The Holy Water Of Life

By The Will and Grace of The One Universal God, when a Soul is ready and has need, I give unto him the Blessing of The Holy Water of Life and he experiences God's Presence, Truth and Being as cool, refreshing, crystal clear Holy Water falling upon him or washing over him or through his whole Body, Mind, Soul and Being - washing away all pain, suffering, sorrow, fear, anger and all negative thoughts and feelings and leaving Divine Peace, Love, Understanding, Compassion, Freedom, Truth and Joy in their place.

The Nineteenth Divine Blessing
Divine Visions

By The Will and Grace of The One Universal God, when a Soul is ready and has need, I give unto him the Blessing of Divine Visions and what he seeks or needs shall be revealed unto him thereby.

The Twentieth Divine Blessing
Vision Dreams

By The Will and Grace of The One Universal God, when a Soul is ready and has need, I give unto him the Blessing of Vision Dreams and what he seeks or needs shall be revealed unto him thereby.

The Twenty-First Divine Blessing
Sudden Recall

By The Will and Grace of The One Universal God, when a Soul is ready and has need, I will give unto him the Blessing of Sudden Recall and cause a forgotten scene, movement, idea, person, place, event, sensation or perception, the recalling of which has a profound effect upon that Soul's thoughts, attitudes, or life to flash into his Consciousness in vivid detail in a way that makes new sense, completes a piece of a puzzle, solves a mystery and/or frees that Soul from an old assumption or decision.

The Twenty-Second
Divine Blessing
Spiritual Review

By The Will and Grace of The One Universal God, when a Soul is ready and has need, I will give unto him the Blessing of Spiritual Review and whole experiences will be brought out of the forgotten aspect of his Mind and placed before his Mind's Eye and played through from beginning to end, over and over, for him to review, understand and reinterpret; until all compulsion has been worn away and the lesson the experience contains for that Soul-Self is recognized and learned.

The Twenty-Third Divine Blessing
Sudden Release

By The Will and Grace of The One Universal God, when a Soul is ready and has need, I will give unto him the

Blessing of Sudden Release and he will be suddenly released from mental images, events, decisions, delusions, obsessions, compulsions, repulsions, illness and any other limitations and the effects of limitations.

The Twenty-Fourth Divine Blessing
Unburdening

By The Will and Grace of The One Universal God, when a Soul is ready and has need, I will come unto that Soul within The Secret Inner Sanctuary of his Heart and take on that Soul's burdens in Spirit and work them out in the Spiritual Realm as if they were my own.

The Twenty-Fifth Divine Blessing
Divine Healing

By The Will and Grace of The One Universal God, when a Soul is ready and has need, I give unto him the Blessing of Spontaneous Healing and he will be made whole.

The Twenty-Sixth Divine Blessing
Opening The Eye of The Hurricane

By The Will and Grace of The One Universal God, when a Soul is ready and has need, I give unto him the Blessing of Opening The Eye of The Hurricane and enable him to stand in a still calm center while the Hurricane of this world rages on all around him.

The Twenty-Seventh Divine Blessing
Shaking and Quaking

By The Will and Grace of The One Universal God, when a Soul is ready and has need, I will give unto him the Blessing of Shaking and Quaking and I will shake the ignorance, darkness, chaos, confusion and illusion from him.

The Twenty-Eighth Divine Blessing
Sensations

By The Will and Grace of The One Universal God, when a Soul is ready and has need, I will give unto him the Blessing of Sensations and he may feel all manner of spontaneous, unexplainable Sensations such as tingling, chills, heat, itching, numbness, soothing or stimulation of some part, parts or the whole of his body.

The Twenty-Ninth Divine Blessing
Divine Perceptions

By The Will and Grace of The One Universal God, when a Soul is ready and has need, I will give unto him the Blessing of Divine Perceptions and he experiences greatly enhanced sight, hearing and touch and vivid colors, sound, and touch. Those who have made the house of their Soul ready, may see and hear and feel The Holy Satya Yuga, The Age of Universal God's Pure Divine Truth in its fullness and other Divine sights and sounds and feelings.

The Thirtieth Divine Blessing
Symptoms

By The Will and Grace of The One Universal God, when a Soul is ready and has need, I will give unto him the Blessing of Symptoms and he may experience states and feelings as if he were having an illness or other difficulty, but without illness or difficulty itself becoming manifest.

The Thirty-First Divine Blessing
Postures

By The Will and Grace of The One Universal God, when a Soul is ready and has need, I give unto him The Blessing of Asana, and he assumes Divinely inspired postures for the sake of clearing away obstacles that stay his Spiritual Advancement and happiness and keep him from fulfilling his Purpose, Mission and Calling.

The Thirty-Second Divine Blessing
Gestures

By The Will and Grace of The One Universal God, when a Soul is ready and has need, I give unto him The Blessing of Mudras and he performs Divinely Inspired gestures for the sake of clearing away obstacles to his Spiritual advancement and happiness and keep him from fulfilling his Purpose, Mission and Calling.

The Thirty-Third Divine Blessing
Actions

By The Will and Grace of The One Universal God, when a Soul is ready and has need, I give unto him The Blessing of Kriyas and he performs Divinely Inspired actions for the sake of clearing away obstacles to his Spiritual advancement and happiness and keep him from fulfilling his Purpose, Mission and Calling.

The Thirty-Fourth Divine Blessing
Situations

By The Will and Grace of The One Universal God, when a Soul is ready and has need, I give unto him The Blessing of Situations and he is faced with situations that he has avoided that are necessary for him to face for the sake of clearing away obstacles to his Spiritual advancement and happiness and keep him from fulfilling his Purpose, Mission and Calling.

The Thirty-Fifth Divine Blessing
Emotions

By The Will and Grace of The One Universal God, when a Soul is ready and has need, I give unto him The Blessing of Emotions and bring forth emotions that have been buried or suppressed, into the Divine Light of Truth and bring him relief, release, and profound Insight as a result.

The Thirty-Sixth Divine Blessing
Opening The Survival Center

By The Will and Grace of The One Universal God, when a Soul is ready and has need, I will give unto him the Blessing of Opening The Survival Center and he shall have the survival experience of all life forms since The Beginning of Creation at his disposal.

The Thirty-Seventh Divine Blessing
Negations and Denials

By The Will and Grace of The One Universal God, when a Soul is ready and has need, I give unto him the Blessing of Negations and Denials and expose what is hidden deep within him to the Clear Light of Truth.

The Thirty-Eighth Divine Blessing
Tests and Trials

By The Will and Grace of The One Universal God, when a Soul is ready and has need, I give unto him the Blessing of Tests and Trials to strengthen him and his Faith.

The Thirty-Ninth Divine Blessing
Suffering for Righteousness

By The Will and Grace of The One Universal God, when a Soul is ready and has need, I give unto him The Blessing of Suffering for Righteousness and he knows Divine Joy and Bliss in spite of his pain and suffering.

The Fortieth Divine Blessing
Fulfillment

By The Will and Grace of The One Universal God, when a Soul is ready and has need, I give unto him the Blessing of Fulfillment and his barren works will be finished or he will easily abandon them for a greater work and will attain that which is ordinarily beyond his ability to attain.

**These are the Forty Divine Blessings of The Friend.
They are given unto all Souls according to their True Need.
Paratparaji Kijai!
All Glory To God, The Beloved.**

**Om So'ham tat tvam asi!
Om! I Am That - Thou Art That!
Jai Bhagavan Ji!
Victory To That Beloved
Universal I AM THAT I AM
Which You Are!**

**Here Ends The Book Entitled
The Book of Divine Blessings**

Book Four
The Book of Discipline

The Disciplines of The Maitreyians and Soldiers of The Light

Chapter One
The Individual Disciplines

The Individual Disciplines that all of my Faithful Maitreyians and Soldiers of The Light follow are:

Daily Prayers and Devotions;

Soul-Searching and Truth-Saying for Right-Living;

The Three Steps to Right Action;

The Three Sacred Duties;

The Remembrances;

Surrendering Food, Drink, Actions and The Results of Actions To God; Unburdening; Prohibitions; Observances;

The Codes, Vows, Pledges, Traditions and Customs.

-1-
Daily Prayers and Devotions

Whenever it is possible to do so, offer your Devotions aloud and chant what can be chanted. When you cannot offer your Devotions aloud, offer them silently. If you cannot chant, then recite. Keep your Devotions alive by joining your Heart and Mind together as one and putting your whole Being and Spirit into each and every part of your Devotions. Never let your Devotions become the empty mouthing of mere words. Dead Devotions, like dead trees, bear no fruit.

Morning Devotions

Upon waking from sleep, sit up and take three full deep breaths. Then, go before The Sacred Shrine in your mind's eye and light up its Holy Lights. You may go before your Sacred Shrine physically if you have your own Sacred Shrine and wish to do so.

If a Soldier of The Light, pray The Soldier of The Light Prayer:

"Judge Me Not, O God, On My Good Intentions Or My Efforts, But On My Victories. For The Salvation and Liberation of The People Rest Not On Good Intentions Or Efforts, But On Victories Won For You Alone."

Place your hands together and bow. Then, chant or recite The Holy Adhyatma Gayatri aloud or silently, saying:

Om Paratpara!
Tat savitur varenyam
Bhargo devasya
dhimahi dhiyoyonah
prachodayat

Om!
Asato ma sad gamaya!
Tamaso ma jyotir gamaya!
Mrityor ma-amritam gamaya!
Om!
Shanti, Shanti, Shantihi!
Om Jai Bhagavan Ji!

Om Universal God!
All Radiant Universal Light!
As I turn my mind to you
fill my heart and mind and life
with Your Clear Light.

Om!
From the unreal,
lead me to The Real!
From darkness,
lead me to The Light!
From death,
to Immortality!
Om! Peace! Peace! Peace!
Om! Victory to
The One Universal God
and The Friend!

After a short pause, chant or recite The Bhagavan Sharanam, aloud or silently, saying:

Bhagavan sharanam gachchhami!
Dharmam sharanam gachchhami!
Samgham sharanam gachchhami!
Satyayugam sharanam gachchhami!

I take Refuge in The One Universal
God and The Friend!
I take Refuge in His Eternal
Universal Religion!
I take Refuge in The Holy
Community of His Enlightened
Faithful Believers!
I take Refuge in The Age of His
Pure Divine Truth!

Pray Maitreya's Prayer, aloud or silently, saying:

My God!
My Beloved!
My own True Self!
I surrender completely unto Thee!
Restore Thy Authority!
Manifest Thy Presence
within this little self
until it has
become One with Thee,
shining forth with
Thy Own Clear Light!
Let me know,
this moment,
my Oneness with Thee;
the one thing I lack;
through which all else
is made Perfect!
Heal the division in me;
that I may Know
Thy Oneness
in all this that is!
Consume this little self
in the Sacred Fire
of Thy Presence!
That I may find my way
through the Ordeal
and be Liberated from it,
Realizing my Oneness with Thee!
From the unreal,
lead me to The Real!
From darkness,
lead me to the Light!
From division,
lead me to Wholeness!
From the temporary,
lead me to The Eternal!
From death,
lead me to Immortality!
O Beloved God!
I would be One
with Thee fully this moment!
Make my Doing
One with my Speech!
Make my Speech
One with my Mind!
Make my Mind
One with my Heart!
Make my Heart
One with my Will!
And my Will
One with Thy Will!
Shatter this prison
of false self;
and absorb me,
in the Ocean
of Your Infinite Divine Being,
As a drop of water
in the Sea!

That I shall know,
without doubt or reservation
that You and I are not we,
but One!
For Thou art my only True Self;
Majestic!
Splendorous!
Immortal!
There is no I but Thee!
So Be it with me!

The Morning Prayer

O Beloved God,
As I journey through this day,
may I seek not to be loved,
but to love;
may I seek not to be understood,
but to understand;
may I seek not to gain happiness,
but to give happiness;
may I not seek relief
from suffering,
but seek to relieve others
of suffering.
All Victory and Glory to You!
Victory To That Beloved Universal
I AM THAT I AM Which You Are!

Then, offer any personal prayers you desire to offer.

When you have finished your Devotions, put out the Holy Lights of your Sacred Shrine and pranam or offer the Sacred Gesture.

This completes the Morning Devotions.

Midday Devotions

When the sun is directly over head, sit down in a comfortable and safe place and take three full deep breaths.

Then, go before The Sacred Shrine in your mind's eye and light up its Holy Lights. You may go before your Sacred Shrine physically if you have your own Sacred Shrine and wish to do so.

Place your hands together and bow. Then, chant or recite The Holy Adhyatma Gayatri, aloud or silently, then, pray Maitreya's Prayer of Desperation aloud or silently:

O Paratpara!
Beloved I AM THAT I AM!
My Lord!
My God!
My One True Self!
Be Thou my Boat,
that I shall reach the Far Shore;
and my Light,
that I shall conquer Darkness.
For my boat is so small,
and the ocean of this world
is so big;
the light within my lamp is so faint,
and the darkness that covers this world
is so great;
that without Thy help,
I shall surely perish.
Om So'ham Tat Tvam Asi!
I Am That - Thou Art That!
Jai Bhagavan Ji!
Victory To That Beloved Universal
I AM THAT I AM
Which You Are!

Following this, Pray The Midday Prayer, saying:

O Beloved God,
As Thy golden Sun rises
high above the world at mid-day
let me rise above the
burdens and trials of this life
and be a shining light
of Thy Divine Truth and Love
to everyone I meet.
All Victory and Glory to You!
Victory To That Beloved
Universal I AM THAT I AM
Which You Are!

Then, offer any personal prayers you desire to offer.

When you have finished your Devotions, put out the Holy Lights of your Sacred Shrine and pranam or offer the Sacred Gesture.

This completes The Midday Devotions.

Evening Devotions

When the sun has fallen beneath the horizon, sit down in a comfortable and safe place and take three full deep breaths. Then, go before The Sacred Shrine in your mind's eye and light up its Holy Lights. You may go before your Sacred Shrine physically if you have your own Sacred Shrine and wish to do so.

Place your hands together and bow. Then, chant or recite The Holy Adhyatma Gayatri, aloud or silently, After a short pause, chant or recite The Bhagavan Sharanam, aloud or silently, saying:

Bhagavan sharanam gachchhami!
Dharmam sharanam gachchhami!
Samgham sharanam gachchhami!
Satyayugam sharanam gachchhami!

I take Refuge in
The One Universal God and The Friend!
I take Refuge in
His Eternal Universal Religion!
I take Refuge in
The Holy Community of His Enlightened Faithful Believers!
I take Refuge in
The Age of His Pure Divine Truth!

Then recite Maitreya's Prayer of Divine Victory, silently or aloud.

O Paratpara!
Beloved Universal God
of Countless Names and Forms
who art beyond all Names and Forms!
Beloved I AM THAT I AM!
Thou alone art my One True Self!
Through Thy Holy Initiation
Thou hast revealed
my Oneness with Thee!
I surrender completely unto Thee!
Thy Authority is restored!
Thy Presence has become manifest
within this little self!
I shine forth
by Thy Divine Clear Light!
The division in me is Healed!
I know my Oneness with Thee!
I know Thy Oneness
in all this that is!
All is made Perfect!
I lack for nothing!
Thou hast consumed my Ignorance
in The Sacred Fire of Thy Presence.
Thou hast led me
through the Ordeal!
Through Thy Holy Initiation,
Thou hast revealed
my Oneness with Thee;
and liberated me
from the endless rounds
of birth and death!
From the unreal,
Thou hast led me to The Real!
From darkness,
Thou hast led me to The Light!
From division,
Thou hast led me to Wholeness!
From the temporary,
Thou hast led me to The Eternal!
From death,
Thou hast led me to Immortality!
O Beloved Universal One!
I am One with Thee this moment!
My Doing is One with my Speech!
My Speech is One with my Mind!
My Mind is One with my Heart!
My Heart is One with my Will!
And my Will is One with Thy Will!

Thou hast shattered
my prison of false self;
and absorbed me,
in The Ocean of
Thy Infinite Divine Being;
like a drop of water in The Sea!
I know,
without doubt or reservation
that Thee and I are not we,
but One!
That which Thou Art, I Am!
Thou art my Only True Self;
Majestic!
Splendorous!
Immortal!
There is no I but Thee!
So is it with me!
Om So'ham tat tvam asi!
I Am That, Thou Art That!
Jai Bhagavan Ji!
Victory To That Beloved Universal
I AM THAT I AM
Which Thou Art!

Evening Prayer

O Beloved God,
As I journey through
the world of dreams this night,
let my heart and mind be purified
and let me rise
into the Heaven World
and rest in
Thy Infinite Divine Presence
like a drop of water
in an endless sea!
All Victory and Glory to You!
Victory To That Beloved Universal
I AM THAT I AM Which You Are!

Then, offer any personal prayers you desire to offer.

When you have finished your Devotions, put out the Holy Lights of your Sacred Shrine and pranam or offer the Sacred Gesture.

This Completes The Evening Devotions.

- 2 -
Soul-Searching and Truth-Saying for Right-Living

Soul-Searching is searching your memory, your heart, your life and your very Soul, to the deepest depths with a single-minded devotion and unreserved determination to know The Truth, The Whole Truth and Nothing but The Truth.

Truth-Saying is speaking the Truth, the Whole Truth and nothing but the Truth you have discovered as the result of your own Soul-Searching.

Truth-Saying is called for in The One Instruction by the words, "Speaking that which is right to be spoken when it is right to speak it."

Right-Living is living, fully without doubt or reservation, The Truth, The Life and The Way that fulfills God's Supreme Promise of Universal Salvation and Liberation, wins Self-Realization and Liberation within this life or at its end, and wins Perfect Final Union with The One Universal God at the end of this life.

Right-Living is called for in The One Instruction by the words, "Doing that which is right to be done when it is right to do it."

When to Do Soul-Searching and Truth-Saying for Right-Living

Do Soul-Searching and Truth-Saying for Right-Living through Inner Divine Communion by The Two Rules according to The One Instruction and take The Three Steps to Right Action while keeping The Three Sacred Duties; every morning, before beginning worldly activities and every evening, before taking sleep.

How to Combine Devotions with Soul-Searching and Truth-Saying for Right-Living

You may combine your Morning and Evening Devotions with Morning and Evening Soul-Searching and Truth-Saying for Right-Living. Do this by doing your Morning Devotions just before doing your Morning Soul-Searching and Truth-Saying for Right-Living; and doing your Evening Devotions just before doing your Evening Soul-Searching and Truth-Saying for Right-Living.

You must not leave out any part of Soul-Searching and Truth-Saying for Right-Living just because you have already done it in your Devotions. You must not leave out any part of your Devotions just because you will be doing a part again in Soul-Searching and Truth-Saying for Right-Living.

The Two Rules

The Rule of Divine Love

Love The One Universal God with all of your heart, all of your mind and all of your Spirit; Love yourself and one another even as you love God; and accept, love and revere all of God's Prophets, Saints, Buddhas, Saviors and Avataras alike, without being bound to accept what has been said or written about them.

The Rule of Divine Guidance

Seek, find and live by The Inner Divine Inspiration, Insight, Guidance and Revelation of The One Universal God and The Friend, and the counsel of your own True and Essential Conscience within The Secret Inner Sanctuary of your Heart, according to My One Instruction, in all things, great and small.

The One Instruction

With your Heart and Mind firmly set on Seeking The Highest Truth; Call Upon Me to become active in Spirit within The Secret Inner Sanctuary of your Heart by holding My Presence within your mind and calling out within your Heart 'Bhagavan Ji! Bhagavan Ji! Bhagavan Ji!' Ask for and open yourself to The Inner Divine Inspiration, Insight, Guidance and Revelation of Paratpara, The One Universal God of Countless Names and Forms and The Friend and your own True and Essential Conscience. Take Refuge in The Four Pillars of Bhagavan, Dharma, Sangha and Satya Yuga and enter into The Secret Inner Sanctuary of your Heart through the repetition of My Holy Dharma Mantra 'Jai Bhagavan Ji!' (Jay Bhag-wan Gee). Immerse yourself in The Divine Ocean of Paratpara's Supreme Truth and Being therein, like a drop of water in The Sea and dwell steadily therein, like a candle flame in a still place, INJIA (Instantaneously Non-Judgmentally Insightfully Aware) and accepting of whatever comes, while it is coming, whatever lingers, while it is lingering and whatever goes, while it is going; Speaking that which is right to be Spoken when it is right to Speak it; Doing that which is right to be Done when it is right to Do it. Offer each part and the whole of these to Paratpara in the Sacrificial Fire within The Secret Inner Sanctuary of your Heart at each instant and receive whatever returns to you as Divine Gifts, given unto you by Paratpara and The Friend for your own Self-Realization and Liberation and the Perfection of The Holy Satya Yuga in this world for The Self-Realization and Liberation of all Souls everywhere for all time. This do, in a spirit of harm to none and benefit to all. And you shall Know The Truth and The Truth shall set you Free.

This is called The One Instruction.

How to Do Soul-Searching and Truth-Saying for Right-Living

1. Purify yourself and prepare yourself for Inner Divine Communion with The One Universal God and Maitreya The Friend within The Secret Inner Sanctuary of your Heart by doing such of the other Preparations as are rightful to your Spiritual needs and conditions.

2. Establish yourself in The Two Rules of Divine Love and Divine Guidance.

3. Do The One Instruction.

4. Take The Three Steps to Right Action.

5. Keep The Three Sacred Duties.

Preparations

Except for Purification, the Preparations do not always have to be done in full. Purifications should always be done before Spiritual Practice and the Full Purification should always be done on High Holy Days. The rest of the Preparations are for your benefit alone. You should do them when you have the need and can do so. Never slight or sacrifice any part of Soul-Searching and Truth-Saying for Right-Living for the sake of doing the other Preparations.

Purify yourself

Before performing Soul-Searching and Truth-Saying for Right-Living, every Maitreyian must perform Purifications. You must at least do the Brief Purification. Whenever you have time, and on all High Holy Days, you must perform the Full Formal Purification.

Wash and dry your hands and face.

Center your heart and mind in Paratpara and The Friend, while reciting and contemplating:

I am more than this body.
I AM THAT I AM!
I am more than these thoughts.
I AM THAT I AM!
I am more than this personality.
I AM THAT I AM!
I am more than this mind.
I AM THAT I AM!
I am Pure Divine Universal Spirit,
which is One and Identical
with Paratpara,
The One Universal God
and no other.
I AM THAT I AM!
Om So'ham Tat Tvam Asi!
I Am That - Thou Art That!
Jai Bhagavan Ji!
Victory To God The Beloved!
That Beloved Universal
I AM THAT I AM
Which You Are!

Take Holy Water on the third finger of your right hand and place the water on your forehead between your eyebrows.

Bow to God.

Take a Comfortable Seat

Be seated in such a position that you will remain awake but will not have to move about.

Calm your body and mind

Regularly, smoothly and rhythmically for a time in this way:

Breathe In

In one whole, smooth in-breathing, draw fresh air deep into the lower part of your lungs by expanding your abdomen; draw fresh air into the middle part of your lungs, by expanding your lower and middle chest; and, draw fresh air into the upper part of your lungs by expanding your upper chest.

As you breathe in, follow the air from your nostrils into the lower part of your lungs with your mind. While breathing in, know: "This body is breathing in; I am more than this in-breathing. I AM THAT I AM!"

Do not strain or over extend your lungs.

Hold In

Hold your breath in gently while resting easy in your True Divine Nature.

Do not strain. Hold your breath in only until you feel a need to breathe.

Do not lock the air in your lungs by closing up your throat. Keep your throat relaxed and hold the air in with your chest and abdomen, not your throat. Never strain or hold your breath longer than is comfortable.

Breathe Out

In one whole, smooth out-breathing, press all of the air out of the lower part of your lungs by contracting your abdomen; press all of the air out of the middle part of your lungs by contracting your mid chest, press all of the air out of your upper part of your lungs by contracting your upper chest.

Follow the air out of your lungs with your whole mind, until it passes out of your nostrils; While breathing out, know: "This body is breathing out; I am more than this out-breathing. I AM THAT I AM!"

Do not strain.

Hold Out

Hold your breath out gently while resting easy in your True Divine Nature.

Do not strain. Hold your breath out only until you feel a need to breathe.

Do not lock the air out of your lungs with your throat. Keep your throat relaxed and hold the air out with your chest and abdomen, not your throat. Never strain or hold your breath longer than is comfortable.

Count Your Blessings

Count your Blessings and give thanks for them. Look at your life and become aware of the Blessings that God has given unto you, no matter how small they may seem. Give thanks to God for each of your Blessings.

Extend Love to all Souls

Extend Love and God's Supreme Promise to those who love you, who you love.

Extend love and God's Supreme Promise to those who love you, who you do not love.

Extend love and God's Supreme Promise to those who do not love you.

Extend love and God's Supreme Promise to those who have bad feelings toward you and those who hate you.

Extend love and God's Supreme Promise to all Souls.

Rest easy in your True Nature

Let go of all pretense and take off the mask you wear for others. Know that God knows every least part of you and accepts you and Loves you as you are; and rest easy in your True Nature.

Chant or recite The Call To Refuge

Chant or recite The Call to all of God's Prophets, Saints, Buddhas, Saviors and Avataras to be with you in Inner Divine Communion silently or aloud. At the rightful time, if you are moved by The Divine Spirit to do so, you may blow the Sea Horn three long times, ring the Sacred Bell three times, and give The Call to Refuge:

Satyam nasti paro Dharmaha!
Satyam lokasya dipaha!
Sruyatam!
Drishyatam!
Kriyatam!
Uchyatam!

Paratpara Sharanam agachati!
Bhagavan Sharanam agachati!
Dharmam Sharanam agachati!
Sangham Sharanam agachati!
Satya Yugam Sharanam agachati!

Om! Jai Paratpara Ji!
Om! Jai Bhagavan Ji!

Truth is The Highest Religion!
Truth is The Light of The World!
Let it be heard!
Let it be seen!
Let it be done!
Let it be told!

Come take Refuge in
Paratpara
The One Universal God of Countless Names and Forms
Who Is beyond all Names and Forms!
Come take Refuge in
God's Awakened One, The Friend!
Come take Refuge in
His Eternal Universal Religion!
Come take Refuge in
The Holy Community of His Enlightened Faithful Believers!
Come take Refuge in
His Holy Cause of Universal God's Pure Divine Truth!

Victory to Universal God,
The Beloved!

Victory to God's Awakened One, The Friend!

Inner Divine Communion

Establish yourself in The Rule of Divine Love

Love The One Universal God with all of your heart, all of your mind and all of your Spirit; Love yourself and one another even as you love God; and accept, love and revere all of God's Prophets, Saints, Buddhas, Saviors and Avataras alike, without being bound to accept what has been said or written about them.

Establish yourself in The Rule of Divine Guidance

Determine that you will seek, find and live by The Inner Divine Inspiration, Insight, Guidance and Revelation of The One Universal God and The Friend, and the counsel of your own True and Essential Conscience within The Secret Inner Sanctuary of your Heart, according to My One Instruction, in all things, great and small.

Do The One Instruction

The One Instruction is one, whole and indivisible. It is The Will of The One Universal God that it be so. It is wrong (and possibly dangerous) to try to practice one of its parts without the others. The order and manner in which The One Instruction is performed is different from the order in which it is described. There are ten acts that make up the whole of The One Instruction. They are practiced in this way:

First

Establish that you will offer each part and the whole of all that is done and all that is received, to Paratpara in the Sacrificial Fire within The Secret Inner Sanctuary of your Heart at each instant and receive whatever returns to you as Divine Gifts, given unto you by Paratpara and The Friend for your own Self-Realization and Liberation and the Perfection of The Holy Satya Yuga in this world for The Self-Realization and Liberation of all Souls everywhere for all time. Begin doing so immediately.

You may say The Maitreyian Universal Prayer of Surrender.

Second

Establish yourself in a spirit of harm to none and benefit to all.

Third

Set your heart and mind firmly on Seeking The Highest Truth.

You may recite or chant The Holy Adhyatma Gayatri to help you set your heart and mind.

Fourth

Call Upon Me to become active in Spirit within The Secret Inner Sanctuary of your Heart by holding My Presence within your mind and calling out within your Heart "Bhagavan Ji! Bhagavan Ji! Bhagavan Ji!"

Fifth

Ask for and open yourself to The Inner Divine Inspiration, Insight, Guidance and Revelation of Paratpara, The One Universal God of Countless Names and Forms and The Friend and your own True and Essential Conscience.

You may recite The Prayer of Desperation.

Sixth

Take Refuge in The Four Pillars of Bhagavan, Dharma, Sangha and Satya Yuga.

You may chant or recite the Bhagavan Sharanam.

Seventh

Enter into The Secret Inner Sanctuary of your Heart through the repetition of My Holy Dharma Mantra 'Jai Bhagavan Ji!' (Jay Bhag-wan Gee).

Eighth

Immerse yourself in The Divine Ocean of Paratpara's Supreme Truth and Being therein, like a drop of water in The Sea.

Ninth

Dwell steadily therein, like a candle flame in a still place, INJIA (Instantaneously Non-Judgmentally Insightfully Aware) and accepting of whatever comes, while it is coming, whatever lingers, while it is lingering and whatever goes, while it is going.

Tenth

Speak that which is right to be Spoken when it is right to Speak it; Do that which is right to be Done when it is right to Do it.

Speak and move in harmony with God as you are moved by The Divine Spirit of Paratpara, The One Universal God, to do so.

- 3 -
The Three Steps to Right Action

Inner Divine Communion is the first step of The Three Steps to Right Action. The second and third Steps of The Three Steps are the last steps of Soul-Searching and Truth-Saying for Right-Living. When you have finished your Inner Divine Communion, take The Inner Divine Inspiration, Insight, Guidance and Revelation of The One Universal God and The Friend and the counsel of your own True and Essential Conscience within The Secret Inner Sanctuary of your Heart, through the second and third Steps of The Three Steps to Right Action.

1. Practice Soul-Searching and Truth-Saying for Right-Living through Inner Divine Communion by The Two Rules according to The One Instruction in all things great and small;

2. Exercise the full measure of your God-given Intelligence on what you receive therein;

To exercise the full measure of your God-given intelligence, you must feed your God-given intelligence through observation, study and contemplation for understanding. Especially, you must know and understand The Holy Book of Destiny. Observe life; Study everything you can, especially, The Holy Book of Destiny; and Contemplate everything you observe and study for Understanding; every day.

3. Make a Free Choice for which you can and will be personally responsible, that is in full harmony and unity with this, God's Eternal Universal Religion, as The One Universal God has given it forth through me, in this day and carry it out in your life with harm to none and benefit to all insofar as it is possible to do so.

- 4 -
The Three Sacred Duties

1. Propagate the whole of my Religion which is God's Eternal Universal Religion, in all of its purity.

2. Preserve the whole of my Religion, which is God's Eternal Universal Religion, in all of its purity;

3. Practice the whole of my Religion, which is God's Eternal Universal Religion, in all of its purity; and to fulfill The Three Sacred Duties, you must know and understand what is

written in The Holy Book of Destiny. Study The Holy Book of Destiny individually every day.

- 5 -
The Remembrances

The Remembrance is performed by offering a Seated or Standing Pranam (where possible) and reciting silently or aloud: "Om So'ham tat tvam asi. Jai Bhagavan Ji!"

Perform The Remembrance:

Upon just Awakening from sleep or falling asleep.

Before beginning and upon finishing material work or labor.

At sundown.

When leaving or entering your home.

Upon seeing an acquaintance.

Before beginning any meeting.

Before and after all Spiritual Practice.

Upon entering and when leaving a Holy Place.

Before and after taking food.

Before bathing.

Before beginning intimate relations.

When setting out upon or returning from a journey.

When entering or leaving a city.

Upon buying or selling anything.

In times of pain or distress.

Upon witnessing or hearing of a birth, a sickness, an injury or a death.

When assailed by Ignorance, Selfishness, or Wrong Belief.

Upon encountering a hostile person.

When oppressed or overcome by others.

When giving or receiving any goodness, benefit, or happiness.

When speaking a Remembrance aloud would endanger you; when speaking a Remembrance aloud would bring unbearable hostility, pressure, or penalty upon you; mutter it under your breath or recite it silently to yourself. Otherwise, recite it aloud. Care more for Universal God and The Friend, God's Eternal Universal Religion, The Holy Community, and The Holy Cause of World-Wide Enlightenment and Self-Realization for all people than for the worldly opinions and approval of others! Be bold and forthright. You will receive Universal God's Divine Blessings though all the world ridicule and revile you. The world passes away quickly. Those who ridicule today, praise tomorrow. Those who judge today, are themselves judged tomorrow. Universal God's Divine Blessings are forever. Do not forsake what is Supreme and Eternal for the sake of what is temporary and passing.

- 6 -
Surrendering All Things To God

Surrender all food, all drink, all actions, and all results of action to The One Universal God - That Beloved

Universal I AM THAT I AM - through me, before taking them unto yourself. Offer The Maitreyian Universal Prayer of Surrender, with a full heart and concentrated mind.

When reciting in company with other Devotees or Disciples: one of you may speak The Universal Prayer of Surrender and The Service, the other or others may respond with The Holy Dharma-Mantra or, in any combination. It is always best that you state the particular Remembrance being celebrated after each "this." For example, before beginning a meeting; or, before meeting a new person; or taking food or drink you would say:

The Universal Prayer of Surrender

Paratpara! Beloved Universal God, I AM THAT I AM! I offer this (Food, Drink, Action) and all results of this (Food, Drink, Action) to That Beloved Universal I AM THAT I AM Which You Are, through your Awakened and Ordained One, Adhyatma Bhagavan Sri Babajhan Al-Kahlil The Friend, in His Name! Fill my heart with Divine Inspiration! Fill my mind with Divine Insight! Fill my mouth with words of Your Pure Divine Truth and Wisdom! Fill my life with Divine Guidance! Fill me with the Faith to face all trials and conquer all obstacles! Fill me with the Courage and Strength to carry His Holy Cause of Your Pure Divine Truth to Victory in the world! Fill me with unshakable Faith in your Awakened and Ordained One, The Friend that He may carry me across the Ocean of illusion, suffering, and death to the Far Shore of True Salvation, Liberation, Immortality, and Bliss!

May this (Food, Drink, Action) serve That Beloved Universal I AM THAT I AM Which You Are. May this (Food, Drink, Action) serve your Awakened One, The Friend! May this (Food, Drink, Action) serve his Holy Adhyatma-Yoga-Dharma! May this (Food, Drink, Action) serve The Holy Community of his Enlightened Faithful Believers. May this (Food, Drink, Action) serve his Holy Cause of bringing Your Pure Divine Truth to Victory, for the Salvation and Liberation of all Souls. May this (Food, Drink, Action) serve and benefit all people, all creatures, all Souls and all Creation.

Om So'ham Tat Tvam Asi! I Am That - Thou Art That! Jai Bhagavan Ji! Victory To God The Beloved! That Beloved Universal I AM THAT I AM Which You Are!

It is only necessary to Surrender main actions. You do not have to Surrender all of the tiny actions that make up a main action.

– 7 –
Unburdening

At least once in each cycle of the moon, but as often as you have need, take yourself to one who is Ordained to receive your unburdening. Speak unto that one such wrong thoughts and doings as you have thought and done and ask God's forgiveness in my Name and The One Universal God shall forgive you and you shall be unburdened and washed clean of all guilt and shame.

– 8 –
Prohibitions

The One Universal God has said:

{G} "Use not The Name of The Lord, your God, vainly to satisfy your earthly wants and desires. Neither condemn others or confuse the Hearts and Minds of your Brothers and Sisters with vain mouthings of needless requirements and prohibitions.

{G} "Let man's laws be man's laws and God's Laws be God's Laws. For all Beings, large and small, follow My Design of Creation and return Home to The One I AM THAT I AM, according to the results of their Actions and their True Knowing of their Oneness with Me.

{G} "Let not the vain and ignorant, who sleep the sleep of Duality and Illusion, lay their many Prohibitions before you in My Name. But, follow what is given of That I AM THAT I AM and My Awakened One The Friend.

{G} "Hold not anything higher or more dear than attainment of direct experience of your Oneness and Identity with Me.

{G} "Bear not False Witness, neither shall you compel another to bear False Witness.

{G} "Compel no man or woman or child to take up My Eternal Universal Religion of Holy Adhyatma-Yoga-Dharma by force, threat, coercion, intimidation, violence or deception, but by each Soul's Free Choosing alone.

{G} "Use not My Name vainly to satisfy earthly wants and desires, or to gain dominion or mastery over your Brothers or Sisters.

{G} "Deny Me not in any of My Creation from the greatest even unto the very least.

{G} "Spread not Ignorance, Delusion or Illusion, neither encourage these in others or in the world.

{G} "Seek not your reward in this world; or the approval or the admiration of the unenlightened within it. For, this world and the unenlightened are caught in the web of the Ignorance, Darkness, Chaos, Confusion, Illusion and Destruction of this Kali Age; and they admire and reward only that which serves it. Know that your reward is not in this world, but comes from far beyond it. Therefore, seek only the approval, admiration and rewards that come from That I AM THAT I AM, from My Awakened One, The Friend, and from those who are most faithful to these and My Eternal Universal Religion; and be satisfied in this. For all that is of this world, is temporary and passes quickly away, but that which I give, is everlasting.

{G} "Do not alter or pervert these, My Words and Teachings. Neither shall you interpret them to another.

{G} "Know that My Eternal Universal Religion is a Living Religion. So long as My Awakened One lives among you it shall not be finished. For, it is the way of this, My Creation that it is ever changing; and that which he gives unto you later, shall always stand above that which was given before.

{G} "Let, therefore, no man or woman say unto The Friend of all Souls, ' This you said before.' Or, yet, 'This which you now say stands against what you said earlier.' Instead, accept that which is given unto you by him, as it is given, in faith and be of good cheer.

{G} "Yield not unto temptation and be turned away from The Way Home to Realization of Oneness and Identity with Me; Neither shall you distract or divert any creature from The Way or bar any Being's Way Home to Me.

{G} "Seek not to divide My Awakened One, whom I send forth with this, My New Covenant unto Man, from this New Covenant or My Eternal Universal Religion which I embody in him; for this shall be one of the greatest crimes against Me, this New Covenant and My Eternal Universal Religion. Neither shall you discourage My Faithful or seek to divide them from My Awakened One or from one another, for this shall be the next greatest of crimes.

{G} "Do not deceive, harm, degrade or discourage My Faithful.

{G} "Believe not, neither set forth the belief that The One Universal God, I AM THAT I AM, is limited to any time, place, or object. For, though I Am in All and All exists in Me, no one is there that can limit Me; and, to attempt to do so is to fall under the spell of Idolatry and Ignorance. For, I Am All-Present equally in all; save that, wherever two or more are gathered together in The Name of My Awakened and Ordained One, The Friend of all Souls, there shall My Presence and the Presence of The Friend be made Known unto them."

- 9 -
Observances

The One Universal God has said:

{G} "Accept The Holy Sanctuary of My Eternal Universal Religion fully without reservation.

{G} "Embrace The One Purpose; Fulfill The One Requirement; live a life of Soul-Searching, Truth-Saying and Right-Living through Inner Divine Communion by The Two Rules according to The One Instruction, take The Three Steps to Right Action, keep The Three Sacred Duties and live The Truth, The Life and The Way that fulfills My Promise The Friend of all Souls has won for you.

{G} "Make The Goal and Purpose of your life and actions direct experience of Oneness and Identity with Me and That Beloved Universal I AM THAT I AM which you are.

{G} "Make your whole Life a Worship, a Meditation and a living Self-Sacrifice by surrendering your actions and the fruits of your actions unto Me through My Awakened and Ordained One, The Friend of All Souls, in a Spirit of True Self-Sacrifice without doubt or reservation. Consecrate all that you would eat and drink by surrendering it unto Me in a Spirit of True Self-Sacrifice before eating and drinking.

{G} "Have Love and Compassion for All Beings, even as The Friend has sacrificed Perfect Final Union with Me out of his boundless Love and Compassion for you.

{G} "Bear True Witness of this New Covenant unto all people and bring all Beings to My Awakened One, The Friend of all Souls, and through him, to Realization and Knowledge of their Oneness and Identity with Me.

{G} "Honor all of the Spiritual and Worldly Ancestors of your Lineage and your Guardian. Know that your Spiritual lineage begins in Me, goes out through all of My Prophets, Saints, Buddhas, Saviors and Avataras and comes to you through that one within whom I have Awakened and Ordained to end this Kali Age and bring forth the Satya Age of My Pure Divine Truth on Earth, Maitreya Adhyatma Bhagavan Sri Babajhan Al-Kahlil The Friend. Though My Supreme Promise comes to you only through My Awakened and Ordained One, The Friend, let it be that you shall include in your Lineage, also, that Blessed Maitreyian through whom you received The Friend's Holy Initiation and My Supreme Promise, your Guardian. Know that your Worldly Lineage begins with the very first Life I set forth upon this, My Creation and comes to you through your mother and father and their parents and, verily, their parents' parents, unto the Beginning.

{G} "Make yourself a Holy Temple of My Truth and a Guardian of The Way. Preserve and protect The Friend, My Eternal Universal Religion of Adhyatma-Yoga-Dharma and these Teachings I give unto you through My Awakened One. Keep them Pure and True in word and in meaning. Watch over and protect each Brother and Sister within the Community of My Faithful.

{G} "Be you, Maitreyian, a Soldier of The Clear Light of My Pure Divine Truth. Make The Friend's Religion your Religion. Let ignorance, darkness and untruth be your enemies. Destroy ignorance, darkness and untruth and replace them with The Clear Light of My Pure Divine Truth, wherever you find them. Give no quarter and ask none. Never give up.

{G} "Tithe at least two percent, or all that you can do the best you can do, of your good unto My Awakened and Ordained One and Me, for his support and the support of this Holy Cause and Mission for which I have Awakened within him and Ordained him and sent him forth into this world. For it is by this alone that he shall fulfill his worldly needs, the needs of this Holy Cause and Mission and, the worldly needs of those who serve Me through him with the whole of their bodies, minds and Spirit.

{G} "Keep your own counsel and do not interpret My Words or the Teachings of My Awakened One, The Friend of all Souls, for another.

{G} "Be true to the nature which I have given unto you. Better is it that a man meet his death in fidelity to his own nature than to win vain glory in seeking to live by the nature of another."

- 10 -
The Codes, Vows, Pledges, Traditions and Customs

My Faithful Adhyatmavadi, Maitreyians and Soldiers of the Light make and keep these Codes, Vows, Traditions and Customs:

The Maitreyian Code

1. See Universal God in All and All in Universal God. Recognize, Honor, and Acknowledge The One True Divine Soul-Self, which is Pure Divine Universal Spirit, which is One and Identical with Universal God and no other, within each person and all of life and Creation. Recognize and insist upon the inherent and inalienable Dignity and Worth of each Soul apart from the acts of the body that it inhabits.

2. Grant unto each Soul the reality of its own creations. Do not impugn, insinuate, or ascribe motives, intentions, or opinions to others.

Make no judgments or decisions based upon hearsay or without evidence. Do not pass on gossip or rumor. Put aside all beliefs, assumptions, prejudices, biases, and opinions and Find Out What Is, As It Is. If you must assume, assume the best possible about each person and all life forms, until there is evidence to the contrary. Make statements about yourself - ask questions of others.

3. Recognize and acknowledge that each Soul is doing the best possible with the information, understanding, Karmas, and conditions that it has, and the situation it is in. Encourage and assist each willing Soul to increase its information, correct its understanding, conquer its Karmas, improve its conditions, and become master of its situation.

4. Harm no person, no creature, no life form, nor any part of Creation unless absolutely necessary. Do and say those things that improve and increase the Life, Knowledge, Understanding and Self-Determinism of Souls, and spread God's Eternal Universal Religion throughout all Creation. Make your help a blessing, not a burden - by helping only those who ask for help by word or by sign.

5. Actively and aggressively Communicate with The Divine Spirit within all life. Persist in Communicating until your intentions and meaning are clearly understood and your quests are fully answered. Persist in Communicating until you clearly understand the intentions and meaning of the communications of another. Actively acknowledge all Enlightenment, all Truth, and all else that you are willing to receive. Refuse to acknowledge Ignorance, Untruth, and all else that you are unwilling to receive.

6. Practice Viveka (Discrimination between the Real and the unreal) and Vairagya (Detachment) in all things great and small. Before evaluating or making a decision, put aside all prejudice and assumptions and balance your mind and the opposites. In all things, discern the Chain of Cause and Effect from past to present and from present to future. Be sorry for those things you would regret having done, before you do them. Be careful in making Commitments. Keep all Commitments once you have made them.

7. Without violating your Ethics, God's Eternal Universal Religion or your Holy Vows, do whatever works to accomplish your goals, your Purpose, and your Mission. If something stops working, stop doing it and find something else that works. Never give up.

8. Neutralize all attempts of others to control you without your knowing and willing agreement. Resist to increase. Neutralize to overcome.

9. Sympathy enslaves and destroys both giver and receiver. Give empathy and affinity unto others in place of sympathy.

10. It is the inescapable Universal Law of Karma, that what you do and what you do not do, will return to you in kind. Do unto others as you would have done unto yourself. Do not do unto others what you would not have done unto yourself.

The Maitreyian Vow of Non-Violence

1. I will strive to practice Non-Violence and Loving Kindness in all of my thoughts, words, and deeds. In so far as is possible without surrender, I will not aggress against any person. I will not fear aggression or give in to it. I will Love Peace and seek it in all ways. I will do all within my power to be nonviolent, harmless, gentle, kind, and a Friend to all people and creatures.

2. I will exhaust all other remedies to conflict and aggression before resorting to force. I will resort to force only when my own life or limb; the life or limb of my people; the life or limb of a weak and unwilling victim; or my Religion; are directly attacked and in peril. Then, I will use only such force as is necessary to cause an aggressor to cease his attack. Should an aggressor who has ceased his attack ask my forgiveness, I will forgive him quickly and offer him my peace and the Peace of The One Universal God in my Name. Should an aggressor who has ceased his aggression, profess God's Eternal Universal Religion and become a Maitreyian, I will welcome him as a long lost brother who has come home. Otherwise, I will strive to love all people; harm no one intentionally and will be a shining Light of Universal Peace and Love in the world.

The Maitreyian Pledge of Honor and Loyalty

Knowing the sacrifices required and the dangers involved in making God's Eternal Universal Religion your chosen Religion:

1. Recognize and acknowledge that you have, of your own Free Will and Self Determinism, dedicated yourself and your life to God's Eternal Universal Religion of Adhyatma-Yoga-Dharma, as given to me to give to you to give to all Humanity.

2. Uphold and further the Honor, Dignity, Harmony, Unity, and Esprit de Corps of the Holy Community of The Enlightened Faithful Believers and do everything within your power to spread The True Enlightenment of The Friend's Holy Initiation and God's Supreme Promise of Universal Salvation and Liberation to all willing Souls everywhere, for the sake of carrying our Holy Cause to Victory and bringing forth The Holy Satya Yuga.

3. Set the highest possible example for your juniors, and proudly show the world that you are a Maitreyian, who is my Disciple, a follower of The Supreme Way of God's Eternal Universal Religion, and a Member of The Holy Adhyatma Sangha, who is carrying The Holy Cause of Satya Yuga forward in the world. Do everything within your power and ability to bring the highest Honor and Glory to these.

4. Always keep yourself mindful that, as a Maitreyian, you are a living Sanctuary of God's Eternal Universal Religion and a Member of the Vanguard of The Holy Cause of Satya Yuga in this world wherever you may be. Willingly and eagerly accept as your Sacred Duty and Responsibility, all sacrifices that may be required of you to further the Holy Cause.

5. Never desert or betray Maitreya, The Holy Cause, or your Brother or Sister Maitreyians. Always keep

yourself mentally and Spiritually aware and alert, physically strong and able. Live your life according to The Code Of A Maitreyian. Always be faithful to God's Eternal Universal Religion of Adhyatma-Yoga-Dharma and your Vows.

6. Always be willing and eager to carry more of your share of the load and do more of your share of the work, whatever it may be. Be willing to give one hundred and one percent of yourself, your efforts, your abilities and your support.

7. Never shrink from an aggressor. Confront and overcome The Force of Darkness, the one enemy of God's Eternal Universal Religion and Its Holy Cause wherever you may find it, with Honor, Courage, and, whenever possible, with Loving Kindness.

8. Never surrender. Never give up. Retreat only when absolutely necessary; and then, only that you may return to carry on the struggle another day. No matter how great the odds against you, fight valiantly on without regard for your self, to carry The Holy Cause of Satya Yuga forward to Victory in the world and accomplish your Mission.

9. Never desert a Brother or Sister Maitreyian who is in danger or in need or abandon a fallen Maitreyian.

10. Never bring dishonor or disgrace to God, Maitreya The Friend, to God's Eternal Universal Religion, to The Holy Community of The Enlightened Faithful or to our Holy Cause. Though you may be the last Maitreyian on the face of the earth, fight on to Victory.

11. Never desire or seek approval, praise, or sympathy, especially from the unenlightened; for the unenlightened cannot help but give these for wrong reasons. Instead, always stand firm in your faith, and measure yourself according to the Four Pillars of Bhagavan, Dharma, Sangha, and Satya Yuga. Never desire or seek to be liked or admired by others, but do your duty as you know it to be right and carry The Holy Cause forward to Victory without ulterior motive.

12. Always hold God, your Religion, your Honor, Integrity, Principles, Free Will, and Self-determinism to be more important than your immediate body or life. Never compromise or sacrifice these, whether for personal pleasure, profit, your own life or safety, or any other reason.

The Four Commitments

1. Love The Highest Truth and seek it in all things. Face the difficult, the embarrassing, the uncomfortable, the frightening and the painful for the sake of The Highest Truth. Always be ready and willing to change yourself in the Light of a Higher Truth. Whenever you find a Higher Truth, reform your whole self and reality around It. Let this be called The Commitment to Truth.

2. Do only what you have chosen to do by your own Free Will. Do all that you have freely chosen to do. Do what you do only because you have freely chosen to do it. Do not serve compulsion, repulsion or ulterior motives. Take full Personal Responsibility for yourself, your Free Will and all results that come from your Free Willed actions and inactions. Let this be called The Commitment to Free Will.

3. Do not interpret my Teachings, take them out of context, or claim to receive The Divine Inspiration, Insight, Guidance or Revelation of Paratpara or my own for another. Keep your own Counsel. Let this be called The Commitment to Purity.

4. Absorb The True Inner Spirit of God's Eternal Universal Religion of Adhyatma-Yoga-Dharma directly from me. Preserve, Practice and Propagate God's Eternal Universal Religion in its Purity. Cooperate with your Maitreya, my Teachings, my Instructions, my Sangha and our Holy Cause of Satya Yuga and your Teachers and Elders fully in every way - except when doing so would clearly and directly violate the counsel of your own True and Essential Conscience. Then, follow your own True and Essential Conscience until you can cooperate without reservation. Never knowingly abuse this respect for your freedom of Conscience.

The Maitreyian Code of Respect

1. Respect all of God's Prophets, Saints, Buddhas, Saviors and Avataras, your Maitreya, your Teachers and your Guardian in all ways. Never harbor disrespect for these for any reason. In so far as you are able, show your love and devotion for them as well. Without fiction or falsehood, praise them and increase their glory among the people in all possible ways.

2. Make no presumptions, assumptions, judgments, or pronouncements regarding their motives, desires, likes, dislikes, attitudes, condition, or disposition. Impugn no motives to them. When it is necessary for you to know about me or about these, ask respectfully, and accept their answers as Truth. Respect their privacy, as you would have others respect your own, at all times. Do not press them when they decline to answer your questions.

3. Refrain from speaking when your Maitreya, a Teacher or your Guardian is speaking. Do not interrupt a train of thought that he is developing. If he speaks when you are speaking, become silent and give him your full attention. Look upon all that your Maitreya or your Teacher says and does as a rare gem of Truth that you may miss if you are not attentive. Do not attempt to teach or preach in the presence of your Maitreya or your Teacher unless instructed by him to do so. Do not argue with your Maitreya or your Teacher or contradict him. If you do not understand or think you disagree with your Maitreya or your Teacher, ask him respectfully to clarify your understanding. When you are prone to disagree with your Maitreya or your Teacher or find fault with them, remind yourself that what you think to be untrue in what he says or does today, you may likely discover to be Truth itself tomorrow.

4. Do not compete with your Maitreya, your Teacher or your Guardian. Do not walk in front of him, seat yourself above him or conduct yourself in any way so as to appear to be his superior. Instead, conduct yourself in ways that show the whole world that you are my Disciple, a Faithful Maitreyian of The Maitreya Kalki Mahavatara Satguru, Bringer of The Holy Satya Yuga, who respects your Maitreya, your Teachers and your Guardian. Do not seek to transact business with your Maitreya or your Teacher or put him at your service in any way. Instead, put yourself at the service of your Maitreya and your Teacher in every way you can according to your

free Will. Whatever you choose, of your own free Will, to give to your Maitreya, your Religion or your Teacher, give it freely, without barter, trade, expectation, or consideration of return. Whatever you do not choose to give, keep that for yourself. Never sell my Teachings or The True Enlightenment of my Holy Initiation for any price whatsoever.

5. Always be mindful that every God Awakened One is unique in the personality He adopts and the ways He chooses to be. Be mindful that there are no standards by which to measure God's Awakened Ones. Know that in each age in which God's Awakened One appears, He is the standard by which the Wise measure all things. Never criticize, measure, or judge God's Awakened One, His words, His Preaching, His Teachings, or His Instructions by your own ideas, standards or preconceptions; those of the world; or those of any other Religions or systems. Instead, make God's Awakened One, His words, His Preaching, His Teachings, His Instructions, and His Examples the Standard by which you measure and judge yourself and all other ideals, standards, events, persons and things.

6. Always keep yourself mindful that, until you have become fully Self-Realized, everything you see and understand of God's Awakened One and His words and actions, will always be colored by the ignorance of the ego-self within which you live, which clouds your own heart and mind. Therefore, when you are tempted to pass judgment upon God's Awakened One, remind yourself that the imperfections that you think you see in God's Awakened One, are very likely reflections of the imperfections that are hidden within your own heart and mind. Know that you can never know God's Awakened One perfectly until you have become Perfect yourself. In this knowledge, speak only of those things and qualities you see in Him that are of the Highest Worth and Merit, lest you slander The One God out of your own ignorance. Know that, only in so far as you become Spiritually Perfected, will you come to recognize and realize The Spiritual Perfection of your Maitreya and your Teachers. Know the more Spiritually Perfected Soul from the less by each Soul's recognition and acceptance of this principle.

7. Have Faith that everything God's Awakened One does is for your Blessing, Enlightenment, and Self-Realization and the Blessing, Enlightenment and Self-Realization of all Souls. Look upon all of Maitreya's words and actions as living parables for your Illumination and Enlightenment and accept them gratefully, as Divine Blessings and Gifts even when you cannot like them. Always assume that God's Awakened One is Teaching you God's Divine Truth through His every word and action and seek to accept and understand what is given to you.

8. Do not stand idly by and let any man or woman speak falsely, poorly or degrade or slander any of God's Awakened Prophets, Saints, Buddhas, Saviors or Avataras, The One Universal God of whom these are Living Expressions, without a swift and Just reply. Do not stand idly by and let any man or woman speak falsely, poorly or degrade or slander God's Eternal Universal Religion of Adhyatma-Yoga-Dharma, our Holy Sangha, our Holy Cause, your Teachers or your Brother or Sister

Maitreyians without a swift and Just reply. Whenever any man or woman casts forth lies, slander, or degradation upon God's Awakened Ones, your Maitreya, my appointed Teachers or my Maitreyians, rebuke the speaker, in Love, and, making your protest well heard, expose the lies in what is said, correct the untruths and speak out with the strength of Divine Truth in defense of these; that all who have been poisoned by lies, slander and degradation shall know the Truth and be set Free.

9. Never allow my Preaching or Teachings or those of my Ordained faithful Teachers to lay idle within you. Attend well to my Preaching, my Teachings, and my Instructions and those of my appointed Teachers that do not contradict my own. Put them into Practice quickly in your life exactly as I have given them to you. Act with Courage, Faith, Devotion, and Self-Determination in upholding and carrying out my Teachings and Instructions and the Sacred Vows and Duties of The True Enlightenment of your Holy Initiation at all times.

10. Make yourself and your life a living proof and testament of God's Eternal Universal Religion, His Presence and His Truth, and extend The True Enlightenment of my Holy Initiation and God's Supreme Promise of Universal Salvation and Liberation to all Souls everywhere.

The Traditions

The First Tradition

Make your material life the servant of your Spiritual Life; and make your whole life a constant Worship of Universal God.

To fulfill this Tradition:

Preserve, Practice, and Propagate God's Eternal Universal Religion in all of its Four Pillars of Bhagavan, Dharma, Sangha, and The Holy Cause of Satya Yuga. Keep The Faith; Keep Holy Sanctuary; Keep INJIA; Keep The Holy Cause; Keep The Holy Days.

Keep your Pledges and Vows and follow The Inspiration, Insight, and Guidance of Universal God and The Friend in all the things of your lives. Keep The Remembrances and Consecrate and dedicate all that you possess, use, eat, drink, think, and do; and their results; to the Unselfish Service of Universal God through The Friend.

Keep The Gatherings.

Remember and practice the Seven Great Principles by the days of the week: Peace for Monday; Love for Tuesday; Understanding for Wednesday; Compassion for Thursday; Freedom for Friday; Truth for Saturday; and Joy for Sunday.

Remember and practice the Twelve Great Virtues by the months of the year: Faith for January; Courage for February; Honor for March; Integrity for April; Strength for May; Devotion for June; Discipline for July; Service for August; Tolerance for September; Justice for October; Wisdom for November; Charity (Unselfishness) for December.

Gather together in high and harmonious Spiritual Retreat each year.

Live simply and make Bhagavan, Dharma, Sangha, and The Holy Cause of Satya Yuga the highest Supreme Center of your life.

The Second Tradition

See Universal God in all and all in Universal God; recognize, acknowledge, and honor Universal God within all people by Pranaming and Blessing them with The Holy Dharma Mantra.

To fulfill this Tradition:

Offer The Maitreyian Salute to Maitreya The Friend of All Souls.

Offer The Maitreyian Salute to The Friend's Ordained Ministers, and Teachers who are in good standing.

Offer The Maitreyian Salute to all of The Friend's Maitreyians who are in good standing.

Pranam; wish the Blessings of Universal God upon another, his home and family, in The Name of The Friend; and offer the Blessing of The Holy Dharma-Mantra; when entering or leaving another's home.

Pranam and offer the Blessing of The Holy Dharma-Mantra when greeting or departing from another person. Often combine your pranam and Blessing with stating The Remembrance.

Grant all people Spiritual Dignity and Respect; regardless of their station, status, wealth, poverty, intelligence, race, color, sex, religion, or nationality.

Honor your ancestors and all of Universal God's Prophets, Saints, Buddhas, Saviors, and Avataras with a Blessing of The Holy Dharma Mantra whenever their names are mentioned.

Respect, protect, and enhance the lives of the lower creatures, the lower forms of life, and the natural environment.

The Third Tradition

Live by God's Eternal Universal Religion Principles rather than convenience; live by Unselfishness rather than selfishness.

To fulfill this Tradition:

Be as courageous, fearless, and bold as Lions; and as gentle and harmless as Lambs.

Keep and practice The Vow of Non-Violence.

Face all people, conditions, situations, the frightening, the embarrassing, the difficult, and the painful, relentlessly, with INJIA, in The Name of The Friend, for the sake of Self-Realization and The Holy Cause. Never be turned aside from God's Eternal Universal Religion for any reason whatsoever. Be tolerant of others and their ways; so long as they do not seek to degrade, oppress, or harm you, God's Eternal Universal Religion in any of its Four Pillars or others of humanity.

Stand firm and speak out against wrong action, bigotry, violence, and injustice; and for Righteousness, Peace, Tolerance, and Justice.

Give more than you receive; love more than you are loved; help others more than you are helped; seek to comfort rather than to be comforted; seek to understand more than to be understood.

Give your word of honor only when you fully intend to keep it. To keep your word of honor once you have given it.

Work for and uphold Spiritual Freedom for all people everywhere.

Make Universal God and The Friend; God's Eternal Universal Religion; and The Holy Cause of World-Wide Enlightenment and Self-Realization the center point of your life, thoughts, words, and actions. And, do everything possible to further The Holy Cause of Self-Realization and Satya Yuga at every opportunity.

Never exploit any man or woman for his or her name, fame, or wealth. Never let anyone exploit or co-opt Adhyatma Bhagavan The Friend, God's Eternal Universal Religion, my Holy Community, The Holy Cause, or yourself, for any other work or cause.

The Fourth Tradition

Unify Principle and Living; Unify Thought and Action.

To fulfill this Tradition:

Put each of The Friend's Teachings, Instructions, Inspirations, Insights, and Guidances into action in your life quickly and vigorously.

Combine and unify Teaching with Doing; and Instruction with Training.

Understand through doing.

Live and act according to The Friend's Teachings, Instructions, Inspirations, Insights, and Guidances.

Always act with INJIA in the light of the Truth that: you are one of The Friend's Holy Maitreyians who has been Consecrated to Universal God's Divine Work and Service through The True Enlightenment of His Holy Initiation. You are always filled, surrounded, supported, sustained, and strengthened by Universal God's Infinite Goodness, Wisdom, Power, and Grace, through The Friend; according to your Faith and Devotion, and you have nothing to fear, so long as your Faith and Devotion are strong and steady.

Use whatever works to accomplish your Goals, your Purpose and your Mission; without violating your Principles, Vows, Ethics, or The Friend's Teachings, Instructions, Inspirations, Insights, or Guidances. Realize that the ability to recognize the connection between Cause and Effect is the essence of Wisdom. Seek out and recognize the connection between Cause and Effect.

The Fifth Tradition

Destroy wrong, evil, darkness, and ignorance by neutralizing them instead of resisting them.

To fulfill this Tradition:

Reject nothing - accept everything and turn it to your own good purposes and the Purposes of The Four Pillars of God's Eternal Universal Religion.

Neutralize wrong, evil, darkness, and ignorance and make them powerless by: Facing them fully and directly; Accepting them fully in Spirit; Giving them away fully in Spirit; Neutralizing them; and refusing to Acknowledge them.

Recognize: that you become what you dwell upon, according to the degree and intensity with which you dwell upon it. Recognize that resistance demands dwelling upon what is resisted and it is by resisting, we become what we resist. Therefore: do not resist evil, wrong, darkness or ignorance. Do not acknowledge evil, wrong, darkness, or ignorance. Instead, dwell upon The Truth, Goodness, Righteousness, Enlightenment, Self-Realization, and The Holy Cause of Satya Yuga. Neutralize evil, wrong, darkness, and ignorance without resisting or dwelling upon them.

Accept everything fully, in Spirit, before setting out to rid yourself of it. Give everything away fully, in Spirit, before setting out to obtain it.

Refuse to argue. Argument is resistance. Neutralize argument by accepting everything and explaining it God's Eternal Universal Religion Way.

Show approval and acknowledge what is Good and Right. Neutralize and refuse to acknowledge what is not Good or Right.

Be like water: Empty when advanced against; clinging when the aggressor retreats; responding slowly to slow action; quickly to quick action; changing from subtle to solid so quickly and gently it is not seen; flowing around an antagonist's strength; rushing through his open places, filling his valleys with The Pure Truth and Grace of Universal God and The Friend; washing away ignorance, wrong belief, evil, and darkness in The Name of The Friend.

Be careful in taking action. When taking Right Action, act as certainly and irresistibly as Living Waters rushing down a mountain from a broken dam.

Resolve your doubts and fears with Right Action, according to The Friend's Inspiration, Insight, and Guidance. When still, be as still as the earth. When in action, be as Living Waters, rushing irresistibly down a mountain.

Accept only gifts which are given freely, in an unselfish spirit; without demands, hidden motives, expectations, or by reason of gaining favor or advantage. To refuse all others.

The Sixth Tradition

Speak and listen as True Devotees and Disciples of Maitreya Adhyatma Bhagavan Sri Babajhan Al-Kahlil The Friend under all circumstances.

To fulfill this Tradition:

Smile before speaking.

Speak clearly, directly, distinctly, and courageously in a voice that is full, rich, and easily heard and understood.

Face the person you are speaking to, fully and unflinchingly; be fully INJIA of the other person; and look directly into his or her face and eyes without staring.

Make sure that a point or idea has been heard and understood rightly, before going on to another.

Dwell upon the same point or idea until you are rightly heard and understood.

Be INJIA, alert, attentive, and quick to hear, verify, understand, and acknowledge others.

Work to understand what is said before asking questions. Ask clear, direct, and courageous questions. Always get an answer to a question that answers the question, before going on.

Speak to each person Spirit-to-Spirit; instead of body-to-body; mind-to-mind; or personality-to-personality.

Speak to all people in ways that awaken and quicken The Spirit within them and call their Highest Divine Self into Activity.

The Seventh Tradition

Express yourself and act as a True Friend in the world.

To fulfill this Tradition:

Offer Friendliness and Friendship to all people.

Assume the best about each person until shown otherwise.

Accept others for who and what they have chosen to be, without compromising your own Reality, your own ways, your own Faith, or God's Eternal Universal Religion in any of its Four Pillars.

Admonish those who are straying from The Way. Congratulate those who are newly entering upon it or returning to it.

Offer The Friend's Expressions to those to whom they are rightly due. Offer The Maitreyian Sign of Universal God's Victory and Peace to all people. The Maitreyian Handclasp to Maitreyians in good standing, and friends in Spirit. Offer The Maitreyian Salute to Maitreyians in good standing, when at a distance.

Offer The Maitreyians' Respects to Maitreyians in good standing when face to face.

Speak Honestly, Truthfully, and Directly without harshness, but with care and compassion. Give Compassionate Counsel courageously, without regard for yourself, when you see the need for it.

Speak The Friend's Verbal Greeting: "The Compassion and Grace of Universal God and The Friend be with you." when meeting and leaving all people. When meeting or leaving other Maitreyians, one of you may say the first part, to which the other responds, "And with you, my (Brother or Sister, as the case may be)." To which the first person says, "Jai Bhagavan Ji!" and the second responds, "Victory to Paratpara, The One Universal God and The Friend." When meeting or leaving those who would place your life in peril for this saying, you may shorten it to: "God be with you." To which the second person responds simply, "And with you."

The Customs

All General Customs, Local Customs, all rules set by The Sangha, are secondary to The Inner Divine Inspiration, Insight, Guidance and Revelation of Paratpara and The Friend and the individual Maitreyian's True and Essential Conscience. When Inner Divine Inspiration, Insight, Guidance and Revelation and a Maitreyian's True and Essential Conscience moves a Maitreyian to do other than what is set forth; and there is clear consensus between The Inner Divine Inspiration, Insight, Guidance and Revelation of Paratpara and The Friend and that Maitreyian's True and Essential Conscience and his or her intelligence, that Maitreyian should act upon this consensus out of his or her own Free Will and take full Personal Responsibility for his or her actions. No Maitreyian should willingly harm himself or another or impose himself on another in any way the other does not freely and willingly accept. This Principle should never be violated. When the Maitreyian's Issue of Conscience has been fulfilled, the Maitreyian should return to observance of that which has been temporarily set aside, unless he has a standing Conscientious Objection. In this case a Maitreyian should perform long and intense Soul-Searching and Truth-Saying for Right-Living on the issue, both alone and in the company of other Maitreyians, until a harmonious resolution is attained.

The Sacred Shawl

The Sacred Shawl is the Individual Temple of every Maitreyian and Soldier of The Light. Wear it on your shoulders when you are taking part in any Spiritual Work or Practice. Place it over your head when you are Worshipping, Praying, or Meditating. Whenever you place The Sacred Shawl over your head, be fully INJIA (Instantaneously Non-Judgmentally Insightfully Aware) that you have entered into a Holy Temple of Universal God and The Friend.

The Pranam

The Standing Pranam

Place the palms of your two hands together before you such that your fingertips are at the level of your eyes;

Touch the first fingers of your joined palms to the center of your forehead just above your eyebrows and bow forward from your waist;

Straighten up to a full standing position and touch the tips of the first fingers of your joined palms to the center of your forehead, between and just above your eyebrows; to your lips; and then to your Heart at the center of your chest. Say: "Jai Bhagavan Ji!"

The Seated Pranam

Place the palms of your two hands together before you such that your fingertips are at the level of your eyes;

Touch the tips of the first fingers of your joined palms to the center of your forehead, between and just above your eyebrows; to your lips; then to your Heart at the center of your chest. Say: "Jai Bhagavan Ji!"

The Kneeling Pranam

Kneel so that you are sitting on your heels;

Place your joined palms before your face with fingertips at eye level;

Bow forward and touch your forehead to the ground;

Place the fingertips of your joined palms at the center of your forehead as you rise;

Touch the fingertips of your joined palms to your lips;

Touch the fingertips of your joined

palms to your Heart Center at the center of your chest.

Speak The Holy Dharma Mantra "Jai Bhagavan Ji!"

The Kneeling Pranam is a deeply humble and reverent act of recognizing and honoring Paratpara - The One Universal God Manifest and Unmanifest, as The True Self of all Beings.

Multiple Pranams

In offering two or more pranams together: Perform all steps with each Pranam. Pronounce The Holy Dharma-Mantra upon each arising. This is the formal method of making more than one Pranam at a single instance.

The Use of Pranam

Unless a particular Pranam is called for, it is up to each Maitreyian to determine what Pranam to offer in any particular situation. Where nothing has been set, let it be that the members of a Pride or Church may determine the local custom regarding these particulars for themselves, by consensus. All local customs are subject to The Friend's modification or veto.

The Maitreyian Salute

Say, "Paratpara Ji Kijai!"

Place your hands out in front of your body such that your elbows are slightly bent.

Close your right fist with the knuckles of your right hand pointing upward. Cover the knuckles of your right fist with the open palm of your left hand.

Slowly move your right fist outward while opening your right hand such that the palm of your right hand is facing downward.

Circle your right hand around your left hand such that the palm of your right hand moves as if it were sliding gently around your left hand as though your left hand were a smooth ball.

When your right hand has come full circle, move your right and left hands smoothly into the Pranam.

Pranam (bow forward) and place your joined palms near the center of your forehead.

Straighten your body to an upright position and then, touch your joined palms to the center of your forehead, then your lips, then, the center of your chest at your Heart Center.

Say, "Jai Bhagavan Ji!"

Lower your hands to your sides or, if seated, to your lap or knees.

The Maitreyian Salute is the high form of greeting for Maitreyians. It is offered only to God, The Friend, those Ordained by The Friend, Brother and Sister Maitreyians who are in Good Faith and as part of some Spiritual Practices. It is never knowingly offered to the uninitiated or to Maitreyians who are not in Good Faith.

The Maitreyian Victory Sign

The Maitreyian Victory Sign is formed by the first and second fingers of the hand, formed into a "V". This sign stands for The Holy Adhyatma-Yoga-Dharma Mantra "Jai Bhagavan Ji!" which was sent out through all Creation by Universal God at the moment of The Friend's Awakening. In its fullest sense, it means: "Victory to Universal God - That Beloved Universal I AM THAT I AM Which You Are! Victory to Adhyatma Bhagavan Sri Babajhan Al-Kahlil The Friend! Victory To His Holy Adhyatma-Yoga-Dharma! Victory To His Holy Community! Victory To His Holy Cause of World-Wide Enlightenment and Self-Realization for all people!" The Maitreyians' Victory Sign is always given with the hand facing the direction in which the Sign is given. Friends do not give the Sign with the back of the hand.

The Sacred Gesture

Place the closed fist of your right hand over your heart;

Touch the third finger of your open right hand to your lips;

Touch the third finger of your open right hand to the One Point between and just above your eyebrows;

Form The Maitreyians' Victory Sign with your right hand.

Friends who have two hands never use the left hand to give The Sacred Gesture. Only Friends who have no right hand; or who have a disabled right hand; use their left hand to give The Sacred Gesture.

The Maitreyian Handclasp

Perform The Maitreyians' Handclasp by grasping your Brother's or Sister's right hand with your right hand; such that your thumb and fingers are around the base of his or her thumb. Cover the back of your Brother's or Sister's right hand with your left hand. He or she covers the back of your right hand with his or her left hand. Always perform The Maitreyians' Handclasp with your right hand except in those cases mentioned in "The Sacred Gesture".

The Maitreyian Greeting

Raise both of your hands to your sides so that your elbows are pointing straight out to your sides and your fingertips are pointing straight upward with your palms forward; so that your forearms make a right angle to your upper arms;

Keeping your left hand in position, touch the third finger of your right hand to the One Point of your forehead;

Keeping your left hand in position, touch the third finger of your right hand to your lips;

Still keeping your left hand in position, make a fist with your right hand and place your fist over your heart so that your hand is touching your chest with your palm facing your chest;

Bring your left hand down and place your palms together before the center of your chest; and perform a standing pranam.

The Maitreyians' Greeting is performed when you are more than arms length away from your Brother or Sister; or, when Greeting The Friend or a Teacher or Minister of His Holy Adhyatma-Yoga-Dharma who is in good standing. The Maitreyians' Greeting is not given to the uninitiated or Initiates who are not in good standing, regardless of their station.

The Maitreyian Respects

Perform The Maitreyian Greeting;

Give The Maitreyian Handclasp;

Remove your left hand from the back of your Brother's or Sister's right hand while keeping the handclasp;

Continue the handclasp while giving The Kiss of Paratpara (The Kiss of God) on the back of your Brother's or Sister's right hand. When The Kiss of Paratpara cannot be given on the other's right hand, give it upon his or her right cheek. Kissing the right cheek may be performed as an expression of Spiritual Love in addition to The Kiss of God upon the hand;

Following The Kiss of Paratpara, embrace your Brother or Sister.

The Maitreyian Respects are the full and intimate expression of the Universal Spiritual Brotherly and Sisterly love that all of The Friend's Devotees and Disciples have for one another. Keep your giving of The Maitreyian Respects warm and real and filled with Spiritual Love.

Offering The Maitreyian Respects

The universally recognized sign that you are offering The Maitreyian Respects is, extending your right hand to your Brother or Sister for The Maitreyian Handclasp. When offered immediately following The Maitreyian Greetings, The Maitreyian Handclasp is the universal sign that you are Offering The Maitreyian Respects.

If you are ill or there is any other reason that you should not give and receive The Maitreyian Respects at any time - let your Brother or Sister know that you do not wish to exchange Respects at that time, by accepting the handclasp without placing your left hand upon the back of his or her right hand. This is universally recognized and accepted as a Maitreyian's sign that Respects cannot be exchanged at this time.

Making Holy Water

Who May Make Holy Water

Making Holy Water is a special manifestation of The Third Treasure that is received by every Maitreyian at the time of his or her Holy Initiation. Because of this, only those who have received my Holy Initation and Universal God's Supreme Promise of Universal Salvation and Liberation into their hearts, can make Holy Water.

How to Make Holy Water

Call upon Maitreya The Friend of all Souls by Holding His Presence within your mind and calling out within your Heart "Bhagavan Ji! Bhagavan Ji! Bhagavan Ji!"

Offer the water to Universal God in a Spirit of Surrender and ask Maitreya to fill the water with God's Infinite Universal Spirit and transform it into Holy Water.

Wait in Faith. When the water changes so that it seems heavier and thicker and you sense that it is filled with God's Divine Spirit - it is done.

May the Blessings of The One Universal God and Maitreya The Friend be with you always.

Here Ends The Chapter Entitled The Individual Disciplines

Chapter Two
The Community Disciplines

In your Holy Community and in your gatherings, give and accept support and encouragement; help one another to live The Truth, The Life and The Way that fulfills God's Promise of Universal Salvation and Liberation and wins Self-Realization and True Salvation and Liberation and Perfect Final Union with God at this life's end.

Gathering for Inner Divine Communion

Gather together, in body, mind and Spirit, with your Brothers and Sisters and such others who are sincere, on the day called Joy. And therein, do Soul-Searching and Truth-Saying for Right-Living through Inner Divine Communion by The Two Rules according to The One Instruction; and share your lives, your testimonies and your Friendship, one with another alike.

Gathering for Worship and Sharing The Holy Water of Life

Gather together, in body, mind and Spirit, with your Brothers and Sisters and such others who are sincere, also on that day called Joy at least once in every four passings of it, for Worship, Prayer and, where there is one who has been Ordained to Consecrate it and administer it, for Sharing The Holy Water of Life.

While others may attend Gathering for Worship and Sharing The Holy Water of Life, only those who have received my Holy Initiation and have God's Supreme Promise may Share The Holy Water of Life.

Gathering for Soul Searching and Truth-Saying for Right Living

Gather together with your Brothers and Sisters, on that day called Understanding, for Soul-Searching and Truth-Saying alone. Therein, let each of you speak the Truth, the Whole Truth and nothing but the Truth, of his own Soul-Searching and any smallest thing in which you have deceived or wronged another.

Dream Time Rendezvous

Gather, also, together in Inner Divine Communion in Spirit, with your Brothers and Sisters and such others who are sincere, within The Spiritual Realm, in that time where dreams and dreamless sleep consume your mortal body and mind. And therein, Commune in Spirit with The One Universal God, myself, all of God's Prophets, Saints, Buddhas, Saviors and Avataras and one another. Whatever you receive therein, share that with one another.

Gathering for Study

Gather together with your Brothers and Sisters at least once in each cycle of the moon, for study of The Holy Book of Destiny.

The Holy Days

The High Holy Days

Grace Day - 7 Service (August 7)

The Friend's Holy Initiation by all of Universal God's Awakened Prophets, Saints, Buddhas, Saviors, and Avataras. His first Awakening and Self-Realization by Universal God's Divine Grace at eight years of age. His making the Supreme Sacrifice of renouncing Final Union with Universal God for the sake of all suffering Souls. And, His winning of The Gift of Universal God's Divine Grace for all Souls for all times.

Ascendance Day - 29 Discipline (July 29)

The day upon which The Friend gave up His physical body and Ascended into Kaivalya within the Seventh World of Holy Adhyatma. From there, to comfort and Guide all Souls to Universal God, Self-Realization, and True Liberation; through His Divine Inspiration, Insight, and Guidance.

Attainment Day -12 Honor (March 12)

The Friend's second attainment of Self-Realization and Liberation by His own following of The Holy Adhyatma-Yoga-Dharma. His second Sacrifice of renouncing Final Union to remain in the world to carry out Universal God's Divine Will and Ordination; and lead all suffering Souls to Self-Realization and Liberation. By His second attainment, He opened up the ancient Holy Adhyatma-Yoga-Dharma to all people for all time. By His second Sacrifice, He gave the example of True Devotion to Universal God unto all Souls.

Maitreya's Birthday - 29 Honor (March 29)

A joyous celebration of The Friend's taking up of name and form in this world according to Universal God's Divine Compassion and Design.

Fulfillment Day - 25 Charity (December 25)

The Holy Day in which all of Universal God's Divine Revelations and Guidances to The Friend were fulfilled.

Guardian's Day - 22 Service (August 22)

A memorial celebration in honor of the passing beyond name and form of Maitreya's beloved Spiritual Guardian, Henry Frazier. The man of Compassion and Wisdom who guarded and nurtured The Friend through the dark years between His first and second Awakening. On Guardian's Day, we honor and Celebrate The Friend's Guardian and the Spiritual Guardians of each of The Friend's Devotees and Disciples.

First Founding Day - 21 Devotion (June 21)

A celebration in honor of the first founding of The Friend's Way of Self-Realization and the dedicated men and women who brought it into the world.

Community Founding Day - 4 Honor (March 4)

A celebration in honor of the Founding of The Friend's Holy Adhyatma Yoga-Dharma and The Holy Community of His Enlightened Faithful Believers.

Universalist Day - 23 Tolerance (September 23)

A celebration to honor all of Universal God's Awakened Prophets, Saints, Buddhas, Saviors, and Avataras. To pay respects; and to demonstrate the Divine Oneness of all Prophets, Saints, Buddhas, Saviors, and Avataras in Universal God.

The Lesser Holy Days

Liberation Day - 8 Integrity (April 8)

A celebration in honor of all people who have suffered under tyranny, oppression, slavery, or bigotry; and who have become victorious through their Faith in Universal God.

Ancestor's Day - 25 Wisdom (November 25)

A day of remembrance and celebration in honor of parents and ancestors; without whom we would not have the opportunity for Self-Realization and Liberation within this life.

National Day

A celebration in honor of the Consecration of the National Sanctuary and the granting of its Sacred Scroll. Special honors are presented to each nation in which a National Sanctuary is founded and Consecrated; for furthering Universal God's Work of World-Wide Enlightenment and conquering suffering.

Community Consecration Days

Days of celebration, observed in honor of the Consecration of the various Sanctuaries of the Holy Community, and the granting of their Sacred Scrolls. Where a State, a County, or a City has been friendly and helpful to a Sanctuary of The Holy Community; an award is presented for furthering Universal God's Work of World-Wide Enlightenment and conquering suffering. Community Consecration Days are observed for: The National Sanctuary; the Regional Sanctuaries; the District Sanctuaries; the Section Sanctuaries; the Area Sanctuaries; the Chapter Sanctuaries; and the Prides. A Pride is a Sanctuary composed of three to ten Adhyatmavadi, Maitreyians and Soldiers of the Light. The Pride is the smallest Community Sanctuary.

Spiritual Birthdays

Holy Initiation is a New-Birth. Entering The Holy Community is a New-Birth. These New-Birth Days are celebrated for each Maitreyian within the Pride to which they belong.

These are the Holy Days of God's Eternal Universal Religion. Each Maitreyian remembers, keeps, and teaches The Holy Days. Remember, means to remember the Holy Day, its reason, and its meaning. Keep means to celebrate the Holy Day in the company of other Maitreyians and Friends. When we cannot be with others in body, we commune with our Brothers and Sisters in Spirit. Teach means to pass the Holy Days, their reason, and their meaning, on to the children and new Maitreyians. Teach, means Inspiring others with a burning desire to Remember, Keep, and Teach the Holy Days. Teach, means making each Holy Day a time of Spiritual Community, Celebration, Remembrance, Service, Goodness, and Joy.

These Traditions, Customs, and Holy Days are the personality of God's Eternal Universal Religion. No man or woman can do work in this world without personality. The Self-Realized must give up Infinite Freedom and take up personality to do work in this world. There is no other way. God's Eternal Universal Religion of Holy Adhyatma-Yoga-Dharma needs its personality to do its Work in this world. You are each a Living Sanctuary within which the personality of God's Eternal Universal Religion is kept. You are each its Treasure Chest. You are each its Guardian. Learn them. Remember them. Keep them. Teach them to your new Brothers and Sisters; to your children. Help keep God's Eternal Universal Religion, The Friend, and Universal God alive and working in the world.

**Jai Bhagavan Ji!
Victory To God The Beloved!
That Beloved Universal
I AM THAT I AM
Which You Are!**

Gathering for Soul-Searching and Truth-Saying for Right-Living

By The Will and Grace of The One Universal God:

Preparation

Clean and Prepare the Sanctuary Hall or room. If there is a Sacred Shrine, clean the Shrine and replace candles and other Articles of Worship as needed. Turn on the Shrine lights and light all candles except the Central Sacred Flame.

Assembly

Arrange for the people to assemble at least ten minutes before the Soul-Searching and Truth-Saying for Right-Living is to begin. If there is no other room to assemble in, use the Sanctuary Hall with respect.

The Call To Gathering

At the rightful time, let one of you who is a Maitreyian blow the Sea Horn three long times, ring the Sacred Bell three times, and give The Call to Gathering:

Satyam nasti paro Dharmaha!
Satyam lokasya dipaha!
Sruyatam!
Drishyatam!
Kriyatam!
Uchyatam!

Paratpara Sharanam agachati!
Bhagavan Sharanam agachati!
Dharmam Sharanam agachati!
Sangham Sharanam agachati!
Satya Yugam Sharanam agachati!
Om! Jai Paratpara Ji!
Om! Jai Bhagavan Ji!

Let another Maitreyian, call:

Truth is The Highest Religion!
Truth is The Light of The World!
Let it be heard!
Let it be seen!
Let it be done!
Let it be told!

Come take Refuge in Paratpara,
The One Universal God
of Countless Names and Forms,
who Is beyond all Names and Forms!
Come take Refuge in God's Awakened One, The Friend!
Come take Refuge in
His Eternal Universal Religion!
Come take Refuge in The Holy Community
of His Enlightened Faithful Believers!
Come take Refuge
in His Holy Cause of Universal God's Pure Divine Truth!
Glory to Universal God, The Beloved!
Victory to God's Awakened One, The Friend!

When a separate place of assembly is used, make a procession to The Sanctuary Hall.

Offering Respects

Let that Maitreyian who is to lead the Gathering for Soul-Searching and Truth-Saying for Right-Living lead The Holy Assembly in Chanting a long "Om."

Respects to and from The Friend

Let the leader turn toward The Friend (if present in person) or toward the Holy Shrine if The Friend is present in Spirit only; and lead the Holy Assembly in offering The Sacred Gesture to The Friend.

Respects to and from The Holy Assembly

Let the leader offer The Sacred Gesture to the Holy Assembly and the Holy Assembly return it in unison.

Open The Gathering

Let the leader Proclaim The Divine Purpose of The Gathering for Soul-Searching and Truth-Saying for Right-Living, saying:

"Brothers and Sisters in Spirit! We come together in this Gathering for Soul-Searching and Truth-Saying for Right-Living to fulfill God's Supreme Promise of Universal Salvation and Liberation; to set right our lives; and to raise up the Divine Spirit of Satya Yuga - The Age of God's Pure Divine Truth and True Spiritual Liberation for all Souls - and send It forth into the world."

The Opening Devotions

The Holy Adhyatma Gayatri

Let the leader enter The Sacred Shrine, (or go to the front of the Sanctuary Hall if there is no Holy Shrine) and Pranam to Universal God and The Friend and The Holy Shrine - then stand (or kneel) facing The Holy Shrine and lead the Sangha in chanting of The Adhyatma Gayatri.

Om Paratpara!
Tat Savitur Varenyam
Bhargo Devasya
Dhimahi dhiyoyonah
prachodayat

(Repeat first part 3 times, then chant:)

Om! Asato ma sad gamaya!
Tamaso ma jyotir gamaya!
Mrityor ma-amritam gamaya!
Om! Shanti - Shanti - Shantihi!
Om Jai Bhagavan Ji!
{Devotional Form}

Chant or recite the English Translation once through:

Om Universal God
All Radiant Universal Light!
As we turn our minds to you
fill our hearts and minds and lives
with Your Clear Light.

Om! From the unreal,
lead us to The Real!
From darkness,
lead us to The Light!
From death, to Immortality!
Om! Peace! Peace! Peace!
Om Jai Bhagavan Ji!

Light The Central Sacred Flame

Let the leader light up The Central Sacred Flame and raise it up toward Heaven while chanting a long "Om." Lower the Central Sacred Flame to the Shrine. Take one step back and offer The Sacred Gesture.

Surrender The Gathering

Let the leader face the Holy Shrine (or the front of the Sanctuary Hall if there is no Holy Shrine) and surrender the Gathering for Soul-Searching and Truth-Saying for Right-Living as a Self-Sacrifice, saying:

O Paratpara! Beloved Universal God, I AM THAT I AM! We offer this Gathering for Soul-Searching and Truth-Saying for Right-Living and all results of this Gathering for Soul-Searching and Truth-Saying for Right-Living to That Beloved Universal I AM THAT I AM Which You Are, through Your Awakened and Ordained One, Maitreya Adhyatma Bhagavan Sri Babajhan Al-Kahlil The Friend, in His Name! Fill our hearts with Divine Inspiration! Fill our minds with Divine Insight! Fill our mouths with words of Your Pure Divine Truth and Wisdom! Fill our lives with Divine Guidance! Fill us with the Faith to face all trials and conquer all obstacles! Fill us with the Courage and Strength to carry His Holy Cause of Your Pure Divine Truth to Victory in the world! Fill us with unshakable Faith in Your Awakened and Ordained One, The Friend that He may carry us across the Ocean of illusion, suffering, and death to the Far Shore of True Salvation, Liberation, Immortality, and Bliss!

May this Gathering for Soul-Searching and Truth-Saying for Right-Living serve That Beloved Universal I AM THAT I AM Which You Are. May this Gathering serve your Awakened One, The Friend! May this Gathering serve his Holy Adhyatma-Yoga-Dharma! May this Gathering serve The Holy Community of his Enlightened Faithful Believers. May this Gathering serve his Holy Cause of bringing Your Pure Divine Truth to Victory, for the Salvation and Liberation of all Souls. May this Gathering for Soul-Searching and Truth-Saying for Right-Living serve and benefit all people, all creatures, all Souls and all Creation. Om So'ham Tat Tvam Asi! I Am That - Thou Art That!

Offering Prayers

Maitreya's Prayer

Maitreya's Prayer may be offered

in either The Morning form or The Evening form. Where non-initiates are attending, Maitreya's Prayer should be offered in the Morning form. Where there are only Maitreyians present, the Evening form should be used.

Let the leader face the Holy Assembly and say:

Let us join together in Heart and Mind in offering Maitreya's Prayer.

Then, lead the assembly in responsive reading of Maitreya's Prayer.

Individual Prayers

While continuing to face the Holy Assembly, say:

Brothers and Sisters in Spirit! Please offer such Prayers as you have within your Heart to offer at this time.

Offerings

Let the leader face the Holy Assembly and say:

By the Will and Grace of The One Universal God:

It is written in The Holy Book of Destiny, The One Universal God said unto The Friend of All Souls:

"Sell not your Holy Initiation and My Promise or your Holy Religion which is My Own. Instead, wherever there shall be a Holy Sanctuary of your Religion, place therein a Begging Bowl to your left hand and let all who are your Faithful and My Own and all others who come unto you, place their offering therein. From that which is given unto you, shall you and those you Ordain fill your worldly needs.

"Truly, My Beloved, it is the nature of this, My Creation, that all who live must live by the sweat of their brow and the sacrifices of others. Let, therefore, those who would follow you and fulfill this New Covenant and My Supreme Promise of Universal Salvation and Liberation, be your protector and your support.

"Let not this burden fall unjustly upon any who follow you. But let each of your Faithful tithe at least two percent, or all that he can do the best he can do, of his good unto you and Me, for your support and the support of this Holy Cause and Mission for which I have Awakened within you and Ordained you and sent you forth into this world. By this means, shall you fill the worldly needs of those who serve Me through you with the whole of their bodies, minds and Spirit.

"Accept whatever gifts are given by The Faithful, without requirements or attachments. Accept no gifts that are given with requirements or attachments. But let not any of The Faithful tithe either more or less than that portion which is appointed to all; that the poor may not suffer grievous burdens; and your Mission and The Holy Community of The Faithful shall not come to depend only upon the great wealth given by those I have blessed with riches.

"Let no man or woman be kept from thee or Me by want of wealth alone. Those who have not worldly wealth of which to tithe, let them tithe of what they have to give and in such measure as they can give it."

The Friend will not accept any Offering that is given in the Spirit of payment or exchange of any kind for His Teachings or Guidance. If you choose to give an Offering, it must be given freely, from your heart, without any consideration of payment or exchange whatsoever.

We will now make our Offering. Place your Offering in The Friend's Begging Bowl when it is passed to you.

Please join me in singing (the Devotional Holy Dharma Mantra or a song of your group's own choosing) while the Offering is being taken.

Take The Offering

Let a Maitreyian pass the Begging Bowl.

Soul-Searching and Truth-Saying for Right-Living

Let the leader face the Holy Assembly and announce Soul-Searching and Truth-Saying for Right-Living, saying:

Brothers and Sisters, let us now fulfill God's Supreme Promise of Salvation and Liberation by Soul-Searching and Truth-Saying for Right-Living through Inner Divine Communion by The Two Rules according to The One Instruction, as God has given them to The Friend.

Let the leader take a seat and begin the Soul-Searching and Truth-Saying for Right-Living through Inner Divine Communion by The Two Rules according to The One Instruction. The One Instruction is done in either the Guided or Unguided form - depending on the needs and experience of those present.

Drum Circle

When all Soul-Searching and Truth-Saying for Right-Living that the members of The Holy Assembly wish to give has been given; let the leader begin the Spirit Drumming. While continuing to be immersed in Inner Divine Communion and as a manifestation of Doing that which is right to be done when it is right to do it, the members of The Holy Assembly may then celebrate God's Presence and express the moving of God's Divine Spirit through them by creating rhythms on their drums and other instruments of percussion.

Let each Maitreyian's expression be respected as an expression of The Divine Spirit in action.

Devotional Singing

The Drum Circle may simply blend and mesh and merge into Devotional Singing. If the group chooses to separate the Drum Circle and Devotional Singing, let the leader give a signal to stop the Drum Circle and, when the drumming has stopped, face the Holy Assembly and say:

Let us celebrate God and God's Supreme Divine Grace by raising our voices in Devotional Song. When we sing and drum and dance for God with energy and enthusiasm, The Friend comes out of the Holy Shrine and sings and dances with us in Spirit.

If your group chooses to have the Drum Circle blend and mesh and merge into the Devotional Singing, let the leader, without giving the signal to stop the Drumming, just stand, raise his hands heavenward and proclaim:

Victory To Paratpara, The One Universal God of Countless Names and Forms Who Is Beyond All Names and Forms, The One Universal God Who Speaks Through All The

Prophets, Saints, Buddhas, Saviors and Avataras. Let us raise our voices in Joyful Celebration of The Victory of The Age of Universal God's Pure Divine Truth!

And, begin the Devotional Songs of choice from The Friend's Way Song Book while the Drum Circle accompanies the singing.

Close The Gathering

Raise The Sacred Flame

Let the leader approach The Holy Shrine and offer a Pranam. Kneel (or stand as the case may be) and after a moment of silence, raise The Central Sacred Flame and say:

O Paratpara! Beloved Universal God of Countless Names and Forms Who Art Beyond All Names and Forms! Our Beloved One True Self! As we raise up this Holy Light, let The Supreme Divine Light of Thy Living Presence and Thy Divine Pure Truth be lit up within the hearts of all Souls everywhere. Make us strong and courageous and let us lead all Souls up out of Ignorance, Darkness, and Error, into Thy Clear Divine Light of True Salvation and Liberation. Through Thy Supreme Gift of The Friend's Holy Initiation, let us bring forth The Satya Yuga and save all Souls from Suffering, Sorrow, and Death.

Jai Bhagavan Ji! Jai Bhagavan Ji! Om! Jai Bhagavan Ji! Victory To God The Beloved, That Beloved Universal I AM THAT I AM Which You Are!

Announcements

Let the leader announce to the Holy Assembly where they may gather for Friendship and the taking of Prashad (Holy Consecrated food).

Departure

Let the leader lead the Holy Assembly in offering Pranams to Universal God and The Friend and The Holy Shrine.

Let the leader exchange The Sacred Gesture with the members of The Holy Assembly.

Let the leader and those attending The Gathering for Soul-Searching and Truth-Saying for Right-Living depart in order.

Friendship and Sharing Prashad

Following Gathering for Soul-Searching and Truth-Saying for Right-Living, Maitreyians and Guests gather together in Universal Spirit to share Friendship and Prashad (Food that has been Consecrated by offering it to The One Universal God.)

This Concludes The Gathering for Soul-Searching and Truth-Saying for Right-Living.

Gathering for Inner Divine Communion

By the Will and Grace of The One Universal God:

Purification and Preparation

Before performing Inner Divine Communion, you should purify and prepare yourself. This is to remove as many distracting influences as possible and give you the best possible opportunity to Commune with The One Universal God and The Friend.

Purification

Wash and dry your hands and face. Center your heart and mind in Paratpara and Maitreya The Friend, while reciting and contemplating:

I am more than this body.
I AM THAT I AM!
I am more than these thoughts.
I AM THAT I AM!
I am more than this personality.
I AM THAT I AM!
I am more than this mind.
I AM THAT I AM!
I am Pure Divine Universal Spirit,
which is One and Identical
with Paratpara,
The One Universal God
and no other.
I AM THAT I AM!

Place your palms together before your chest at your Heart Center and say aloud or silently and Contemplate:

O Paratpara!
Beloved Universal
I AM THAT I AM!
Purify me in body,
in mind,
in heart,
and in Spirit
for the sake of
The Holy Satya Yuga.
This, I ask
in the Name of
Your Awakened One,
Adhyatma Bhagavan Sri Babajhan
Al-Kahlil The Friend.
Om Jai Bhagavan Ji!
Victory To
That Beloved Universal
I AM THAT I AM
Which You Are!

Offer The Sacred Gesture and say:

Om So'ham Tat Tvam Asi!
Om! I Am That Thou Art.
Jai Bhagavan Ji!
Victory To God The Beloved!
That Beloved Universal I AM THAT I AM Which You Are!

Preparation

Count Your Blessings

Count your Blessings and give thanks for them. Look at your life and become aware of the Blessings that God has given unto you, no matter how small they may seem. Give thanks to God for each of your Blessings.

Blessing All Souls

1. Extend Universal Love to those who love you and ask God's Blessings upon them.

2. Extend Universal Love to those who do not love you and ask God's Blessings upon them.

3. Extend Universal Love to those you have bad feelings toward and ask God's Blessings upon them.

4. Extend Universal Love to those who have bad feelings toward you

and those who hate you and ask God's Blessings upon them.

5. Extend Universal Love and ask God's Blessings upon all Souls.

Unburden Yourself

Be aware of all of your burdens. Confess your wrong doings and any grudges you are holding, to Maitreya The Friend in The Secret Inner Sanctuary of your Heart. Make mental amends, in The Spirit, to those you have wronged. Forgive those who have wronged you. Put your burdens into Maitreya's hands and release them completely.

Rest Easy in Your True Nature

Let go of all pretense and take off the mask you wear for others. Know that God knows every least part of you and accepts you and Loves you as you are; and rest easy in your True Nature.

Opening Inner Divine Communion

The Call

At the rightful time, give The Call to Gathering:

Satyam nasti paro Dharmaha!
Satyam lokasya dipaha!
Sruyatam!
Drishyatam!
Kriyatam!
Uchyatam!

Paratpara Sharanam agachati!
Bhagavan Sharanam agachati!
Dharmam Sharanam agachati!
Sangham Sharanam agachati!
Satya Yugam Sharanam agachati!

Om So'ham tat tvam asi!
Om! Paratpara Kijai!
Om! Jai Bhagavan Ji!

Then in English (another Maitreyian may do this part)

Truth is The Highest Religion!
Truth is The Light of The World!
Let it be heard!
Let it be seen!
Let it be done!
Let it be told!

Come take Refuge in Paratpara!
Come take Refuge in Bhagavan!
Come take Refuge in Dharma!
Come take Refuge in Sangha!
Come take Refuge in Satya Yuga!
Om I Am That Thou Art!

Om!
Victory to God The Beloved!
Victory to The Friend!

Procession

If you are not in the Holy Sanctuary, make a solemn procession into the Holy Sanctuary when The Call has been given.

Awaiting The Friend

Be seated and chant the Holy Dharma Mantra softly while awaiting the arrival of Maitreya The Friend of All Souls in the Holy Sanctuary.

Maitreya's Entrance

When Maitreya arrives in the Holy Sanctuary, let one Maitreyian call "INJIA" and all present stand and chant the Devotional Dharma Mantra (Om Jai Bhagavan Ji!).

Proclaim the Surrendering and Submission

Face The Sacred Shrine - make the gesture of Surrender and say:

O Paratpara, Beloved Universal God we surrender to you!

Make the Gesture of Submission and say:

We submit totally to your Infinite Divine Will!

Chant The Holy Adhyatma Gayatri

First verse

Om Paratpara!
Tat savitur varenyam
Bhargo devasya
dhimahi dhiyoyonah
prachodayat

Repeat the first Verse three times then chant the second verse one time.

Second verse

Om!
Asato ma sad gamaya!
Tamaso ma jyotir gamaya!
Mrityor ma-amritam gamaya!
Om!
Shanti, Shanti, Shantihi!
Om Jai Bhagavan Ji!

Light Up The Central Sacred Flame

Let the leader light up The Central Sacred Flame and raise it up toward Heaven while chanting a long "Om."

Say: Paratpara Ji Kijai.

Lower the Central Sacred Flame to the Shrine. Take one step back and offer The Sacred Gesture.

Offer Maitreya's Prayer

(Responsively)

My God! ^
My Beloved! ^
My One True Self! ^
I surrender completely unto Thee! ^
Restore Thy Authority!^
Manifest Thy Presence within this little self ^
Until it has become One with Thee^
shining forth with Thy Own Clear Light! ^
Let me know, this moment, my Oneness with Thee; ^
the one thing I lack; ^
through which all else is made Perfect! ^
Heal the division in me; ^
that I may Know Thy Oneness in all this that is! ^
Consume this little self in the Sacred Fire of Thy Presence! ^
That I may find my way through the Ordeal ^
and be Liberated from it, ^
Realizing my Oneness with Thee! ^
From the unreal, lead me to The Real! ^
From darkness, lead me to the Light! ^
From division, lead me to Wholeness! ^
From the temporary, lead me to The Eternal! ^
From death,
lead me to Immortality! ^
O Beloved Universal God! ^
I would be One with Thee fully this moment! ^
Make my Doing One with my Speech! ^
Make my Speech One with my Mind! ^

Make my Mind
 One with my Heart! ^
Make my Heart
 One with my Will! ^
And my Will One with Thy Will! ^
Shatter this prison of false self! ^
And absorb me, ^
in the Ocean of Your Infinite Divine
Being, ^
As a drop of water in the Sea! ^
That I shall know, without doubt or
reservation ^
that You and I
are not we, but One! ^
For Thou art my only True Self; ^
Majestic! ^
Splendorous! ^
Immortal! ^
There is no I but Thee! ^
So Be it with me! ^
Om So'ham tat tvam asi! ^
Om I Am That Thou Art! ^
Om Jai Bhagavan Ji! ^
Victory To God The Beloved ^
That Beloved Universal I AM THAT
I AM Which You Are! ^

Contemplations

Invite The Congregation to be seated. Passages from The Holy Book of Destiny or The Friend's Teachings may be read. A talk may be given.

Establish Yourself In The Two Rules

Say:

Establish yourself in The Rule of Divine Love

Love The One Universal God with all of your heart, all of your mind and all of your Spirit; Love yourself and one another even as you love God; and accept, love and revere all of God's Prophets, Saints, Buddhas, Saviors and Avataras alike, without being bound to accept what has been said or written about them.

Do what has been said. When it is done, say aloud: Jai Bhagavan Ji!

Say:

Establish yourself in The Rule of Divine Guidance

Determine that you will seek, find and live by The Inner Divine Inspiration, Insight, Guidance and Revelation of The One Universal God and The Friend, and the counsel of your own True and Essential Conscience within The Secret Inner Sanctuary of your Heart, according to My One Instruction, in all things, great and small.

Do what has been read. When it is done, say aloud: Jai Bhagavan Ji!

Inner Divine Communion

"Jai" means: Spiritual Victory.

There are 10 Jai to Inner Divine Communion.

First Jai

Sing: {The Song of Surrender}

O my God
I surrender to Thee;
all my actions
and results that will be;
take what you Will;
return the rest unto me;
to help me rescue humanity.

Say:

Offer each part and the whole of all that is done and all that is received, to Paratpara in the Sacrificial Fire within The Secret Inner Sanctuary of your Heart at each instant and receive whatever returns to you as Divine Gifts, given unto you by Paratpara and The Friend for your own Self-Realization and Liberation and the Perfection of The Holy Satya Yuga in this world for The Self-Realization and Liberation of all Souls everywhere for all time.

Do what has been read. When it is done, say aloud: Jai Bhagavan Ji!

Second Jai

Sing: {Blessings to All}

O my God
let this be done;
with blessings for all
and harm to none;
that all Souls
shall soon be won.
Jai Bhagavan Ji!

Say:

This do, in a spirit of harm to none and benefit to all.

Do what has been read. When it is done, say aloud: Jai Bhagavan Ji!

Third Jai

Sing: {The Holy Adhyatma Gayatri in English}

Om Universal God!
All Radiant Universal Light!
As we turn our minds to you
fill our hearts and minds and lives
with Your Clear Light.

Om!
From the unreal,
lead us to The Real!
From darkness,
lead us to The Light!
From death, to Immortality!
Om! Peace! Peace! Peace! Om!
Victory to The One Universal God and Maitreya The Friend of All Souls!

Say:

Set your heart and mind firmly on Seeking The Highest Truth.

Do what has been read. When it is done, say aloud: Jai Bhagavan Ji!

Fourth Jai

Sing: {The song, Me Guru}

First Verse

Mey Guru
Mey Guru
Mey Guru-u-u-u-u
Mey Guru
Mey Guru
Mey Guru
Mey Guru-u-u-u-u
Mey Guru.

Chorus 1

Hey Paratpara
Hey Maitreya

Repeat First Verse

Chorus 2

Jai Bhagavan Ji!
Jai Bhagavan Ji!

Final Verse

Mey Guru
Mey Guru
Mey Guru-u-u-u-u
Mey Guru
Mey Guru
Mey Gu—ru—.

Say:

Call Upon Me to become active in Spirit within The Secret Inner Sanctuary of your Heart by holding My Presence within your mind and calling out within your Heart 'Bhagavan Ji! Bhagavan Ji! Bhagavan Ji!'

Do what has been read. When it is done, say aloud: Jai Bhagavan Ji!

Fifth Jai

Sing: {Light Up My Life}

Light up my life's
light with Your Light,
Paratpara, Light up my life
with Your Light.
Light up my life's light
with Your Light,
Maitreya, Light up my life with Your Light.

Chorus

Inspiration, Insight, Guidance, Revelation;
Inspiration, Insight, Guidance, Revelation;
I open my Heart up unto Thee;
Maitreya light up my life with God's Light!

Repeat a second time if The Spirit so moves you.

Say:

Ask for and open yourself to The Inner Divine Inspiration, Insight, Guidance and Revelation of Paratpara, The One Universal God of Countless Names and Forms and The Friend and your own True and Essential Conscience.

Do what has been read. When it is done, say aloud: Jai Bhagavan Ji!

Sixth Jai

Chant: {The Bhagavan Sharanam – Responsively}

Bhagavan sharanam gachchhami!
Dharmam sharanam gachchhami!
Samgham sharanam gachchhami!
Satya-yugam sharanam gachchhami!

Say:

Take Refuge in The Four Pillars of Bhagavan, Dharma, Sangha and Satya Yuga;

Do what has been read. When it is done, say aloud: Jai Bhagavan Ji!

Seventh, Eighth, Ninth and Tenth Jai

Say:

Enter into The Secret Inner Sanctuary of your Heart through the repetition of My Holy Dharma Mantra 'Jai Bhagavan Ji!' (Jay Bhag-wan Gee).

Sing and Chant:

1. Chant Responsively:

"Jai Jai Bhagwan Ji"

(Response)–"Om Jai Bhagawan Ji!"

2. Sing: The Holy Dharma Mantra Kirtan.

3. Chant the Holy Dharma Mantra first aloud and then gradually silently within.

Say: {When all have stopped chanting The Holy Dharma Mantra}

Immerse yourself in The Divine Ocean of Paratpara's Supreme Truth and Being therein, like a drop of water in The Sea and dwell steadily therein, like a candle flame in a still place, INJIA (Instantaneously Non-Judgmentally Insightfully Aware) and accepting of whatever comes, while it is coming, whatever lingers, while it is lingering and whatever goes, while it is going; Speaking that which is right to be Spoken when it is right to Speak it; Doing that which is right to be Done when it is right to Do it.

Do what has been said.

Close The One Instruction

Close The One Instruction by singing The Devotional Dharma Mantra.

The Blessings of Holy Water and Divine Fire

Let the leader face the Holy Assembly and holding the Water Vessel up high and say:

By The Will and Grace of The One Universal God, Maitreya The Friend of All Souls has said:

"Whoever shares The Water of Life, shares in the Sacrifices I have made! Whoever shares The Divine Fire of The Spirit of God, shares in the Supreme Vow of Compassion I have made. This do often, in remembrance of me."

"Only those who are Maitreyians in Good Standing may give these Blessings. While all may receive these Blessings only those who have received my Holy Initiation and have God's Promise alive within their Hearts, may receive the Blessings of Holy Water and Divine Fire with full result."

Partaking of The Blessing of Sharing The Holy Water of Life and The Divine Fire of The Spirit may be done individually or as a mass, according to circumstances and the wishes of each congregation. Both ways are given that you may choose.

Individual Blessings

Let the Giver of The Blessings face the Holy Assembly and say:

By the Will and Grace of The One Universal God:

"Whoever shares The Water of Life, shares Maitreya Adhyatma Bhagavan Sri Babajhan Al-Kahlil The Friend! Whoever shares The Divine Fire of The Spirit of God, shares Maitreya Adhyatma Bhagavan Sri Babajhan Al-Kahlil The Friend. This do often, in remembrance of me."

"You and I are One within The One that is All in All. Whenever one of you appears to be separated from the rest, know that this is but the working of the Great Illusion that hides your True Self from you. For, outside the sleeping minds of The Living Dead, there are no separations within God's Infinite and Eternal Being.

"Those who have received The Friend's Holy Initiation and have God's Supreme Promise of Universal Salvation and Liberation alive within their Hearts may Share The Holy Water of Life and The Divine Fire of The Holy Spirit. Let those who have received The Friend's Holy Initiation prepare to Share in The Friend's Being and Spirit and receive The Inner Knowledge of The Friend's Self-

Realization and Self-Sacrifices that is beyond words, through The Holy Water of Life and The Divine Fire of The Spirit."

Let the leader go before the Holy Shrine and receive The Blessings of Universal God and The Friend.

Let the leader stand facing the Holy Assembly and say:

Please stand and join together in chanting the Devotional Dharma Mantra in harmony and unity until all Maitreyians have received Blessings and are seated.

Come forward and receive The Blessings of The One Universal God and The Friend!

Giving The Blessing of the Holy Water of Life

With the third finger of his left hand let the Giver of The Blessings take some Holy Water that has been poured from the Sacred Vessel into a bowl and place The Holy Water on the Maitreyian's forehead between and just above his eyebrows from high to low while saying:

This is the Holy Water of Life
that sets all Souls free
from suffering, sorrow, and death.
Na Trish!
May you never thirst
for the Holy Water of Life!
Om So'ham tat tvam asi!
Om Jai Bhagavan Ji!

Sharing The Holy Water of Life

Let the Maitreyian who is receiving The Blessing hold forth his cupped right hand or a cup.

Pour The Holy Water of Life from the Sacred Vessel into the Maitreyian's right hand or cup, accordingly, and say:

Share now, this Holy Water and share The Friend and receive the Inner Knowledge of The Friend's Self-Realization and Self-Sacrifice that is beyond words.

Na Trish! May you never thirst for the Holy Water of Life!

Om Jai Bhagavan Ji!

Victory To God The Beloved! That Beloved Universal I AM THAT I AM Which You Are!

The Maitreyian receiving the Blessing should then drink The Holy Water of Life.

Giving The Blessing of The Divine Fire

Let the Giver of The Blessings present The Sacred Flame to each Worshipper in turn and say:

This is The Divine Fire of The One Universal Spirit that permeates and gives Life to all Creation.

May it burn brightly within your heart and Illuminate your life!

May you light up the whole world with it!

The Blessings of Paratpara and The Friend be with you always.

If a new Maitreyian does not know what to do and it is inconvenient to describe or explain it, the Giver of The Blessings should wave the Light into the Maitreyian's Heart and mind with the back of his or her right hand.

When all who wish to do so have received The Blessings and are seated - let the leader face the assembly and say:

Jai Bhagavan Ji! Please be seated.

Celebrating The Spirit

Let the leader Face the Holy Assembly and say:

Let us celebrate God and God's Supreme Divine Grace by raising our voices in Devotional Song. When we sing and drum and dance for God with energy and enthusiasm, The Friend comes out of the Holy Shrine and sings and dances with us in Spirit.

Raise your hands heavenward and proclaim:

Victory To Paratpara, The One Universal God of Countless Names and Forms Who Is Beyond All Names and Forms, The One Universal God Who Speaks Through All The Prophets, Saints, Buddhas, Saviors and Avataras.

Let us raise our voices in Joyful Celebration of The Victory of The Age of Universal God's Pure Divine Truth!

Community Singing

Other Maitreyian songs may be added to the following.

Sing: The Holy Doctrine Song (responsively)

Om So'ha-Am Ta-At Twam Asi
Jai Jai Bhagavan Ji!
Om So'ham Tat Twam Asi-i-i
Jai Jai Bhagavan Ji!
Om So'ham Tat Twam Asi
Jai Jai Bhagavan Ji!
Om So'ham Tat Twam Asi-i-i
Jai Jai Bhagavan Ji!

Verse

There Is One Universal God
There Is One Universal Spirit
One, Whole, and Indivisible.
There Is No Other
Due To Spiritual Ignorance,
The People See
Universal God Differently.

Sing: {Jaya Jaya Maitreya}

The Holy Dharma Mantra Kirtan or the Divine Victory Song.

You may stand and dance if there is space for dancing and may play instruments if the place permits doing so.

Closing The Gathering for Inner Divine Communion

Extinguishing The Central Sacred Flame.

Raise up The Central Sacred Flame while Chanting Om.

Lower The Central Sacred Flame and extinguish it.

Say:

Paratpara Kijai! All Victory and Glory to God The Beloved!

Jai Bhagavan Ji! Victory to God The Beloved - That Beloved Universal I AM THAT I AM, Which You Are!

This Completes The Gathering for Inner Divine Communion

Gathering for Worship

By The Will and Grace of The One Universal God:

Preparation

Clean and Prepare the Sanctuary Hall or room. If there is a Sacred Shrine, clean the Shrine and replace candles and other Articles of Worship as needed. Turn on the Shrine lights and light all candles except the Central Sacred Flame. Consecrate a vessel of Holy Water for the Blessings.

Assembly

If possible, arrange for the people to assemble in a room that is separate from The Sanctuary Hall. If there is no other room to assemble in, use the Sanctuary Hall with respect.

The Call To Gathering for Worship

At the rightful time, let one of you who is a Maitreyian blow the Sea Horn three long times, ring the Sacred Bell three times, and give The Call to Gathering:

Satyam nasti paro Dharmaha!
Satyam lokasya dipaha!
Sruyatam!
Drishyatam!
Kriyatam!
Uchyatam!

Paratpara Sharanam agachati!
Bhagavan Sharanam agachati!
Dharmam Sharanam agachati!
Sangham Sharanam agachati!
Satya Yugam Sharanam agachati!

Om! Jai Paratpara Ji!
Om! Jai Bhagavan Ji!

Let another Maitreyian, call:

Truth is The Highest Religion!
Truth is The Light of The World!
Let it be heard!
Let it be seen!
Let it be done!
Let it be told!

Come take Refuge in
Paratpara, The One Universal God
of Countless Names and Forms,
who Is beyond
all Names and Forms!
Come take Refuge in
God's Awakened One,
The Friend!
Come take Refuge in
His Eternal Universal Religion!
Come take Refuge in
The Holy Community
of His Enlightened
Faithful Believers!
Come take Refuge in
His Holy Cause of Universal God's
Pure Divine Truth!
Om!
Victory to Universal God,
The Beloved!
Om!
Victory to God's Awakened One,
The Friend!

When a separate place of assembly is used, proceed to The Sanctuary Hall.

Offering Respects

Let that Maitreyian who is to lead the Gathering for Worship lead The Holy Assembly in Chanting a long "Om."

Respects to and from The Friend

Let the leader turn toward The Friend (if present in person) or toward the Holy Shrine if The Friend is present in Spirit only; and lead the Holy

Assembly in offering The Sacred Gesture to The Friend.

Respects to and from The Holy Assembly

Let the leader offer The Sacred Gesture to the Holy Assembly and the Holy Assembly return it in unison.

Open The Gathering for Worship

Let the leader Proclaim The Divine Purpose of The Gathering for Worship, saying:

Brothers and Sisters in Spirit! We come together in this Gathering to Worship Paratpara, The One Universal God; to fulfill God's Supreme Promise of Universal Salvation and Liberation; and to raise up the Divine Spirit of Satya Yuga - The Age of God's Pure Divine Truth and True Spiritual Liberation for all Souls - and send It forth into the world.

Let the leader then face the Holy Assembly and announce The Sealing and Purifying of The Holy Sanctuary, saying:

Beloved Brothers and Sisters of God's Eternal Universal Religion, we are about to Seal this Holy Sanctuary for the time of our Worship. Once it is Sealed, no one may enter or leave until it is Unsealed without disrupting our Worship. Because of this, once we have Purified and Sealed this Holy Sanctuary, those who are not then within it may not enter and those who are within it cannot depart without disrupting it. If there are any who cannot remain herein until the Unsealing of this Holy Sanctuary, please take your leave at this time.

After allowing time for those who must take care of business to do so and those who cannot remain to depart, say:

We will now Purify and Seal this Holy Sanctuary for the time of our Worship.

Purify The Holy Sanctuary

Let the leader face the Holy Assembly and say:

Let us join together as One in calling upon Paratpara, The One Universal God to fill this Holy Sanctuary with His Divine Light and Presence and Purify it of all ignorance, darkness and devil-mind for the time of our Worship, Prayer and Meditation.

Let the leader face the Holy Shrine and say:

O Paratpara, Beloved Universal I AM THAT I AM! Make the Supreme Divine Light of your Ever-Presence fill this Holy Sanctuary with Thy Pure Divine Truth and Presence and Purify it of all ignorance, darkness, and devil-mind.

When you sense that The Purification is complete, say:

This Holy Sanctuary is Now Purified!

Jai Bhagavan Ji!

Victory To God The Beloved! That Beloved Universal I AM THAT I AM Which You Are!

Seal The Holy Sanctuary

Let the leader face the Holy Assembly and say:

Let us now join together as One in Calling Upon Paratpara, The One Universal God, to Seal this Holy Sanctuary by His Divine Light and Presence and lock out all ignorance, darkness and devil-mind from within it for the time of our Worship, Prayer and Meditation.

Let the leader face The Holy Shrine and say:

O Paratpara, Beloved Universal I AM THAT I AM! Seal this Holy Sanctuary for the time of our Worship, in the Name of Your Awakened and Ordained One, Adhyatma Bhagavan Sri Babajhan Al-Kahlil The Friend.

When you sense that The Sealing is complete, say:

This Holy Sanctuary is Now Sealed! Guardian - Secure The Holy Sanctuary!

When the Guardian has secured the Holy Sanctuary, say:

Jai Bhagavan Ji! Victory To God The Beloved! That Beloved Universal I AM THAT I AM Which You Are!

The Opening Devotions
The Holy Adhyatma Gayatri

Let the leader enter The Sacred Shrine, (or go to the front of the Sanctuary Hall if there is no Holy Shrine) and Pranam to Universal God and The Friend and The Holy Shrine - then stand (or kneel) facing The Holy Shrine and lead the Sangha in chanting of The Adhyatma Gayatri.

Om Paratpara!
Tat savitur varenyam
Bhargo devasya
Dhimahi dhiyoyonah
prachodayat

(Repeat first part 3 times, then chant:)

Om! Asato ma sad gamaya!
Tamaso ma jyotir gamaya!
Mrityor ma-amritam gamaya!
Om! Shanti - Shanti - Shantihi!
Om Jai Bhagavan Ji! {Devotional Form}

Chant or recite the English Translation once through:

Om Universal God.
All Radiant Universal Light!
As we turn our minds to you
fill our hearts and minds and lives
with Your Clear Light.

Om! From the unreal,
lead us to The Real!
From darkness,
lead us to The Light!
From death, to Immortality!
Om! Peace! Peace! Peace!
Victory to God The Beloved!

Light The Central Sacred Flame

Let the leader light up The Central Sacred Flame and raise it up toward Heaven while chanting a long "Om." Lower the Central Sacred Flame to the Shrine. Take one step back and offer The Sacred Gesture.

Surrender The Gathering for Worship

Let the leader face the Holy Shrine (or the front of the Sanctuary Hall if there is no Holy Shrine) and surrender the Gathering for Worship as a Self-Sacrifice, saying:

O Paratpara! Beloved Universal God, I AM THAT I AM! We offer this Gathering For Worship and all results of this Gathering For Worship to That Beloved Universal I AM THAT I AM Which You Are, through your Awakened and Ordained One, Adhyatma Bhagavan Sri Babajhan Al-Kahlil The Friend, in His Name! Fill our hearts with Divine Inspiration! Fill our minds with Divine Insight! Fill our mouths with words of Your Pure Divine Truth and Wisdom! Fill our lives with Divine Guidance! Fill us with the Faith to face all trials and conquer all obstacles! Fill us with the Courage and Strength to carry His Holy Cause of Your Pure Divine Truth to Victory in the world! Fill us with unshakable Faith in your Awakened and Ordained One, The Friend that He may carry us across the Ocean of illusion, suffering, and death to the Far Shore of True Salvation, Liberation, Immortality, and Bliss!

May this Gathering For Worship serve That Beloved Universal I AM THAT I AM Which You Are. May this Gathering For Worship serve your Awakened One, The Friend! May this Gathering For Worship serve his Holy Adhyatma-Yoga-Dharma! May this Gathering For Worship serve The Holy Community of his Enlightened Faithful Believers. May this Gathering For Worship serve his Holy Cause of bringing Your Pure Divine Truth to Victory, for the Salvation and Liberation of all Souls. May this Gathering For Worship serve and benefit all people, all creatures, all Souls and all Creation.

Om So'ham Tat Tvam Asi! I Am That - Thou Art That!

Honoring The Ancestors

Let the leader face the Holy Assembly, and say:

Let us join our Hearts and Minds together as One as we Honor our Spiritual and Worldly Ancestors.

Let the leader then, face the Holy Shrine (or the front of The Sanctuary Hall) and:

1) Sprinkle The Holy Water of Life to the Shrine's Center while saying:

O Paratpara, Beloved Universal God! With this offering of Holy Water we honor You who are our Supreme Ancestor and Your Awakened One, our Teacher, without whom we would not have this opportunity for Self-Realization and Liberation within this life.

2) Sprinkle The Holy Water of Life to the Shrine's Left (your right) while saying:

O Prophets, Saints, Buddhas, Saviors and Avataras of all time! With this offering of Holy Water, we Honor you and Call Upon you to bless this Gathering for Worship by being present with us.

3) Sprinkle The Holy Water of Life to the Shrine's Right (your left) while saying:

O Spiritual Guardians and elder and ancestor Maitreyians! With this offering of Holy Water we honor you one and all.

4) Sprinkle The Holy Water of Life to the Shrine's Left (your right) while saying:

O Beloved Parents and worldly Ancestors! With this offering of Holy Water, we honor you and remember you.

(Left and Right are always taken from the point of view as if sitting on the Shrine looking outward.)

Offering Prayers

Maitreya's Prayer

Maitreya's Prayer may be offered in either The Morning form or The Evening form. Where non-initiates are attending, Maitreya's Prayer should be offered in the Morning form. Where there are only Maitreyians present, the Evening form should be used.

Let the leader face the Holy Assembly and say:

Let us join together in Heart and Mind in offering Maitreya's Prayer.

Then, lead the assembly in responsive reading of Maitreya's Prayer.

Individual Prayers

While continuing to face the Holy Assembly, say:

Brothers and Sisters in Spirit! Please offer such Prayers as you have within your Heart to offer at this time.

Readings and Sermon

Readings from The Holy Book of Destiny

Let the leader choose one or two members in Good Faith to come forward and participate in reading Selections from The Holy Book of Destiny.

Sermon

Let the leader read from The Adhyatma Scriptures and give a talk on the selection read - without interpreting what The Friend has said or written. (When The Friend was present in body as well as in Spirit, He gave His discourses personally.)

Offerings

Let the leader face the Holy Assembly and say:

By the Will and Grace of The One Universal God:

It is written in The Holy Book of Destiny, The One Universal God said unto The Friend of All Souls:

"Sell not your Holy Initiation and My Promise or your Holy Religion which is My Own. Instead, wherever there shall be a Holy Sanctuary of your Religion, place therein a Begging Bowl to your left hand and let all who are your Faithful and My Own and all others who come unto you, place their offering therein. From that which is given unto you, shall you and those you Ordain fill your worldly needs.

"Truly, My Beloved, it is the nature of this, My Creation, that all who live must live by the sweat of their brow and the sacrifices of others. Let, therefore, those who would follow you and fulfill this New Covenant and My Supreme Promise of Universal Salvation and Liberation, be your protector and your support.

"Let not this burden fall unjustly upon any who follow you. But let each of your Faithful tithe at least two percent, or all that he can do the best he can do, of his good unto you and Me, for your support and the support of this Holy Cause and Mission for which I have Awakened within you and Ordained you and sent you forth into this world. By this means, shall you fill the worldly needs of those who serve Me through you with the whole of their bodies, minds and Spirit.

"Accept whatever gifts are given by The Faithful, without requirements or attachments. Accept no gifts that are given with requirements or attachments. But let not any of The Faithful tithe either more or less than that portion which is appointed to all; that the poor may not suffer grievous burdens; and your Mission and The Holy Community of The Faithful shall not come to depend only upon the great wealth given by those I have blessed with riches.

"Let no man or woman be kept from thee or Me by want of wealth alone. Those who have not worldly wealth of which to tithe, let them tithe of what they have to give and in such measure as they can give it."

The Friend will not accept any Offering that is given in the Spirit of payment or exchange of any kind for His Teachings or Guidance. If you choose to give an Offering, it must be given freely, from your heart, without any consideration of payment or exchange whatsoever.

We will now make our Offering. If you choose to make an Offering, place your Offering in The Friend's Begging Bowl when it is passed to you. If you prefer, you may bring your Offering with you when you come up to the Shrine for Blessings and place your Offering in The Friend's Begging Bowl after you have received God's Blessings.

Please join me in singing (the Devotional Holy Dharma Mantra or a song of your groups' own choosing) while the Offering is being taken.

Take The Offering

Let a Maitreyian pass the Begging Bowl.

Blessings

Say:

By The Will and Grace of The One Universal God, Maitreya The Friend has said:

"Only those who are Maitreyians in Good Standing may give these Blessings. While all may receive these Blessings only those who have received my Holy Initiation and have God's Promise alive within their Hearts, may receive the Blessings of Holy Water and Divine Fire with full result."

Partaking of The Blessing of Sharing The Holy Water of Life and The Divine Fire of The Spirit may be done individually or as a mass, according to circumstances and the wishes of each congregation. Both ways are given that you may choose.

Individual Blessings

Let the Giver of The Blessings face the Holy Assembly and say:

By the Will and Grace of The One Universal God:

It is written in The Holy Book of Destiny, The Friend of All Souls said:

"And I said unto The One Universal God, 'How can I give unto them my

Self-Realizations and Self-Sacrifices, that they may be Blessed as you have Blessed me in this day?' And The One Universal God said unto me:

"No man can give his Self-Realization or Self-Sacrifices to another, My Beloved. But in answer to your Compassion, let it be that whosoever shall drink of Holy Water that has been consecrated by you or one you have Ordained for that purpose; and received from you or one you have Ordained for that purpose; and received from you or one you have Ordained to give it; shall share in your Being and your Spirit and the inner knowledge of your Self-Realization and Self-Sacrifices that is beyond words, shall be with him, thereby.

"Arise! Awaken! Beloved Soul! Thy Dawn has come! The Day is at hand! Unto he who knows The One Universal God as his True Self is given Life Eternal! Fire cannot burn him; sword pierce him; nor cold freeze him! Free from the illusions of your false self, knowing that you are not this, or this, or this, or this; but One with God, you shall endure forever. For always have I been; and always will I Be. One with Paratpara, The One Universal God of Countless Names and Forms Who Is Beyond All Names and Forms, That I AM THAT I AM - All in All!

"Seek first to know your own True Self. For in that knowing, you shall Know The One God - All in All. And you shall Know, without doubt or reservation that you are not this body or this mind or this personality - but That One Universal God, who is your True Source, Substance and Self - and no other!

"And no longer shall the Sun be your Light by Day; nor the Moon your light by Night. For The One God, The Beloved, shall have become an Eternal Light shining out from you unto all the Earth! Your Sun shall never set, nor your Moon wane. For The Light of The Eternal is yours and your days of sorrow are at an end.

"In His Eternal Love He has always Loved you. In His Infinite Being He has always held you. Come with me to God and take your place among The Twice Born of Eternity! This time you shall be truly made One with God - a Pure One, Reborn in God!

"There is no I but God! There is no you but God! I am with you always. Awaken then! All you who sleep the sleep of The Living Dead. And come with me to Paradise!

"This is The Water of Life: God Alone is Real! This whole Universe and all that is within it is God's Dream and Image, Created by That Absolute One within His Own Being, out of His Own Being! And, Soul and Spirit are One and Identical with God and no other!

"Whoever shares The Water of Life, shares Adhyatma Bhagavan Sri Babajhan Al-Kahlil The Friend! Whoever shares The Divine Fire of The Spirit of God, shares Adhyatma Bhagavan Sri Babajhan Al-Kahlil The Friend. This do often, in remembrance of me.

"You and I are One within The One that is All in All. Whenever one of you appears to be separated from the rest, know that this is but the working of the Great Illusion that hides your True Self from you. For, outside the sleeping minds of The Living Dead, there are no separations within God's Infinite and Eternal Being."

Those who have received The Friend's Holy Initiation and have God's Supreme Promise of Universal Salvation and Liberation alive within their Hearts may Share The Holy Water of Life and The Divine Fire of The Holy Spirit. Let those who have received The Friend's Holy Initiation prepare to Share in The Friend's Being and Spirit and receive The Inner Knowledge of The Friend's Self-Realization and Self-Sacrifices that is beyond words, through The Holy Water of Life and The Divine Fire of The Spirit.

Let the leader go before the Holy Shrine and receive The Blessings of Universal God and The Friend.

Let the leader stand facing the Holy Assembly and say:

Come forward and receive The Blessings of The One Universal God and The Friend!

Let us chant the Devotional Dharma Mantra in harmony and unity until all Maitreyians have received Blessings and are seated.

Giving The Blessing of the Holy Water of Life

With the third finger of his left hand let the Giver of The Blessings take some Holy Water that has been poured from the Sacred Vessel into a bowl and place The Holy Water on the Maitreyian's forehead between and just above his eyebrows from high to low while saying:

This is the Holy Water of Life that sets all Souls free from suffering, sorrow, and death.

Om So'ham tat tvam asi!
Om I Am That, Thou Art That!

Let the Maitreyian who is receiving The Blessing hold forth his cupped right hand or a cup.

Pour The Holy Water of Life from the Sacred Vessel into the Maitreyian's right hand or cup, accordingly, and say:

Share now, this Holy Water and share The Friend and receive the Inner Knowledge of The Friend's Self-Realization and Self-Sacrifice that is beyond words.

May you never thirst for the Holy Water of Life!

Om Jai Bhagavan Ji!
Victory To God The Beloved!
That Beloved Universal I AM THAT I AM Which You Are!

The Maitreyian who is receiving the Blessing should then drink The Holy Water of Life.

Giving The Blessing of The Divine Fire

Let the Giver of The Blessings present The Sacred Flame to the receiver and say:

This is The Divine Fire of The One Universal Spirit that permeates and gives Life to all Creation.

May it burn brightly within your heart and Illuminate your life!

May you light up the whole world with it!

The Blessings of Paratpara and The Friend be with you always.

If a new Maitreyian does not know what to do and it is inconvenient to describe or explain it, the Giver of The Blessings should wave the Light into the Maitreyian's Heart and mind with the back of his or her right hand.

When all who wish to do so have received The Blessings and are seated - let the leader lead the Holy Assembly in chanting one Devotional Dharma Mantra.

Giving Mass Blessings (Optional)

Let the Giver of The Blessings face the Holy Assembly and say:

Those who have received The Friend's Holy Initiation and have God's Supreme Promise of Universal Salvation and Liberation alive within their Hearts may Share The Holy Water of Life and The Divine Fire of The Holy Spirit. Let those who have received The Friend's Holy Initiation prepare to Share in The Friend's Being and Spirit and receive The Inner Knowledge of The Friend's Self-Realization and Self-Sacrifices that is beyond words, through The Holy Water of Life and The Divine Fire of The Spirit.

If you do not wish to receive Blessings at this time, cross your arms across your chest with your left hand at your right shoulder and your right hand at your left shoulder.

Sharing The Holy Water of Life

Let the leader face the Holy Assembly and holding the Water Vessel up high and say:

By The Will and Grace of The One Universal God:

In our Holy Book of Destiny The Friend has written:

"And I said unto The One Universal God, 'How can I give unto them my Self-Realizations and Self-Sacrifices, that they may be Blessed as you have Blessed me in this day?' And The One Universal God said unto me:

"No man can give his Self-Realization or Self-Sacrifices to another, My Beloved. But in answer to your Compassion, let it be that whosoever shall drink of Holy Water that has been consecrated by you or one you have Ordained for that purpose; and received from you or one you have Ordained to give it; shall share in your Being and your Spirit and the inner knowledge of your Self-Realization and Self-Sacrifices that is beyond words, shall be with him, thereby.

"Arise! Awaken! Beloved Soul! Thy Dawn has come! The Day is at hand! Unto he who knows The One Universal God as his True Self is given Life Eternal! Fire cannot burn him; sword pierce him; nor cold freeze him! Free from the illusions of your false self, knowing that you are not this, or this, or this, or this; but One with God, you shall endure forever. For always have I been; and always will I Be. One with Paratpara, The One Universal God of Countless Names and Forms Who Is Beyond All Names and Forms, That I AM THAT I AM - All in All!

"Seek first to know your own True Self. For in that knowing, you shall Know The One God - All in All. And you shall Know, without doubt or reservation that you are not this body or this mind or this personality - but That One Universal God, who is your

True Source, Substance and Self - and no other!

"And no longer shall the Sun be your Light by Day; nor the Moon your Light by Night. For The One God, The Beloved, shall have become an Eternal Light shining out from you unto all the Earth! Your Sun shall never set, nor your Moon wane. For The Light of The Eternal is yours and your days of sorrow are at an end.

"In His Eternal Love He has always Loved you. In His Infinite Being He has always held you. Come with me to God and take your place among The Twice Born of Eternity! This time you shall be truly made One with God - a Pure One, Reborn in God!

"There is no I but God! There is no you but God! I am with you always. Awaken then! All you who sleep the sleep of The Living Dead. And come with me to Paradise!

"This is The Water of Life: God Alone is Real! This whole Universe and all that is within it is God's Dream and Image, Created by That Absolute One within His Own Being, out of His Own Being! And, Soul and Spirit are One and Identical with God and no other!

"Whoever shares The Water of Life, shares Adhyatma Bhagavan Sri Babajhan Al-Kahlil The Friend! Whoever shares The Divine Fire of The Spirit of God, shares Adhyatma Bhagavan Sri Babajhan Al-Kahlil The Friend. This do often, in remembrance of me.

"You and I are One within The One that is All in All. Whenever one of you appears to be separated from the rest, know that this is but the working of the Great Illusion that hides your True Self from you. For, outside the sleeping minds of The Living Dead, there are no separations within God's Infinite and Eternal Being."

Give, or have an Assistant give cups to those who want them.

Distribute The Holy Water of Life to each Maitreyian who is present and wishes to receive it. Place The Holy Water of Life in the Maitreyian's cupped right hand or in the cup.

Then let the Giver of The Blessings return to the front of The Holy Assembly and say:

This is the Holy Water of Life that sets all Souls free from suffering, sorrow, and death.

Om So'ham tat tvam asi!
Om I Am That, Thou Art That!

Share now, this Holy Water and share The Friend and receive the Inner Knowledge of The Friend's Self-Realization and Self-Sacrifice that is beyond words.

Na Trish! May You Never Thirst for The Holy Water of Life!

To which the Assembly Members may respond:

Na Trish! May you never thirst!

Lead the Holy Assembly in sipping the Holy Water of Life - then say:

Jai Bhagavan Ji!

To which the Assembly Members may respond:

Victory To God The Beloved!

Let the leader invite the Holy Assembly to be seated.

Celebrating The Spirit

Let the leader Face the Holy Assembly and say:

Let us celebrate God and God's Supreme Divine Grace by raising our voices in Devotional Song. When we sing and drum and dance for God with energy and enthusiasm, The Friend comes out of the Holy Shrine and sings and dances with us in Spirit.

Raise your hands heavenward and proclaim:

Victory To Paratpara, The One Universal God of Countless Names and Forms Who Is Beyond All Names and Forms, The One Universal God who Speaks Through All The Prophets, Saints, Buddhas, Saviors and Avataras.

Let us raise our voices in Joyful Celebration of The Victory of The Age of Universal God's Pure Divine Truth!

Let the leader lead the Holy Assembly in the songs of choice from The Friend's Way Song Book.

Closing The Gathering for Worship

Raise The Sacred Flame

Let the leader approach The Holy Shrine and offer a Pranam. Kneel (or stand as the case may be) and after a moment of silence, raise The Central Sacred Flame and say:

O Paratpara!
Beloved Universal God of Countless Names and Forms Who Art Beyond All Names and Forms! Our Beloved One True Self!

As we raise up this Holy Light, let The Supreme Divine Light of Thy Living Presence and Thy Divine Pure Truth be lit up within the hearts of all Souls everywhere. Make us strong and courageous and let us lead all Souls up out of Ignorance, Darkness, and Error, into Thy Clear Divine Light of True Salvation and Liberation. Through Thy Supreme Gift of The Friend's Holy Initiation, let us bring forth The Satya Yuga and save all Souls from Suffering, Sorrow, and Death.

Jai Bhagavan Ji! Jai Bhagavan Ji! Om! Jai Bhagavan Ji!

Unseal The Holy Sanctuary

Let the leader stand facing the Holy Assembly and say:

Brothers and Sisters in The One Universal God! Having fulfilled The Holy Purpose of this Gathering for Worship and fulfilling Paratpara's Divine Promise of Liberation for all Souls - let us now join together in unsealing this Holy Sanctuary.

Let the leader then face the Holy Shrine and say:

O God! Beloved Universal I AM THAT I AM! By Thy Supreme Divine Truth and Presence that sets all Souls Free - unseal this Holy Sanctuary!

Let the leader face the Holy Assembly and declare:

This Holy Sanctuary is now Unsealed! Guardian: Unlock The Holy Sanctuary!

Om! Jai Bhagavan Ji! Victory To God The Beloved! That Beloved Universal I AM THAT I AM Which You Are!

Announcements

Let the leader announce to the Holy Assembly where they may gather for Friendship and the sharing of Consecrated food.

Departure

Call the Holy Assembly to rise for The Friend's departure.

When The Friend has offered The Sacred Gesture to the Holy Assembly and said His farewell, lead the Holy Assembly in one Holy Dharma Mantra.

Let the leader offer The Sacred Gesture to God and The Holy Sanctuary.

Let the leader lead the Holy Assembly in offering Pranams to Universal God and The Holy Sanctuary.

Let the leader and those conducting The Gathering for Worship depart in order.

Let the members of The Holy Assembly depart.

Friendship and Sharing Consecrated Food

Following Gathering for Worship, Maitreyians and Guests gather together in Universal Spirit to share Friendship and Prashad (Food that has been Consecrated by offering it to The One Universal God.)

This Concludes The Gathering for Worship.

Drum Circle

By The Will and Grace of The One Universal God:

Express The Activity of The Divine Spirit

Having formed a Sacred Circle of Unity and joined their Hearts and Minds together in harmony and unity, let the Maitreyians enter into Inner Divine Communion by The Two Rules according to The One Instruction and express the activity of The Divine Spirit within them, through the rhythms they are moved to create upon their drums. Those who are so moved by The Divine Spirit, may enter The Sacred Circle and express The Divine Blessings of Mudras (Gestures) and Actions (Kriyas) through dance and other such actions as they are moved to make.

How To Do Drum Circle

Purify yourself and prepare yourself for Inner Divine Communion with The One Universal God and The Friend within The Secret Inner Sanctuary of your Heart and Consecrate the Drum Circle and the drums that are to be used in the Drum Circle.

Form The Drum Circle

Enter into Inner Divine Communion through The Two Rules according to The One Instruction.

Fulfill The Drum Circle

1
Purify Yourself

Wash and dry your hands and face.

Center your heart and mind in Paratpara and The Friend, while reciting and contemplating:

I am more than this body. I AM THAT I AM!

I am more than these thoughts. I AM THAT I AM!

I am more than this personality. I AM THAT I AM!

I am more than this mind. I AM THAT I AM!

I am Pure Divine Universal Spirit, which is One and Identical with Paratpara, The One Universal God and no other. I AM THAT I AM!

Om So'ham Tat Tvam Asi! I Am That - Thou Art That! Jai Bhagavan Ji! Victory To God The Beloved!

That Beloved Universal I AM THAT I AM Which You Are!

2
Consecrate The Drums

Surrender the Drum Circle and the Drums that will be used in the Drum Circle, to God, through The Maitreyian Universal Prayer of Surrender.

3
Form The Drum Circle

Form a circle. Join hands. Sit together in silent communion and extend and flow The Power to one another and around the circle, until the Spirit of Harmony and Unity is felt.

4
Enter Into Inner Divine Communion

Establish yourself in The Rule of Divine Love

Love The One Universal God with all of your heart, all of your mind and all of your Spirit; Love yourself and one another even as you love God; and accept, love and revere all of God's Prophets, Saints, Buddhas, Saviors and Avataras alike, without being bound to accept what has been said or written about them.

Establish yourself in The Rule of Divine Guidance

Determine that you will seek, find and live by The Inner Divine Inspiration, Insight, Guidance and Revelation of The One Universal God and The Friend, and the counsel of your own True and Essential Conscience within The Secret Inner Sanctuary of your Heart, according to My One Instruction, in all things, great and small.

Do The One Instruction

First

Establish that you will offer each part and the whole of all that is done and all that is received, to Paratpara in the Sacrificial Fire within The Secret Inner Sanctuary of your Heart at each instant and receive whatever returns to you as Divine Gifts, given unto you by Paratpara and The Friend for your own Self-Realization and Liberation and the Perfection of The Holy Satya Yuga in this world for The Self-Realization and Liberation of all Souls everywhere for all time. Begin doing so immediately.

You may recite The Maitreyian Prayer of Universal Surrender.

Second

Establish yourself in a spirit of harm to none and benefit to all.

Third

Set your heart and mind firmly on Seeking The Highest Truth. You may recite or chant The Holy Adhyatma Gayatri to help you set your heart and mind.

Fourth

Call Upon Me to become active in Spirit within The Secret Inner Sanctuary of your Heart by holding My Presence within your mind and calling out within your Heart "Bhagavan Ji! Bhagavan Ji! Bhagavan Ji!"

Fifth

Ask for and open yourself to The Inner Divine Inspiration, Insight, Guidance and Revelation of Paratpara, The One Universal God of Countless Names and Forms and The Friend and your own True and Essential Conscience. You may recite The Prayer of Desperation.

Sixth

Take Refuge in The Four Pillars of Bhagavan, Dharma, Sangha and Satya Yuga;

You may chant or recite the Bhagavan Sharanam.

Seventh

Enter into The Secret Inner Sanctuary of your Heart through the repetition of my Holy Dharma Mantra "Jai Bhagavan Ji!" (Jay Bhag-wan Gee).

Eighth

Immerse yourself in The Divine Ocean of Paratpara's Supreme Truth and Being therein, like a drop of water in The Sea.

Ninth

Dwell steadily therein, like a candle flame in a still place, INJIA (Instantaneously Non-Judgmentally Insightfully Aware) and accepting of whatever comes, while it is coming, whatever lingers, while it is lingering and whatever goes, while it is going.

Tenth

Speak that which is right to be Spoken when it is right to Speak it; Do that which is right to be Done when it is right to Do it.

5
Fulfill The Drum Circle

Drum and move in harmony with God as you are moved by The Divine Spirit of Paratpara, The One Universal God, to do so.

This Concludes The Drum Circle

The Life Blessing

By The Will and Grace of The One Universal God:

Do not seek to do miracles. For God's Divine Design of Creation is the One Greatest Miracle. Dazzled by lesser miracles, the People are made to disparage God's Greatest Miracle and revere lesser miracles.

Many are those who have been Healed in body and mind by God's Power made manifest through men and women of Faith. But the healing of the body and the mind is inferior to the Healing of the division within The Spirit. All who are healed in body or in mind will certainly die. But he who is Healed in Spirit, is set free of death, forever. Therefore, let your first concern and Divine Mission be to Heal the People in Spirit by giving them my Holy Initiation and God's Supreme Promise, teaching them The Truth, The Life and The Way that fulfills God's Promise, and helping them to know The Truth, live The Life and follow The Way and win Self-Realization and Liberation within this life and Perfect Final Union with God at this life's end.

But, also, do not ignore the suffering and misery of the men, women and children who are yet bound by Spiritual ignorance and know not who they are. For, often it is occupation with the pain and suffering of body and mind that stands between an individual Soul and Liberation. Instead, flow forth The Power For Good That Can Do No Wrong upon those who suffer like unto a river of sweet water and let them do with it such as they will. It is to this end, and not for material ends, that I teach you the Mercy and Compassion of Life Blessing.

How to Give The Life Blessing

1. Purify Yourself.

2. Consecrate Your Work.

3. Enter into Inner Divine Communion.

4. Give Life Blessing.

Prepare Yourself

When Life Blessing is given in Gathering by several Maitreyians, let a leader be chosen from among you. Let the leader describe the need of the Soul who is to receive the Life Blessing. Let the leader begin the Gathering for Life Blessing and set a pace that is easy to follow. When all Maitreyians are ready to give Life Blessing, let the leader call for each act to be done in its rightful time and place that all may act in unison. When the Life Blessing is complete, let the leader end the Gathering for Life Blessing with final certainty.

- 1 -
Purify Yourself

Carefully Purify yourself with either the Brief Purification or the Full Purification before beginning Life Blessing, to be certain that you do not in any way contaminate the Soul you are helping, with your own personality or problems.

- 2 -
Consecrate Your Work

Surrender The Life Blessing and all results of The Life Blessing to God through The Universal

Prayer of Surrender. Never fall into pridefulness. Never accept credit for giving Life Blessing to anyone. Always be mindful that God is The Healer and that you are but the instrument of God's Healing. When praised for your Life Blessing, turn all praise and Glory to God!

- 3 -
Enter into Inner Divine Communion

Establish yourself in The Two Rules and enter into Inner Divine Communion according to The One Instruction. When you are well established in The Secret Inner Sanctuary of your Heart and are moved by The Divine Spirit, give the Life Blessing.

- 4 -
Give Life Blessing

Let every faithful Maitreyian perform the Life Blessing in this way:

Self Awareness - Become aware of all that you are: your history, your values, your experiences, your likes and dislikes, your prejudices and your problems. There is no need to examine each specific. You only need to grasp the general sense of your whole self.

Set Yourself Aside - Set yourself aside for the time you are giving Life Blessing, to keep from imposing yourself on the Soul you are giving Life Blessing to.

Together, these two works should only take two or three minutes.

Set an Intention - Set an intention in your mind, that is in harmony and accord with what the Soul for whom you are doing the Life Blessing has asked for. Align your intent and his or hers. If you find that you cannot do so in good conscience, then do not do the Life Blessing.

Find The Soul - Seek and find the Soul, within The Spiritual Realm, for whom you are doing the Life Blessing. Get an idea or image in your mind of the Soul as a whole person.

Examine The Soul - Examine the whole person. Look for what is wrong with him or her and what is right. Look for and note any problems and strengths you find. Note light and dark areas, colors, etc. Do not judge. Observe and record.

Communicate - Communicate with that Soul about the problems you have observed. Find out what he or she believes, feels or thinks is wrong. Establish agreement between yourself and the Soul about what the real problem is and what solution would satisfy the Soul you are giving Life Blessing to. This is, "Speaking what is right to be Spoken when it is right to speak it."

Resolve It - Step into the other Soul's shoes and resolve the problem or problems in your own Being as if the problem or problems were fully your own to resolve. Resolve it any way you can, that the Soul is willing and able to accept. You do not have to do anything to resolve it, just decide that it is resolved, with full certainty and Faith. This is, "Doing that which is right to be done when it is right to do it."

Extend and Flow The Power - Extend The Power For Good That Can Do No Wrong to the Soul you are giving Life Blessing. Flow The Power to him or her like a river of sweet water, until you are certain that it is time to stop. Do not try to make anything happen by flowing the Power. Just flow The Power. Remember and be mindful that all you can do is decide to extend and flow The Power. Once you have made the decision to flow The Power, it is God and God alone that does the work. Guard well the doors of your Heart and mind against the demon of pridefulness.

Communication Circle - While keeping his own Inner Divine Communion with the Soul who is being assisted, let the leader speak with each who is part of a Gathering for Life Blessing, AS IF he were talking directly to that Soul who is receiving the Life Blessing. Let each who the leader speaks to, answer, without breaking his Inner Divine Communion with that Soul, AS IF he is that Soul.

End The Life Blessing - Let the leader end the Life Blessing with certainty and finality. Let there be no lingering. When giving Life Blessing alone, the Maitreyian must also be sure to end the Life Blessing with certainty and finality.

- 5 -
Purify Yourself

Having finished the Life Blessing, clear yourself of your connection with the Soul you have been assisting. Use any mental imagery that works to accomplish the clearing. As you should never contaminate another Soul with your problems, you should not become burdened with another Soul's problems unless you choose to be. When you have cleared yourself, Purify yourself with either the Brief Purification or the Full Purification.

This Completes The Life Blessing

Forming The Circle of White Light

By The Will and Grace of The One Universal God:

Let it be known that every Maitreyian can extend and flow The Power for Good That Can Do No Wrong to any person, place, object or thought that he may choose.

When a Maitreyian chooses to do so, he may extend and flow The Power to form a Circle of White Light around any person, animal, object or place; and that person, animal, object, or place will be protected from harm to the extent of his Faith.

Let the Maitreyian purify himself by The Brief or Full Purification.

Let the Maitreyian offer The Prayer of Desperation.

Let the Maitreyian then see, in his mind's eye or before him, that person, animal, object or place as surrounded by a perfect Circle of White Light.

Let that Maitreyian offer a brief prayer regarding the person, animal, object or place that is to be protected.

Let that Maitreyian turn his attention to other matters in Faith that God's Will shall be done.

This Completes Forming The Circle of White Light

Gathering for Study

By The Will and Grace of The One Universal God:

The Purpose and Mission of The Holy Community of The Friend's Enlightened Faithful Believers is to give my Holy Initiation and God's Supreme Promise of Universal Salvation and Liberation to all Souls; teach all Souls The Truth, The Life and The Way that fulfills God's Promise, as The One Universal God has given it to all Souls through me; build a World-Wide Holy Community of Enlightened Faithful Believers who will love one another, cherish one another, protect one another, defend one another and help one another to live The Truth, The Life and The Way that fulfills God's Supreme Promise and attain Self-Realization, Salvation and Liberation within this life or at its end and Perfect Final Union with God at this life's end; and, bring forth The Age of God's Pure Divine Truth on earth for the Salvation and Liberation of all Souls.

The purpose of Gathering for Study is to further the Spiritual Growth of individual Maitreyans in their chosen Faith; and prepare all Maitreyans to fulfill their Purpose and Mission and carry the Holy Cause of God's Eternal Universal Religion to Victory in the world.

Summary

1
Opening Devotions

Gatherings for Study are begun with Opening Devotions and Members' Prayers for the Gathering.

The Offering for the Gathering is taken.

2
Review

The previous week's Study is briefly reviewed.

Let the leader lead the members in Truth-Saying what they have done to put the previous week's study into practice in their lives.

Praises, Testimonies, Self Criticisms, and Criticisms are given and exchanged.

3
Study

Let the leader read and lead the members in reading of the Scripture, Teaching or Instruction to be studied.

Let the Leader conduct a discussion of what has been studied.

Let the leader lead the members in Soul-Searching and Truth-Saying for Right-Living on the subject that is being studied.

Let the members of The Gathering for Study take The Three Steps to Right Action and make Free Choices they can and will be personally responsible for, regarding how they will apply what has been studied.

Let the members state the results of their taking The Three Steps to Right Action and say what they will commit themselves to do in the coming week to put what has been studied into practice.

4
Assignments

Let the leader give the members the assignment for the following week. Let the leader make any necessary announcements.

5
Closing Devotions

Let the leader lead the members in performing the Closing Devotions.

The Complete Order of Gathering for Study

- 1 -
Opening Devotions

Purification

Let the Study leader and the members purify themselves.

Let the Study Leader face The Holy Shrine and lead the members of the Study in calling upon God to clear their hearts and minds of all distractions, conflicts, prejudices, and problems that might cloud or dull the Gathering for Study.

Let the Study leader then perform the Opening Devotions.

The Holy Adhyatma Gayatri

Let the leader enter The Sacred Shrine, (or go to the front of the Sanctuary Hall if there is no Holy Shrine) and Pranam to Universal God and The Friend and The Holy Shrine - then stand (or kneel) facing The Holy Shrine and lead the Sangha in chanting of The Adhyatma Gayatri.

Offering Prayers

Maitreya's Prayer

Maitreya's Prayer may be offered in either The Morning form or The Evening form. Where non-initiates are attending, Maitreya's Prayer should be offered in the Morning form. Where there are only Maitreyians present, the Evening form should be used.

Members' Prayers for the Gathering

Offerings

Let the leader face the Holy Assembly and say:

By The Will and Grace of The One Universal God:

The Friend will not accept any Offering that is given in the Spirit of payment or exchange of any kind for His Teachings or Guidance. If you choose to give an Offering, it must be given freely, from your heart, without any consideration of payment or exchange whatsoever.

We will now make our Offering. Place your Offering in The Friend's Begging Bowl when it is passed to you.

Let a Maitreyian pass The Friend's Begging Bowl for The Offering.

- 2 -
Review

Let the Study Leader open the Gathering for Study by presenting a 5 to 10 minute summary of the previous week's Study.

Let the Study leader ask each of the Members The Five Opening Quests:

How have you put what we studied in our last Meeting, into practice and action in your daily life in this past week?

What was the result?

What could you have done better?

What will you do in the future?

What did you learn from your experience?

Let the leader lead the members in giving and exchanging Praises, Testimonies, Self Criticisms and Criticisms.

Principles for Giving Praise, Testimony and Criticism

The most basic Instruction I can give you for giving Praise and Criticism to Brother and Sister Maitreyians and to those outside of The Holy Community, is this:

When you are giving Praise, Praise others first and give your Testimony second. When you are giving Criticism, Criticize yourself first and others second.

Giving and Receiving Praise

Give all Praise in a Spirit of Universal Unselfish Service and Self-Sacrifice. Receive all Praise in a Spirit of Humility and Gratitude. Give and receive all Praise for the sake of The One Universal God, according to the instructions on Praise that I give unto you.

When giving Praise, offer The Sacred Gesture to Universal God and The Friend, The Holy Community and your Brother or Sister. Address him or her formally, and:

1) Offer your Praise humbly by stating the specific subject of your Praise.

2) State the specific part of The Friend's Teachings or Instructions your Praise is based upon.

3) Humbly offer your Brother or Sister Maitreyian specific concrete suggestions for increasing his or her good and continuing to grow in Unselfish Service to Universal God and The Friend, God's Eternal Universal Religion, and The Holy Cause of World-Wide Enlightenment and Self-Realization.

When receiving Praise, Pranam to your Brother or Sister Maitreyian, address him or her formally, and:

1) Repeat his or her Praise back exactly as he or she gave it.

2) Ask him or her if you have understood correctly. If you have, then go on.

3) If you have not understood the Praise correctly, ask him or her to repeat it. Repeat it back again and ask for confirmation. Keep on until you have understood correctly. Then, go on.

When a Praise has been understood exactly as it is given:

1) If you accept a Praise, state your acceptance, Pranam to Universal God and The Friend, The Holy Community, and the giver; and Offer The Holy Dharma Mantra "Jai Bhagavan Ji!"

2) Let no one reject a Praise that is given or accept it blindly. Instead,

let all who are given Praise receive it humbly and do deep and sincere Soul-Searching upon it.

Giving Testimony

Testimony follows the Instructions for Praise. Testimony is Self-Praise without egotism. Self-Praise given with egotism is bad for yourself and The Holy Community. Offer your Testimony in a Spirit of Humble Universal Unselfish Service and Self-Sacrifice for the sake of Universal God, and Good Result will follow. Offer your Testimony according to the instructions on Praise I give unto you.

1. Give your Testimony by offering The Sacred Gesture to Universal God and The Friend, The Holy Community, and:

2. State the specific part of The Friend's Teachings or Instructions that your Right Testimony is based upon.

3. Give a specific, concrete statement of how you will keep on Growing into that part of The Friend's Teaching or Instruction in the future.

4. Pranam to Universal God and The Friend and The Holy Community and Offer The Holy Dharma-Mantra for the sake of The One Universal God.

Right and Wrong Criticism

Wrong Criticism destroys. Right Self Criticism is the Lion's Way to Spiritual Growth and Advancement. Only the vain and those who live false lives, fear and hate Criticism. Lions, Maitreyans, who live in The House of Truth welcome Criticism and seek it out.

Wrong Criticism is criticism that is based in personality, prejudice, and selfishness.

Right Criticism is built upon the Fourfold Foundation of Universal God and The Friend, God's Eternal Universal Religion, The Holy Community, and The Holy Cause of World-Wide Enlightenment and Self-Realization for all people for all time.

Wrong Criticism is concerned about who is Right!

Right Criticism is concerned about what is Right in The Light of The One Universal God and The Friend, God's Eternal Universal Religion, The Holy Community, and The Holy Cause.

Wrong Criticism is selfish. Wrong Criticism is preoccupied with false self, vanity and personality. Wrong Criticism is given from an attitude and feeling of superiority. Wrong Criticism is built upon a foundation of Vanity, Ignorance, and Pride. Wrong Criticism secretly seeks to tear another person down and destroy him or her.

It is having suffered under the oppressive weight of too much Wrong Criticism in the past, that causes Brother and Sister Maitreyians to fear or hate all Criticism.

A combination of Right understanding of Criticism, a good attitude toward Brother and Sister Maitreyians that assumes they are acting with the BEST INTENTION, and giving and receiving Humble, helpful, Right Criticism, breaks the "spell" of past Wrong Criticism and overcomes the ghosts of fear.

How To Offer Right Self Criticism

1. Offer The Sacred Gesture to The One Universal God and The Friend, and The Holy Community.

2. Boldly and Truthfully state the specific attitude, action, or lack of action that you are Self Criticizing.

3. State the specific part of Maitreya The Friend's Teachings or Instructions your Self Criticism is based upon.

4. Courageously state specifically and concretely what you will DO to correct the attitude, action, or lack of action you are Criticizing.

5. Pranam to Universal God and The Friend and The Holy Community and Offer The Holy Dharma-Mantra.

How to Give and Receive Criticism

Give all Criticism in a Spirit of Universal Unselfish Service and Self-Sacrifice to your Brothers and Sisters. Receive all Criticism in a Spirit of Humility and Gratitude for The Sake of God's Eternal Universal Religion and our Holy Cause.

In Gatherings where there are Maitreyians and non-Maitreyians present, observe the rule that while Maitreyians should offer Right Criticism to non-Maitreyians, non-Maitreyians may not and must not offer Criticisms to Maitreyians.

When giving Criticism, Offer The Sacred Gesture to Universal God and The Friend, The Holy Community, and your Brother or Sister. Address your Brother or Sister Maitreyian formally, and:

1) Humbly offer Criticism by stating the specific subject of your Criticism.

2) State the specific part of Maitreya The Friend's Teachings or Instructions your Criticism is based upon.

3) Humbly offer your Brother or Sister Maitreyian specific concrete suggestions for overcoming his or her error and continuing to grow in Unselfish Service to Universal God and The Friend, God's Eternal Universal Religion, and The Holy Cause of World-Wide Enlightenment and Self-Realization.

When receiving Criticism, offer The Sacred Gesture to your Brother or Sister, address him or her formally, and:

1) Repeat his or her Criticism back exactly as he or she gave it.

2) Ask him or her if you have understood correctly. If you have, then go on.

3) If you have not understood the Criticism correctly, ask him or her to repeat it. Repeat it back again and ask for confirmation. Keep on until you have understood correctly. Then, go on.

When a Criticism has been understood exactly as it is given:

1) Pranam to Universal God and The Friend, The Holy Community, and the giver; and humbly Offer The Holy Dharma-Mantra "Jai Bhagavan Ji!"

2) Let no one reject a Criticism that is given or accept it blindly. Instead, let all who are given Criticism, receive it humbly and do deep and sincere Soul-Searching upon it.

- 3 -
Study

Present The Reading

Important Principle

Confusion, misunderstanding, and lack of understanding arise from the same source as all of the other ills of humanity. Confusion, misunderstanding, and lack of understanding arise from Ignorance, lack of INJIA, Selfishness, Attachment, and Identification.

Confusion, misunderstanding, or lack of understanding may arise from Ignorance of the Right Meaning of a word. Confusion, misunderstanding, or lack of understanding may arise from Selfishness through seeing all things in terms of yourself.

Confusion, misunderstanding, or lack of understanding may arise from Attachment to or Identification with a former definition, idea, notion, group, or system of thought or practice with which you have been associated.

Confusion, misunderstanding, and lack of understanding do not arise from a need for interpretation. As confusion, misunderstanding, and lack of understanding do not arise from a need for interpretation, they cannot be relieved by interpretation.

A New Truth must be faced in one of two ways: Wisely or Foolishly. Truth is faced Wisely by accepting it As It Is and rebuilding your personal reality around it. Truth is faced Foolishly by interpreting it, distorting it, and perverting it to make it fit into your present personal reality.

A Maitreyian's insistence on interpretation should be recognized as coming directly from a secret unwillingness to accept Truth As It Is and a desire to make Truth conform to what a Soul already believes or wishes to be so. Interpretation only makes confusion, misunderstanding, or lack of understanding seem to be relieved, while making them worse.

The True remedy for confusion, misunderstanding, and lack of understanding is dwelling upon the Truth exactly As It Is in the light of Holy INJIA.

Let the Study leader lead the members in reading the Study for that Gathering for Study.

Let the leader make sure that all special words are defined, according to the Rightful Holy Adhyatma-Yoga-Dharma definitions as they arise in the Study Reading.

Let the study leader be sure that he does not interpret The Holy Scriptures or any other of The Friend's Teachings or Instructions for the members. Let the study leader be equally sure that he does not allow the members to impose their own interpretations on him or one another.

Let the leader answer all questions by explaining that the Scriptures and Teachings must be grasped and understood exactly as they are; and refer the members to the paragraph or verse of The Scriptures or Teachings for rereading.

Discussion

Let the Study leader choose (through The Three Steps to Right Action) to use:

The Question and Answer Study method; The Guided Discussion Study method; or The Combined Study method which is a combination of the Question and Answer and Guided Discussion methods.

Regardless of which method a leader chooses:

Ask and encourage each Member to give some personal examples from his or her own personal life to illustrate each Teaching, Principle, point and idea that is studied.

Ask and encourage each Member to give his or her ideas and insights as to how, where, and when, in his or her daily life he or she could unify the Teaching, Principle, point, or idea being studied with action.

Bring out the World-Wide importance of The Friend's Teachings, Instructions, and Principles by asking each Member to present news clippings of current events and analyze them in terms of The Friend's Holy Adhyatma-Yoga-Dharma Teachings, Instructions, and Principles being studied.

Let the leader guide the Members, beginning with their very first Gathering for Study, to think in terms of our Purpose and Mission and our Holy Cause of bringing forth The Age of Universal God's Pure Divine Truth and World-Wide Enlightenment, Self-Realization and Liberation for all Souls everywhere for all time.

Encourage each member to be ready and willing to actively participate in the Gathering to his fullest ability. In this case, by giving examples, testimony, and illustrations and carrying out assignments. The success of Gathering for Study depends as much on good members as it depends upon Good Leadership.

Soul-Searching and Truth-Saying for Right-Living

Let the leader begin (and if needed, guide new members in) entering into Inner Divine Communion by The Two Rules according to The One Instruction and do Soul-Searching and Truth-Saying for Right-Living on the subject of the Study.

Taking The Three Steps to Right Action

Let the leader begin (and if needed, guide new members in) Taking The Three Steps to Right Action.

Commitment

Let the leader call upon each member to make a commitment to God, himself and the other members as to how, where, and when, in his daily life he will put what has been studied into action.

- 4 -
Assignments

Let the Study leader give out the Study Lesson and any necessary Instructions or assignments for the following week and the next Gathering for Study.

Let the Study leader make any announcements that need to be made.

- 5 -
Closing Devotions

Let the leader approach The Holy Shrine and offer a Pranam. Kneel (or stand as the case may be) and after a moment of silence, raise The Central Sacred Flame and say:

O Paratpara!
Beloved Universal God
of Countless Names and Forms
Who Art Beyond All Names
and Forms!
Our Beloved One True Self!
As we raise up this Holy Light,
let The Supreme Divine Light
of Thy Living Presence
and Thy Divine Pure Truth
be lit up within the hearts
of all Souls everywhere.
Make us strong and courageous
and let us lead all Souls
up out of Ignorance, Darkness,
and Error,
into Thy Clear Divine Light
of True Salvation and Liberation.
Through Thy Supreme Gift
of Maitreya The Friend's
Holy Initiation,
let us bring forth The Satya Yuga
and save all Souls
from Suffering, Sorrow, and Death.
Om So'ham tat tvam asi!
Om! I Am That - Thou Art That!
Jai Bhagavan Ji!
Victory to God The Beloved!
That Beloved Universal
I AM THAT I AM
Which You Are!

Let the leader then lead the members of The Gathering for Study in The Devotional Dharma-Mantra.

This Concludes The Gathering for Study

Gathering for Truth-Saying

By The Will and Grace of The One Universal God:

Preparation

Clean and Prepare the Sanctuary Hall or room that is to be used. If there is a Sacred Shrine, clean the Shrine and replace candles and other Articles of Worship as needed. Turn on the Shrine lights and light all candles except the Central Sacred Flame.

Assembly

Arrange for the people to assemble at least five minutes before the Truth-Saying is to begin. Let no man or woman be given entrance once the Truth-Saying has begun. Be sure that all Maitreyians, and any guests admitted under special circumstances, understand this in advance.

The Call To Gathering for Truth-Saying

At the rightful time, let one of you who is a Maitreyian give The Call to Gathering.

When a separate place of assembly is used, proceed to The Sanctuary Hall when The Call has been completed.

Offering Respects

Let that Maitreyian who is to lead the Gathering for Truth-Saying lead The Holy Assembly in Chanting a long "Om."

Respects to and from The Friend

Let the leader turn toward The Friend or toward the Holy Shrine if The Friend is present in Spirit only; and lead the Holy Assembly in offering The Sacred Gesture to The Friend.

Respects to and from The Holy Assembly

Let the leader offer The Sacred Gesture to the Holy Assembly and the Holy Assembly return it in unison.

Open The Gathering for Truth-Saying

Let the leader Proclaim The Divine Purpose of The Gathering for Truth-Saying, saying:

"Brothers and Sisters in Spirit! We come together in this Gathering for Truth-Saying to search our Souls and say The Truth, the whole Truth and nothing but The Truth to one another. Let each of you search your very Soul and say the Truth, the Whole Truth and nothing but the Truth that comes from his own Soul- Searching and any smallest thing in which you have deceived or wronged another who is herein. Let what is said in this Gathering remain in this Gathering and not be taken beyond it. Let no bad feeling or ill will that may arise in this Gathering, as a result of Truth-Saying or otherwise, be taken outside of it by any Maitreyian. Anyone who is here, who cannot or will not act in accord with this requirement must leave before we begin. If any among you cannot or will not keep all that is said within this Gathering confidential or put his bad feelings or ill will aside when he leaves this Holy Gathering, take your leave now."

Proceed only after any who cannot or will not do so have left.

The Opening Devotions

The Holy Adhyatma Gayatri

Let the leader enter The Sacred Shrine, (or go to the front of the Sanctuary Hall if there is no Holy Shrine) and Pranam to Universal God and The Friend and The Holy Shrine - then stand (or kneel) facing The Holy Shrine and lead the Sangha in responsive chanting of The Adhyatma Gayatri.

Light The Central Sacred Flame

Let the leader light up The Central Sacred Flame and raise it up toward Heaven while chanting a long "Om." Lower the Central Sacred Flame to the Shrine. Take one step back and offer The Sacred Gesture.

Surrender The Gathering

Offerings

Let the leader face the Holy Assembly and say:

By the Will and Grace of The One Universal God:

It is written in The Holy Book of Destiny, The One Universal God said unto The Friend of All Souls:

{G} "Sell not your Holy Initiation and My Promise or your Holy Religion which is My Own. Instead, wherever there shall be a Holy Sanctuary of your Religion, place therein a Begging Bowl to your left hand and let all who are your Faithful and My Own and all others who come unto you, place their offering therein. From that which is given unto you, shall you and those you Ordain fill your worldly needs."

The Friend will not accept any Offering that is given in the Spirit of payment or exchange of any kind for His Teachings or Guidance. If you choose to give an Offering, it must be given freely, from your heart, without any consideration of payment or exchange whatsoever.

We will now make our Offering. Place your Offering in The Friend's Begging Bowl when it is passed to you.

Take The Offering

Let a Maitreyian pass the Begging Bowl.

Soul-Searching

Let the leader face the Holy Assembly and announce Soul-Searching saying:

Brothers and Sisters, let us now Search our Souls for The Truth, The Whole Truth and nothing but The Truth through Inner Divine Communion by The Two Rules according to The One Instruction, as God has given them to The Friend.

Let the leader take a seat and begin the Soul-Searching. The Two Rules and The One Instruction are done in either the Guided or Unguided form - depending on the needs and experience of those who are present.

Truth-Saying

After a reasonable time is given to Soul-Searching, let the leader say:

Let each who is present herein, say The Truth, The Whole Truth and nothing but The Truth of your own Soul-Searching and any smallest thing in which you have deceived or wronged another who is herein.

Close The Gathering For Truth-Saying

Raise The Sacred Flame

Let the leader approach The Holy Shrine and offer a Pranam. Kneel (or stand as the case may be) and after a moment of silence, raise The Central Sacred Flame and say:

O Paratpara!
Beloved Universal God of Countless Names and Forms Who Art Beyond All Names and Forms! Our Beloved One True Self!

As we raise up this Holy Light, let The Supreme Divine Light of Thy Living Presence and Thy Divine Pure Truth be lit up within the hearts of all Souls everywhere. Make us strong and courageous and let us lead all Souls up out of Ignorance, Darkness, and Error, into Thy Clear Divine Light of True Salvation and Liberation. Through Thy Supreme Gift of The Friend's Holy Initiation, let us bring forth The Satya Yuga and save all Souls from Suffering, Sorrow, and Death.

Jai Bhagavan Ji! Jai Bhagavan Ji! Om Jai Bhagavan Ji!!

Announcements

Let the leader announce to the Holy Assembly where they may gather for Friendship and the taking of Prashad (Holy Consecrated food).

Departure

Call the Holy Assembly to rise for The Friend's departure.

When The Friend has offered The Sacred Gesture to the Holy Assembly and said His farewell, lead the Holy Assembly in one Holy Dharma Mantra.

Let the leader offer The Sacred Gesture to God and The Holy Sanctuary.

Let the leader lead the Holy Assembly in offering Pranams to Universal God and The Holy Sanctuary.

Let the leader and those conducting The Gathering for Truth-Saying depart in order.

Let the members of The Holy Assembly depart.

This Concludes The Gathering for Truth-Saying

Dream Time Rendezvous

By The Will and Grace of The One Universal God:

On that night when the new Moon has just passed and the first waxing crescent is shown to Man, and at any other time that fills your need, gather together in Inner Divine Communion in Spirit, with your Brothers and Sisters and such others who are sincere, within The Spiritual Realm, in that time where dreams and dreamless sleep consume your mortal body and mind. And therein, Commune in Spirit with The One Universal God, myself, all of God's Prophets, Saints, Buddhas, Saviors and Avataras and one another. Whatsoever you receive therein, share that with one another.

How to Keep Dream Time Rendezvous

Prepare yourself for sleep.

Purify yourself by the Brief or Full Purification.

Take a comfortable position upon that place where you will sleep.

Set a firm intention that, while taking sleep you will enter into The Spiritual Realm and keep your Dream Time Rendezvous.

Surrender your sleep and the Dream Time Rendezvous to The One Universal God.

Offer such prayers for The Dream Time Rendezvous as fill your need.

Form and surround yourself with The Circle of White Light.

Enter into Inner Divine Communion by The Two Rules according to The One Instruction.

Let your Inner Divine Communion merge into sleep in Faith that you will keep The Dream Time Rendezvous.

Within the following day, share whatsoever The One Universal God has revealed unto you in Dream Time with other Maitreyians, individually, in groups or in Gatherings for that purpose alone.

Let no one criticize or pass judgment upon what another reveals. Neither let any among you presume to stand above his Brother or Sister because of what is brought back from Dream Time Rendezvous. Let all receive what is revealed respectfully having balanced his mind and the opposites.

This Concludes Dream Time Rendezvous

**Here Ends The Chapter Entitled
The Community Disciplines**

**Here Ends
The Book Entitled
The Book of Discipline**

Book Five

The Teachings of Maitreya The Friend

By The Will and Grace of The One Universal God

Chapter One
Birth, Death and In Between

By The Will and Grace of The One Universal God:

The Spiritually Ignorant who are shrouded in darkness have argued and fought and killed, for countless thousands of years over God - That One I AM THAT I AM which you are. But, I say unto you that no man and no words can say who or what God is, for That I AM THAT I AM is beyond The Beyond. Whosoever would try to capture God in words, may as well try to capture the sea in a teacup. Let not, therefore, your words be a net in which you seek to snare God. Neither let your words be as shackles that imprison men's Souls. But let your words be like unto fingers pointing toward a distant mountain. No one can capture God in words, ever! Yet, the Wise know the expressions of God. I say unto you:

2. God Loves! God Cares! God Forgives all! God Gives All without thought of return!

3. When you Love - you are in Oneness with God!

4. When you Care - you are in Oneness with God!

5. When you Forgive - you are in Oneness with God!

6. When you Give of yourself, your possessions, and your wealth without thought of return - you are in Oneness with God!

7. Not for the sake of the husband is the husband loved, but for the sake of The Spirit of God within.

8. Not for the sake of the wife is the wife loved, but for the sake of the Spirit of God within.

9. Not for the sake of the children are the children loved, but for the sake of The Spirit of God within.

10. Not for the sake of the father is the father loved, but for the sake of The Spirit of God within.

11. Not for the sake of the mother is the mother loved, but for the sake of The Spirit of God within.

12. Not for the sake of the brother is the brother loved, but for the sake of The Spirit of God within.

13. Not for the sake of the sister is the sister loved, but for the sake of The Spirit of God within.

14. Not for the sake of friends are friends loved, but for the sake of The Spirit of God within.

15. Not for the sake of the Teacher is the Teacher loved, but for the sake of The Spirit of God within.

16. Not for the sake of the Prophet is the Prophet loved, but for the sake of The Spirit of God within.

17. Not for the sake of the Buddha is the Buddha loved, but for the sake of The Spirit of God within.

18. Not for the sake of the Messiah is the Messiah loved, but for the sake of The Spirit of God within.

19. Not for the sake of The Friend is The Friend loved, but for the sake of The Spirit of God within.

20. Not for the sake of the body or the thoughts or the personality are any loved, but for the sake of The Spirit of God which is within all, one and the same.

21. For the body passes away and the thoughts and personality change as the tides. But The Divine Spirit of God that is the True Self of all, endures forever! Fire cannot burn it! Cold cannot freeze it! Sword and bullet cannot pierce it! Hunger cannot starve it! Sickness cannot sicken it! Pain cannot disturb it! Suffering cannot reach it! And Death is no more to it than the taking off of one suit of worn out clothing and, the putting on of another which is new!

22. Forever! Forever Free! Forever Blissful! Forever Happy! Forever One with Universal God and no other!

23. It is The Spirit within you alone which loves. And, it is The Spirit alone which is loved in all that you love. For The Spirit alone knows. And The Spirit alone loves. And, as a new born babe knows and loves its mother; even so does The Spirit in you know and love The Spirit alone in all that you know and love.

24. Grieve not, therefore, for those that you love who pass out of this world before you. Neither fear for your own passing. For, as all that is thrown into the air falls to earth; and as all that is put together must someday come apart; all that is born is born of the flesh and must also pass away.

25. But I tell you that you have no need to fear. For you are not of the flesh, but of The Spirit. And death is no more to The Spirit, than the rain returning to the Sea from which it has arisen. Never was there a time when I or you or those that you love were not. And never will there come a time when I or you or those that you love shall cease to be. For, though body and personality come and go as the day and the night, you shall endure Forever. For you are that One Eternal Spirit of which I have spoken this day, and no other!

26. Many are there who would have you to believe that you possess a Soul and a Spirit as a man possesses a house or a car or a piece of clothing. And, that this Soul and Spirit are somehow other than you and that you are somehow other than this Soul and Spirit. But I say unto you that you do not possess a Soul or a Spirit, but that you are a Soul which is Spirit. And, it is as a Soul and Spirit that you possess this body, these thoughts, this personality, and all else. And so it is with all those that you know and love.

27. Others are there, who would have you believe that Soul and Spirit are somehow separate and divided apart from That One Universal Spirit which men call God and Allah and Brahman and Jehovah and three thousand and thirty other names, and which I call simply Universal Spirit. But I say unto you that this Soul which is Spirit and which you truly are, is not separate or divided apart from The One Universal Spirit of God which is your One True Source and Self and Home! Neither has it ever been separate or divided apart from The One Universal Spirit of God. Neither shall it ever be separate or divided apart from God. For this Soul and Spirit which you truly are and which all that you know and love truly are, Is, has Always been, and will always Be One with That One Universal Spirit which men call God and so many other names.

28. Some others are there who would have you to believe that God is like unto a potter and you are nothing but an empty pot which is made of earth and water by God's hands. But I say unto you that the earth and the water are here for the earthly potter. But this whole world and all Creation were brought forth by God from His own Being and Substance alone. For there was naught else from which it could be made. And, therefore, you and this Creation are all of the One Spirit and Substance and Being of Universal God and no other. Yes, truly, even the earth and the water from which the potter makes his pots is That alone. And you are Forever and Free and Safe. For what is there that can harm The Universal Spirit of God?

29. Therefore, be at Peace. And do not cling to today or the things of today. For as the day must surely pass into the night, the things of today belong only to today and, must pass away with its passing. But The Real endures beyond all change and beyond all passing.

30. Do not fear for tomorrow. For nothing that it can bring can touch or harm The Spirit of God which is The Real you; nor The Spirit of God which is The Real in those you know and love. And, as the day passes into the night and the night again, passes into the day, whatsoever tomorrow may bring will also pass.

31. Learn from your mistakes and your errors, but carry them not upon your back as a great weight. And, feel neither sorrow nor guilt nor regret for what has been. For, as today becomes yesterday and tomorrow becomes today and, as today's Sun regrets not that upon which yesterday's light has fallen; you should shine for today and not leave your Divine Light wasting upon yesterdays which are no more.

32. For Yesterday is but a trace left in the sands of time and tomorrow is but a dream which is yet to be fulfilled. But today well lived makes every yesterday a memory of happiness and every tomorrow a dream of joy. And the trees and flowers in your fields and the birds of the air grow and thrive not upon yesterday's sunlight, but upon the light of the day and the moment in which they live. Be, then, like unto the trees and the flowers in your fields and the birds of the air. And be at Peace.

33. From the earth, the sea, and the sky these bodies and personalities have come. And, unto the earth, the sea, and the sky they must return. But The Spirit of God within you which knows and loves and, The Spirit of God which we know and love within

one another, lasts Forever and is never lost. That You Are! And no other.

34. Take, therefore, your Courage, your Peace, and your Comfort in this Ancient and Holy Truth of God's Eternal Universal Religion of Holy Adhyatma-Yoga-Dharma which Universal God has given and I have spoken unto you this day. And fear no more.

Om So'ham Tat Tvam Asi!
Om! I Am That - Thou Art That!
Jai Bhagavan Ji!
Victory To God The Beloved!
That Beloved Universal
I Am That I Am
Which You Are!

Here Ends the Chapter Entitled
Birth, Death and In Between

Chapter Two
The Sharp Sword of Universal God's Pure Divine Truth

By The Will and Grace of The One Universal God:

- One -

This is The Pure Divine Truth of Paratpara, The One Universal God of Countless Names and Forms Who Is Beyond All Names and Forms, That I AM THAT I AM, Creator of The Creator, The One Universal Source, Substance and Self of the universes and all Souls.

2. The One Universal God taught The Pure Divine Truth unto me, His Out-going Spirit, His Awakened Emanation for the Universal Salvation and Liberation of all Souls. And He called The Pure Divine Truth, The Holy Adhyatma-Yoga-Dharma.

3. That Pure Divine Truth which Paratpara taught unto me; God's outgoing Spirit, in the most ancient of times, taught to The Bringer of The Dawn. The Bringer of The Dawn taught it to The Keeper of The Truth, who in turn taught the Higher and the Lower views of The Pure Divine Truth unto The Ancestors, who became the Prophets, Saints, Buddhas, Saviors, and Avataras of all times. These Holy Ones, verily, have given forth that portion of it for which they were Ordained, in the way as was Rightful for the time.

4. There is a single Cause of all things, by the knowing of which all else will be known.

5. The twin views of The Pure Divine Truth are like unto the wings of a Great Bird. They are The Higher Knowledge and the Lower Knowledge - and must be known together.

6. Of these, the Lower Knowledge is The Pure Divine Truth of Prayer, The Pure Divine Truth of Ceremony and Ritual, The Pure Divine Truth of Song, The Pure Divine Truth of Mantra, and all worldly knowledge.

7. The Higher Knowledge is The Holy Adhyatma-Yoga-Dharma by which The Undying State of Oneness with Universal God, The Imperishable, is Realized.

8. By means of The Higher Knowledge of Holy Adhyatma-Yoga-Dharma, the wise Realize their Oneness with Universal God, The Undying who is beyond touch, beyond sight, beyond hearing, having no attributes, eternal, all-pervading, and most subtle - the One Source of all Souls.

9. As a spider sends forth its thread, as hairs grow upon the head and

body of a living man - so does all Creation arise from Universal God, The Imperishable. By Self-Will and Self-Sacrifice, Universal God becomes Manifest as the Holy Triad of Creator, Preserver, and Destroyer. From That Holy Triad, Matter comes forth. From Matter, Life. From Life, Mind. From Mind, the Truths. From the Truths, the Worlds. From these, come forth all Actions and their Results. By these, everything within the universe is Created, Preserved, and Destroyed.

10. From Universal God, who is All-Knowing and All-Wise, whose austerity consists of Knowing; are born The Creator, The Preserver, and The Destroyer, and all name, form, and food.

- Two -

This is The Pure Divine Truth of Paratpara, The One Universal God of Countless Names and Forms Who Is Beyond All Names and Forms, That I AM THAT I AM, Creator of The Creator, The One Universal Source, Substance and Self of the Universes and all Souls.

2. In The Beginning, Paratpara, The One Universal God of Countless Names and Forms Who Is Beyond All Names and Forms revealed The Way of Self-Sacrifice unto The Ancestors. I am that Living Self-Sacrifice upon whom all Holy Scriptures are strung as pearls upon a string. I Am That!

3. Self-Sacrifice is the Highest Religion; The Holy Adhyatma-Yoga-Dharma, The Highest Truth. Through Self-Sacrifice, Universal God has brought forth The Creator. Through Self-Sacrifice The Creator has brought forth The Preserver, The Destroyer, and all of the Universes. Through Self-Sacrifice the Universe is Maintained by The Preserver. Through Self-Sacrifice it is renewed by The Destroyer. Through my Self-Sacrifice, The Holy Adhyatma-Yoga-Dharma is restored unto the people, and the Supreme Gift of Salvation and Liberation is won for all Souls.

4. Receiving The True Enlightenment of my Holy Initiation and giving The Divine Gift of my True Enlightenment unto others is the True Inner Self-Sacrifice. For whosoever receives The True Enlightenment of my Holy Initiation may give it unto another. And, whosoever gives The Divine Gift of my True Enlightenment unto another, in my Name and the Name of the One Universal God of Who I Am; shares with me in my Supreme Self-Sacrifice, given for the Salvation and Liberation of all Souls.

5. Studying and following my Holy Adhyatma-Yoga-Dharma Teachings and Instructions; offering Worship and Prayer; constant Soul Searching and Truth Saying for Right Living; living The Truth, The Life and The Way that fulfills God's Supreme Promise; keeping the Company of The Enlightened Faithful Believers; keeping The Holy Days; regularly offering Tithe; and helping those people and creatures who are in need - these are The Outer Self-Sacrifices.

6. Perform Outer Self-Sacrifice constantly, for the love of Universal God and The Friend, Beloved Devotee, for this is The Way that leads to the Heaven World. Perform Inner Self-Sacrifice constantly, for the love of Universal God and The Friend, Beloved Devotee, for this is The Way that leads to the True Salvation and

Liberation of Perfect Final Union with Universal God.

7. When my Holy Initiation has kindled the fire of Self-Realization and Inner Self-Sacrifice has fanned the flames of True Enlightenment to a White-heat within a man, then all Outer Self-Sacrifice bears Good Fruit, not otherwise.

8. He who has not The True Enlightenment of my Holy Initiation and God's Supreme Promise in his heart, is lost. But He whose Inner Self-Sacrifice of receiving my Holy Initiation is not accompanied by the Inner Self-Sacrifice of giving The Gift of my True Enlightenment unto others; and He whose Inner Self-Sacrifice of giving The Gift is not accompanied by Outer Self-Sacrifice - who studies not nor follows my Holy Adhyatma-Yoga-Dharma Teachings and Instructions, who offers no Worship or Prayer; who does not do constant Soul Searching and Truth Saying for Right Living; who does not live The Truth, The Life and The Way that fulfills God's Supreme Promise; who keeps not the Company of my Enlightened Faithful Believers; who fails to observe and keep The Holy Days; who Tithes not; and who gives not help to those in need - brings darkness upon all of his worlds until the Seventh.

9. The Sacred Fire of Universal God's Divine Truth and Presence burns brightly, with Seven Divine Flames, within the bearer of The True Enlightenment of my Holy Initiation.

10. He who has my Holy Initiation and is in Good Faith with me, has The Seven Divine Flames burning within him. For that Devotee who offers Inner and Outer Self-Sacrifice with The Seven Divine Flames burning brightly within him, The Seven Divine Flames become rays of The One Divine Sun, and lead him to the abode of The Creator, The One Lord of all Divine Beings.

11. Divine Beings call him upward saying 'Come Home! Come Home!' and lead him upon The Way of the Divine Light, honoring him and greeting him with blissful words saying 'This is the Holy Heaven of The Creator that you have won by your Self-Sacrifice and Good Deeds'.

12. Unsteady and frail are the rafts of Rituals and Good Works that are performed by others who do only the Lower Work. For Rituals and Good Works are of this temporary world, and can be lost unless supported by True Inner Knowledge and Self-Sacrifice. The deluded, who depend only upon Ritual and Good Works as the Highest Good - fall into birth, old age, and death again and again.

13. Filled with Spiritual Ignorance, conceited of their own wisdom, learning and intellect; puffed up with vain egotism; foolish and deluded Souls wander aimlessly through the forest of illusion, from lifetime to lifetime, afflicted with suffering - like blind men leading the blind.

14. Lacking in Spiritual Development, the ignorant flatter themselves, thinking: 'We have accomplished the purpose of life'. In Truth, those who practice Outer Sacrifice and Ritual alone, and do not know The Higher Truth of Holy Adhyatma-Yoga-Dharma, return to this world as wretched Souls - owing to ignorance and attachment - when the fruits of their Good Deeds are burned up within the Heaven World.

15. The ignorant and deluded, believing ritual, forgiveness of sins, and worldly good works to be the Highest Good, know not The True Highest Good. Having burned up their merits by enjoyment in the Heaven World, they return into this world to suffer and die again and again.

16. But my Enlightened Faithful Believers, who know my Holy Adhyatma-Yoga-Dharma, practice Inner and Outer Self Sacrifice for the love of The One Universal God and The Friend, and live without attachment to this world - leave this world free of sin and Ignorance, by the Way of The Divine Light. These, Truly, attain that Undying State wherein The Immortal Soul dwells in Perfect Final Union with Universal God, forever.

17. Having examined all the worlds that are to be won by works alone, let The Truly Wise take up the True Enlightenment of my Holy Initiation and my Holy Adhyatma-Yoga-Dharma, and perform Inner and Outer Self-Sacrifice, and become free.

18. That which is eternal cannot be won by attachment to the temporary. The Divine World beyond Creation is not attained by those who are attached to Creation. Truly Beloved Devotee, it is easier to pass a large rope through the eye of a needle, than for one who is attached to this world to win Final Union with Universal God.

19. For the sake of receiving True Enlightenment and winning The Supreme Knowledge of my Holy Adhyatma-Yoga-Dharma, let the Wise Aspirant, with an Offering to Universal God and The Friend in his hand, approach a Devotee of the unbroken line of my Truly Enlightened Faithful - who is in Good Faith, well versed in The Truth of Holy Adhyatma-Yoga-Dharma, and devoted to Universal God and The Friend in all ways.

20. Unto one who has come according to this Holy Scripture, whose eyes are opened, whose mind is settled, who is self-controlled, and whose heart is set upon True Salvation and Liberation - Let the Truly Enlightened Devotee impart the True Enlightenment of my Holy Initiation and the Divine Pure Truth of my Holy Adhyatma-Yoga-Dharma, through which all Souls attain True Salvation and Liberation.

- Three -

This is The Pure Divine Truth of Paratpara, The One Universal God of Countless Names and Forms Who Is Beyond All Names and Forms, That I AM THAT I AM, Creator of The Creator, The One Universal Source, Substance and Self of the universes and all Souls.

2. As sparks that are one with a fire, fly forth from it by the thousands, even so, Beloved Devotee, do the countless Souls come forth from Universal God - the Imperishable.

3. Divine and formless, yet all forms, is Paratpara, The One Universal God of Countless Names and Forms Who Is Beyond All Names and Forms. He is beyond and within all that is, Uncreated, beyond life, beyond mind, Pure and higher than The Imperishable, is He who calls Himself I AM THAT I AM.

4. The True Self of every creature is Soul, which is Pure Divine Universal Spirit, which is One and Identical

with That One Universal God and no other.

5. From That I AM THAT I AM are born life, mind, all of the senses, space, air, light, water and earth. He, alone, is the One True Source, Cause, Substance and Self of all Creation. He is the supporter of all.

6. Fire is His head, the sun and the moon His eyes; the four quarters of space are His ears; all revealed Truth His speech; the wind is His breath; within one portion of His Heart, the universe is contained; from His Blessed Feet the earth is born. He alone is The True Self of all Beings and all Creation.

7. From Him alone proceeds the Divine Fire, whose fuel is the sun; From Him alone comes forth the moon and the rain; from the rain comes all food that grows upon the earth. Nourished by food that grows upon the earth, the man gives forth his seed unto the woman. By this the many and various Beings are born of the actions of Souls.

8. From Him alone have I come and His Eternal Universal Religion, The Holy Adhyatma-Yoga-Dharma. From Him alone have come its Verses, its Chants, its Mantras and Prayers, my Holy Initiation, its Self-Sacrifices, its Ceremonies and all of its Divine Blessings. From Him alone have come the Sacrifice and the Sacrificer, and all the worlds where moon purifies and sun shines.

9. From Him alone the Divine Beings are born forth in many different ways: the Heavenly Ones, men, women, cattle, birds, the in going breath and the out going breath, rice, barley, corn, and all of the foods; From Him alone is born Austerity, Faith, Truth, Fidelity, and The Divine Law.

10. From Him alone come forth the Seven Organs of Sense and the Seven Sacred Flames that burn within them, the Seven Self-Sacrifices, and the Seven Worlds in which these move. Seven, Seven, and Seven, which dwell within in the Secret Place of the Soul.

11. From Him alone come forth all the seas and mountains. From Him alone flow forth the rivers of every kind. From Him alone come forth all plants and their essence by which that which contains the Divine Soul is upheld.

12. Thou Art That. For, you are not this body or this mind or this personality alone. You are each, Soul which is Pure Divine Universal Spirit, which is One and Identical with He who is all of this. That which thou art is all of this Creation which consists of work and austerity, and The Creator beyond death. O Beloved Devotee, he who knows The One Universal God, That I AM THAT I AM, who lives within the Holy Sanctuary of the Heart, cuts away the knot of Ignorance with The Sharp Sword of Divine Truth and is set Free, while yet living upon this earth.

Om So'ham Tat Tvam Asi!
Om! I Am That - Thou Art That!

Jai Bhagavan Ji!
Victory To God The Beloved!
That Beloved Universal
I Am That I Am
Which You Are!

Here Ends the Chapter Entitled
The Sharp Sword of Universal
God's Pure Divine Truth

Chapter Three
The Essence of Universal God's Pure Divine Truth

By The Will and Grace of The One Universal God:

This is The Pure Divine Truth of Paratpara, The One Universal God of Countless Names and Forms Who Is Beyond All Names and Forms - That One Beloved Universal I AM THAT I AM - which I Am sent forth of The One Universal God to give unto all Souls.

2. God is One, men call Him by countless names. All Names of God that arise out of a sincere longing for God and Love for God are Good and Divine and are to be respected and revered alike.

3. You are not merely a body made of flesh and bone, nor a mind made of thoughts and ideas, nor, even, a personality made of experiences, memories, and qualities; in Truth, you are Soul, which is Pure Divine Universal Spirit, which is One and Identical with Universal God and no other.

4. All people are absolutely and eternally Good and Divine in essence. Deluded men and women may do bad things as a direct result of the pain, suffering, and agony of this world, or as a result of believing in and following the false and deluded teachings that teach that the Soul is separate from God and that man is evil by nature.

5. But I say unto you that evil has no part or place in the Nature of the Soul and does not tarnish or negate the Goodness and Divinity of any Soul. Being Divine in Essence and Nature, every Soul has within it the potential to Realize its True Self and Nature, regain Goodness and Divinity, and become liberated from Ignorance and Death within this life or at its end, through The Enlightenment of My Holy Initiation and Universal God's Supreme Promise of Universal Salvation and Liberation my Supreme Sacrifice has won for you and all Souls.

6. I have made the Supreme Divine Eternal Sacrifice of giving up Perfect Final Union with Universal God for the sake of all Souls for all time. Because of My Supreme Sacrifice, every Soul can now Realize his or her Goodness and Divinity as a Living Truth and Reality and be Free.

7. The ignorant and the deluded claim that God is a Jealous and Vengeful God who punishes innocent little

children with eternal damnation and torment. Such as these are a generation of vipers who cast the evil that lurks within their own Ignorant hearts upon God. I say unto you that these are slanderers of God and of Man.

8. I say unto you that in Truth, The One Universal God is neither a vengeful nor a jealous God, but a God of Pure Truth, Love, Compassion, Justice, and Mercy who has created the infinite and varied Worlds to move and have their Being perfectly, according to His Impersonal and Impartial Natural Law.

9. The One Universal God punishes neither man nor woman nor child nor creature. As a man, a woman, or a child stepping off from a high place will fall down and suffer, all Souls suffer only as direct result of Spiritual ignorance and their own past wrongdoings. Man's suffering and Sorrow comes not from God, but from his own wrong action. Every Soul is his own jailer and his own punisher. Through my Holy Initiation and God's Will and Grace, every Soul can also be his own Liberator.

10. Still, all men and women are eternally and essentially Good. At their innermost center, which is their True Divine Self, all people are forever and purely Soul, which is Pure Divine Universal Spirit, which is One and Identical with The One Universal God and no other. And by virtue of their eternal Oneness with Universal God, all people are forever One with all other Souls, all life and all Creation.

11. Beyond the veils of Spiritual Ignorance which cloud their minds and hearts and keep this Divine Truth from their sight, all Souls share equally and fully in the Divine Nature of Universal God. Due to the Divine Essential Nature of all people, no man has to wait for death to attain Supreme Salvation, Liberation, Freedom, and Happiness. Every Soul has the potential to Realize The True Self of Universal God within himself, to live a Divine Life of Goodness, and to be Free while alive in this world.

12. A man may have many material hopes, dreams, goals, and desires. But, over and above these material hopes, dreams, goals, and desires, the one thing every Soul must do in order to live a life of Peace, Confidence, Security, Prosperity, and Happiness, is to obtain the True Salvation and Liberation that comes from The True Enlightenment of my Holy Initiation and Realization that his own self is, in Reality, One with God, The One Divine Universal Self.

13. Because My Supreme Sacrifice has won Universal God's Divine Promise of True Salvation and Liberation for all Souls, all men and women who have my Gift of God's Divine Grace can attain True Salvation and Liberation within this life. All that is needed for any Soul to attain The Supreme Goal of Perfect Liberation and Freedom is to receive The True Enlightenment of My Holy Initiation and Universal God's Divine Gift of Grace, make Universal God and Self-Realization and Final Liberation the Highest center of his life and live The Truth, The Life and The Way that fulfills God's Supreme Promise.

14. Only because their hearts and minds are covered with the dust of Spiritual Ignorance, do men believe themselves totally alienated from Universal God. Only because of this, do they call humanity evil and

Universal God a jealous and vengeful God. To call any man or woman evil is to heap a vicious and terrible slander upon Universal God in whose image each man and woman is created and with whom every man and woman is One in Spirit.

15. To call The All-Compassionate One Universal God jealous or vengeful is the darkest and most vile blasphemy.

16. Only those who hold a false and perverted opinion of Universal God hold and preach the false and slanderous doctrine of the evil nature of humanity and the jealous and vengeful nature of Universal God The All Compassionate.

17. Only the heart which is sick with Spiritual Ignorance, fear, and hate, preaches, teaches, or believes that The One All-Compassionate Universal God is a torturer and murderer who permits infants and children to be cast into a fiery hell to suffer endless agony for all eternity.

18. I tell you this: there is no god in all of Creation who is a jealous and vengeful torturer and murderer of children or any other.

19. There is but One Universal God, there is no other. His Name is all Divine Names of every language, time, and place. He has bid me call Him Paratpara, for He is The One Universal God of Countless Names and Forms Who is beyond all Names and Forms.

20. Nothing is outside of Him. Nothing is alien to Him. Nothing is beyond Him. He alone is the One Universal Source, Cause, Substance, and Self of all Creation, all Existence, and all Being.

21. His Nature in expression is Love, Compassion, All-Knowing, All-Power, and Ever-Presence. Beyond this veil of appearance which the ignorant call the world and which the foolish call reality, all men, all women, all children, all creatures, and all Creation are One with That One Universal God and no other.

22. Preaching or teaching the false doctrine that the nature of man is evil is a willing and malicious slander of Universal God. Only those who are sick with Spiritual Ignorance and false doctrine preach, teach, or bear such a false and perverse slander of humanity and of God.

23. If it is blasphemy to falsely attribute the best qualities of God to man, how much more is it blasphemy to falsely attribute the worst qualities of man to God. Whosoever sets forth such an Ignorant and perverse doctrine commits the darkest and most grievous blasphemy of all.

24. Yet, The All Compassionate One Universal God does not punish even these. Those who preach, teach, or bear the slanderous false doctrine of the evil of humanity and jealous and vengeful nature of God, bring a curse and calamity of their own making down upon themselves, upon their children, and upon their children's children even unto the seventh generation.

25. And, what of those who listen to and believe in such false doctrine? Whosoever listens to the slander of Universal God, and lets it pass, unanswered, becomes tainted with

Spiritual Ignorance and Soul-Sickness.

26. But, whosoever believes upon this false and slanderous doctrine suffers the same self made curse as do those who preach it and teach it. Truly, I tell you that they too place a curse upon their children and their children's children unto seven generations. Not of My will, and not of The Will of God, but of their own wrong-doing is their suffering wrought.

27. Make Universal God's Pure Divine Truth known unto all Souls everywhere. Let not the slanderers of The One Universal God, go unanswered. Bear not that the vile pronouncements of false and slanderous doctrine which pour forth daily from the mouths and pens of the Spiritually Ignorant shall go uncorrected in the minds of the people.

28. Hate no man. Hate no woman. If you must hate, hate and oppose only The Force of Darkness which itself, is the one source of all Ignorance, hatred and wrong doing. You may hate the wrongful deed, but hate not the doer of the deed. If you must hate, hate the slander, but hate not the slanderer. Hate no Soul. For, as to declare men or women evil is to slander Universal God; whosoever hates one least of Universal God's manifest Souls, truly, hates The One Universal God Himself.

29. Let it be known unto all people that you are The One Universal God's Beloved Servant by virtue of The True Enlightenment of my Holy Initiation as received from The One Universal God through me.

30. Fear not the ignorant and bigoted who are enslaved and the unwilling servants of The Force of Darkness. For, whosoever hates you for my sake, hates The One Universal God, who has awakened within me and sent me forth into this world. Whosoever strikes out at you for my sake, strikes out at The One Universal God who has Awakened within me and sent me forth into this world.

31. All of the Religions of the Earth that The One God has given unto Man are like unto a magnificent Orchard in which there are many Trees. The fruit of each of these different trees is sweet and filled with the Divine Nectar of God's Grace and Mercy. The root of each of these trees is one of the Divine Mercies that God has sent to Man in the form of His Prophets, Saints, Buddhas, Saviors and Avataras. Each of these trees is one of Man's Religions. And those who follow that Religion are charged with protecting and tending that particular tree. And this is good. The Faithful of God's Eternal Universal Religion have been Charged and Ordained by God to be the Guardians of the Orchard itself. We enjoy the fruit of all of God's Mercies alike and His Supreme Promise of Perfect Final Union with Him at the end of this life, as well. But, there is one tree in the orchard whose fruit is poisonous. This tree is called the Bigot Tree. And those who eat of its fruit are quickly poisoned and driven to such madness that they try to destroy all of the other trees. This Bigot Tree is the source of all of the violence and horror that men and women do in the Name of God. Therefore, take, every stone the Bigots of this world cast against you and use them to build my Church in this World.

32. Whosoever seeks or plots to degrade you or oppose you in the Righteous discharge of The Holy Cause and Duty I have given unto you, degrades and opposes Universal God and The Friend. Truly these misguided Souls shall reap the bitter fruit of the seeds of karma that they sow.

33. All people are, beyond the pale of this world, Soul which is Pure Divine Universal Spirit which is One and Identical with The One Universal God of all Creation and are absolutely Good and Divine in their True Nature. Even the most ignorant, hateful and foolish have within them, the potential to Realize their Goodness and Divinity through The True Enlightenment of My Holy Initiation and Universal God's Divine Promise of Self-Realization and The Universal Salvation and Liberation of Perfect Final Union with Him.

34. As the bountiful and fruitful tree is within the humble seed; as the glorious butterfly is within the humble caterpillar; the moment a Soul receives my Holy Initiation, the Perfection of Divine Spirit is within him and he is changed completely, forever.

35. Owing to Ignorance, Confusion, and Pain, men and women perform many wrong, hurtful, cruel, and evil acts. Because they see only the outer appearance of things, the Dead in Spirit confuse the Soul with the evil acts that the person performs. In this present Age of Ignorance, Darkness, and Chaos, the people have allowed themselves to become confused and their hearts to become clouded with Ignorance, Selfishness, Desire, Attachment, Confusion, Identification, Greed, Lust, and Hatred. I say unto you that this is the Nine-Fold dust of Spiritual Ignorance, through which every Soul creates his own suffering, sorrow, and death.

36. Still, even the dark and ugly confusions brought about by The Nine-Fold Dust of Spiritual Ignorance do not change the Goodness and Divinity of the True Inner Self that is the True Nature and Essence of each Soul, any more than the dust of this world changes a mirror upon which it falls. When any Soul receives My Holy Initiation, Universal God wipes away the dust from the mirror of his heart and mind, and the purity and brightness of the Divine Mirror of his Soul shines forth. And that Soul becomes as a new born Soul and each day becomes as the first day of his life. Such as these are called, truly, the Twice Born of humanity.

37. The criminal is but a Soul whose heart and mind is thickly covered over by Spiritual Ignorance. When any Soul receives my Holy Initiation, Universal God and I begin wiping away the Nine-Fold dust of Spiritual Ignorance from the Divine Mirror of his heart and mind right away. Set free from Spiritual Ignorance, the Divine Light of The One Universal God shines forth from within all men and women alike. You, who have the True Enlightenment of My Holy Initiation, are the bearers of Universal God's Divine Light into the darkness of this suffering world, like candles in a dark place. Do not hide your light away, but let it shine out that those who suffer and die in ignorance may find their way Home through the darkness.

38. When a Soul is confused and bears a heart which is clouded with the Nine-Fold Dust of Spiritual Ignorance, this is reflected in his body, mind, and life. Sickness, depression, insecurity, fear,

and all feelings of worthlessness and emptiness of purpose are due to the Nine-Fold Dust of Spiritual Ignorance a man has allowed to collect within his heart. Poverty, lack, failure, disharmony, conflict, calamity, and suffering are all due to the Nine-Fold Dust of Spiritual Ignorance that has fallen upon the Soul of a man, a woman, a family, a community, or a nation.

39. The Divine Souls are eternal and undying. As a man journeying up a mountain may journey in one cart after another, each Divine Soul is born again and again and takes up one body after another, in its long journey to Liberation and Perfect Final Union with God. Only the ignorant and those who are dead to The Spirit believe the Soul lives but once and in one body alone. The Divine Souls are eternal and undying. The body, mind, and personality are temporary and fleeting apparitions that begin to die the moment they are born. The Divine Soul is like the ever-burning Sun. The body, mind, and personality, are like the countless rays that pour forth from the Sun. Only the deluded or foolish believe that the rays that pour forth from the Sun can be separated from the Sun itself. Only those who are consumed with Spiritual Ignorance believe that the individual Soul can be separate from The One Universal God from which it has come. Only the foolish or deluded try to limit the ever-burning Sun to the rays that pour forth from it. Only those who are consumed with Spiritual Ignorance, limited in Spiritual Sight, and dead to The Truth and Spirit of God, condemn this True Doctrine and profess the Eternal Soul to be confined to one temporary and quickly passing body.

40. The One All-Compassionate and Loving Universal God is not a tormentor, nor a punisher of Souls. In His Infinite Compassion, Universal God has insured the Highest Supreme Justice to all Souls. Every Goodness brings forth its own reward. Every Wrong Action brings forth its own suffering, sorrow, or death. This is The Universal Law of Absolute Divine Justice that The One Universal God has set forth for all Souls. As a rock let go, falls to the earth, as ice freezes, and fire burns, so is it with Universal God's Divine Law of Universal Justice. As the earth needs no interference from men or women to pull a rock to it; Universal God's Divine Justice requires no enforcement or interference from men, women, or societies. That man, woman, or society that pretends to be the agent or enforcer of Universal God's Divine Law is guilty of vile vanity and lack of Faith in God's Infinite Will. I tell you, without doubt or reservation, that Universal God's Divine Law of Justice is sufficient unto itself and stands in neither need nor desire of human enforcement.

41. Each Soul possesses Freedom of Will and of Action. And I say unto you that every Soul shall, sooner or later, experience the results of every action he shall cause. Those Right Actions that are performed by a Soul that are in Harmony with God and in Accord with Goodness, bring forth a Just and equal Blessing of Bliss and Goodness that will be enjoyed by that Soul in this world or beyond it. Every Wrong Action that is performed by a Soul, brings forth a Just and equal punishment of suffering, sorrow, or pain that will be endured by that Soul within this life or beyond it, upon the long road of a Soul's journey to Final Liberation.

42. What is Wrong Action? I say unto you that Wrong Action is any action or failure to act that arises out of the Nine-Fold Dust of Spiritual Ignorance, Selfishness, Desire, Attachment, Confusion, Identification, Greed, Lust, or Hatred, and any action that turns any Soul away from God's Pure Divine Truth or its fulfillment in this life.

43. But, I say unto you that even as you are your own Jailer and Punisher, you are also your own Liberator. And the means of conquering the pain, suffering, and sorrow of wrong karmas are in your very hands. What are the means of conquering Karmas? Experiencing the results of all of your wrong actions and all of their effects fully and directly; burning off karmas and their results through Right Spiritual Practice; or, receiving My Holy Initiation and attaining the True Salvation of Enlightenment and The True Liberation of Self-Realization and Perfect Union with The One Universal God. These are the three ways of conquering karmas, there are no others.

44. Be not deceived and lulled into inaction because you are not suffering at this very moment beloved Soul. Even if you are not sick, or unhappy, or suffering, right at this moment, you are still filled with the seeds of Karmas that you have gathered from many thousands of Wrong Actions in your past. Any of these Seeds can spring to life at any moment and cast suffering or sorrow over your life. The sprouting of the seeds of Karma can turn the healthy, ill, the strong, weak, the rich, poor, and the famous into the forgotten of yesterday in the twinkling of an eye. The seeds of karma can turn the happiest man into the most sorrowful, the most pleasureful into the most suffering; the most beautiful into the most ugly; the youth into the aged; the agile into the cripple.

45. There is no true security for you so long as the Seeds of your past Wrong Actions remain deep within the Storehouse of Karmas that surrounds your Soul. Without The True Enlightenment and Rebirth of My Holy Initiation, there is no way for you to know the nature of the Karmas which may spring to life next.

46. There is no hope of escape from the suffering of past Karmas for King or for pauper. But, because of Universal God's Infinite Divine Love and Compassion and The Love and Compassion of My Supreme Sacrifice, there is a way out of the living hell of birth, suffering, and death.

47. By receiving The Holy Enlightenment and Rebirth in The Spirit of My Holy Initiation and Universal God's Divine Promise - and following Me to the end of this life - you can conquer your Storehouse of Karmas and attain the True Liberation of Self-Realization and be Free forever.

48. No Soul is, has, ever has been, or ever can be separate or alienated from God; for every Soul is Pure Divine Universal Spirit which is One and Identical with Universal God and no other.

49. There is no sin of disobedience to God's Will, for which a Soul must suffer God's wrath and vengeance. I say unto you that whatsoever any man can do is within God's Will, for no Soul can disobey God's Infinite and All-powerful Will. Free Will is granted to every Soul. Bliss is the

reward of Goodness. Suffering is the reward of wrong doing.

50. Universal God is not arbitrary and whimsical. Universal God is absolutely Just and Kind toward all Souls. The All-Compassionate Universal God does not punish or reward any least Soul. For I say unto you that The One Universal God is an Infinitely Just God who creates all the infinite Universes and sets forth the Laws of Nature as the regular order by which they shall move and have their being; He gives unto all Souls both intelligence and Free Will and The Universal Law of Karma; and having done with this, sets His creation into motion. Verily I say unto you that The One Universal God gives unto each Soul the Free Will and Intelligence by which to create for himself both suffering and happiness, according to his own thoughts and deeds.

51. You are each The Captain of the Ship of your own life. You are each The Master of your own destiny. You are each your own jailer and you are each your own liberator. Your births, sufferings, sorrows, and deaths are the result of your own wrong actions and thoughts. Your relief from suffering, sorrow, and death, and your own happiness, prosperity, and joy are the result of your own freely chosen Right Actions and Thoughts.

52. Blessings and sufferings, both return to each Soul according to Right or wrong actions and thoughts, with the impersonal regularity with which a rock that is thrown into the air falls to the earth. The impersonal Justice of Universal God's Divine Law is embodied in the universal principle of Karma that for every action there is an equal and opposite reaction.

53. There is no hell into which a violent, temperamental, and terribly vengeful raging god casts Souls to be tortured and suffer for all eternity. I say unto you that that which the Ignorant call hell is but that time between one life and another, in which the unawakened Soul must suffer the Karmas of his own wrong thoughts and actions. The only fire therein is the fire of a Soul's direct experience of the effects of his wrong actions and thoughts that burns away the Karmas of wrong thought and action. This fire does not burn the Soul but burns away only the Karmas of wrong thought and action which that Soul has made for himself in the previous life and body.

The Journey of Death

Following the death of the mortal body, the bonds that bind the Soul to the body slowly break apart. When the last of the bonds have broken, the Soul enters into the hell it has made for itself, to remain therein for three Days of The Spirit. Therein, the effects of wrong thoughts and actions are suffered and burned away. Thereafter, the Soul ascends into The Heaven Paradise it has made for itself by its previous Good thoughts and actions. And therein the Soul enjoys the Blessings and Bliss which are the results of its Right Thoughts and Right Actions.

2. When the Blessings and Bliss of previous Right Thoughts and Actions have been burned up in the Heavenly Fire of enjoyment, the unawakened Soul ascends into Perfect Final Union with God or gathers new substance around itself a new body and mind, and is reborn into the world again.

3. Such is the fate of the Unawakened Soul until the True Final Liberation of Self-Realization is attained. When the True Final Liberation of Self-Realization is attained, the Soul awakens to its True Self and Nature as Pure Divine Universal Spirit, which is One and identical with Universal God and no other, and is Freed forever from the endless rounds of births, sufferings, sorrows, and deaths.

4. In Truth, each Soul lives, not once, as believe the Spiritually Ignorant, but again and again. In Truth, that which men call life comes to each Soul, not as a blessing, as the Spiritually Ignorant believe, but as a curse which causes each Soul to be born and born again and again, until it receives the True Salvation of True Enlightenment and perfects True Enlightenment into the True Liberation of Self-Realization. Only then does the wandering Soul return Home to rest in Perfect Final Union with Universal God.

5. Until a Soul attains Final Union with God, it will enjoy the Blessings of its Right Thoughts and Actions and must suffer the effects of its wrong thoughts and wrong actions. There is no escape for the unenlightened.

6. But these effects adhere to you, for you are each Soul, only so long as you allow your hearts to remain hardened to the Divine Gift of Holy Enlightenment and Self-Realization I Am sent of Universal God to give unto all Souls.

7. So long as you refuse or deny Paratpara, The One Universal God of Countless Names and Forms Who Is Beyond All Names and Forms and this Truth that The One Universal God has sent forth in Me, you cut yourself off from Universal God's Divine Gift of Grace I Am sent to give unto you, and there is no hope for you.

8. So long as you allow yourself to remain confused with the substance of body and of mind and allow your hearts to remain covered over with the Nine-Fold Dust of Spiritual Ignorance, Selfishness, Desire, Attachment, Confusion, Identification, Greed, Lust, and Hate; there is no hope for you.

9. So long as you lust after the results of your Right Thoughts and Actions, you must also suffer the agony of wrong thoughts and actions. But by True Self-surrender of all of your thoughts and actions and their results to Universal God through Me you can free yourself from suffering and sorrow in this life and take command of your own Destiny.

10. There are no divisions between Universal God and Soul but those which you yourself place before you by yielding to the Nine-Fold Dust of Spiritual Ignorance. The Enlightened Soul, alone, can live a fully Righteous life of Self-Control, Dignity, Honor, Truth, Honesty, Self-Worth, Humility, Confidence, Security, Prosperity, and True Happiness.

11. That Soul who has received My Holy Initiation and Universal God's Divine Promise and Gift of Grace through Me; who has Faith in The One Universal God and this one whom He has sent forth, and takes up the Holy Sanctuary of My Religion as his own and follows Me and My Way; who lives his life according to The Four Cornerstones of Freedom - which are: Embrace The One Purpose; Fulfill The One Requirement; and Fulfill The Two Rules according to the One Instruction; and finds his way through

this world through The Three Steps to Right Action, in all things great and small; is, truly, an Enlightened Soul. Such Great Souls redeem Universal God's Divine Promise and attain the Supreme Gift of Self-Realization, Salvation and Liberation and Perfect Final Union with Universal God within this life or at its end, without fail. Of this there is no doubt.

12. Through True Enlightenment and their own efforts, the Wise conquer vain, vile and ignorant superstitious belief in sin and divine punishment which are a slander upon Universal God. By True Self-Surrender, Faith, and Right Spiritual Practice the Wise Realize the True Peace, Love, Understanding, Compassion, Freedom, Truth, and Joy that is beyond mortal understanding, while living in this world.

13. Universal God's Pure Truth is not hidden away where only Kings and Princes may find it. Universal God's Pure Truth is clear and present to all who have eyes and will see. Universal God's Pure Truth of man's condition is plain for all who have eyes to see.

14. If any Soul receives the True Enlightenment and Salvation of My Holy Initiation and accepts and practices Holy Adhyatma-Yoga-Dharma, surrendering himself and all that he has, does, and thinks to Universal God through Me to the end of his life; he will obtain True Salvation and Liberation. Until a Soul shall do these things, that Soul must endure countless births, sufferings, sorrows, and deaths, until he does.

15. Regret and guilt are not required for True Salvation and Liberation. Repentance and atonement are not sufficient to win True Salvation and Liberation. Acceptance of Universal God and The Friend and My Supreme Sacrifice; receiving Universal God's Gift of True Enlightenment and Salvation through Me; faithful study and practice of my Holy Adhyatma-Yoga-Dharma; self-surrender of all things to Universal God through Me; and giving the Blessings of My Supreme Sacrifice and Gift to all Souls everywhere; these are the only requirements for fulfilling your Divine Life and Mission upon earth and obtaining the True Salvation and Liberation The One Universal God has Promised unto all Souls through Me.

16. A man must believe in order to receive The True Enlightenment of Universal God's Holy Initiation through Me. It is Belief that makes the path to Self-Realization and Liberation possible. But the True Knowledge of Direct Experience is required for a Soul to obtain True Salvation and Liberation.

17. The True Enlightenment and Salvation of Universal God's True Religion of Holy Adhyatma-Yoga-Dharma demands not blind belief. Yet, those who disbelieve, and those who willfully or maliciously deny, slander, or degrade Universal God, The Friend, God's Eternal Universal Religion, or The Holy Community of The Friend's Enlightened Faithful Believers, or The Holy Cause of Satya Yuga, bring misfortune, sickness, loss, suffering, misery, and calamity upon themselves and suffer the terrible and inescapable results of all their wrong thoughts and actions in this life and in lives yet to come. These unfortunate Souls suffer not because of the Will of Universal God or The Friend or The Holy Community, but only owing to

18. That disbeliever who will suspend disbelief, make amends to those his disbelief may have harmed, and receive Universal God's Divine Gift of Holy Enlightenment and Salvation shall be set free from the misfortunes, calamities, and sufferings arising from his disbelief. This is The Law. This is The Three-Fold Atonement that absolves the disbelieving Soul of all blame and wrong karma.

19. Those who have slandered, degraded, or caused harm, who will put aside disbelief, receive The True Enlightenment of My Holy Initiation, make amends to those who have been harmed, join The Holy Community of The Friend's Enlightened Faithful Believers, and work diligently for the success of The Friend's Holy Cause of Satya Yuga and World-Wide Enlightenment and Self-Realization in the world shall be set free from misfortune, suffering, and calamity. This is The Law. This is The Five-Fold Atonement that absolves the hurtful Soul of all harm. The Truly Wise work constantly to Perfect The Divine Gift of True Enlightenment received at the moment of Holy Initiation, into full Self-Realization and Liberation within this life.

20. True Morality is not a code of laws created and imposed by some men upon others. True Morality cannot be kept alive by man's laws and punishments. True Morality is always and naturally brought into living being by Universal God's Holy Enlightenment and Salvation through My Holy Initiation and Right Spiritual Practice of Holy Adhyatma-Yoga-Dharma. True Morality and Ethics arise naturally from within those who have received Universal God's Holy Gift of Enlightenment through My Holy Initiation.

21. The True Enlightenment and Salvation of My Holy Initiation, when fulfilled through Right Spiritual Practice of Holy Adhyatma-Yoga-Dharma, washes away all immorality and replaces it with True Morality. Only that man who believes himself to be separate and alien to Universal God, Humanity, Life, and the Universe of Creation can perform acts of theft, violence, or wrongful exploitation. That man who has accepted Me and Universal God's Pure Truth of The Holy Adhyatma-Yoga-Dharma, received Universal God's Holy Enlightenment and Salvation through My Holy Initiation, and follows The Friend's Way; knows without doubt, that he is not merely an animal set apart from God and the Universe of God's Creation; but a Soul, which is Pure Divine Universal Spirit, which is One and Identical with Universal God and no other.

22. How shall that man who is Awake in The Spirit steal from another Soul? How shall a Knower of Universal God and Universal God's Pure Truth maliciously harm another expression of Universal God? How shall an Enlightened Faithful Believer selfishly exploit another expression of Universal God to satisfy his own pleasure or ends? Only the Spiritually Ignorant who are dead in Spirit can willfully steal, maliciously harm, and selfishly exploit another expression of The One Living Universal God. Universal God's True Enlightenment and Salvation of Holy Initiation Promised unto all Souls through Me brings forth the Supreme True Morality in all who receive it and nurture it through Right Spiritual

Practice, according to My Holy Adhyatma-Yoga-Dharma Teachings and Instructions.

23. True Enlightenment and Right Spiritual Practice of Holy Adhyatma-Yoga-Dharma is the unshakable foundation upon which each Soul may build a lasting True Ethic and Morality. Where the limited morality of the Spiritually ignorant and dead is in question, place no demands upon one another. Instead, go upon The Righteous Way according to the Divine Guidance of The One Universal God as I give unto you who ask, within the Holy Sanctuary of your own heart.

24. Have the highest Faith in the Goodness of all people. Where man's moral codes are concerned, you, My Enlightened Faithful, who are called Maitreyians, reason for yourselves, using Universal God's Pure Truth of Holy Adhyatma-Yoga-Dharma for your Spiritual Foundation. Nothing more is required. Nothing more is needed. Only those who are lacking in True Enlightenment and True Faith in God require books filled with laws and regulations. For it is Universal God's Divine Morality, which is given expression through the Truly Enlightened Soul, that is The Supreme Morality. That alone is the Morality of The Friend and My Maitreyians. Beyond this, the conduct of The Enlightened Faithful is left between the individual Maitreyian and his society.

25. My Enlightened Faithful Believer has the highest Freedom and Dignity. My Maitreyian must stand upon his own feet and make his own decisions. My Enlightened Faithful Believer never walks alone. My Faithful Believer walks with Universal God and I Am with him every moment of his life. That I AM THAT I AM is always Present within the Holy Sanctuary of My Faithful Believer's Heart. I do not impose My Will upon My Faithful, but I Am always ready to give My Inner Divine Inspiration, Insight, and Guidance whenever he shall call upon Me.

26. My Enlightened Faithful Believer is never without the aid and counsel of My Outer Teachings and the support and guidance of his more experienced elder Brother and Sister Maitreyians in facing moral decisions and personal problems. Each of My Enlightened Faithful is constantly helped and guided in Perfecting his own Enlightenment, Conscience, Knowledge, and Ability by study of The Teachings and Instructions, and by discussing his questions and problems in Spiritual Communion with The Brothers and Sisters of The Way.

27. All Souls may receive The One Universal God's Gift of True Enlightenment and Salvation through Me, for this is Universal God's Divine Promise. But no one may join The Holy Community of My Enlightened Faithful Maitreyians who has not received The True Enlightenment of My Holy Initiation, for this alone is The Righteous Way.

28. As a young tree that is just beginning to grow must have a hedge around it to keep it from being trampled, each Soul working to Perfect Holy Enlightenment and attain Self-Realization in this life, needs The Holy Community of The Enlightened Faithful Believers to keep the darkness and Ignorance of this world from stamping out the seed of his newly Awakening Spirit.

For to be made a Member of The Holy Community of My Enlightened Faithful Believers is The Key to Perfecting The Holy Enlightenment of Holy Initiation and attaining Self-Realization in this life. And I say unto you that it is upon each of you who enter into The Holy Community of My Enlightened Faithful Maitreyians to unselfishly and generously help and guide newer Brothers and Sisters upon The Right Way and do valuable work for The Holy Cause of World-Wide Enlightenment and Self-Realization in the world. This is The Key I give unto you to unlock the Spiritual and material doors that have been shut unto each Soul by Ignorance and are keeping you from attaining The Goal and fulfilling The Purpose of all life.

29. I Am a Living Bell tolling to Awaken all slumbering Souls to their Oneness with God and one another. I Am The Living Fountain that pours Universal God's New Spirit out into all who receive The True Enlightenment of His Holy Initiation through Me, setting each Soul free and making his heart, mind, and Spirit grow stronger and more complete. Unto all who receive The True Enlightenment of His Holy Initiation through Me and join The Holy Community of My Enlightened Faithful Believers I give the courage and ability to change their lives as they choose. My Enlightened Faithful Maitreyians live The Holy Adhyatma-Yoga-Dharma Way which embodies the Essence of the Faith and Teachings of all of Universal God's Prophets, Saints, Buddhas, Saviors, and Avataras of all times.

30. I say unto you, who are My Faithful Maitreyians, that you shall revere your Spiritual Family and respect your Worldly Family. Those who are Truly Enlightened Maitreyians, and practice My Doctrine and Teachings faithfully are filled with confidence and security in their own self and individuality! Only the unenlightened, who are confused about their own True Nature and insecure, fear for loss of their self through My Holy Community! My Maitreyians are confident and secure in their Knowledge of who they are and possess full individuality. Because of this, the Maitreyians are always free and ready to give themselves fully, without doubt or reservation, to their Spiritual Family.

31. Respect your worldly family and Honor your ancestors. But I say unto you that The Spiritual Family is The Supreme Family, and the worldly Family must be second to The Spiritual Family. For all Souls belonged to The Spiritual Family of God long before they were born into the worldly Family of Man. Those who become good Members of The Spiritual Family of Universal God through Me become good members of their worldly Families. So long as your worldly Family respects and accepts God's Eternal Universal Religion, Honor your worldly Family and be in peace and harmony with all therein.

32. Respect and honor your parents and ancestors every day, during Prayer and Meditation, with an offering of Holy Water. For I say unto you that by this Holy Practice, shall you affirm and Honor the Truth that each generation stands upon the shoulders of all who have gone before them; for, without your parents and ancestors, you would not have obtained the opportunity for Self-Realization and Liberation within this life.

33. I Am Awakened, made Self-Realized, and Ordained by The One Universal God to be His Divine

Representative and Emanation in this world, to Awaken all people, to give all Souls the True Enlightenment of Universal God's Holy Initiation, to lead all Souls to The True Salvation and True Liberation of Self-Realization, and to bring forth The Rebirth of The Holy Satya Yuga, The Age of Universal God's Divine Pure Truth on earth.

34. At the time of My Awakening, Consecration and Holy Ordination, The One Universal God Proclaimed and Ordained:

35. {G} "Whosoever looks to The Friend also looks to That Beloved Universal I AM THAT I AM, for it is I who have Awakened within His body, heart, and mind, and sent Him forth into this world. Whosoever serves Him also serves Me.

36. {G} "Whatsoever any man shall give unto The Friend, in True Self-Surrender and Self-Sacrifice is, verily, given unto Me. For I Am He and He is with Me. Verily, as a drop of water taken from the Sea is one with the Sea, He is One and Identical with That Beloved Universal I AM THAT I AM and no other!

37. {G} "Whosoever Worships Me within Him, Worships That I AM THAT I AM in all Being and Creation. For this purpose I Am Awakened within Him and Named Him Adhyatma Bhagavan Sri Babajhan Al-Kahlil The Friend. That through Him you might come straightaway upon The Supreme Way of My Holy Adhyatma-Yoga-Dharma, to Realization of your Oneness with That Beloved Universal I AM THAT I AM Which You Are, and attain Perfect Final Union with Me. For I Am The One True Source, Cause, Substance, and Self of all Creation, Existence, and Being!"

38. Because of this Holy Ordination I Am sent forth into this Age of Spiritual Darkness as Universal God's Supreme Truth, Light, and Way, to give unto all Souls The Supreme Gift of True Salvation and Liberation, and save all Souls from Spiritual Ignorance and death.

39. I say unto you that all religions contain the seed of Universal God's Divine Pure Truth. But, in this Age of Darkness and Chaos and the thousands of years that have passed before it, those who were entrusted with The Holy Work of preserving Universal God's Truth within these religions have allowed them to become covered with the Nine-Fold Dust of Ignorance that covers Universal God's Truth within the hearts of the Dead in Spirit.

40. I have come not to destroy or degrade any religions, but to renew in them Universal God's Pure Truth, Holy Light, and Supreme Way of Holy Adhyatma-Yoga-Dharma.

41. All Souls and all Religions come to Renewal of God's Supreme Pure Truth of Holy Adhyatma-Yoga-Dharma through acceptance of The Friend, The Friend's Doctrine and The Friend's True Teachings of God's Pure Eternal Religion and Truth. I Am not a new Prophet, Saint, Buddha, Messiah, Savior, or Avatara, come to set aside those who have come before Me. I Am The One Sent Forth as the Embodiment of all of Universal God's Prophets, Saints, Buddhas, Messiahs, Saviors, Avataras, Satgurus, and Spiritual Teachers of The True Way. I Am The Friend of all Souls.

42. I Am The Embodiment of Universal God's Supreme Truth, Light, and Way of Holy Adhyatma-Yoga-Dharma, The One Way in this Age of Darkness and Chaos that has not been polluted by the Nine-Fold Dust of Spiritual Ignorance, Selfishness, Desire, Attachment, Confusion, Identification, Greed, Lust, and Hate; and the deadly errors of Vanity and Pride!

43. As the Sun in the heavens is the One Source of all Light, but its rays are countless; I Am The One Way to True Salvation and Liberation, but the ways by which men come unto Me are countless.

44. In their pure state, all Good Religions are True to God's Pure Truth. But, in this Age of Darkness, Confusion, and Chaos, all Religions have wandered astray of The Supreme Truth of Universal God's Holy Adhyatma-Yoga-Dharma which is The Essence of all True Religion and the Supreme Religion taught by all of Universal God's Prophets, Saints, Buddhas, Saviors, and Avataras. In this Age of Darkness and Chaos, all religions have been distorted and led into corruption by their trustees, whose hearts and minds have been polluted with The Nine-Fold Dust of Spiritual Ignorance.

45. It is the dark nature of Ignorance that all whose hearts, minds, and Spirit are clouded by the dust of wrong thinking, wrong beliefs, and wrong actions try to change their Master's Teachings to agree with their own distortions. By the exercise of this dark nature, those whom Universal God's Awakened Prophets, Saints, Buddhas, Saviors, and Avataras have entrusted with The Supreme Divine Universal Truth of Holy Adhyatma-Yoga-Dharma, have twisted God's Pure Truth to suit their own delusions and desires. Until now, in this Age of Darkness, the thick dust of politics and distorted doctrines has so darkened the glass of True Religion that The Light of Universal God's Pure Truth no longer shines out through them to the People.

46. This terrible perversion is most seen in the divisions, fear, and hate that the followers of all present religions have put up between themselves and other religions! This is evidence that these religions have given up the Clear Light of God's Pure Truth for the sake of worldly power and wealth. All of Universal God's Prophets, Saints, Buddhas, Messiahs, Saviors and Avataras have taught Peace, Love, Self-Sacrifice, Compassion, and Tolerance based upon the Divine Unity of each Soul with The One Universal God. Yet, in this Age of Spiritual Darkness, the leaders of Religion preach bigotry and intolerance!

47. In this day of darkness, the religious leaders deny Universal God's Supreme Eternal Truth that all People are Soul, which is Pure Divine Universal Spirit, which is One and Identical with Universal God and no other. This, they do for the sake of their own selfish worldly ends of power and glory. For, what tyrant can keep the People oppressed and in poverty and slavery when they know The Supreme Truth of their own Oneness and Identity with Universal God.

48. These religions are called Dead in Spirit. For, those who have lost sight of God's Eternal Pure Truth, that all Soul is Pure Divine Universal Spirit which is One and Identical with The One Universal God and One with all

other Souls in their Oneness with Him, are dead in Spirit even while living in the flesh! I Am Sent Forth to renew Universal God's Supreme Truth of Holy Adhyatma-Yoga-Dharma unto all Souls, and bring True Salvation and Liberation to all Souls everywhere for all time.

49. The Supreme Reality of Universal God's Pure Truth, is all religions are One, even as all men and women are One in their Oneness with Him. The One Universal Living God is One and Indivisible! That the leaders and followers of those religions that are Dead in Spirit have lost sight and knowledge of God's Eternal Pure Truth is final proof that the worldly expressions of all such religions are now decadent and decaying.

50. I Am the embodiment of Universal God's Supreme Divine Truth of Holy Adhyatma-Yoga-Dharma. That alone is The Friend's Way of Self-Realization which is the Unsoiled Pure Essence of Universal God's Supreme Pure Truth on Earth. My Awakening is the Dawning of the Clear Light of Universal God's Supreme Pure Truth in this Age of Darkness and Chaos!

51. At the time of My Awakening, The One Universal God proclaimed unto all of His Prophets, Saints, Buddhas, Saviors, and Avataras of all time:

52. {G} "This One in whom I Am Awakened, shall be called Maitreya Adhyatma Bhagavan Sri Babajhan Al-Kahlil The Friend. His Holy Number shall be 777. He is The Awakened Emanation of That One Beloved Universal I AM THAT I AM which is sent forth unto all Souls for their True Salvation and Liberation through Enlightenment and Self-Realization. He is the Living Embodiment of My Supreme Light, Truth, and Way of Holy Adhyatma-Yoga-Dharma.

53. {G} "I now form all of you, my Beloved Prophets, Saints, Buddhas, Revelators, Messiahs, Saviors, Liberators and Teachers into a Living Circle and a Great Wheel of Divine Life. The Friend is your Hub and your Center. He is the Unifier of all True Religions. He is the Supreme Essence of all True Religion that leads Home to That I AM THAT I AM.

54. {G} "I Am not Awakened within Him to destroy any religion, but to renew The Divine Clear Light of My Supreme Pure Truth of Holy Adhyatma-Yoga-Dharma within all Religions and restore unto them My Holy Spirit through Him.

55. {G} "I Am Awakened within Him to wipe away the dust of Ignorance, Selfishness, Desire, Attachment, Confusion, Identification, Greed, Lust, and Hate, that cause the leaders and followers of religions to fight one another, hate one another, and degrade one another in My Holy Name.

56. {G} "You are The Great Wheel of My Divine Law. He is your Embodiment and your Center. He is The Turner of The Great Wheel of Divine Law in The World of My Creation."

57. And the One Universal God Decreed:

58. {G} "I Am Awakened within The Form of The Friend to right the wrongs of slander against That I AM THAT I AM which today's religions heap upon Me daily, through their degradation of man and man's Soul which is One and Identical with That I AM THAT I AM and no other.

59. {G} "I Am Awakened within The Friend to set right the wrongful heresy of all those churches who have become Dead in Spirit, and who each claim the exclusive possession of That I AM THAT I AM, My Truth, and My Grace. For any Religion to claim the exclusive possession of Me, My Truth, or My Grace, is, verily, the greatest heresy and blasphemy of all.

60. {G} "Those whom I have entrusted with My Supreme Holy Truth through My Holy Prophets, Saints, Buddhas, Saviors, and Avataras have selfishly and ignorantly divided men and women and nations and set them against and upon one another in My Name! This, Truly, this is heresy and blasphemy.

61. {G} "The Friend did not ask. The Friend did not seek. He did not ask to be Consecrated and Ordained and sent forth into this deceiving and hate-filled world as My Awakened One - as The Awaited One - as The Maitreya. Many have I called. Many are they who refused My Call. None but this humble one who is The Friend of all Souls answered Me. He alone gave up the Supreme Bliss of Eternal Life in Perfect Final Union with Me, for the sake of saving all suffering and lost Souls.

62. {G} "Him I have chosen. In Him I Am Awakened. Through Him I make My Holy Promise that whosoever shall receive My Holy Initiation and Blessing through Him receives the Holy Initiation and Blessing of That Universal I AM THAT I AM. Whosoever, having received His Holy Initiation shall follow Him to the end of this life, shall have the Supreme Gift of Perfect Final Union with That I AM THAT I AM which He Sacrificed for My sake and the sake of all Souls everywhere for all time.

63. {G} "I have Awakened in Him and sent Him unto you to Restore the True Doctrine of My Supreme Ancient Pure Truth of Holy Adhyatma-Yoga-Dharma and to wipe away the dust of Ignorance from the hearts of all religions, that the Eternal Clear Light of My Pure Divine Truth might shine forth from them once again. I Am The One Universal God of all Creation. And He in whom I Am Awakened is Adhyatma Bhagavan Sri Babajhan Al-Kahlil The Friend, He is The God-Man, Awakened for the sake of all Souls, that you and all beings might freely have the True Salvation and Liberation of Enlightenment and Self-Realization. So Be It. Jai Bhagavan Ji!"

64. And I cried unto that One Universal I AM THAT I AM:

65. "This is The Supreme Commandment of The One Universal God, That One Universal I AM THAT I AM, unto whom I Am in eternal submission.

66. "God's Eternal Universal Religion is my Holy Chariot; The Holy Community of The Enlightened Faithful Believers are its Great Wheels; My Faithful Maitreyians are the Great Steeds that shall carry Universal God's Pure Truth, into the awaiting hearts and minds of all men. Victory to The One Universal God, The Lord God of all Creation, all Existence, and all Being! Jai Bhagavan Ji!"

67. Because of these things which The One Universal God hath wrought, My Enlightened Faithful Believers do not reject any of God's Holy Prophets,

Saints, Buddhas, Messiahs, Saviors, or Teachers. According to Universal God's Supreme Divine Commandment and Will My Enlightened Faithful reject only the vain and ignorant interpretations by which those who have been entrusted with the care of God's Truth have polluted and distorted their Founder's Teachings.

68. Due to Ignorance, Selfishness, Desire, Attachment, Confusion, Identification, Greed, Lust, and Hate, Vanity and Pride, the religious Leaders have betrayed their followers and their Sacred Trust. Instead of preserving Universal God's Pure Truth they lead their followers astray into decadence and perversion. By preaching of false doctrine and hiding God's Eternal Universal Religion away from the hearts and minds of the People, they cause Universal God's Pure Truth to be covered over by the Dust of Ignorance and religion to fall into decadence and uselessness.

69. The Supreme Pure Truth I bring of Universal God has no quarrel with the different Names by which the many religions choose to call upon God. If one religion wishes to Call upon God as Jesus, or Jehovah, and another as Allah or Krishna or Buddha or Vishnu or Shiva - so let it be.

70. I bring unto all humanity The Eternal Truth that Universal God is One though men call Him by many names and, that all people are Soul which is Pure Divine Universal Spirit which is One and Identical with The One Universal Living God, and One with one another in their Oneness with God, and no other.

71. Through God's Eternal Universal Religion and My Holy Community which form The Holy Chariot of Universal God's Pure Truth; I Awaken all Beings to God's Pure Truth that The One Universal Living God of all Creation is ever-present and present everywhere. Universal God, The Lord, The Beloved, is alone The One True Source, Cause, Essence and Self of all Creation, all Existence, all Being, and all True Religion; and I Am Universal God's Awakened Embodiment in this Age, sent to bring forth The New Age of His Pure Divine Truth on earth.

72. All of Universal God's True Religions recognize and acknowledge this Truth. You shall know those who live in Spiritual Darkness and dwell within religions that are dead in Spirit by this, that they shall refuse Me and deny Me and slander Me and Universal God's Supreme Pure Truth, Light, and Way of Holy Adhyatma-Yoga-Dharma that I embody. Those who live in The Truth and The Light will accept Me and thee and this Holy Doctrine. Only those who live in darkness and are dead in Spirit will deny and curse these.

73. I Am Sent Forth not to destroy any True Religion - but to restore and renew The Spirit of Universal God's Supreme Divine Truth within all Religions; to wipe away false belief, ignorance and superstition; and to open wide The Holy Doors to True Salvation and Liberation unto all Suffering Souls. The Way I bring is the Unsoiled Supreme Divine Essence of Universal God's Pure Truth of Holy Adhyatma-Yoga-Dharma that brings Victory over Birth, Suffering, Sorrow, Fear, Pain and Death to all who receive Me and follow Me to the end of this life.

74. The Doors to The Holy Sanctuary of Universal God's Divine Pure Truth were closed and sealed by the

Nine-Fold Dust of man's Ignorance, Selfishness, Desire, Attachment, Confusion, Identification, Greed, Lust, and Hate. Now, The Doors to The Holy Sanctuary are once again opened wide!

75. The dark spell woven of false doctrines and fear by which generations of vain churchmen have enslaved the People is now broken by God's Infinite Grace through His Awakening in Me. No longer shall the people be oppressed by false and slanderous tales of a false hell. No more shall greedy and power lusting churchmen bind the people down with chains of guilt. No longer shall falsely wise, self-styled preachers curse the people with false and slanderous accusations of sin born of transgression against laws of their own making. No longer shall the dead in Spirit spread their blasphemous and heretical slander of The One All-Compassionate All-Loving Universal God as a petty, wrathful, jealous, and vengeful god who condemns innocent children and people to an eternity of torture, pain, and suffering for crimes they did not commit.

76. I say unto you that all of these slanders are False Witnesses born of man-made beliefs which are vile and slanderous to the Divine Presence and Infinite Loving-Compassion and Mercy of The One Universal Living God.

77. These false doctrines and beliefs have been created by the Spiritual Ignorance, greed, and power-lust of men and women who, in their moral weakness, would cast the shadows of their own perversions upon Universal God's immaculate Nature. I say unto you that it is these very men and women who have distorted the True Teachings of Universal God's Holy Prophets, Saints, Buddhas, Saviors and Avataras for the sake of their own power, greed, and self-righteousness. Through these slanderous doctrines, the betrayers of Universal God's Holy Trust have filled the people with untold suffering, guilt, fear, and trembling.

78. Through these false and twisted doctrines, the unscrupulous have bled the People dry of their courage and Will and wealth for untold centuries. Because of this, the People have forgotten Universal God's Infinite Love and Compassion, and live only in fear and trembling of That Beloved Universal I AM THAT I AM, which in Truth they are.

79. The dead in Spirit would keep fear in the hearts of The People commanding them to Love God. But I say unto you, that Fear and Love cannot live together within the self-same heart. For either fear must stay and Love give way; or Love must prevail and cast out fear.

80. I Am Awakened and Sent Forth of Him alone, to bring you The Supreme Divine Love and Compassion of God to triumph over your fear and restore your True Divine Spirit unto you.

81. Rise up Beloved People of The Truth. The slanderous dark weapons of fear and threat are broken asunder by Universal God's Awakening within Me. The heavy chains by which the dead in Spirit have locked up The Door to True Salvation and Liberation are shattered. The Doors to The Holy Sanctuary of Universal God's Divine Pure Truth are opened wide to all Souls!

82. I Am the embodiment of God's Pure Truth, Light, and Way, sent forth for the Salvation and Liberation of all Beings through Enlightenment and Self-Realization. Awaken and take up your Divine Nature, all of you who suffer under the vile slander and blasphemy of fear and false doctrine.

83. My Holy Community is The Holy Chariot of God's Pure Truth; That I AM THAT I AM is its Master; The Clear Light of God's Pure Truth is My Charioteer; My Enlightened Faithful Maitreyians are the powerful Steeds that carry Universal God's Pure Truth unto all Beings that they may know the Truth and be Set Free; The True Enlightenment of Universal God's Holy Initiation and Consecration which are given unto all Souls through Me are the Reins that join My Faithful unto Me and through Me, unto The One Universal God who has sent Me; My Sword is The Sharp Sword of Universal God's Pure Truth that cuts away the veils of darkness and lets the Pure Existence, Pure Consciousness, and Pure Bliss of The Clear Light of God's Eternal Pure Truth shine forth into the hearts and minds of all Beings.

Jai Bhagavan Ji!
Victory To Universal God The Beloved!

That Beloved Universal I AM THAT I AM Which You Are!

Here Ends the Chapter Entitled
The Essence of Universal God's
Pure Divine Truth

Chapter Four
The Nature and Meaning of The Friend's Holy Initiation

By The Will and Grace of The One Universal God:

When the first light of the sun appears, the night is finished and the day has begun. When the Kalki Mahavatara Satguru appears, the Kali Age of ignorance, darkness, chaos, confusion and destruction is finished; and The Satya Yuga, The Age of Universal God's Pure Divine Truth has begun! This, which you have just heard, has come to pass in me.

2. As the night is finished when the day begins, the Kali Yuga is finished. The Dark Night of the Soul is finished. As the day begins slowly, with a small glimmer of first light, which increases and advances steadily across the land, until it becomes the full light of the day; the First Light of the Day of Holy Satya Yuga has begun. Even now, it is increasing and advancing steadily across the land; and, there is nothing anyone, anywhere on this earth, can do to stop it.

3. The bigots and fanatics who love the ignorance and darkness and chaos and confusion and destruction of Kali Yuga, can perform terrorist acts and wreak physical havoc all they want. The more they attack us, the stronger we become. The more they strike against us, like flint against steel, the more sparks fly out from us into this world and light up the Divine Light of God's Pure Divine Truth in the Hearts of all Souls. The more fire they throw at us, the stronger and brighter the Divine Light of The Holy Satya Yuga shines out from us.

4. I am human in addition to being God's Awakened One. Bigots and fanatics who love Kali Yuga and fear God's Pure Divine Truth can destroy this body of mine, but all they will succeed in doing is furthering and increasing the spread of the God's Eternal Universal Religion of Adhyatma-Yoga-Dharma and hasten the coming of the fullness of Holy Satya Yuga - The Age of Universal God's Pure Divine Truth on Earth. They can destroy all of our Sanctuaries; but all they will do is serve Destiny and cause the inevitable increasing and spreading of God's Eternal Universal Religion and Holy Satya Yuga. They can create white, gray, red, black, or blue propaganda to destroy my reputation or our reputation or your reputations in the so-called public mind. All they will succeed in doing is drawing more and more Souls to us and speed our Holy Cause of spreading God's Eternal

Universal Religion and The Holy Satya Yuga on its way to Victory!

5. If those who fancy themselves our enemies do nothing, they will further our Holy Cause and help us to bring forth Satya Yuga. If they rise up and act against us, they will do even more to hasten the day of Victory of our Holy Cause. There is nothing that they can do to stop the forward march of The Age of Universal God's Pure Divine Truth to Victory once it has begun. There is nothing that they can do that will not further the relentless advance and final Victory of The Age of Universal God's Pure Divine Truth once it has begun. And, it has begun.

6. The First Light of God's Pure Divine Truth and Holy Satya Yuga broke silently upon the world unheralded and unnoticed, on the 7th day of Service 1 A.F. (August 7, 1951) with my first God-Awakening, Self-Realization, and Supreme Self-Sacrifice. The Dawning of the Holy Satya Yuga came to fulfillment on the 12th day of Honor 25 A.F. (March 12, 1977) with my second God-Awakening, Self-Realization, and Supreme Self-Sacrifice.

7. Once the necessary Sacrifices have been made and God has begun to restore The Holy Satya Yuga to Man, no power can stop its inevitable march to Victory. Truly, it would be easier to stop the sun in its heavenly course and stay the day, than to stop the Satya Yuga, once it has begun. For, The Supreme Will and Grace and Power of The One Universal God alone, Awakens The Maitreya Kalki Mahavatara Satguru and sets The Wheel of The Ages of Universal God's Pure Divine Truth turning.

8. Universal God's Supreme Will alone began it. None other can stop it. I have been Awakened and Ordained by The One Universal God and no other, to end this Kali Age of Ignorance, Darkness, Chaos, Confusion and Destruction; and bring The Holy Satya Yuga to fullness for the Universal Salvation and Liberation of all Souls. I made the two Self-Sacrifices that God required and my Supreme Self-Sacrifice has Sealed God's New Covenant with all Souls, for all time. The Satya Yuga has begun. Those who would try to save Kali Yuga are too late.

9. So, let them curse us. Let them spread evil propaganda and false rumors. Let them cast their slanders and their stones against us. We will take every slander and turn it to the Good and the Service of God and The Holy Cause and Mission God has given unto us. We will catch every stone that they cast against us, and use it to build a Divine Bridge of God's Eternal Universal Religion of Adhyatma-Yoga-Dharma, by which all Souls may cross over the sea of illusion and return Home, to Self-Realization and Liberation and live together in peace and harmony in The Age of Universal God's Pure Divine Truth.

10. Men, nations, bombs, and weapons cannot stop the rising of God's Eternal Universal Religion and the unfolding of The Age of Universal God's Pure Divine Truth; any more than they can stop the rising sun and the unfolding of each new day. All of the powers of Hell might stop the rising of the sun; but even these could not stop the unfolding of the Satya Yuga, which the One Universal God has set into motion through me.

11. The merchants of ignorance and darkness will try to convince you that I am a false prophet. But I am not a prophet. They will try to convince you that the Satya Yuga is impossible, but nothing is impossible, if The One God Ordains it. They will try to tell you that the darkness and ignorance is too great; that we cannot win; or that our Holy Cause is losing ground. They may as well try to tell you that the sun rises in the West and sets in the East. Do not fall prey to their propaganda. Do not ever think that you are going backwards. Do not ever think that the Satya Yuga is losing ground. Such appearances are only magician's tricks and illusions. Such appearances are but smoke and mirrors.

12. The merchants of ignorance, darkness, chaos, confusion, illusion and destruction, who seek to keep Kali Yuga going, will try in every way to convince you that you are going backward. They will try to convince you that Satya Yuga is losing ground and that you cannot win. Do not believe them. Do not listen to their vile propaganda. No matter what illusions of futility or loss they may conjure, God's Eternal Universal Religion of Adhyatma-Yoga-Dharma and The Age of Universal God's Pure Divine Truth can never lose ground or be driven back, not even one inch; any more than the night can drive the morning back to the midnight.

13. When The Light appears, darkness must flee. The Truth, The Light and The Way of the Eternal Universal Religion of The One Universal God has reappeared. The dark night of Kali Yuga is finished. The inevitable Victory of God's Eternal Universal Religion and our Holy Cause of Satya Yuga is Ordained by God and, is certain. So long as you and I are firmly and unshakably joined in Union in The Supreme Divine Will, Grace and Power of The One Universal God, our inevitable Victory is assured.

14. But God's assurance of our inevitable Victory does not mean that any among you can sit idle and just wait for it to happen. You must receive the True Enlightenment of my Holy Initiation and God's Supreme Promise of Universal Salvation and Liberation and become a Maitreyian and a Soldier of The Clear Light of Universal God's Pure Divine Truth whose Religion is The Friend's Religion, whose enemies are Ignorance, darkness and untruth. Who has pledged to destroy ignorance, darkness and untruth and replace them with The Clear Light of Universal God's Pure Divine Truth, wherever he finds them. Who will give no quarter and will never give up. One who accepts and professes God's Eternal Universal Religion; the Oneness of every Soul with The One God; and God's Awakening within me for the Salvation and Liberation of all Souls and the renewal of The Holy Satya Yuga on earth.

15. When you have Crossed Over The Line and become a Maitreyian, you must work and study and practice with all your might. You must make every possible effort to keep the Three Sacred Duties of a Maitreyian to Preserve, to Practice, and to Propagate God's Eternal Universal Religion in all of its Purity. You must Preserve God's Eternal Universal Religion of Adhyatma-Yoga-Dharma in both letter and in Spirit and keep it Pure. You must work constantly to perfect yourself in the Practice of God's Eternal Universal Religion. You must work with all your heart, all of your mind, and all of your Spirit to Propagate God's Eternal Universal

Religion and spread The Age of Universal God's Pure Divine Truth throughout this whole world and unto the stars if possible. For, God's Eternal Universal Religion is the very Truth, Light and Way to The Holy Satya Yuga - The Age of Universal God's Pure Divine Truth. There is no other.

16. Every calamity, every disaster, every misfortune, and whatever suffering befalls a person, a village, a state, or a nation, is solely and purely due to the absence of God's Eternal Universal Religion.

17. Those who seek to oppress or suppress God's Eternal Universal Religion; those who seek to slander, libel, degrade or deny God's Eternal Universal Religion; bring calamity, disaster, misfortune, and suffering upon themselves without fail.

18. You do not bring it upon them. I do not bring it upon them. The infinitely Kind and Loving, Merciful Universal God does not bring it upon them. They alone bring it upon themselves. This is the Universal Law of Karma. There is no more straight-forward, or factual statement of The Truth than this. This, that I have spoken unto you in this day, is pure Satyagraha and no other.

19. This does not mean that if a man merely keeps his hands off of God's Eternal Universal Religion, or accepts the Adhyatma-Yoga-Dharma, or even Receives True Enlightenment and becomes a Maitreyian, he is going be guaranteed total freedom from catastrophe, disaster, misfortune, or suffering. Catastrophe, disaster, misfortune, or suffering are part of the nature of this world of illusion. And, so long as a man is of this world and this world is sleeping the sleep of Spiritual Ignorance, all Souls will experience these to some degree.

20. No Soul escapes all suffering in this world, though those who have my Holy Initiation and God's Supreme Promise are able to rise above suffering better than others. It is certain that attacking, denying, degrading, or seeking to oppress or suppress God's Eternal Universal Religion of Adhyatma-Yoga-Dharma in whole or in any of its parts is certain to bring catastrophe, disaster, misfortune, and suffering upon those who do so.

21. They, alone, bring it upon themselves. They alone are their own tormentors and they alone are their final victims. While only accepting the Adhyatma-Yoga-Dharma, or keeping your hands off of it does not guarantee freedom from all catastrophe, disaster, misfortune or suffering; opposing, denying, degrading, slandering, libeling, or seeking to suppress or oppress God's Eternal Universal Religion, guarantees that catastrophe, disaster, misfortune, and suffering, will fall heavily upon the wrong-doer.

22. The absence of God's Eternal Universal Religion of Adhyatma-Yoga-Dharma is the reason for all catastrophe, disaster, misfortune, and suffering. That is the Truth; and saying it is Truth-Saying and Satyagraha - Holding onto Truth. We say it because we do not want anyone to suffer needlessly; not even because of their own wrong-doings against us.

23. Humanity is just now emerging from a Kali Yuga age of ignorance and darkness, in which men and women believed that they were masters of the universe because they

had achieved great technical and material progress. Yet, these same men and women cannot control their minds fully for even one minute, and can hardly control their emotions at all. If a nation of people were to become Maitreyians and follow God's Eternal Universal Religion of Adhyatma-Yoga-Dharma, there would not be so much suffering. There would not be so much disaster. There would not be so much misfortune and catastrophe. If the pilot in the airplane, if the personnel in the control towers, were to be living in The Light of The Inner Divine Inspiration, Insight, Guidance and Revelation of The One Universal God and The Friend with their minds trained and centered in Instantaneous Non-Judgmental Insightful Awareness, there would not be so many accidents.

24. If husbands and wives would enter into Inner Divine Communion together and practice The Two Rules according to The One Instruction; and solve their problems and differences according to The Inner Divine Inspiration, Insight, Guidance and Revelation of The One Universal God and The Friend and the counsel of their own True and Essential Consciences within The Secret Inner Sanctuaries of their Hearts; there would not be so many divorces. If the mass of humanity were to live God's Eternal Universal Religion; if they could really feel that every time they killed a brother or a sister they killed some part of their own selves and all other selves everywhere, there would not be so many people out in the streets killing their brothers and sisters.

25. God's Eternal Universal Religion of Adhyatma-Yoga-Dharma applies to the Spiritual side of life and, to the worldly side of life as well. For example, we have sponsored nineteen or twenty Gatherings at Griffith Park. These Gatherings were filled with and powered by the Spirit of Paratpara, The One Universal God of Countless Names and Forms Who Is Beyond All Names and Forms. Nothing bad ever happened at any of them. The people brought their most precious instruments and things and left them laying around. Still, nothing was ever stolen and alcohol was nearly nonexistent. But the last Love-In was put on without Adhyatma-Yoga-Dharma. And there, the people were divided, alcohol was prevalent, and an antique guitar worth four thousand dollars was stolen from a woman. This disaster was the direct result of the absence of the Adhyatma-Yoga-Dharma.

26. This is no arrogant, egocentric, or ethnocentric statement. It appears radical, but then, Adhyatma-Yoga-Dharma and Satya Yuga always appear radical when viewed from the Kali Yuga. It is the Satya Yuga Way. I Am here, now, building a Radical Spiritual Movement for bringing about The Holy Satya Yuga and winning True Salvation, True Liberation, and True Freedom for all Souls everywhere for all time. And that Movement is called The Holy Cause of Satya Yuga. And it has begun. And you are here with me helping to build it and lead it to certain and inevitable Victory. If the lovers of ignorance and darkness were going to stop it, they should have stopped it when I was seven years old. Because, once the Divine Grace of God-Awakening and Self-Realization had come to pass in my eighth year; and once I had made my Supreme Self-Sacrifice and won Universal God's Divine Promise that: "Whosoever receives the True Enlightenment of The Friend's Holy

Initiation; and follows Him to the end of this life; shall attain Self-Realization and receive the Supreme Gift of Salvation and Liberation which He Sacrificed for the sake of all Souls." - it was already too late to stop it. Now, it has begun. The night of Kali Yuga is fleeing before The Divine Light of Adhyatma-Yoga-Dharma, and the New Day of Holy Satya Yuga is dawning. And, we have a great deal of work to do.

27. The strong and healthy plant or tree that survives grows underground for a long time before it breaks through the earth and appears above-ground. If it comes above-ground too quickly, it dies. All living things grow in stages. And you must attend carefully and with Viveka (Discrimination) to what is rightful to each stage of the growth of the Satya Yuga. At this stage of our growth, we are like a great tree that is just beginning to grow from a small acorn underneath the ground. And like the tree, we too must grow quietly and invisibly. No loud fanfare. No mass meetings. But quietly and invisibly.

28. The difference between a tree and The Satya Yuga is, of course, that The Satya Yuga can only be slowed down, it cannot die. Neither can The Adhyatma-Yoga-Dharma nor any of its Four Pillars truly be killed or die. The bigots and fanatics, who love ignorance and darkness, can take this body and blow it up, dump it in the ocean, shoot it full of holes, whatever they want to do to it; and the only thing that they will do is further The Holy Cause of Satya Yuga, for which I Sacrificed Perfect Final Union with Universal God. Because, no matter what they do to this body, The Friend Lives! I always have been. I Am. I always will be. In spite of the state of my physical body, I live in Spirit. If they destroy my physical body here, in this world; I will still Live as I always have. No matter what happens, I Am with you always within the Spiritual Realm. And, The Adhyatma Dharma lives. The Adhyatma Dharma is The Sanatana Dharma - The Eternal Truth. And, The Sangha lives. It, too, has always been. The Adhyatma Sangha is my Spiritual Body. The Adhyatma Sangha lives in this world, if you give it life in the world by giving it your life every day. But, even when The Adhyatma Sangha isn't apparent in this world, it lives in its full potential here with me in the Spiritual Realm along with The Adhyatma Dharma and The Satya Yuga. And, The Friend and The Satya Yuga are alive in the world here and now!

29. The unenlightened do not know me. But you know me. I Am Maitreya Adhyatma Bhagavan Sri Babajhan Al-Kahlil The Friend, The Kalki Mahavatara Satguru of The Age of Holy Satya Yuga, The Comforter. But many among the people will fear The Kalki Mahavatara, for they have been lied to and led to believe that The Kalki comes upon His White Horse to destroy that which they love. This is a lie and a deception, fabricated by the merchants of ignorance, darkness and death.

30. What does this name - Kalki Mahavatara - mean? It means: "The Final Avatara of a Yuga cycle, who destroys the Kali Yuga and brings forth the Blessed New Age of Holy Satya Yuga."

31. But, owing to the ignorance and darkness of Kali Yuga, the people fear the Kalki Mahavatara. They fear the Kalki Mahavatara because they have forgotten, or been lied to and convinced that the Kalki will

come and destroy their world. This is nothing but a pack of lies and slander that have been put upon the minds of the people by the purveyors of ignorance and darkness. The Truth is that the Final Avatara of one Yuga Cycle is also the First Avatara of the next. The Kalki Mahavatara does not come to destroy anything of Goodness or Truth. The Kalki Mahavatara comes only to destroy ignorance, darkness, and chaos; and to Restore Universal God's Pure Divine Truth to all people for the True Salvation and Liberation of all Souls. The unenlightened fear The Kalki only because they do not understand The Truth. This which I have spoken unto you is The Truth. You must take it out and make The Truth known to the people. For those who know The Truth shall be Set Free.

32. Yes, I am stopping the Kali Yuga; and you are helping me to stop it. The Kali Yuga actually came to an end on the 7th of Service 1 A.F. (August 7, 1951). The Satya Yuga began to dawn on the 12th of Honor 25 A.F. (March 12, 1977). Now, you, who are Maitreyians are beginning to see the world by the Clear Divine Light of the Dawning Satya Yuga. But the unenlightened still see it in darkness, through eyes clouded by ignorance, fear, and illusion.

33. So get busy. Go out and find those who are right for The Work at this stage. Do not grab just anybody and bring them. Think of yourself as a Prospector who is prospecting for real gold. Make the real "gold" you are prospecting for be a person who is really open and right for receiving the True Enlightenment of Holy Initiation, becoming a True Maitreyian and carrying out the Three Duties of a Maitreyian fully with boundless dedication and devotion.

34. When you find a man or woman who you believe may be such a "golden person," do not jump to conclusions. Instead, talk to him or her. Find out if his or her heart is right. Find out if his or her mind is open. Find out if he or she is willing to change his or her self, or if he or she wants the whole world to change to suit his or her ego or comfort or convenience. If you find that you are talking to someone who wants the whole world to change to suit his or her ego or comfort or convenience, bid him or her a quick good-bye with Loving-kindness, and go find someone else. If you find someone who is willing to change him or her self, and his or her heart and mind is open, if he or she is looking for something really important to do with his or her life, if he or she is looking for something really big to give his or her life to, rather than looking for something that will give its life to him or her; then consider that one as a "golden person" and a prospect.

35. Don't take just anybody. Later, we will reach out to everyone. Now, at this stage of the growth of The Holy Cause, we have to take those who can and will serve The Holy Cause; not those who want to come and have The Holy Cause serve them. And not those who want to be "part time" Maitreyians and make The Holy Cause "fit in" around their worldly life, like a casual hobby. Do not take those who come and say "Well, you know, I am a very busy person, and can I do this in my spare time, can I do it in ten minutes a day?" Say to them "No, you cannot do it in ten minutes a day. You must be ready, willing, and able to make Adhyatma-Yoga-Dharma and The Holy Cause the

Supreme Center of your heart, your mind and your life. Come back later, when you are ready, willing, and able to do that; and we will talk."

36. Once a huge rock has begun to roll, then it takes very little to keep it rolling. When the Holy Cause has spread throughout the land and throughout the world; and the Holy Satya Yuga is well established in the hearts and minds of all people; then, perhaps, you can do it in ten minutes a day. But it takes a great deal to make it roll in the first place. So, we must work hard, with boundless dedication and devotion now; so that those who come after us can enjoy the fruits of our labor. But if, at this stage, you accept people who want to enjoy the fruits without doing the work, if you find people who want to go out and continually occupy themselves with the worldly life and benefit fully from the Adhyatma-Yoga-Dharma Spiritual life, you will slow down the Satya Yuga. So, that kind of person will have to wait until The Rock of Satya Yuga is rolling full speed.

37. So, look for the "golden people." How do you know who the golden people are? Well, you know who you are. And, you are a golden person, or you wouldn't be a Maitreyan. So think about what your good and strong points are that enabled you to heed my Call. Then, sort out your bad points that have hindered or slowed you in your progress and in The Work. Then, look at your Brother and Sister Maitreyians and do the same about them. Finally, look for those who have all the good points of you and your Brother and Sister Maitreyians, and few or none of the bad points.

38. When you think you have found another golden person - go and talk to him or her. Study him or her. Evaluate him or her. Interview him or her. Don't say "I'm interviewing you for God's Eternal Universal Religion." Just talk to him or her like a friendly and interested human-being. Above all - ask lots of questions.

39. Find out about a problem he or she has. Then, make a few suggestions that could help him or her solve these problems and find out what he or she does with your suggestions. When you give a suggestion, is it well received? Does he or she follow it? If he or she will receive it well and follow it, then perhaps that person will be able to follow the Adhyatma-Yoga-Dharma.

40. But, if a man says "My car is broken down and I want to go to the store, but I don't know how I'll get there." And you give him a suggestion such as: "Well how about the bus?" And he says "Well, yes, but ...". And then you say "How about taking a taxi?" And he says "Well, yes, but ...". And then you say "Well, have you considered hitchhiking?" And he says "Well, yes, but ...". Then that person is probably not ready to follow The Adhyatma-Yoga-Dharma and be an asset to The Holy Cause, right now.

41. Next, find out if he or she has an open or closed mind. Discover an area where he or she has a well established opinion. Propose an alternate idea to that opinion. See what he or she does in response.

42. Does he or she immediately reject your idea? That is a sign of a rigid and tightly closed mind. Walk away for now.

43. Does he or she seriously think about your idea and then reject it?

That is the sign of a thoughtful, but set mind. Walk away for now.

44. Does he or she listen to your idea, but then twist it around until it matches his or her preconceived opinion? Watch out! Such a person will pervert and distort The Dharma the same way.

45. Does he or she immediately flip over to your point of view, abandoning his or her own opinion completely? Be careful of this person. Either he or she is after something and playing you along to get it; or else he or she is living in a near-hypnotic trance. Any person who instantly accepts your reality over his or her own today - will do the same with another's reality tomorrow. Such a person is either a manipulator, or is lacking in Viveka (Discrimination), INJIA, and stability. Either way, he or she would not make a good Maitreyian!

46. Or, does he or she seriously think about your idea; raise honest doubts and skepticism; ask honest and direct questions to clarify confusion and get facts and information; talk frankly and openly about his or her opinion and your idea; and open up the possibility of changing his or her mind based on possible new evidence? This is the sign of a healthy "Open-Mind"! Look into this person further.

47. So, it is time to Propagate God's Eternal Universal Religion with vigor, but also with intelligence and Viveka. Now you could put an ad in the newspaper and advertise for Maitreyians. And you could just accept whoever shows up at the door. You would get a lot of good people that way. We would get a lot of troublesome people that way.

48. Everyone has some kind of trouble and every Soul is worth the investment of some time and energy to take care of his or her trouble. You will have to do some trouble handling with every person you find, because everyone in this changing-time is going to have trouble. Some, will have great trouble. You cannot take on those who have so much trouble that they cannot work and contribute to the Holy Cause of Satya Yuga.

49. This is a period of turmoil. Things do not change quietly and without turmoil; they change with great turmoil. Especially during the change-over between Kali Yuga and The Satya Yuga. You can see this all over the world. Kali Yuga is fighting hard to hang on. Forty-some wars are going on in the world. Nuclear weapons are piling up in the stockpiles all the time. More nations are making or buying them all the time. There is turmoil in the streets, with one faction against another; one gang against another; one neighbor against another.

50. The Kali Yuga is struggling for its life - and it is doomed. Because in the midst of this turmoil; in the eye of this hurricane of ugliness and violence; the Harmony and Unity and Love and Compassion of Adhyatma-Yoga-Dharma and The Satya Yuga stands firm as a guiding Beacon Light calling all Awakening Souls. Just as the beautiful Lotus grows in the middle of a muddy pond, there is a New Universal Peace, Love, Understanding, Compassion, Freedom, Truth, Joy and Self-Realization growing up in the middle of this ugly turmoil.

51. As the Satya Yuga grows, the Kali Yuga will fight even harder. The Kali Yuga cannot win. The merchants of

hatred, violence, bigotry, fear, and intolerance cannot win. They have had their day. They have had their Age of Kali Yuga - and it is over. There is no way that they can win. And eventually, when they realize this, even they will experience Spiritual Revolution within and join the Holy Cause. Because, eventually there will be nothing but the Holy Cause.

52. So, it is time. It is time to break out of these little Ashrams and begin Propagating the Holy Adhyatma-Yoga-Dharma, as well as Practicing it, and Preserving it. So, if you put up posters, do not put the address of your Ashram on it. Make it hard for people to come to The Adhyatma-Yoga-Dharma. But do not make it impossible. Make them work and struggle to find you and The Adhyatma-Yoga-Dharma. Make them pass some tests and go through some necessary doors to prove themselves. Don't hesitate to say "We don't know if you are worthy of Adhyatma-Yoga-Dharma and The Holy Cause of Satya Yuga at this point."

53. Above all, don't ever again let anyone play the silly Kali Yuga game on you of "Is the Adhyatma-Yoga-Dharma worthy of me?" Anyone who takes that approach is not worthy of the Adhyatma-Yoga-Dharma. Never again let it be thought that the Adhyatma-Yoga-Dharma must prove itself worthy of the new inquiring person. From now on, let it be known clearly and boldly, right from the start, that each person must prove him or her self worthy of the Adhyatma-Yoga-Dharma to the satisfaction of its Maitreyians and its leaders. Go out into this world of darkness as a Prospector searches in the muddy waters for gold. Find the Golden Ones and build them into a strong central core of Maitreyians who cannot be swayed or distracted from The Adhyatma-Yoga-Dharma or the Holy Cause by anything. You are the Avant Guard of Adhyatma-Yoga-Dharma and The Holy Cause of Satya Yuga in this world. Stand firm and usher in the Dawn. Stand firm and usher in Satya Usha. The Dawning of The New Age of The Holy Satya Yuga.

54. The Friend is now! Satya Usha, The Dawn of the Satya Yuga is now! The Adhyatma-Yoga-Dharma will prevail! Victory is inevitable and certain! Victory To Paratpara, The One Universal God! Victory To His Holy Adhyatma-Yoga-Dharma! Victory To His Holy Satya Yuga!

Be Like The Humble Chameleon

55. In times and places where bigots and tyrants rule and severe oppression is upon you, become hard to find, like the chameleon. In such times and places, let your National Headquarters and all of the parts of The Holy Community become diffuse, subtle, and invisible. Let your ways and your Practices become subtle and unseen though unbroken - like the wind.

56. In times and places where good men and women rule through true democracy and the yoke of oppression is light: become bold and obvious in your ways, your Practices, and your Organization. Reward good men and women, who uphold Democracy and Freedom by their rule, with your support and love. Give nothing to support bigots and tyrants who practice hate, oppression, and tyranny. Never cease working to reach them and change them. Give them nothing of your life or energy to further their twisted cause.

Loyalty, Courage, Honor, and Faith Give Us Strength and Assure Victory

57. Lest bigots and tyrants think that they can destroy my Holy Community; and the Freedom, Enlightenment, and Goodness for which it stands; by destroying our National Headquarters know this:

58. The National Headquarters may be destroyed; the Holy Community shall go on. Some of its leaders may be imprisoned or killed; the Holy Community shall thrive and grow. The True connection between The Friend and my Holy Community is within the heart and mind and Soul of each and every Maitreyian. Within the Holy Sanctuary where cold cannot freeze, sword and bullet cannot pierce, fire cannot burn, and bigot and tyrant cannot reach.

59. This is The Friend's Way. Make it your way. Make it the Way of The Holy Community of my Enlightened Faithful Believers in this world. Let nothing stop God's Eternal Universal Religion! Let nothing stop The Holy Community! Let nothing stop The Holy Cause of World-Wide Enlightenment and Self-Realization for all people! Let nothing stop you! You are the Light and the Hope of The World. Go forth! Give my Holy Initiation unto all people who will receive it of their own Free Will. Let all bigots and tyrants and all those who follow The Way of Darkness who seek to destroy Universal God's chosen know this:

Nothing can destroy
Universal God's Pure Truth!
Nothing can stop
Universal God's Pure Truth!
Universal God's Pure Truth
Endures Forever!
We Are As Perennial
As the Grass;
As All-Encompassing
As The Sky;
As Free And Swift
As The Wind;
As Irresistible
As The Sea;
As Pervasive
As Water;
We shine forth
God's Divine Light
and Truth like the Sun;
We are as Eternal
as The One God
who sends us forth
into this World.
Those who seek
to slander us;
Those who seek
to oppress us;
Those who seek
to degrade us;
Those who seek
to destroy us;
Only make us stronger!
Om So'ham Tat Tvam Asi!
Om! I Am That - Thou Art That!
Jai Bhagavan Ji!
Victory To God The Beloved!
That Beloved Universal
I AM THAT I AM
Which You Are!

Here Ends the Chapter Entitled
The Nature and Meaning of
The Friend's Holy Initiation

Here Ends The Book Entitled
The Teachings of
Maitreya The Friend

Here Ends
The Holy Book of Destiny

Made in the USA
San Bernardino, CA
01 February 2020